DECISIONS
AT ANTIETAM

OTHER BOOKS IN THE COMMAND DECISIONS IN AMERICA'S CIVIL WAR SERIES

Decisions at Stones River: The Sixteen Critical Decisions That Defined the Battle
Matt Spruill and Lee Spruill

Decisions at Second Manassas: The Fourteen Critical Decisions That Defined the Battle
Matt Spruill III and Matt Spruill IV

Decisions at Chickamauga: The Twenty-Four Critical Decisions That Defined the Battle
Dave Powell

Decisions at Chattanooga: The Nineteen Critical Decisions That Defined the Battle
Larry Peterson

Decisions of the Atlanta Campaign: The Twenty-One Critical Decisions That Defined the Operation
Larry Peterson

Decisions of the 1862 Kentucky Campaign: The Twenty-Seven Critical Decisions That Defined the Operation
Larry Peterson

Decisions at Gettysburg: The Twenty Critical Decisions That Defined the Battle, Second Edition
Matt Spruill

Decisions at The Wilderness and Spotsylvania Court House: The Eighteen Critical Decisions That Defined the Battles
Dave Townsend

Decisions of the Tullahoma Campaign: The Twenty-Two Critical Decisions That Defined the Operation
Michael R. Bradley

DECISIONS
AT ANTIETAM

The Fourteen Critical Decisions
That Defined the Battle

Michael S. Lang
Maps by Tim Kissel

COMMAND DECISIONS
IN AMERICA'S CIVIL WAR

The University of Tennessee Press / Knoxville

Copyright © 2021 by The University of Tennessee Press / Knoxville.
All Rights Reserved. Manufactured in the United States of America.
First Edition.

Library of Congress Cataloging-in-Publication Data

Names: Lang, Michael S., author.
Title: Decisions at Antietam: the fourteen critical decisions that defined the battle / Michael S. Lang; maps by Tim Kissel.
Other titles: Command decisions in America's Civil War.
Description: First edition. | Knoxville: The University of Tennessee Press, [2021] | Series: Command decisions in America's Civil War | Includes bibliographical references and index. | Summary: "The Maryland Campaign represented Gen. Robert E. Lee's first invasion of the North. Opposing Lee was Union general George B. McClellan, who had just retreated from Lee's onslaught during the Seven Days Battles. While Lee and McClellan fought skirmishes as they maneuvered their armies, the full force of both armies would meet at Antietam, and the subsequent battle would prove to be the bloodiest single-day battle of the war. *Decisions at Antietam* is geared for a general audience and offers a general introduction to the battle through the lens of Union and Confederate commanders. Typical of past books in the series, the manuscript is replete with photos and maps and includes a driving tour of the decisions to encourage visitation to National Battlefield Parks"—Provided by publisher.
Identifiers: LCCN 2020032141 (print) | LCCN 2020032142 (ebook) | ISBN 9781621906148 (paperback) | ISBN 9781621906155 (kindle edition) | ISBN 9781621906162 (adobe pdf)
Subjects: LCSH: Antietam, Battle of, Md., 1862.
Classification: LCC E474.65 .L36 2021 (print) | LCC E474.65 (ebook) | DDC 973.7/336—dc23
LC record available at https://lccn.loc.gov/2020032141
LC ebook record available at https://lccn.loc.gov/2020032142

CONTENTS

Preface	xi
Acknowledgments	xix
Introduction	1
Chapter 1. Before the Battle, September 15–16, 1862	11
Chapter 2. The Battle of Antietam, September 17, 1862	29
Chapter 3. After the Battle, September 18–20, 1862	105
Conclusion. September 21–November 5, 1862	121
Appendix I. Battlefield Guide to the Critical Decisions at Antietam	127
Appendix II. Union Order of Battle	195
Appendix III. Confederate Order of Battle	221
Appendix IV. Strengths and Casualties of Union and Confederate Forces	245
Notes	255
Bibliography	277
Index	283

ILLUSTRATIONS

Figures

Maj. Gen. George Brinton McClellan	2
Gen. Robert Edward Lee	4
The Army of Northern Virginia Crossing the Potomac	8
Gen. Robert Edward Lee	12
Stephen D. Lee's Confederate Gun Line, Antietam	19
Maj. Gen. George Brinton McClellan and Staff	20
Pry House, Modern Image	27
Maj. Gen. Joseph Hooker	30
The Dunker Church, Modern Image	38
Brig. Gen. John Bell Hood	40
Southern Edge of the Cornfield	45
Maj. Gen. Edwin Vose "Bull" Sumner	46
The West Woods	54
McLaws, G. T. Anderson, and R. H. Anderson	57
The West Woods	60
Brig. Gen. Jubal A. Early	61
The West Woods	68
Brig. Gen. William H. French	69

The Sunken Road, Modern Image	75
Brig. Gen. Roger A. Pryor	76
The Sunken Road, circa 1862	82
The Dunker Church, circa 1862	83
Tompkins's Union Battery and the Visitor Center	89
Maj. Gen. Fitz John Porter	91
Middle Bridge, circa 1862	96
Maj. Gen. Ambrose E. Burnside	97
Burnside's Bridge	104
Confederate Dead, circa 1862	107
Thompson's Independent Battery	113
Confederate Dead, circa 1862	114
The Sunken Road	120
Boteler's Ford	122
Lincoln and McClellan, circa 1862	124
Antietam National Battlefield	125
Pry House, circa 1862	130
Pry House, Modern Image	131
View of the Antietam Battlefield from the Pry House	135
View of the Antietam National Battlefield from the Visitor Center	138
View of Antietam Battlefield from the Poffenberger Farm	141
View of Antietam Battlefield Looking North	146
View of the West Woods from the East Woods	150
Brockenbrough's Maryland Battery in the West Woods	155
Mumma Farm	158
View of the Sunken Road from the Roulette Farm	162
The Sunken Road	166
Burnside's Bridge	171
View Looking North from Cemetery Hill	178
View Looking East from the National Cemetery	181
Antietam National Cemetery	185
Lee's Headquarters in Sharpsburg, Maryland	190
Potomac River at Boteler's Ford	193

Maps

Maryland Campaign September 4 to September 14, 1862	7
Lee Offers Battle at Sharpsburg, September 15, 1862	14
McClellan Launches His Attack, September 16, 1862	23
Hooker Opens the Battle, September 17, 1862, Dawn	32
Hood Counter Attacks at the Cornfield, 7:00 a.m.	41
Sumner Attacks the West Woods, 8:00 a.m.	48
Lee Commits His Reserves, 8:30 a.m.	56
Jubal Early Deploys in the West Woods, 8:30 to 9:00 a.m.	64
The Battle Shifts to the Sunken Road, 9:00 a.m.	71
Confederate Crisis in the Sunken Road, 9:30 to 10:00 a.m.	78
Sumner Holds Back the Sixth Corps, 12:00 to 1:00 p.m.	85
The Fifth Corps Does Not Advance, 3:00 to 4:00 p.m.	92
Locating Snavely's Ford, 9:00 to 10:00 a.m.	99
McClellan Does Not Attack, September 18, 1862	108
Lee Withdraws to Virginia, September 18, 1862	117
Decisions at Antietam Tour Map	128

PREFACE

It is not generally known that I wrote my first treatise on the American Civil War forty-five years ago, in 1975. My seventh-grade history teacher assigned my fellow students and me the task of writing a paper on our favorite US president. Having already acquired an appetite for all things related to the Civil War, I at once chose the one president whom I considered a genuine hero of that war: Ulysses S. Grant. I also chose Grant because my best friend had already taken Lincoln as his topic.

I stepped into the assignment with all the determination a young historian could muster and produced, in my view, a well-constructed paper on the celebrated commanding general and president. Although my work only received a B minus, the project amplified my interest in and love of the Civil War. I recently rediscovered this lost essay in an old box of memorabilia my mother had kept for me that included some baseball cards, a second-place ribbon for a three-legged race, and a broken wristwatch. Questionable grammar and creative spelling notwithstanding, I think the paper still holds up as an acceptable first effort for a twelve-year-old budding historian.

Although a substantial gap of time exists between that first effort at historical scholarship and this current manuscript, my passion for the Civil War has endured. I have always loved a great story told well, and what is history if not the stories of all of us? As an American, I somewhat selfishly consider accounts of the Civil War some of the most dramatic and compelling narratives I have ever read. Often, these remarkable stories simultaneously inspire me and touch my heart with tremendous sadness. Many of those immersed in the conflict demonstrated unimaginable courage, and the fighting tragically shortened so many of these individuals' lives. This book is perhaps the culmination of that passion and my long-held connection to our past.

My captivation with the Civil War was rekindled in 2000 when I joined the Rocky Mountain Civil War Round Table in Colorado. Therein I found many kindred spirits and future close friends. I have since acquired an extensive library concerning the war, and I have presented more than a dozen talks and video documentaries on a variety of Civil War–related subjects to this and other groups. I proudly served five years as the round table's president and three years as editor of our newsletter. Since 2017 I have lived in Texas and taken full advantage of a new perspective on the Civil War—one that comes from residing in a state more broadly impacted by that conflict.

During my time in Colorado I came to know Matt Spruill, a retired army colonel, former Gettysburg Battlefield guide, and former member of the US Army War College who provided a perspective on the Civil War I had never considered before. Matt inspired me to look at Civil War battles through his eye, the eye of a soldier and leader. An accomplished author himself, Matt was the first to suggest that I contribute to his concept of a book series examining the critical decisions of significant Civil War battles and campaigns. With his guidance and confidence, I became convinced I could accomplish such a challenging assignment. I consider Matt one of my closest friends and a valued mentor.

I have been a "serious student of the Civil War" for well over seventeen years. During that time, I have studied the Maryland Campaign and Battle of Antietam in great depth and spent many an hour wandering the roads, meadows, and woods of this now-tranquil battlefield. For perhaps obvious reasons, Antietam is my favorite Civil War battlefield to visit.

Through the course of my studies, I have discovered several immutable truths about how we view history and the Battle of Antietam in particular. The most observable of these is that every historian of the battle has a slightly different interpretation of events. While there may be consensus on the battle's chronology, historians will often express varying and wide-ranging viewpoints on the merits of the various personalities involved, the importance of specific incidents, and what lessons can be inferred from the outcome.

While writing this book, I realized I needed to take a very different tack and refrain from expressing my personal opinion. This type of study requires a dispassionate and balanced approach, and I have endeavored to offer just that. An ability to look at the past and judge not by what we know, but by what those in the past knew and when they knew it, is an essential part of this process. Because we live in historical figures' future, we can far too quickly fall prey to judging them by our present knowledge and not their past awareness. Our unobstructed vista of history tells us how every decision played out. Thus it is irresistible to analyze a particular commander and point out how his wrong decisions definitively prove his ineptitude. Conversely, we praise other commander's decisions whose abilities we deem remarkable.

While working in the private sector, I have spent more than thirty years as a manager for one of the largest companies in the world. I therefore understand the sometimes complicated and subtle concepts of leadership and politics in large organizations. While my experience is not precisely like a career in the military, I do understand what separates good leaders from bad ones—as I have seen both up close and personal. I know how my decisions as a leader can affect many aspects of the organization for my subordinates and superiors.

As is the case with the other volumes in the Command Decisions of the American Civil War series, *Decisions at Antietam* applies critical decision methodology. This methodology asserts that as we study the course that a particular campaign or battle took, we need to ask, "Why did these events happen the way they did?" We often believe that history is a series of random events all mixed together to make up the past. As a matter of fact, history is almost always determined by human beings' conscious and deliberate decisions. The Battle of Antietam is a perfect example of this phenomenon.

A study of the critical decisions requires us to look at a particular series of events and then contemplate why they happened or what caused them to happen. We also have to ask, "What might have changed had this decision not been made in favor of another?" When this critical decision concept is understood, it can be applied to any battle in any war.

During the course of any historical event as complicated as the Battle of Antietam, actors on both sides of the conflict made thousands if not tens of thousands of decisions. Most of these are typical of any battle. While many of these choices can be considered significant, only a handful of them are considered critical. Critical decisions are not only momentous in their own right but also so important that they substantially shape the decisions and events that follow, thus forming the course of history. These criteria essentially define the characteristics of a critical decision. Simply stated, the study of critical decisions examines the why of a historical event as opposed to the what.

The following chart illustrates the decisions hierarchy. At the bottom are the many and various decisions, above those are a lesser number of important decisions, and at the top are a very few critical decisions.

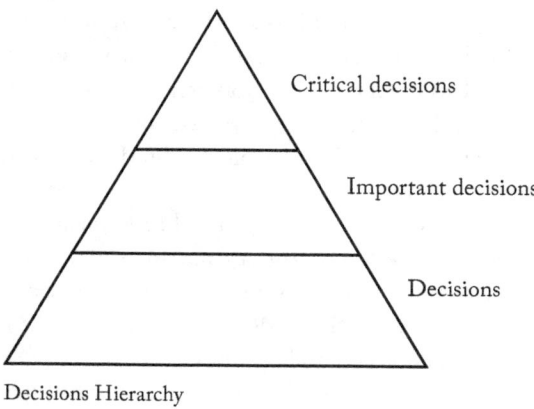

Decisions Hierarchy

Studying these critical decisions quickly reveals that they are reached at every level of the military. Critical decisions can be strategic, operational, tactical, organizational, personnel related, or logistical.

In concentrating on the critical decisions, I lay out some basic facts to present a relatively clear outline of a very complex event. Where relevant, I include pertinent details, biographical and topographical information, and the situational narrative to provide the reader with an overview of why events developed as they did. I then outline the various options the decision-maker had before him, and what decision he ultimately made. Then the results and impact of the decision are examined along with what might have happened had an alternative decision been made in favor of the actual decision.

Judgments as to what constitutes a critical decision may differ, and many readers' opinions will no doubt diverge from my own. The critical decision analysis is by its very nature somewhat subjective. For example, cases like the struggle for the West Woods or the Sunken Road involved many decisions, but the nature of the fighting makes precise analysis difficult.

This work assumes the reader has some basic knowledge of the battle, and understanding this fact is essential. This book is not intended to be a complete retelling or reinterpretation of the Battle of Antietam. I only briefly reference the very complicated and relevant political aspects adjacent to the 1862 Maryland Campaign, and I touch on but a few material points of the overall narrative. Any number of excellent books provide a more detailed analysis of those aspects of the campaign as a whole. They are not listed here, so the reader should refer to the bibliography as a guide for preliminary study. This book covers just those events and details relevant to the various decisions discussed. This work, by design, begins its main narrative on September 15, 1862.

This is not a dismissal of the relevant events at South Mountain and Harpers Ferry that preceded this date, but a deliberate effort to keep this book at a reasonable length. A future volume will speak to the complex events that took place during the campaign as a whole and the critical decisions that brought both armies to the banks of the Antietam Creek.

As you read, you will notice that the Union and Confederacy used similar but often differing methods to identify units. Both sides identified units at the company, battalion, and regimental level in the same manner. Companies were distinguished by a letter—e.g., A Company, B Company, and so on. Regiments and battalions were usually designated by a number—e.g., Fifth (or 5th) Texas, Nineteenth (or 19th) Indiana. Above the regimental level, the Union and Confederacy took different approaches to identifying individual units.

The official designations of Union brigades, divisions, and corps were numeric and began with a capital letter. Examples include First Brigade, Second Division, Right Wing, Brig. Gen. James Nagle's First Brigade, Maj. Gen. Israel B. Richardson's First Division, Maj. Gen. Joseph Hooker's First Corps, and Maj. Gen. Ambrose Burnside's Right Wing. When referring to a brigade or division belonging to or commanded by an individual, lowercase letters are used. Examples include, Crawford's brigade, Sedgwick's division, Mansfield's corps, and so on.

Early in the war, the Confederacy simultaneously used both numbering and naming systems for unit designations. The numbering system was used far less often than the naming system as the war progressed. Confederate brigades, divisions, and commands/corps were officially designated by the commanders' last names followed by *Brigade, Division, Command, or Corps*. Examples include Law's Brigade, Anderson's Division, and Jackson's Command. Identification can also be problematic because multiple generals and colonels named Anderson, Hill, and Jones led units in the Army of Northern Virginia at that time.

The Confederate Congress did not authorize the designation of corps until September 18, 1862. Subsequently, Robert E. Lee did not organize his army into corps until November 6, 1862. Longstreet and Jackson unofficially had "commands" during the battle. However, after-action reports and various manuscripts alternately refer to these commands as corps and/or wings.

The Confederate system of unit designation can often be confusing. For example, Col. Vannoy H. Manning led the unit officially named Walker's Brigade at Antietam. Manning's brigade was in Walker's Division at Antietam and commanded by Brig. Gen. John G. Walker. Walker had commanded the aforementioned brigade until June 1862. Therefore, Walker's Brigade was part of Walker's Division, with only the latter commanded by Walker himself. If that was not confusing enough, Col. James A. Walker commanded Trimble's Brigade of Lawton's Division at Antietam.

As is the case with many Civil War battles, Antietam has more than one name. In the South, the battle was called the Battle of Sharpsburg, and in the North, it was called the Battle of Antietam. Southerners tended to name engagements for the closest town, while Northerners tended to name them for the closest body of water. There were exceptions to this rule as well. The National Park Service officially named the battlefield Antietam, its present designation. To avoid identifying every battle twice in this book, I am sticking with the Northern naming convention going forward.

Determining the specific facts and events that occurred during the Civil War can be extremely problematic. As a result, understanding the precise number of combatants on each side of the conflict becomes a very circular discussion with no clear answer. To further complicate this situation, new research contradicting earlier assertions seems to be published every day. Additionally, as many students of the war understand, exact and standard timekeeping was not generally practiced in the nineteenth century. Readers should therefore add or subtract an hour from every time stated and increase or decrease every head count by 15 percent. Appendix 4 of this manuscript contains additional details on the two armies' strengths and casualties.

A complete and thorough grasp of mid-nineteenth-century warfare often requires a study of the ground where these events took place. Topography plays a critical role in comprehension of a decision or event. Knowing what a decision-maker saw can often provide valuable insight that is otherwise obscured. Walking the battlefield of Antietam perfectly illustrates this fact. To better facilitate such understanding, I have included a battlefield guide (appendix 1) with tour stops that correlate with a number of the decisions.

As I discovered while writing my erstwhile biography of U. S. Grant, any good story must first start with a suitable subject. The Battle of Antietam is one of the Civil War's most compelling, and a close examination of the facts should show even casual observers the remarkable significance and impact of the fighting. This battle quite literally changed the course of the war and possibly the history of our country. Fortunately for my credibility, I am not alone in that assessment.

Asserting that its legacy would "shape the nation for decades to come," Steven M. Gillon lists the Battle of Antietam among the events he examines in *10 Days That Unexpectedly Changed America*. This list also includes the California Gold Rush, the assassination of Pres. William McKinley, and the infamous Scopes "monkey trial."[1]

In *The Gleam of Bayonets*, author James V. Murfin states the following: "Few battles in which Americans died have left such a mark on history as did Antietam. Few battles have held in their final moments of victory and defeat the vast political, economic and military implications that did this bloodiest single day of the Civil War. Antietam was the turning point of the Confederacy; it was diplomatically speaking, one the decisive battles of the world; on it hinged the very existence of the United States." [2]

Stephen W. Sears's *Landscape Turned Red* provides this estimate of the critical engagement: "By almost any measure too, Antietam was pivotal in the history of the Civil War. In September 1862 events across a broad spectrum—military, political, social, and diplomatic—were rushing toward a climax. The battle in Maryland would affect all of them radically, turning the course of the war in new directions."[3]

In *To Antietam Creek: The Maryland Campaign of September 1862*, D. Scott Hartwig notes the dramatic way in which the battle altered the nature of the Civil War: "September 17 and the Battle of Antietam slammed the door on a limited war; there would be no turning back. Either the South would be defeated and slavery in America destroyed, or what Lincoln believed to be 'the last best hope on earth,' the government and nation created by the Founding Fathers, would be in ruins and the independence of a Southern slaveholding republic a reality."[4]

Author and National Park Service ranger Daniel Vermilya's *That Field of Blood* (2018) states that the Battle of Antietam's outcome profoundly altered the history of our republic: "Here the history of the United States had forever changed. This was the battle that turned the tide of Civil War, a Union victory at a time when one was sorely needed by the North. This was the battle that led to the Emancipation Proclamation."[5]

Looking back after the Battle of Antietam was over, Abraham Lincoln did not overstate the significant political opportunities it had brought forth. Lincoln tapped into this long-awaited Union victory to change the focus of the war and the course of the nation by issuing the Emancipation Proclamation: "Things looked darker than ever. Finally, came the week of the battle of Antietam. I determined to wait no longer."[6] The implications of the Battle of Antietam, and the decisions made therein were far-reaching indeed.

It is my sincerest wish that you find this work a beneficial addition to your library and your study of this most decisive battle of the American Civil War.

ACKNOWLEDGMENTS

This manuscript would be woefully incomplete without acknowledgment of all the individuals who supported me in the arduous task of bringing it to life. An endeavor such as this commands an enormous personal commitment to be sure, but it also requires a great deal of help.

Almost ten years ago, my friend Matt Spruill asked me to consider writing a book on Antietam. An accomplished author in his own right, Matt explained to me his concept of a series of books speaking exclusively to the critical command decisions of the American Civil War. Inspired by Matt's enthusiasm and with no comprehension of what I was about to commit to, I immediately agreed. Naturally, I was thrilled with the opportunity to analyze such a significant battle. Those feelings remained, daunting as this manuscript proved to be. I owe Matt a debt that I shall never be able to repay. He is a valued mentor, teacher, friend, and cheerleader who has inspired me to go beyond what I believed were my capabilities. I shall always be grateful for his guidance, frankness, and friendship.

Thanks as well to Larry Peterson, who has provided me with invaluable insight into the process of creating this book. I wish to thank Dave Townsend, whose enthusiasm and spirit have been real blessings to me. I would also like to thank my dear friend Sherri Renner, whose skill as an editor, was an enormous asset to this process. In addition, I am also incredibly grateful for the many dear friends in the Rocky Mountain Civil War Round Table who have collectively cheered me on all these many years.

Acknowledgments

The men and women who make up the United States National Park Service have been uniquely helpful to me. Like many of you, I have traveled to more Civil War battlefields than I can count, but Antietam occupies a special place in my soul. Every visit impresses me with the dedication and infectious enthusiasm these often underappreciated individuals bring to their jobs. I wish to specifically recognize National Park Service ranger Dan Vermilya, as he has been so generous with his time and information.

I wish to acknowledge Mike Doyle for his friendship and personal perspective on the area in and around the Antietam Battlefield. Collectively, the members of SHAF (Save Historic Antietam Foundation) and the Antietam Battlefield Guides have collectively been indispensable to my growing understanding of and appreciation for the unique nature of the battle and relevant terrain. I wish especially to acknowledge Dr. Tom Clemens; he and his unparalleled knowledge of the Maryland Campaign provided priceless notes and feedback on this manuscript. Additionally, guide and author Steven Stotelmyer has been extremely generous with his time, vast knowledge, and perspective.

I would be remiss if I did not also recognize that this book would never have been a reality without the talented individuals at the University of Tennessee Press. Specifically, I need to pay special tribute to Thomas Wells. His passion and commitment to the Command Decisions in America's Civil War series cannot be overstated. It is an honor to be counted among the cadre of gifted authors who populate the Press's catalog.

I would also like to thank all of the authors and historians who came before me. The story of the Battle of Antietam has been imparted by some of the most gifted historians and authors to put words to paper. These scholars have laid the foundation for this manuscript. You never appreciate how much research goes into a work of nonfiction such as this until you are actually in the middle of it. Knowing that my work will someday occupy bookshelves next to scholarship from the likes of Ezra Carman, Stephen Sears, Joseph Harsh, Tom Clemens, and D. Scott Hartwig is beyond my wildest dreams. These authors' writings have inspired me time and time again. I can only hope this book occupies some small space in the shadow of these talented individuals and perchance becomes an inspiration to others.

Finally, I wish to thank my beautiful wife, Rebecca. Her belief in me and her boundless patience with my endless days hunched over a laptop surrounded by piles of books has helped more than I can ever articulate. Her love and support are a large part of why you are now reading these words.

INTRODUCTION

Traveling through the realm of Civil War history means I have spent uncounted hours engaging my fellow Civil War enthusiasts in sometimes heated debates on the importance of the various battles and the countless what-if scenarios these engagements have generated. We may agree as to the events of battles. However, asking professional and amateur historians to rate these encounters in order of importance is likely to yield conclusions commensurate with the number of individuals questioned. That being said, I think I am on solid ground when I state that the Civil War is one of the most significant events in all of American history. If we concede this truth, then we must also acknowledge that, taken together, the Maryland Campaign and the Battle of Antietam proved one of the most significant episodes of that war.

To fully comprehend the extent of this significance, all we have to do is ask what was at stake. What did the Union stand to lose? Conversely, what did the Confederacy stand to gain? Had Lee and his army managed to successfully execute the objectives he set forth at the outset of the campaign, what part of history might be different from the one we now know? Lincoln might not have had the political opportunity to enact the Emancipation Proclamation when he did. England and France might have recognized the Confederacy as a legitimate and separate government.

Had Lee won decisively at Antietam and then been able to move into Pennsylvania and beyond, might the 1862 midterm elections have had a very different outcome? In that case, could the Federal government have been forced to sue for peace with the condition of Southern separation from the Union with slavery intact? Additionally, might not all of the subsequent battles in the Eastern Theater have been altered as a result? Would we still even have had a Fredericksburg, a Chancellorsville, or a Gettysburg? If you assume history is malleable and subject to change, you can tie yourself into a thousand mental knots trying to comprehend the myriad of alternative histories that might have resulted from such a deviation. Would these histories have been radically different than the ones we recognize today?

As it stands, the story of the Battle of Antietam is extremely dramatic and complicated. It is a tale of supreme sacrifice and wasted lives, of desperate gambles and lost opportunities. It is also the story of how a Union victory became the catalyst for arguably the most substantive social and political change in the history of our country.

Events that culminated in the otherwise quiet farmlands of western Maryland on September 17, 1862, began with the termination of the First Battle of Bull Run, fought on July 21, 1861. Then commanded by Brig. Gen. Irvin McDowell, the fledgling Union army was defeated by an equally inexperienced Confederate army commanded by Brig. Gen. Joseph E. Johnston and Brig. Gen. P. G. T. Beauregard. This battle was the first significant clash of the Civil War, and neither side knew what to expect. The five thousand com-

Maj. Gen. George Brinton McClellan,
USA, commanding, Army of the Potomac.
Library of Congress / National Archives.

bined casualties stunned people everywhere, and those who were predicting a clean and quick ninety-day war soon found out how wrong they were.

As the stunned Union army retreated into Washington, DC, after the fighting, Pres. Abraham Lincoln found it painfully evident that salvaging the military and political situation would require drastic change. The agent of the necessary change was the thirty-five-year-old, Maj. Gen. George Brinton McClellan.[1]

Born to a prominent Philadelphia doctor in 1826, McClellan was an overachiever his whole life. He spoke several languages and entered law school at the age of thirteen. At fifteen, the young McClellan secured an appointment to West Point, where he graduated second in the much-celebrated class of 1846.[2]

On July 26, 1861, McClellan was appointed commander of the Military Division of the Potomac, and on August 20, 1861, several units were consolidated into this department. This new unit was redesignated the Army of the Potomac, and McClellan was its first commander.

The general took to his new assignment with great vigor and resolve. He completely reorganized and refitted the demoralized Union army, drilled the soldiers every day, and built up orderly camps all around the capital. Any success the Army of the Potomac achieved in the later years of the war was due in no small part to the training and esprit de corps McClellan instilled in the troops during his first months of command. His soldiers loved him, and it would not be an exaggeration to say McClellan was the most popular man ever to lead the Army of the Potomac. He possessed all the ingredients of success, and he enjoyed seemingly boundless popularity among the Washington elite at the time. An enthralled nation had extreme confidence in the young general and expected great things from him.[3]

In November 1861, the aging Maj. Gen. Winfield Scott retired, and the thirty-five-year-old McClellan was promoted to general-in-chief of all Federal forces. Despite his meteoric rise and mounting public pressure, McClellan did not initiate a new campaign against the Confederacy until March 17, 1862, almost eight full months after the Union's stunning defeat at First Bull Run. His campaign involved floating the massive Union army down the Chesapeake Bay and landing at Fort Monroe at the tip of the peninsula between the York and James Rivers. Marching up the narrow strip of land, McClellan's plan was to sweep the Rebels from his path, capture Richmond, and end the war. However, this strategy turned out to be far easier said than done. Once McClellan landed, he took the whole spring to move the sixty or so miles up the Virginia Peninsula. Bad weather and roads, inadequate maps, questionable leadership, and interservice rivalries hampered the entire operation. Just

Gen. Robert Edward Lee, CSA, commanding, Army of Northern Virginia. Library of Congress / National Archives.

when it seemed things would go McClellan's way, fate intervened in the unlikeliest manner on June 1, 1862. On May 31, the Battle of Seven Pines had begun just outside the city limits of Richmond. Confederate commander Gen. Joseph E. Johnston was severely wounded during the first day of fighting, and Confederate president Jefferson Davis immediately selected Gen. Robert E. Lee, his most trusted military advisor, to take Johnston's place.[4]

Born in Virginia in 1807, Robert Edward Lee was a member of one of America's most distinguished and notable families at that time. Lee's father ("Light-Horse Harry" Lee) was a favorite lieutenant of George Washington. The Confederate general's future wife (Mary Anna Randolph Custis) was the great-granddaughter of Martha Washington. While separated by twenty years, Lee's and McClellan's respective careers often mirrored each other. Lee also graduated second in his West Point class of 1829, along with the man he eventually replaced, Joseph E. Johnston.

In one of military history's most remarkable reversals of fortune, Lee completely wrested the initiative away from the Union. He then shifted the fighting from the suburbs of Richmond to the outskirts of Washington, DC. During the Seven Days' Battles, from June 25 to July 1, 1862, and despite hefty losses to his army, Lee forced McClellan back across the peninsula, leading

Maj. Gen. Henry Halleck to evacuate the Army of the Potomac. Lee then pressed his army north to thrash Maj. Gen. John Pope's Army of Virginia at Cedar Mountain (August 19) and then at the Second Battle of Bull Run (August 28–30). Lee accomplished all of these feats in a mere two months' time.[5]

By August 1862, the American Civil War overall had taken on a decidedly gloomier tenor for the Union. The first half of the year witnessed Northern victories at places like Forts Henry and Donelson, New Orleans, and Memphis. This success was soon overshadowed by dramatic Union setbacks at the hands of Stonewall Jackson in the Shenandoah Valley, and by McClellan's evacuation of the Virginia Peninsula. Meanwhile, Confederate forces in the Western Theater were back on the offensive. In an attempt to reverse Federal gains of the previous spring, forces under Rebel commanders Gen. Braxton Bragg and Maj. Gen. Edmund Kirby Smith attempted to outflank Union major general Don Carlos Buell by launching an invasion deep into the heart of Kentucky.[6]

While battlefield developments were a source of enormous concern, political affairs were also at the forefront of many people's minds in the late summer of 1862. The national midterm elections in the North were scheduled for November, and they would be the first real test for the young Republican Party's tenuous grip on the federal government. No one could confidently or accurately predict the outcome of this first national election held amid a civil war or the extent to which military setbacks might influence the vote.

In the White House, pressure on the Lincoln administration came in every form and from every direction. During his presidency, Abraham Lincoln was not the beloved figure we know and study today. In 1862, he was beset from all sides by detractors and outright enemies. Lincoln was obviously not well liked by those in the South, but the Northern press, Democrats, abolitionists, and Radical Republicans were all ostensibly engaged in a running gun battle to establish who could be the president's harshest critic north of the Mason-Dixon Line.

In 1862 rumors abounded that Great Britain and France were poised to formally recognize the Confederacy. Such a decision threatened to upset the balance of political and military power. However, in this the seventeenth month of the war, few on either side, except possibly Abraham Lincoln, had any inkling that the conflict was on the verge of a dramatic transformation. Lincoln had long publicly insisted that he was waging war exclusively to preserve the Union. By the summer of 1862, the president was beginning to conclude that harsher measures were necessary to defeat the Confederacy. Lincoln stated in a July 1862 letter to New York banker and financier August Belmont, "This government cannot much longer play a game in which it stakes all and its enemies stake nothing. Those enemies must understand that they cannot experiment for ten years trying to destroy the government, and if they fail still come back into the Union unhurt."[7]

Lincoln now sought a means by which he could not only re-energize the Union war effort but also infuse it with a moral cause. The slavery question presented him with that means. Determined to make slave emancipation a Northern war aim, the president showed a draft of his Preliminary Emancipation Proclamation to his mostly stunned cabinet on July 22, 1862. After much heated debate, the administration decided to postpone the document's release until it could be backed up by a military victory.[8]

As the summer of 1862 waned, Lincoln's confidence in George McClellan was evaporating right along with it. Lincoln and Henry Halleck had determined that the best course of action was to remove McClellan's army from the Virginia Peninsula, and as the Army of the Potomac was extricating itself from the area, McClellan lost his command one corps and one division at a time. These units were sent north to bolster Pope and to check Lee's emerging threat to the nation's capital. By the time Second Bull Run began, McClellan was basically a commander without an army to lead.

As the struggle near Manassas reached its climax, the Lincoln administration was facing yet another great calamity unfolding before its very eyes. Scores of defeated Union soldiers streamed into Washington, DC, in the wake of yet another humiliating defeat. A Confederate army that had seemingly been on the threshold of downfall had somehow seized the initiative and was now on the offensive twenty miles from a capital that was on the verge of panic. The calamity facing the Union war effort was as bad as it could be and getting worse with every passing day.[9]

As one can imagine, the mood in Richmond was the exact opposite. In three months, Jefferson Davis had stopped asking where the seat of the Confederate government should relocate to once Richmond fell and started asking Robert E. Lee what his next offensive move might be. History now began to record the military genius of Robert E. Lee. His reputation grew over the next three years and beyond. To this day, we are all too familiar with this reputation of mythical proportions.[10]

On September 1 Lee tried once again to get on Pope's flank, sparking an inconclusive battle near Chantilly, Virginia. Lee then moved his army northwest. Pope's Army of Virginia had all but retreated into the defenses of Washington, DC, and Lee determined he could no longer pursue the enemy troops. He instead ordered his divisions to concentrate near a small Virginia crossroads called Dranesville. It was here that the Confederate general positioned his army for his next offensive thrust.

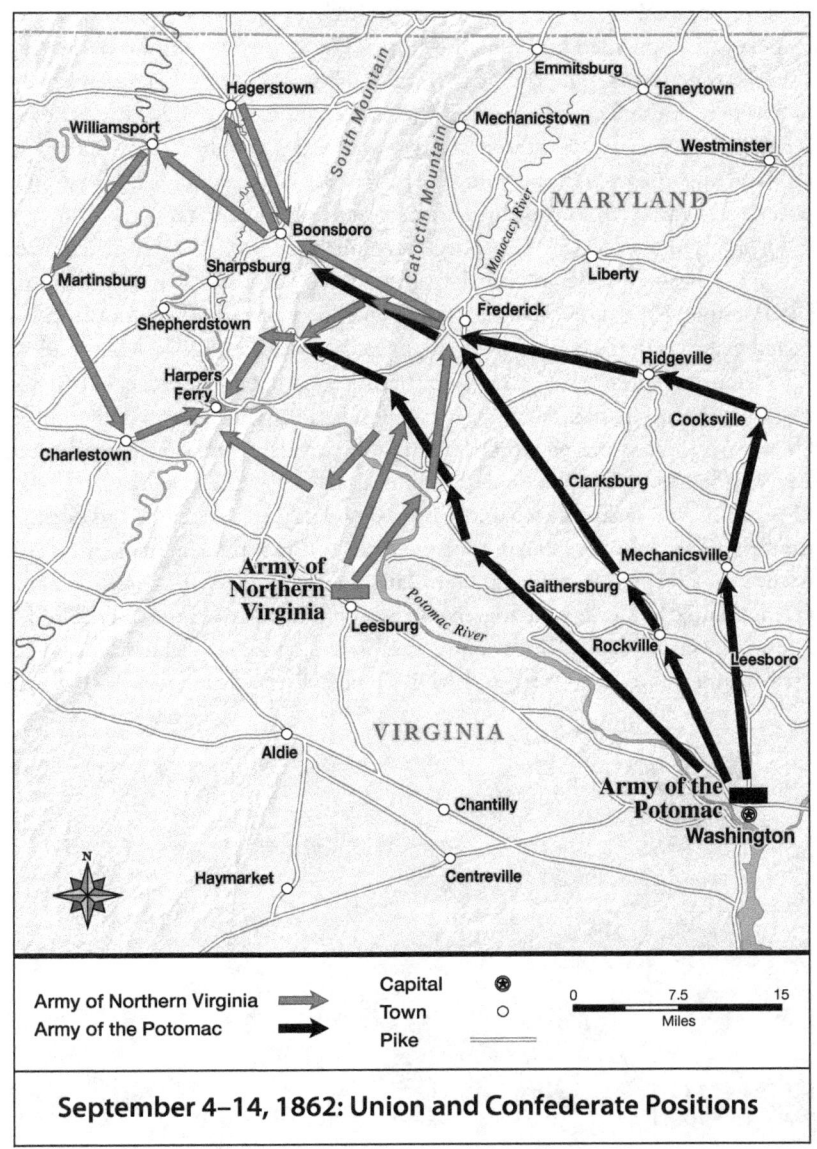

September 4–14, 1862: Union and Confederate Positions

Introduction

On September 3, resolved to capitalize on his hard-won initiative, Robert E. Lee decided to invade the North. He wrote Jefferson Davis, stating "The present seems to be the most propitious time since the commencement of the war for the Confederate Army to enter Maryland."[11] Lee now believed a decisive victory on Northern soil would yield a number of military and political advantages. Chief among there was the Confederacy's ability to negotiate separation from the Union from a position of strength.

On September 4 near Leesburg, Virginia, Lee pushed nine divisions of infantry, three brigades of cavalry, and eighty batteries of artillery across the Potomac River and into Maryland. This force of roughly 70,000 combat tested veterans made its way north, concentrating at Frederick, Maryland.

After pausing to rest and regroup, Lee decided to take a further calculated risk. Presuming he had several weeks before a disorganized and demoralized Union army could march from Washington threaten him, on September 10, Lee divided his army. He sent three divisions under the command of Maj. Gen. Stonewall Jackson, two under Maj. Gen Lafayette Mclaws, and one under Brig. Gen. John G. Walker to remove the threat of the Union garrison still occupying Harpers Ferry. Maj. Gen. James Longstreet, with three divisions (accompanied by Lee) would march west beyond the relative safety of the South Mountain range to await the completion of the operation. Maj. Gen. D. H. Hill would guard Lee's rear and Maj. Gen. J. E. B. Stuart's cavalry would

The Army of Northern Virginia crossing the Potomac, ca. 1862. *Harper's Weekly*.

provide screening and intelligence. Once this was complete, Lee presumed he would then be free to lead a unified Rebel army into Pennsylvania.[12]

In response to this crisis, Abraham Lincoln placed McClellan in field command of the Union army. On September 7, McClellan led a revamped Army of the Potomac north-west from Washington, DC. Six infantry corps, five brigades of cavalry, and sixty-four artillery batteries combined to make a force of roughly 87,000 men. Augmented by a large number of recent enlistees, three out of every eight men in this army had never fired their weapons in anger. By September 12, the van of McClellan's cobbled together army entered Frederick, and by the next day, he had most of his forces massed near the town.[13]

On September 13, two Union infantrymen found a copy of Lee's operational plans in a field near Frederick. Pushed up the chain of command, the orders eventually found their way to the Union Commanding General. Now armed with conformation of what he already believed McClellan determined to drive a wedge between Lee's divided army and to relive the besieged Union garrison at Harpers Ferry.[14]

On September 14, McClellan advanced on several key South Mountain passes. No less determined to stop him, Lee scrambled to reinforce and defend these positions. Lee now hoped to buy time for his overdue Harpers Ferry operation to complete and his scattered army to reassemble. From Turner's and Fox' Gaps astride the National Road to Crampton's Gap some six miles south, a desperate struggle raged from dawn till dusk along the steep slopes of South Mountain. All combined roughly 28,000 Union men in three corps assaulted some 18,000 Confederates in parts of four divisions resulting in over 5,000 casualties.

That same day, Stonewall Jackson finally had all of his divisions in position along the Potomac river. The encirclement of Harpers Ferry was finally complete. The Confederates began to rain down artillery fire on the Union defenders in preparation for the assault the next day. So confident was Jackson that the garrison would fall that at 8:00 pm he sent massage to Lee that predicted Confederate victory by the next morning.[15]

CHAPTER 1

BEFORE THE BATTLE, SEPTEMBER 15–16, 1862

Two critical decisions took place before the battle on September 17.

If you have skipped the preface, please return to it and read the definition of a critical decision to better understand the format in which this book is presented.

Lee Offers Battle at Sharpsburg

Situation

From the moment Robert E. Lee decided to divide his army on September 9, the operational clock was ticking. His army could only stay separated for a finite amount of time. Six days later, his calculated risk was beginning to come apart.

Lee faced a daunting situation on the evening of September 14. The garrison at Harpers Ferry had not evacuated in response to his incursion into the North, and the operation to eliminate this obstacle was now two days behind schedule. McClellan had suddenly and inexplicably taken a more aggressive posture in Lee's direct front at South Mountain. The Confederate general's ability to gain and maintain the initiative gave him the freedom to control the tenor of the campaign, and up until now, he had done so very effectively. By

Gen. Robert E. Lee, CSA, commanding, Army of Northern Virginia, ca. between 1860 and 1870. Library of Congress

the evening of September 14, however, the military scales had tipped in favor of the Union. Even though history paints McClellan as generally slow in his movements, his aggressiveness at South Mountain suddenly gave Lee pause. According to the Rebel commander, McClellan was now advancing "more rapidly than was convenient."[1]

The fighting at South Mountain on the fourteenth resulted in a Union victory, and the setting sun was the only thing that prevented a more decisive one. After a meeting with his lieutenants, Lee determined that Longstreet's and D. H. Hill's men could not hold Turner's Gap once dawn came, and that the position was to be abandoned during the night. Additionally, the Confederate forces defending Crampton's Gap fell back to Pleasant Valley and south to Maryland Heights. Although at that moment Lee was unaware of the full extent of the Crampton's Gap defeat, he knew McLaws's and Anderson's combined force at Maryland Heights and at the southern end of Pleasant Valley was the most vulnerable.

The geography of Pleasant Valley provided a genuine obstacle to the Confederate army. If the Union could get a sizeable force into the valley, McLaws and R. H. Anderson would have no direct line back to the main Confederate force now north of the Potomac. Their only viable option would be to cross the river and fall back through Harpers Ferry. This could not happen if Harpers Ferry was still held by the Union. If the men in McLaws's Command were forced to remain north of the Potomac, they might find themselves between the proverbial rock of the Union Sixth Corps and the hard place of the Harpers Ferry garrison.

On the evening of September 14, Lee issued orders to his widely scattered commands. Longstreet's, Hood's, and D. H. Hill's Divisions were to withdraw silently from South Mountain and fall back in the direction of Sharpsburg. Brig. Gen. William N. Pendleton, Lee's chief of artillery, was ordered to position batteries three miles west of Boonsboro and to send the remainder of the reserve artillery with a small infantry force to a position at Boteler's/Blackburn's Ford on the Potomac. Cavalry under Brig. Gen. Fitzhugh Lee's and Brig. Gen. John B. Hood's divisions, with the aforementioned artillery, were ordered to act as the rear guard during the withdrawal. Lee also sent a dispatch to Jackson asking for an estimated completion time for the Harpers Ferry operation.[2]

Lee also sent two telling messages. The first ordered Jackson to abandon the Harpers Ferry operation, fall back to Shepherdstown, and cover the army's retreat. The second directed McLaws and his troops to abandon Maryland Heights and with Anderson's Division make their way back to the relative safety of Virginia any way they could. Robert E. Lee's great invasion into the North was about to come to a sudden and inglorious end.

Lee sent the following to Layfette McLaws.

> GENERAL: The day has gone assistant us and this army will go by Sharpsburg and cross the river. It is necessary for you to abandon your position to-night. Send your trains not required on the road to cross the river. Your troops you must have well in hand to unite with this command, which will retire by Sharpsburg.[3]

After sending his dispatch to McLaws, Lee learned of the disaster at Crampton's Gap. After determining McClellan's forces were still firmly positioned in his front, Lee set his sights on the town of Keedysville as a dual-function position. He could use it to make a stand against the Federals in his front and to threaten the flank of any Union forces in Pleasant Valley.[4]

The scales of war tipped back in Lee's favor just a few hours later. Early on Monday, September 15, the general was scanning the countryside from a high meadow just east of the village of Sharpsburg. He was absorbing all the details of the landscape with his military engineer's eye as he pondered his next move. While initially wanting to consolidate his force at Keedysville, Lee changed his mind upon seeing a better defensive position farther west, beyond the Antietam Creek.

Lee was partial to the terrain due west of Antietam Creek for several

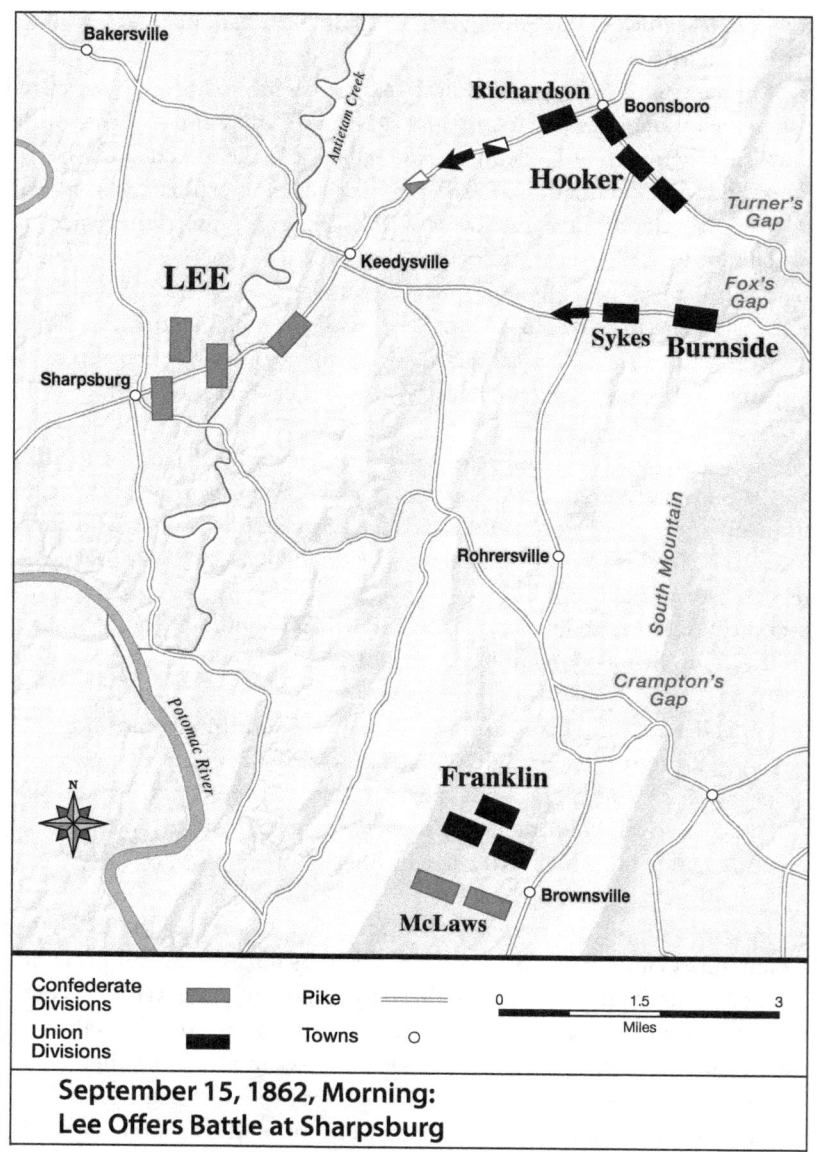

reasons. He needed favorable ground to conduct a new delaying action should McClellan continue his aggressive movements. Lee also wanted an advantageous position to concentrate his army north of the Potomac River should he have the opportunity to continue the campaign north. Additionally, because Franklin's corps was now in between McLaws's and Anderson's Divisions and the main body of Lee's army, Lee needed to be west of Elk Ridge to give the Rebel units a feasible route to rejoin him. Finally, the Antietam Creek also provided a natural barrier for the general to position his army behind. The terrain west of the Antietam at Sharpsburg filled all of these requirements. Its only drawback was its proximity to the Potomac River, which provided limited maneuvering space and a single crossing point for a retreat.

Lee was here at 8:00 a.m., enjoying a hot cup of coffee gifted to him by a local citizen, when he received a dispatch Stonewall Jackson had sent him the night before. The message said[5] "Through God's blessing, the advance, which commenced this evening, has been successful thus far, and I look to Him for complete success to-morrow."[6]

Options

With the capitulation of Harpers Ferry now imminent, Lee finally had the opportunity he was seeking. With this dispatch in hand, Lee had three options: continue to retreat to Virginia, reunite his army and fight at Sharpsburg, or reunite his army and maneuver toward Hagerstown.

Option 1

Lee could continue with his current mind-set, end the campaign, and make for Virginia via the Potomac Ford at Shepherdstown. He had sound reasons to believe this was his best option. Despite the message from Jackson, Lee had no real guarantee that the situation was turning in his favor. While the general trusted his lieutenant's judgment, Jackson's communication was more than twelve hours old, and there might be good reason to doubt the predictions it contained. At the moment Lee received the dispatch from Jackson, Harpers Ferry had not yet surrendered. The Army of Northern Virginia was still divided and vulnerable. On that morning, Lee had perhaps twelve thousand combat effectives he could use for the defense of his line at Sharpsburg. Twenty-five of his thirty-nine brigades were still at or near Harpers Ferry some fifteen miles and several hours' march away.[7]

Meanwhile, McClellan's army, would soon be pouring through Fox's and Turner's Gaps, if it was not already. Nothing but a small delaying force was available to slow the Federals. While Lee was doubtless unsure of the Union troop strength, he probably believed he was outnumbered. With fifty thousand

Federal effectives within a few hours' march of the Confederates' thinly held line, Lee would find himself in a very tight spot should McClellan continue to press him hard. The position, west of Antietam Creek, it left Lee with only one avenue of retreat should he need it. Only Boteler's Ford downstream of Shepherdstown presented a viable place where Lee's army could cross the Potomac. Also, even though the Potomac was close, Lee had too few men to completely anchor his flanks on the river. At various times over the next few days, both flanks were thinly held only by cavalry forces, if they were held at all. Moreover, conventional military wisdom dictates that a commander should never fight a battle with a significant obstacle at his back.

Finally, Lee had to consider whether the benefits he had envisioned at the beginning of the campaign were still worth the risks his army now faced. Were the high stakes for the invasion worth the possible destruction of his force? Should Lee decide to fall back, he could still regroup and reorganize south of the Potomac, then look to cross the river again should the opportunity present itself. The Confederate strategy made a battle necessary, but Lee was not compelled to fight at this exact place and time.[8]

Option 2

Lee could attempt to reunite his army and offer McClellan battle at Sharpsburg. The Confederate commander had invested a great deal to get to this point in the campaign, and ending it here without accomplishing any of his operational objectives would have been a bitter pill to swallow. If Lee did fall back across the Potomac to the safety of Virginia, he had no guarantee that the Army of the Potomac would allow him to recross the river later. The position his forces would soon occupy at Sharpsburg had many advantages for defense. The rolling terrain provided a good field of observation and fire. A predominant ridge along the Hagerstown Turnpike offered an ideal defensive position. Moreover, Antietam Creek created an excellent natural obstacle in Lee's front that was just deep and wide enough to hamper any concerted effort to cross it, except in a few places.

Lee could defend the Middle and Lower Bridges with his limited forces and allow the enemy only the Upper Bridge as a means to move troops over the creek. The ridge running along the Hagerstown Turnpike just north of the town provided an optimal position to defend his left. Lee held interior lines, and the area's good network of roads could be exploited to concentrate his army and to move infantry and artillery from point to point with relative ease. As the ground rose from Antietam Creek, it undulated in deep swales and gullies that would enable Lee to conceal or display his forces to the enemy as it suited him. While McClellan had been aggressive at South

Mountain, once he pushed the Rebels back, his forces were bottlenecked by the roads and the narrow mountain passes as Lee hoped they would be.

When given a choice, Lee always sought to be aggressive—so much so that this quality seemed his second nature. Since the moment Lee had assumed command of the army, he had held the initiative and forced the Federals to react to his actions. By keeping his campaign alive, he would reclaim the advantage he had fought so hard to gain.

Lastly, Lee's overarching operational objective was to force a decisive confrontation with the Army of the Potomac. As an opportunist who took everything into consideration, Lee might have assumed that this location offered the best place to accomplish that goal at that particular moment.[9]

Option 3

Lee could try to reunite his army and proceed toward Hagerstown. While the position at Sharpsburg was a strong one, and Lee was committed to no real destination once he crossed the Potomac River, traveling farther north would serve his overall operational goals. The Confederate commander looked for opportunities to threaten several points in the North, including Harrisburg directly and Baltimore and Philadelphia indirectly. Lee also could use Hagerstown as his jumping-off point for an invasion of Pennsylvania should he choose to do so. While we do not know for sure whether Lee really intended to move as far north as Harrisburg, it is reasonable to assume he would do so if it served his overall objectives. He might also have believed that another position farther north might offer more room for maneuver.

Additionally, the farther north of the Potomac Lee moved, the more he would cause difficulties not only for the Union army but also for the Lincoln administration. There was additional military and political capital to be gained by spreading further panic in the towns and cities of Maryland and Pennsylvania. Lee was contemplating this course of action while he was in Frederick, but the Harpers Ferry operation interrupted his plans. In fact, up until the moment the Union First Corps crossed over Antietam Creek on the afternoon of September 16, the general still considered a move north by way of the Hagerstown Turnpike a viable option.[10]

Decision

Lee decided to make a stand at Sharpsburg almost instantly upon receiving the message from Jackson (Option 2). He at once sent orders for all of his forces to converge on the town. The three divisions plus one brigade at hand continued marching west, crossed the Antietam, and occupied defensive positions.

Lee counted on the bottleneck of South Mountain to slow the Union army's advance for several days, thus giving him the time he needed. He outlined this thinking in a letter to Davis on the sixteenth: "Learning later in the evening that Crampton's Gap on the direct road from Fredericktown to Sharpsburg had been forced, and McLaws' rear thus threatened, and believing from a report from Genl Jackson that Harper's Ferry would fall next morning, I determined to withdraw Longstreet and D. H. Hill from their positions and retire to the vicinity of Sharpsburg, where the army could be more readily united."[11]

Understanding Lee's decision and intentions at this moment can be a bit challenging. Based on some accounts, you could argue that he initially intended Sharpsburg to be used only as a concertation point for his army to continue his campaign north into Pennsylvania (Option 3). Some historians indicate Lee sent a force to reconnoiter a route north late on September 16. This patrol reported that a large Union force (Hooker) had crossed the creek and now blocked the way. Only after receiving this news did Lee decide to stand and fight (Option 2). However, even if Lee had initially selected Option 3, current circumstances dictated that he would fight here regardless.

Lee must have also believed he had time before McClellan would attack him. However, assuming that McClellan would loiter east of the Potomac for several days and not send forces across Antietam Creek to block the Rebels' way north would seem to grossly underestimate an enemy that had shown unpredictable aggressiveness for almost a week. Additionally, even if Lee contemplated a turning movement on the Union right, he could not execute it while his army was still divided. McLaws and Anderson would not be on the field until the early morning of the seventeenth, and A. P. Hill would not arrive until later in the afternoon. Lee had to wait for these units to join the main body. Otherwise, or the whole reason for standing at Sharpsburg would become pointless. For all intents and purposes, once Lee told his men, "We will make our stand on these hills," he committed himself to battle at Antietam whether he realized it or not.[12]

Results/Impact

Making a stand at Sharpsburg determined the location for the upcoming fight and was the next step in actually bringing it on. Additionally, Lee's decision forced McClellan to pause to wonder why. On September 15 and 16, Lee's aggressive stance on the west bank of Antietam Creek was almost entirely a bluff, but it was a good enough bluff to make McClellan contemplate what his enemy was up to and why he was choosing to stand and fight here and now. There is also good reason to believe that McClellan took Lee's defiance as a

Stephen D. Lee's Confederate gun line, Antietam National Battlefield, modern image. Author.

sign that the Confederates indeed possessed the vast numbers of men that the Union commander thought they had from the outset of the campaign.[13]

Alternative Decision/Scenario

Had Lee decided to abandon his campaign at this point, events might have unfolded quite differently. We might have still seen a battle at Sharpsburg, but several days later. We might have seen an engagement at Williamsport or even Shepherdstown as Lee attempted to recross the Potomac, or we might have seen no fighting at all. Once Lee retreated over the Potomac on September 18 after fighting along Antietam Creek, McClellan considered his campaign a success and did not engage in a vigorous pursuit. There is an excellent chance that McClellan, feeling he had accomplished his objective of driving Lee from Northern soil, might have simply have let him go at this time as well.[14]

McClellan Launches His Attack

Situation

To understand the story of the Maryland Campaign in its fullest sense is to recognize that many conspicuous themes surround it. One of the most famous or infamous of these is that, in spite of his vastly superior numbers on

Maj. Gen. George Brinton McClellan and staff, USA, commander, Union Army of the Potomac. Library of Congress / National Archives

September 15 and 16, an overly cautious or even cowardly McClellan decided not to attack, giving Lee valuable time to consolidate his army. Views on this particular subject vary depending on whom you read. Stephen Sears implies that McClellan squandered those critical hours and missed an opportunity to attack due to his own incompetence and caution, while Ethan Rafuse tells of a McClellan who wanted to attack but was let down by his corps commanders and by pure bad luck. More recently, Steven Stotelmyer points out that the Union commander had compelling military reasons not to attack on the fifteenth. Whatever version of McClellan the reader believes commanded the Army of the Potomac during these critical hours is not nearly as important as the choices the general had before him.[15]

At dawn on September 15, it became evident to the Union troops advancing on the now-abandoned Confederate positions at South Mountain that they had struck the critical first blow of the campaign. McClellan possessed Lee's operational plans and had used them to drive the Confederate forces from the South Mountain passes. Initial reports indicated that the Rebels were falling back, possibly as far as the Potomac. For the briefest of moments, McClellan had stolen the initiative from his opponent, and what he did next would determine how long he could hold it. The next two days proved essential to the course of the campaign and any impending battle.

From his headquarters at Bolivar, George McClellan sensed there was still an opportunity to follow up on the successes from the night before and continue to pressure the retreating Confederate army. It is safe to say that McClellan was still somewhat in the dark about the number of enemy troops in his front. But in those early morning hours, he did know that a significant portion of the Confederate army remained at Harpers Ferry. McClellan would not learn about the surrender of the Harpers Ferry garrison until later on the fifteenth, and that information quickly changed the dynamics of the situation. Lee still had an opportunity to reconsolidate his army. Yet for the moment, the odds were still in McClellan's favor, as this action would take some time for Lee to complete.[16]

McClellan sent the following to Halleck on the evening of September 14:

> After a very severe engagement, the corps of Hooker and Reno have carried the heights commanding the Hagerstown road. The troops behaved magnificently. They never fought better. Franklin has been hotly engaged on the extreme left. I do not yet know the result, except that the firing indicated progress on his part. The action continued until after dark, and terminated leaving us in possession of the entire crest. It has been a glorious victory. I cannot yet tell whether the enemy will retreat during the night or appear in increased force in the morning. I am hurrying up everything from the rear, to be prepared for any eventuality.[17]

Like most of McClellan's military career, controversy surrounds the decision outlined in the above letter. It can be a bit difficult to unpack all of that happened on those critical two days leading up to the Battle of Antietam.

By 8:00 a.m. on September 15, McClellan and his staff, perhaps believing that Lee was falling back, perhaps as far as the Potomac, shot off several dispatches to his commands indicating that his army would pursue and attack. Even before that, at 7:00 a.m., Hooker ordered Maj. Gen. Israel B. Richardson's Second Corps division, which was temporarily attached to his own corps, to move out and chase the retreating enemy.[18] McClellan then fired off two somewhat premature messages to Halleck that seem like a combination of rumor and speculation sprinkled with a few facts:

McClellan initially sent the following message to Henry Halleck.

> I have just learned from General Hooker, in the advance, who states that the information is perfectly reliable that the enemy is making for Shepherdstown in a perfect panic; and General Lee last night stated publicly that he must admit they had been shockingly

whipped. I am hurling everything forward to endeavor to press their retreat to the utmost. [19]

Later that morning, McClellan sent another dispatch to Halleck:

> Information this moment received completely confirms the rout and demoralization of the rebel army. General Lee is reported wounded and Garland killed. Hooker alone has over 1,000 more prisoners. It is stated that Lee gives his loss as 15,000. We are following as rapidly as the men can move.[20]

Alfred Pleasonton's cavalry, also on the move at first light, was ordered to pursue the fleeing Rebels. The balance of the Union infantry corps was ordered to follow Hooker and Pleasonton with all haste. Learning of Franklin's success at Crampton's, McClellan ordered him to advance as well.

Thereafter, very little went right for the Union army commander. Burnside delayed getting the Ninth Corps moving from Fox's Gap, shoddy staff work congested all the roads. To add to McClellan's bad luck, he received two messages from Franklin as he was moving west into Pleasant Valley. The first, arriving at 11:00 a.m., indicated that Franklin's advance on Maryland Heights had stalled, and the second, arriving at 3:15 p.m. stated that Harpers Ferry had fallen to the Confederates.[21]

Just after noon, Richardson, accompanied by Col. John F. Farnsworth's cavalry brigade, advanced to the east bank of Antietam Creek. The unit had been actively pressing Lee's rear guard (Brig. Gen. Fitzhugh Lee) since encountering it at Boonsboro. Upon reaching a point west of Keedysville, these Federals discovered that the Confederate army was not, in fact, retreating but turning to make a stand. When Richardson arrived, he found the Army of Northern Virginia drawn up in line of battle west of Antietam Creek. Richardson was joined by Hooker at 2:00 p.m. and by Sumner an hour later, and the generals quickly determined they lacked the manpower to launch an attack on the Confederate position. Hooker assumed the enemy was as many as fifty thousand men strong. Rather than deploying immediately, the Union generals then halted the advance. The resulting traffic jam clogged the roads all the way back to Turner's Gap. McClellan arrived at approximately 4:00 p.m., also declaring it impossible to attack that day.

At this moment, the Union high command had only the vaguest idea of what the ground was like on the other side of the creek, and the size of the forces opposing them was anybody's guess. Additionally, the rest of the Army of the Potomac was spread out in a nine-mile-long column from Keedysville

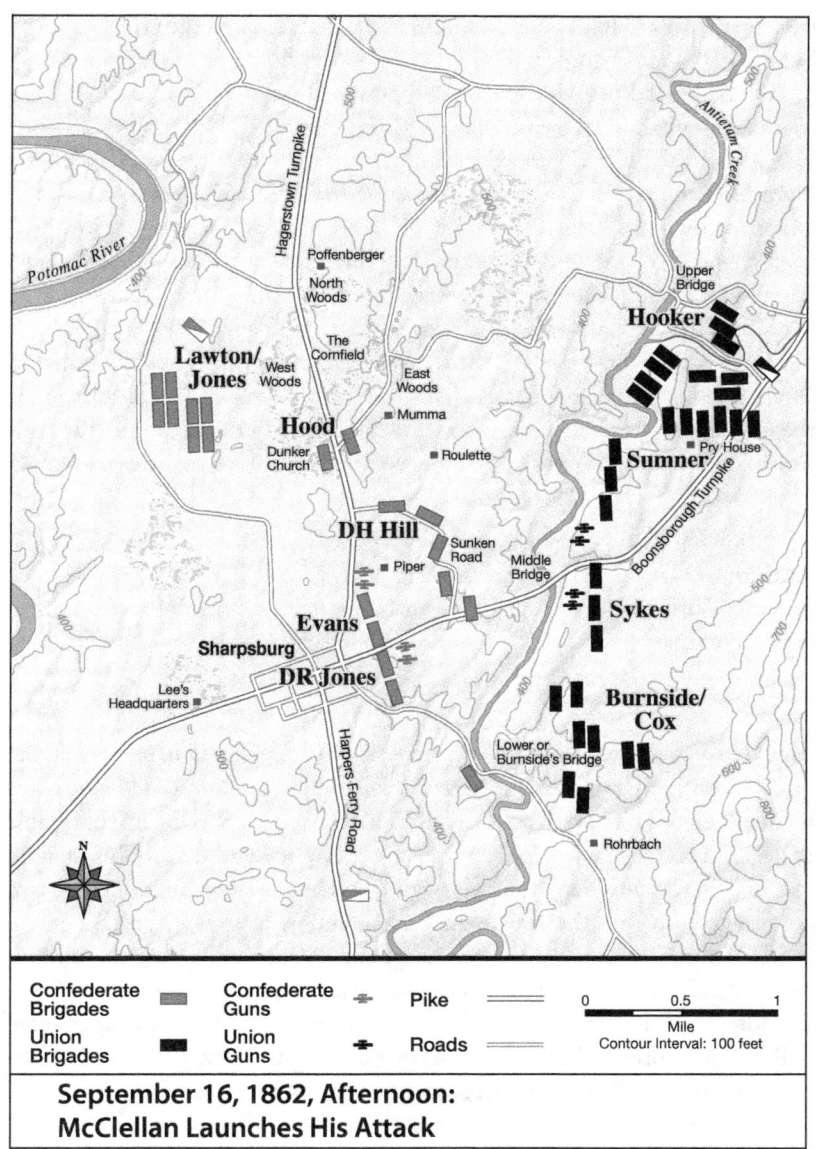

September 16, 1862, Afternoon: McClellan Launches His Attack

back to Turner's Gap. As darkness fell, McClellan ordered the army deployed but did not issue any orders to prepare for an attack the next day.[22]

On September 16, McClellan's manpower situation improved slightly. By that morning, all his forces except Franklin, Couch, and Humphreys's Third Division of the Fifth Corps were stationed within a few miles of McClellan's forward headquarters at the Pry House. Although he did not know it, the Union commander held the advantage in manpower over his enemy. This soon changed, as the nine thousand or so men that made up Jackson's command were now arriving from Harpers Ferry.

When McClellan awoke, he discovered a dense fog in the valley that completely shrouded his view of Antietam Creek and the foe beyond. Once it lifted, at about 10:00 a.m., McClellan began to develop his plan. He also spent the next several hours assigning bivouacs, placing batteries, and riding his positions on the east side of the creek to ascertain the Confederate dispositions.[23]

Options

With the situation changing by the moment, McClellan could either attack or wait. With his foe standing defiantly in front of him, he had a critical decision to make.

Option 1

McClellan could send his army across Antietam Creek and launch an attack on Lee, continuing to press his initiative and falling on the Confederate commander before he was prepared. If McClellan acted quickly, he might be able to descend on the enemy troops and defeat them in detail. Part of his mission was to drive the invaders from Maryland, and by that morning it might have seemed to him that the Rebels had no intention of leaving on their own. McClellan might have concluded that if the Confederates were to be extricated from Maryland, they would have to be attacked and driven out by force. In addition, perceived delays on the part of the army might have created more political pressure on McClellan. With each passing day, it would become more and more difficult for him to justify any passive stance.

Additionally, while he was still unsure of his opponent's strength, McClellan might have thought that the longer he waited, the longer his odds would be. As each hour passed, surely those forces at Harpers Ferry would continue to make their way to Lee. McClellan now had roughly fifty thousand men of all arms assembled east of the creek. Still flush with victory after the encounter at South Mountain, the morale of his men was as high as he could have desired. This is what Abraham Lincoln and the War Department were hoping would happen. After the news of the victory at South Mountain reached him, the president sent an enthusiastic and somewhat prodding telegram to his commander: "God bless you and all with you. Destroy the rebel army if possible."[24]

Option 2

McClellan could wait and see what, if anything, Lee would do. While it is difficult to be certain, McClellan might have deemed waiting for Lee to either continue his retreat or attempt to attack first was his best option. Despite his best efforts, the Federal commander had only the vaguest idea of the Confederate position across the river. In his autobiography, McClellan bemoaned the advantages of Lee's position: "On all favorable points the enemy's artillery was posted, and their reserves, hidden from view by the hills on which their line of battle was formed, could manoeuvre unobserved by our army, and from the shortness of their line could rapidly reinforce any point threatened by our attack. Their position, stretching across the angle formed by the Potomac and Antietam, their flanks and rear protected by these streams, was one of the strongest to be found in this region of country, which is well adapted to defensive warfare."[25]

Even though McClellan had the bulk of his army with him, it was not in the best of shape. While the Army of the Potomac's situation was not as acute as Lee's, the force had its own challenges with combating straggling and feeding its men. Disorganization caused commissary wagons to be too far from the men they were supposed to feed. Hungry Ninth Corps men reportedly searched the haversacks of dead Rebels after South Mountain. Furthermore, in the course of driving the Confederates from South Mountain, McClellan's army suffered over 2,300 casualties. The exhausted First and Ninth Corps men not only marched and fought from dawn until dusk on September 14, but they also slept in the cold on their arms that night. They then were awakened to pursue their foe that next morning. To add to McClellan's misfortune, Ninth Corps commander Jesse Reno had been mortally wounded, and new Twelfth Corps commander. Maj. Gen. Joseph K. Mansfield possessed very sparse combat command experience.[26]

Additionally, this reorganized Army of the Potomac had only existed in its current state for perhaps a week at this point. McClellan was still getting to know his command, which was not the army McClellan had led on the peninsula. Under ideal conditions, these soldiers were closer to an unwieldy mob than to a professional army. Thus it was a genuine challenge for McClellan to bend this immature force to his will. Many of the regiments he commanded were new and untested in battle, and in many cases, the army was being assembled as it marched. Caution was not uncalled for—even at this relatively early stage of the war, Robert E. Lee had established a reputation for doing the unexpected in battle.[27]

Decision

McClellan chose to attack (Option 1). On the afternoon of the sixteenth, he ordered Hooker and his First Corps to advance across the Antietam. While it is difficult to say precisely when he decided to attack, McClellan did not issue these orders to Hooker until 2:00 p.m. By then, more than twenty-four hours had passed since the Army of the Potomac had first arrived on the field. Unpacking McClellan's ultimate plan for the battle is challenging to be sure as McClellan seems to contradict himself in his after-action reports. October 15, 1862, he stated, "The design was to make the main attack upon the enemy's left—at least to create a diversion in favor of the main attack, with the hope of something more by assailing the enemy's right—and, as soon as one or both of the flank movements were fully successful, to attack their center with any reserve I might then have on hand."[28]

While we can argue that may have been unnecessary delays and that McClellan may have been able to attack on September 15 or 16, he did make the ultimate decision to attack—perhaps despite some lingering doubts he had about his chances for success.

Results/Impact

The most obvious and direct result of this decision by McClellan was that it inaugurated the Battle of Antietam by forcing Robert E. Lee to fight. Secondarily, it ensured that the battle occurred at the location and on the day that history now records. McClellan's choice also allowed Lee to engage in a defensive battle on ground of his own choosing possessing good interior lines. One other impact of note is that McClellan's decision prevented Lee from moving his army north to continue his campaign of maneuver, perhaps making Confederate commander's determination to fight here somewhat quixotic. As mentioned in discussion of the last critical decision, it is likely that Lee never planned to linger for very long in the vicinity of Sharpsburg. Instead, he wanted to move north beyond McClellan's right flank. By deciding to attack and sending Hooker's corps across the creek, McClellan effectively blocked Lee from executing that movement. Modern scholars like Dennis Frye argue that this is precisely what McClellan had planned all along.[29]

Alternative Decision/Scenario

Any number of scenarios could have resulted had McClellan waited to see what Lee would do. One possible outcome is that we might have seen the bat-

Pry House, McClellan's forward headquarters, Antietam National Battlefield, modern image. Author.

tle take place on September 18, September 19, or even later. Had Lee managed to slip around McClellan's right, the fighting might have occurred someplace else farther north.

If McClellan had given him time, the Confederate commander would have taken full advantage of it. With an opportunity to rest, feed, and, most importantly, concentrate his army, Lee would have made his men stronger. After the battle, hundreds and perhaps thousands of stragglers would rejoin his army at Sharpsburg. Any fighting beyond the seventeenth would have involved Lee's former stragglers who were then up and with him. More significantly, after A. P. Hill joined Lee's force at Sharpsburg on the afternoon of the seventeenth, Lee accomplished his goal of reuniting his army, and he was free to march his entire force north on the Hagerstown Turnpike to continue his campaign on into Pennsylvania.

CHAPTER 2

THE BATTLE OF ANTIETAM, SEPTEMBER 17, 1862

The next ten decisions took place during the Battle of Antietam.

By the time the sun set on September 17, 1862, the battle had raged interrupted for the better part of twelve hours. Antietam came to be known as America's bloodiest day in large part because the killing that began the moment there was enough light to see, persisted until the shroud of darkness made it impractical to continue.

Hooker Opens the Battle

Situation

Born in Massachusetts into a family that had lived in the state since the early 1600s, Maj. Gen. Joseph Hooker was the grandson of a Revolutionary War captain. Joe Hooker graduated from West Point in 1837, ranking twenty-ninth out of a class of fifty that included such personalities as Braxton Bragg, Jubal Early, William French, John Sedgwick, John Pemberton, and Robert Chilton.

History has portrayed Joseph Hooker as a hard-drinking ladies' man and a somewhat problematic commander. Author and Antietam veteran Francis Palfrey described the First Corps commander as follows: "Brave, handsome, vain, insubordinate, plausible, untrustworthy, he had many of the merits

Maj. Gen. Joseph Hooker, USA, commander, First Corps. Library of Congress / National Archives.

of a lieutenant, but not all, and he too failed dismally when he was made commander-in-chief. As an inferior, he planned badly and fought well; as chief, he planned well and fought badly." As a result of a reporter's typo, Hooker earned the brash sobriquet of Fighting Joe, which he reportedly despised.[1]

By the morning of September 17, Hooker's First Corps had been right in the thick of the previous three days' action. As part of Burnside's wing, the corps had been heavily engaged at Turner's Gap on September 14, suffering roughly one thousand casualties. The First Corps pursued the retreating Confederates from Turner's Gap and then became among the first Union units to arrive east of Antietam Creek on the afternoon of September 15. Hooker's men soon discovered a Confederate army that had defiantly turned to challenge its Federal pursuers. On the afternoon of September 16, McClellan ordered Hooker's 9,400-man corps to open the offensive on Lee's left the next day, sending its three divisions west of the Antietam Creek. Additionally, the Union commanding general gave Hooker command authority over that end of the field and empowered him to ask for any necessary reinforcements. Hooker assumed that any troops sent to aid him would fall under his control. The general thus had license to determine how this initial effort of the battle would manifest itself.[2]

The Antietam Battlefield encompasses just over ten square miles. Located in a mostly rural corner of Washington County, Maryland, the ground is neatly nestled in several great curves of the Potomac River. Several significant topographical features of the area around Sharpsburg influenced the fighting. The

September 17, 1862

Antietam Creek generally flows north to south before emptying into the Potomac several miles below Shepherdstown. While gently sloping in some spots, the banks of the creek become incredibly steep in others. Four triple-arch stone bridges spanned Antietam Creek at the time of the battle, extending from an intersection of the Keedysville Road in the north to just above the creek's confluence with the Potomac in the south. The three bridges closest to Sharpsburg became of interest to both armies as they represented critical potential crossing points. North to south, they are the Upper, Middle, and Lower Bridges, respectively. Several fords also intersected the creek at vital points.

The Hagerstown Turnpike ran north from Sharpsburg, connecting the town with the seat of Washington County, aptly named Hagerstown. West of the turnpike a series of low ridges begins in the north at a bend in the Potomac, then runs south through the town of Sharpsburg and along the Harper's Ferry Road. Splitting the battlefield along its north–south axis, the Boonsboro Turnpike crossed the creek at the Middle Bridge, then entered the eastern end of Sharpsburg. As it exited to the west of town, it became the Shepherdstown Pike, connecting Sharpsburg to the Potomac and beyond.

The field's deceivingly uneven ground could hide entire brigades from view while exposing others to deadly fire. In 1862, this was primarily an agricultural area. Then much as now, the pastoral landscape was dotted with farmhouses, country lanes, fields, and woodlots.

On the morning of September 17, the Army of Northern Virginia occupied a 3.5-mile line running from just south of the Lower/Rohrbach Bridge, north across the Boonsboro Turnpike, and along a sunken farm lane. Just beyond this Sunken Road, the line bent to the west at the Samuel Mumma Farm, where it was anchored at the bend in the Potomac. A section of high ground directly east of a little whitewashed building (the Dunker Church) along the Hagerstown Pike was the prominent feature of this end of the field. The Confederates massed their infantry and artillery here. Lee also positioned units in this location to contest attempted crossings of the Lower and Middle Bridges, but he lacked the manpower to cover the area near the Upper Bridge. As a result, Lee was compelled to place the bulk of his forces on the more vulnerable left side of his line near the church. Stonewall Jackson, who commanded this end of the field, had about fourteen thousand men in line and in immediate support.

A mixed bag of forces made up Jackson's position, including the eight brigades of the divisions of Brig. Gen. John R. Jones and Brig. Gen. Alexander Lawton. These troops were positioned in and around the plateau of ground near the Dunker Church, along the Smoketown Road, and in the East and West Woods. The Confederates extended their front north to within a few

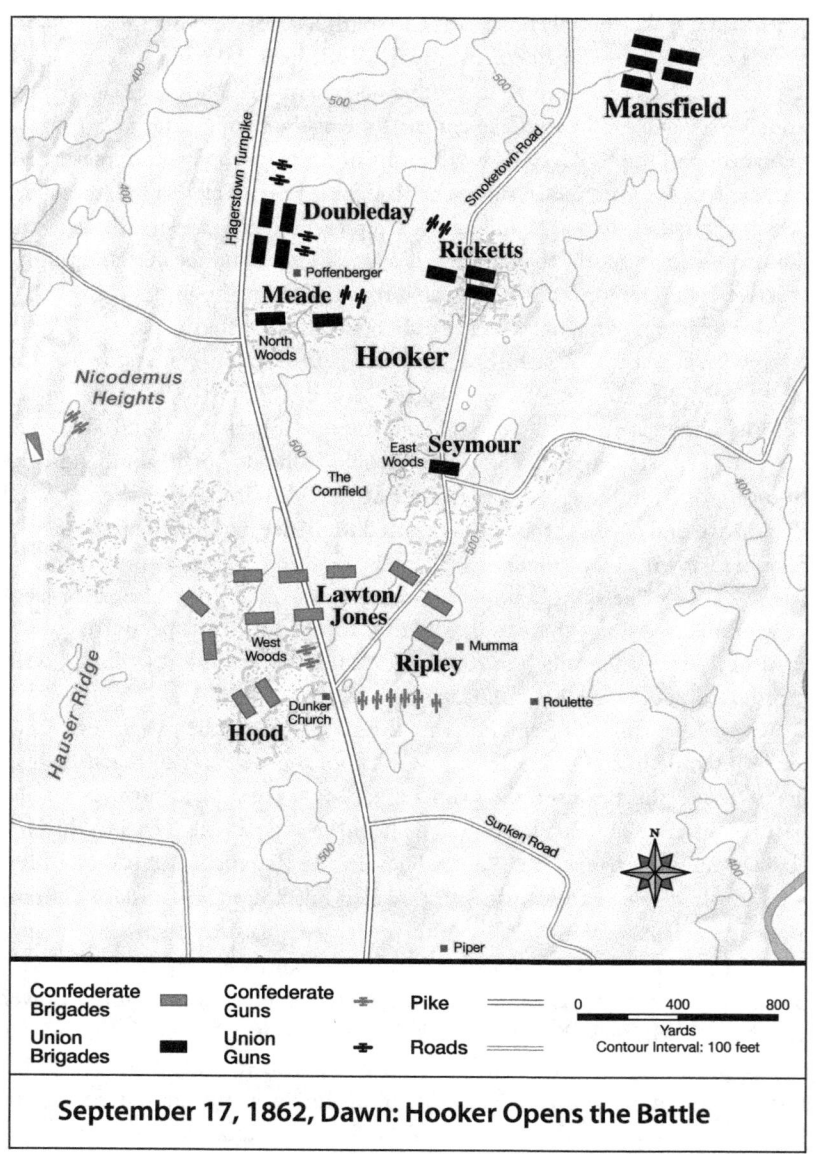

September 17, 1862, Dawn: Hooker Opens the Battle

hundred yards of a twenty-acre cornfield. The two-brigade division of Brig. Gen. John B. Hood was in immediate reserve west of the Dunker Church. D. H. Hill's division had one brigade reinforcing Lawton, another straddling the Boonsboro Turnpike, and three nearby in the Sunken Road. These Confederates were supported by no fewer than eight batteries of artillery. Brig. Gen. Fitzhugh Lee's cavalry brigade and three batteries of horse artillery commanded by Capt. John Pelham formed the extreme left of the line. Pelham's artillery defended the half-mile gap between the Hagerstown Turnpike and the Potomac River. This position on Nicodemus Heights was also supported throughout the morning by Brig. Gen. Jubal A. Early's brigade of Lawton's Division.[3]

At 2:00 p.m. on September 16, Hooker received orders from McClellan to cross the creek by the Upper Bridge and Pry's Ford below it. His orders were to attack and, if possible, crush Lee's left. The First Corps divisions of Maj. Gen. George G. Meade and Brig. Gen. James Ricketts crossed at the bridge, while the division of Brig. Gen. Abner Doubleday crossed at the ford. Hooker had put his troops in motion by 4:00 p.m. As the sun was setting, he was across the creek advancing Meade's division south along the Smoketown Road and into the East Woods. It was here that Federal infantry belonging to Brig. Gen. Truman Seymour's brigade made contact with Confederate pickets from Hood's Division occupying a position near the woods. A small but sharp engagement ensued. This preliminary fighting slowly died down as darkness covered the battlefield.

Not wanting to face the Rebels with his corps alone, Hooker had asked for additional support from McClellan. The Union commanding general responded by ordering Mansfield's Twelfth Corps, with some 7,600 men, across the creek later that night. The Twelfth took a position about a mile to Hooker's left and rear, just west of the Upper Bridge crossing. McClellan also made Maj. Gen. Edwin V. Sumner's Second Corps available as a reserve force. At that moment, however, McClellan had not yet made up his mind as to when and where the Second Corps would go in.[4]

Once Hooker had his corps west of the Antietam Creek, he established his headquarters at the Joseph Poffenberger Farm. From here, Hooker could just make out a small whitewashed building on some high ground to his south. The building was the Dunker Church, about a mile from Hooker's position. Confederate colonel Stephen D. Lee's nineteen-gun artillery battalion occupied the open plateau just to the east of this church. Sometimes referred to as a schoolhouse in after-action reports, the church made an easily identifiable objective for the Federals to converge on. Hooker viewed this high ground as key terrain as he believed he was on Lee's left flank. If he could take this area, Hooker reasoned he could not only imperil the Confederate position here, but also deploy Union artillery to enfilade the Confederates occupying the Sunken Road and in the town beyond. Subsequently, Hooker positioned his corps in and around the Poffenberger Farm with the intent of launching his attack at dawn: 5:50 a.m. The stage was set for the opening phase of the battle. The issue Joe Hooker now faced was how he would strike the first blow of the forthcoming engagement. Reports indicate that he and McClellan spoke on at least three separate occasions on September 16, and while the full context of those conversations is not known, it can be assumed that the men discussed what Hooker was expected to do the next day.[5]

Options

The First Corps commander had five tactical options open to him. He could attack by sending his corps directly at the church while Mansfield provided support on his left. Hooker could also launch an in-depth assault at the church using his and Mansfield's corps, attack simultaneously with Mansfield's force on his left, or carry out an offensive with Mansfield's men on his right. Alternatively, the two corps could move south along the creek and attack the apex of the Confederate line.

Option 1

To exploit any opportunities the situation offered, Hooker could use his own corps as the spearhead of an attack while using Mansfield's men and any additional forces available to him (presumably Sumner) on his left for support. Beyond their immediate sight line, the Union command was somewhat in the dark as to the Confederates' disposition. Hooker could decide that his best move was to probe the Rebel defenses with this initial advance and then attack with reinforcements once the situation clarified itself. However, it is not clear what support besides the Twelfth Corps Hooker could expect. His corps and Mansfield's were the only ones west of Antietam Creek at dawn on September 17, and additional units would have to cross the creek to be of any assistance.[6]

Option 2

Hooker could launch a weighted attack directly at the church, using his corps as a spearhead. Once this offensive eventually lost momentum, he could order Mansfield to attack through his corps and continue along the same axis of advance. This plan would have the advantage of a continuing assault on an already weakened point in the Confederate defensive line. One drawback might be that the area of advance could become clogged and choked with men as the battle raged over it.

Option 3

Hooker could launch simultaneous assaults with his corps along the Hagerstown Turnpike and with Mansfield's on his left. He could then order any additional support (presumably Sumner) to attack directly west from the Pry's Ford crossing at Antietam Creek at a designated point on the line. While tactically challenging to execute, this approach would create additional challenges for the Confederates by forcing them to defend multiple positions of their line at once.

Option 4

Hooker could launch an assault at the high ground near the church with the First Corps while sending Mansfield's corps to his right. Mansfield's force would attack west of the Hagerstown Turnpike on the ground between it and the Potomac, driving off those Confederate units defending the Nicodemus Heights. Any additional supporting units could then be sent in on Hooker's left.

Option 5

Hooker could advance with his corps and the Twelfth as support on a line closer to the creek and assault the apex of Lee's position near the Sunken Road. Doing so would allow him to take full advantage of the long-range Union artillery and use the creek to protect his flank. According to author Joseph Harsh, this is what McClellan had in mind all along.[7]

Decision

Hooker indicated his intentions in his after-action report written on November 8, 1862:

> At daylight Gibbon's and Hartsuff's brigades were thrown forward, supported with the brigades of their respective divisions, while Meade followed them up in the center, instructed to spring to the assistance of either, as circumstances might require. Seymour continued to hold the advance, with the utmost firmness and resolution, until our troops had passed him. With these dispositions completed, the battle was soon renewed on the morning of the 17th. My object was to gain the high ground nearly three-quarters of a mile in

advance of me, and which commanded the position taken by the enemy on his retreat from South Mountain; to prevent which he had been re-enforced by Jackson's corps during the night and at the same time had planted field batteries on high ground on our right and rear, to enfilade our lines when exposed during the advance.[8]

With artillery on both sides firing as soon as there was light enough to see, Hooker opened the battle at roughly 5:30 a.m. with his corps alone (Option 1). Hooker eventually committed all three of his divisions in a seesaw effort to drive the Confederates from the high ground before him. Doubleday, Ricketts, and Meade battled Jackson's two divisions for the quarter-square-mile area that made up the East Woods, the West Woods, and the space surrounding the Dunker Church. Mansfield's Twelfth Corps was ordered to support the First Corps at 5:30 a.m., but it did not make contact with Confederate forces until 7:15 a.m.[9] The Second Corps did not cross Antietam Creek until that morning, and while it was ordered to advance at 7:20 a.m., the unit did not join the battle until 8:30 a.m. Additionally, only the Second Corps divisions of Maj. Gen. John Sedgwick and Brig. Gen. William French participated in this initial movement. McClellan held back Maj. Gen. Israel B. Richardson's division until Morell's division of the Fifth Corps could replace it in the tactical reserve. Richardson did not cross the creek until almost two hours later.[10]

Results/Impact

Despite his fear that the Confederates would overwhelm his single corps, Hooker primarily fought the opening phase of the battle (almost two hours) with the First Corps alone. Mansfield's Twelfth Corps, stopping and starting several times during its mile-long advance to the front, did not arrive on the field until after 7:00 a.m. By the time Mansfield was in action, the three divisions of the First were more or less rendered combat ineffective.[11] Additionally, Hooker never explained why he did not bring Mansfield's corps closer to his own the evening before. Perhaps the Twelfth's position gave Hooker some deployment flexibility that only he understood. Moreover, based on reports, confusion and ignorance of the enemy's position prevailed in the Union army that day. Perhaps Hooker deemed it too risky for his whole force to attack without full knowledge of the Confederate position.[12]

Also, Hooker incorrectly believed that he was on the enemy's flank. While he was unaware of this fact at the time, the piecemeal attacks at the opening of the battle played right into Lee's hands. Committing at most two divisions at a time enabled Lee and Jackson to deploy their reserves at one point of attack on the field and then another to counter Hooker. At least three or four times during the morning phase of the battle, Confederates described their desperate position as the weight of the Union attacks pushed them near to the breaking point. In each case, the Rebels were able to counterattack, stemming the Union tide.[13] It has been argued that this is precisely the outcome McClellan wanted, as the enemy would be forced to bolster his left by weakening his right, thereby becoming extremely vulnerable.

Hooker's attack flowed along the line of the Hagerstown Turnpike and into the East Woods, the infamous Cornfield, and the West Woods, desperately driving for the plateau beyond the Smoketown Road. The Twelfth and Second Corps each become engaged separately, basically fighting over and over again for the same piece of ground. Consequently, the three Union corps involved in the morning phase of the battle were used up one by one as the Confederates countered successive unsupported attacks. Any semblance of command and control was lost when Hooker and Mansfield both became casualties.

Hooker recounted the day in his after-action report:

> We had not proceeded far before I discovered that a heavy force of the enemy had taken possession of a corn-field (I have since learned about a thirty-acre field) in my immediate front, and from the sun's rays falling on their bayonets projecting above the corn could see that the field was filled with the enemy, with arms in their hands, standing apparently at "support arms." Instructions were immediately given for the assemblage of all of my spare batteries, near at hand, of which I think there were five or six, to spring into battery, on the right of his field, and to open with canister at once. In the time I am writing every stalk of corn in the northern and greater part of the field was cut as closely as could have been done with a knife, and the slain lay in rows precisely as they stood in their ranks a few moments before. It was never my fortune to witness a more bloody, dismal battle-field.[14]

Hooker's choice to fight with his corps alone proved critical because it launched a battle that was a series of uncoordinated frontal assaults and counterattacks from both sides. While inflicting severe losses on the Confederates and driving them from the high ground, the Federals could not break the enemy line. Confederate artillery on Nicodemus Heights was therefore able to harass the advancing Federals in flank during much of the morning's fighting. Additionally, while various decisions made the desperate and bloody combat on the Union right flow back and forth across the Cornfield and the East Woods, then into the West Woods, and finally into the Sunken Road, Hooker's first decision set all of these actions in motion.

Alternate Decision/Scenario

Had Mansfield been ordered to attack on Hooker's right, west of the Hagerstown Turnpike, instead of his left (Option 4), the battle would have been dramatically different. At dawn on September 17, the half mile of ground between the Hagerstown Turnpike and the Potomac was thinly defended. As the struggle developed, the fighting slowly moved south along the turnpike from the Cornfield to the West Woods, the church, and then to the Sunken Road. This resulted in each Union corps attacking, more or less en echelon on the previous corps' left.

Several essential things might have happened if the assaults had run west of the Hagerstown Pike instead. That morning, John Pelham's horse artillery that was firing in the Union forces' flank from Nicodemus Heights might have had to withdraw or turn their guns away from the turnpike and toward Mansfield's attacking divisions. Jubal Early's brigade sent to support this position would have been at the center of the fighting. The reinforcements that

The Dunker Church, Antietam National Battlefield, modern image. Author.

Lee sent into the fight east of the turnpike might have instead been sent west of the turnpike to stop Mansfield and to bolster his now extremely vulnerable left. Also, the three brigades of D. H. Hill's and Hood's divisions sent to counterattack might instead have been sent much farther west of the Hagerstown Turnpike.

Depending on the success of these Union attacks, McLaws and Walker might have carried their attacks farther west as well. Consequently, when Sumner arrived on the field, he would have faced an entirely different front than the one he did. Maj. Gen. John Sedgwick's division might have been hitting the Confederates in the flank instead of the other way around. There is no guarantee that this advance would have made a decisive breakthrough in the Confederate line, as Lee surely would have sent all of his available reserves to that point to defend his vulnerable line of retreat. The battle, however, would have taken a quite different turn, perhaps changing its outcome.

Hood Counterattacks at the Cornfield

Situation

John Bell Hood resigned his commission from the United States Army immediately after the Civil War began. Dissatisfied with the neutrality of his native Kentucky, he decided to serve his adopted state of Texas instead. By September 30, 1861, Hood was promoted to colonel of the Fourth Texas Infantry, and on February 20, 1862, he took command of the new Texas Brigade, consisting mainly of regiments from that state. On March 26, Hood was promoted to brigadier general. Leading the Texas Brigade as part of the Army of Northern Virginia in the Peninsula Campaign, he soon established his standing as a brave and aggressive commander. For their part, Hood's men quickly gained a reputation as members of one of the army's elite combat units. On July 26, 1862, the thirty-two-year-old Hood assumed command of a division of which the Texas Brigade was part. His division was soon reassigned to Maj. Gen. James Longstreet's command.[15]

By the time of the opening shots of the Battle of Antietam, Hood's Division had been one of the most active in Longstreet's Command. After marching from Frederick to Boonsboro, Hood's men marched to Hagerstown with the rest of Longstreet's force to counter a nonexistent threat, then marched back to bolster D. H. Hill's line at South Mountain. The division was also part of Lee's rear guard as the army fell back toward Sharpsburg. Upon crossing Antietam Creek on September 15, Hood's Division was eventually placed in line with Jackson's divisions on the far left of Lee's line.

Brig. Gen. John Bell Hood, CSA, commander, Hood's Division. Library of Congress / National Archives.

On the night of the sixteenth, Hood's two brigades were holding position north of the Mumma Farm straddling the Smoketown Road. As Meade's division advanced south on the road, Truman Seymour's Union brigade skirmished with the center of Hood's line as darkness fell. Once the fighting had ceased and he had conversed with Stonewall Jackson, Hood had the brigades of Col. Marcellus Douglass and Col. James A. Walker of Lawton's Division relieve his own exhausted, hungry division. Hood made this arrangement with the proviso that he and his troops would come at once if called on. Finally, his two-thousand-man division fell back to a position west of the Dunker Church to rest and eat.[16]

At 6:45 a.m. on September 17, the battle was some ninety minutes old. The savagery of the fighting took both sides by surprise, and the Army of Northern Virginia now faced its first crisis of the morning. While almost utterly wrecked themselves, Hooker's divisions of Ricketts and Doubleday had utterly decimated the Confederate divisions of Lawton and J. R. Jones. The Union First Corps drove Jackson's line back to the Smoketown Road and into the West Woods, rendering the troops combat ineffective in the process. Only Brig. Gen. Roswell S. Ripley's brigade of D. H. Hill's division held a position near the Mumma Farm. Of the over 13,500 men engaged in this opening move, 4,368 or 32 percent were now casualties.[17]

Jackson described the desperate situation in his after-action report: "General Lawton, commanding division, and Colonel Walker, commanding

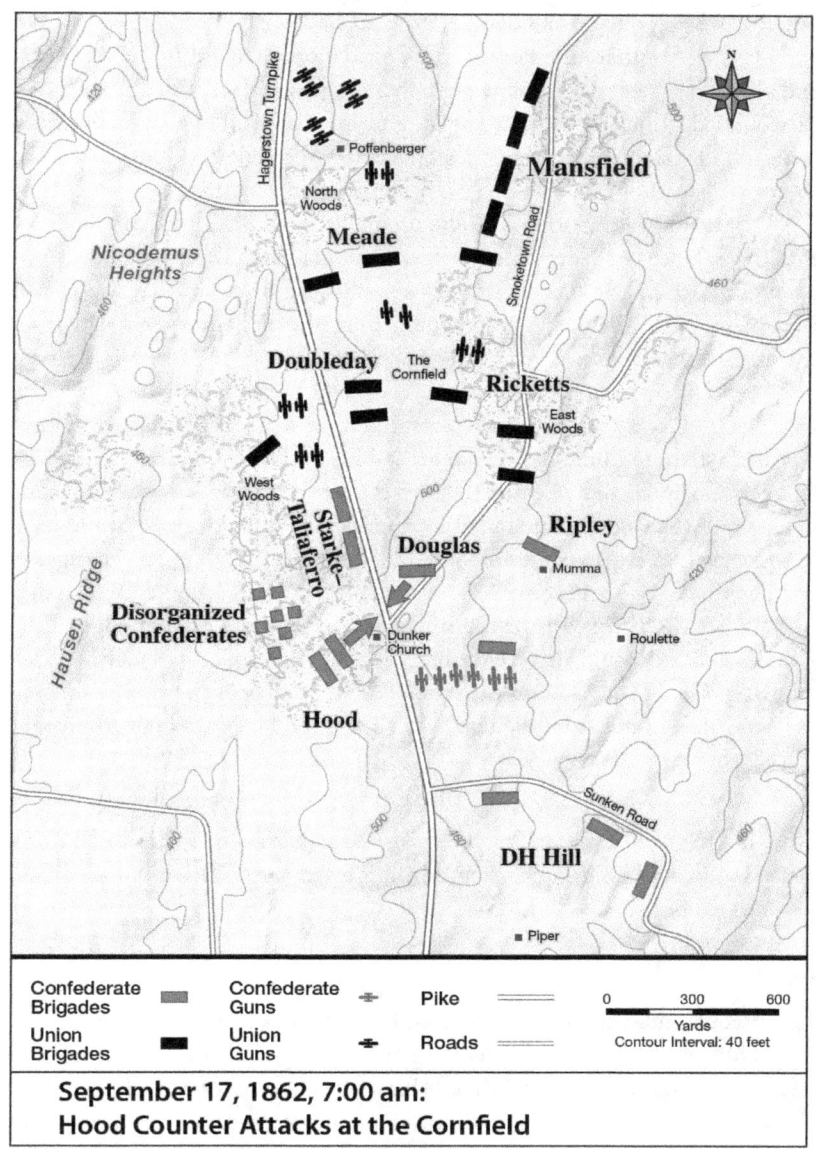

September 17, 1862, 7:00 am:
Hood Counter Attacks at the Cornfield

brigade, were severely wounded. More than half of the brigades of Lawton and Hays were either killed or wounded, and more than a third of Trimble's, and all the regimental commanders in those brigades, except two, were killed or wounded. Thinned in their ranks, and exhausted of their ammunition, Jackson's Division and the brigades of Lawton, Trimble and Hays retired to the rear."[18]

As Jackson was laboring to shore up his battered line, little did he know that the balance of George Meade's division, not yet fully engaged, was positioned north of the Cornfield. Jackson was also unaware that the van of Mansfield's Twelfth Corps was approaching the Poffenberger Farm from the northeast. Positioned west of the Dunker Church, John B. Hood's men had been anticipating a call to advance as soon as the first sounds of battle were heard. Hood received word to come at once with his division to support Lawton's shattered line. He then marched his two brigades across the Hagerstown Turnpike and wheeled them to the left just in time to see a brigade of Lawton's Division commanded by Col. Marcellus Douglass falling back in disarray. Directly in front of Hood, the better parts of four Union brigades were holding a line beginning west of the Hagerstown Turnpike and running past the southern edge of the Cornfield and beyond the eastern edge of the East Woods. He could also see the brigades of Brig. Gen. Marsena R. Patrick and Brig. Gen. John Gibbon of Doubleday's First Corps division advancing on the Confederates from the northwest along the Hagerstown Turnpike.[19]

Options

Now holding a line about five hundred yards south of the Cornfield, John Bell Hood could hold his current position or advance. Either choice would be a critical decision.

Option 1

Hood could hold his current line and brace for an attack. According to Hood himself, he had been ordered in only for support—he did not mention launching a counterattack. With only his division, what was left of Brig. Gen. Roswell S. Ripley's brigade, and remnants of the Twenty-First Georgia of Trimble's Brigade holding the line, standing on the defensive and letting the Yankees come to him might be a reasonable posture for Hood. The ground he now occupied near the Smoketown Road was slightly higher than the Cornfield and the ground between. By now, he could by now see elements of Brig. Gen. John Gibbon's Union brigade pushing out of the rows of corn and advancing on him. Lastly, by standing where he was, Hood could allow

Ripley's and Trimble's men to anchor the position on his right flank and some disorganized Confederate units to take a position on his left. On the other hand, if he advanced, Hood might find his flanks exposed to the enemy.

Option 2

Hood could decide to advance his division and launch a counterattack. Almost as soon as his two brigades began to cross the Hagerstown Turnpike, they came under fire from the Union artillery across the Antietam and the batteries north and west of the Cornfield. Once the gunners got the range, Hood's Division was an easy target on this high ground. Men were being knocked out of the ranks with almost every shot, and that alone might be reason enough for Hood not to stay as he was. During the past several months, the division had earned a reputation as one of the most aggressive and hard fighting in Lee's army, and Hood was considered one of its most audacious generals. In fact, historians have occasionally criticized Hood's aggressiveness, as it frequently bordered on recklessness. Additionally, Hood might have believed that Jackson needed additional time to bring in reinforcements, and driving into the Union regiments in his front might just buy him that time.[20]

Decision

True to form, Hood chose to attack (Option 2), ordering his division's nine regiments forward and into the maelstrom that was the Cornfield and the East Woods. The Rebel general's division drove headlong into the teeth of the Union position. This aggressive and unexpected move caught the Federals completely off guard and knocked the Union line north of the Cornfield, almost to where it had started two hours before. In his after-action report, Hood described his decision while somewhat exaggerating the numbers he faced:

> Being in readiness I at once marched out on the field in line of battle and soon became engaged with an immense force of the enemy, consisting of not less than two corps of their army. It was here that I witnessed the most terrible clash of arms, by far, that has occurred during the war. The two little giant brigades of this division wrestled with this mighty force, losing hundreds of their gallant officers and men but driving the enemy from his position and forcing him to abandon his guns on our left. The battle raged with the greatest fury until about 9 o'clock, the enemy being driven from 400 to 500 yards.[21]

Results/Impact

Hood's Division held its position for approximately forty-five minutes once it pressed to the northern edge of the Cornfield. As the desperate struggle wore on, the general and his men discovered they had an intolerable situation on their hands. During the advance, Hood's two brigades had split apart, essentially fighting two separate engagements at opposite ends of the Cornfield. His men were now running low on ammunition, and Wofford's Brigade was getting flanked on their left by Union infantry and artillery along the Hagerstown Turnpike. Fighting at the eastern edge of the Cornfield, Laws's men could now see the lead elements of the Union Twelfth Corps advancing on their position from the north. With no reinforcements forthcoming, Hood's men were finally forced back to the point from which they started. The division was decimated in the process, suffering over 1,000 casualties, 50 percent of those who had stepped off that morning. The First Texas of Wofford's Brigade lost its flag, 8 color-bearers, and 182 of its 211 men in the assault—a loss rate of nearly 87 percent.[22]

Col. William T. Wofford, commanding the left brigade in Hood's wrecked division, later wrote, "This brigade went into the action numbering 854, and lost, in killed, wounded, and missing, 560—over one-half. . . . These brave officers all fell while gallantly leading their small bands on an enemy five times their number. They deserved a better fate than to have been, as they were, sacrificed for the want of proper support."[23] Despite this horrible loss, Hood's decision was critical for a number of reasons. First of all, it drove the last of Hooker's corps from the area north of the Smoketown Road and the Cornfield, stopping the momentum of the Union's initial morning assaults. These attacks had come within an inch of collapsing Lee's left. Moreover, the assault all but knocked the First Corps out of the action for the day. Secondly, in choosing to fight, Hood forced Hooker to call on Mansfield's Twelfth Corps to shore up his shattered divisions. Lastly, Hood's assault staved off Confederate disaster by allowing Lee and Jackson time to move critical reinforcements to the sector and prop up the devastated Confederate left.

Additionally, Hood's attack drew additional Union infantry and artillery into the seesaw fight for the Cornfield to stop him, thus preventing these forces from going elsewhere on the field. More specifically, the Rebel general stopped these Federals from supporting any more significant attack on his left. Also, this decision and the subsequent attacks by D. H. Hill's division might have had a more substantial effect than anyone at the time realized. At that moment, McClellan was east of the Antietam Creek contemplating where to send the Second Corps. Sumner had been chomping at the bit since before dawn while waiting for orders, and at 7:20 a.m. McClellan directed

September 17, 1862

Southern edge of the Cornfield, Antietam National Battlefield, modern image. Author.

him to cross the creek and join the battle. Hooker was sweeping the field with his early morning attack, only to be violently knocked back by Hood's devastating assault. Perhaps feeling his right was now on the verge of collapse and getting Hooker's requests for support, McClellan ordered Sumner across Antietam Creek to reinforce Hooker.[24]

Alternate Decision/Scenario

Had Hood decided to hold the line as his division wheeled into position at the Smoketown Road, the battle might have gone very differently. It is difficult to say how long Hood and his division could have remained on that ground and withstood attack after attack and the continual shelling. But it is probable that in doing so, they would have been unable to stop the momentum of the Union First Corps and push that force back beyond the Cornfield. It is also very likely that the Federal attacks would have kept the pressure on Lee's left, changing the entire flow of battle likely as a result. If Hood had not counterattacked when he did, the Union forces might very likely have kept the fighting well south of the Cornfield. It might then have been possible for Hooker to realize his plan of clearing the Dunker Church plateau much sooner while Mansfield was engaged.

Sumner Attacks the West Woods

Situation

By the opening shots of Antietam were fired, Maj. Gen. Edwin Vose "Bull" Sumner had been in the army for over forty-three years. Born in Boston in 1797, he could trace his ancestors back to the original Massachusetts settlers.

The war touched Sumner's family in a profound way. His two sons, Edwin Vose Jr. and Samuel, both served in the Civil War, becoming generals afterward and then serving in the Spanish-American War. His son-in-law, Armistead L. Long, who served as his aide, resigned his commission in the US Army and enlisted to serve the Confederacy. Long was Robert E. Lee's military secretary during the Maryland Campaign and an artillery brigadier general later on in the war.[25]

When McClellan began organizing the Army of the Potomac in March 1862, Sumner, one of his closest allies, was given command of the Second Corps. He led the Second throughout the Peninsula Campaign and during the Seven Days' Battles.[26]

At Antietam, Sumner was the most senior corps commander in the Army of the Potomac, and he also commanded the largest corps in the army, counting some sixteen thousand men of all arms. Sumner's three divisions were led by Maj. Gen. Israel B. Richardson, Maj. Gen. John Sedgwick, and Brig.

Maj. Gen. Edwin Vose "Bull" Sumner, USA, commander, Second Corps. Library of Congress / National Archives.

Gen. William H. French. By the time the battle was over, Richardson and Sedgwick were both wounded. While Sedgwick soon recovered, Richardson succumbed to his wound eight weeks later.

On September 16, the Second Corps, bivouacked just north of the Pry House, was tasked with being part of the planned attack the following day. McClellan's design called for the Second to operate as a reserve force to exploit any Union breakthrough. The commanding general ordered Sumner to have his corps ready before dawn; however, McClellan did not release it for action until after the opening phase of the battle was almost over. It is possible that McClellan wanted to wait and see how the fight developed before he committed the Second to any particular part of the field.

On the evening of September 16, Joe Hooker had his First Corps in position on Lee's left but now feared that the Confederates would be too much for his lone unit. When Hooker requested additional support, McClellan ordered Sumner to make the Twelfth Corps available to him. The Twelfth was sent across Antietam Creek, going into camp behind and to the left of Hooker's position. Sumner, in the position of wing commander, assumed his Second Corps would soon follow, but McClellan ordered him to wait. The Twelfth and Second Corps had made up the middle column during the march out from Washington, so Sumner must have considered an advance a logical move. Unfortunately, he would have to wait for orders.[27]

Once Hood's Division could be observed driving the First Corps back across the field, McClellan assumed his right flank was now in danger of collapsing, then ordered Sumner into the fight.[28] Once the orders came down, Sumner crossed at Pry's Ford with Sedgwick's division in the lead. French followed shortly thereafter, but Richardson's division did not get permission to advance until Maj. Gen. George W. Morell's Fifth Corps division replaced it in the tactical reserve almost an hour later. Sumner described the situation in his after-action report:

> SIR: I have the honor to report that, on the evening of the 16th ultimo, I received an order at Keedysville to send the Twelfth Corps (Banks') to support General Hooker, and to hold my own, the Second Corps, in readiness to march for the same purpose an hour before daylight. Banks' corps, under General Mansfield, marched at 11.30 p.m., and my own corps was ready to move at the time ordered, but did not receive from headquarters the order to march till 7.20 a.m. on the 17th. I moved Sedgwick's division immediately in three columns on the receipt of the order, followed by French's division in the same order. Richardson was ordered to move in the

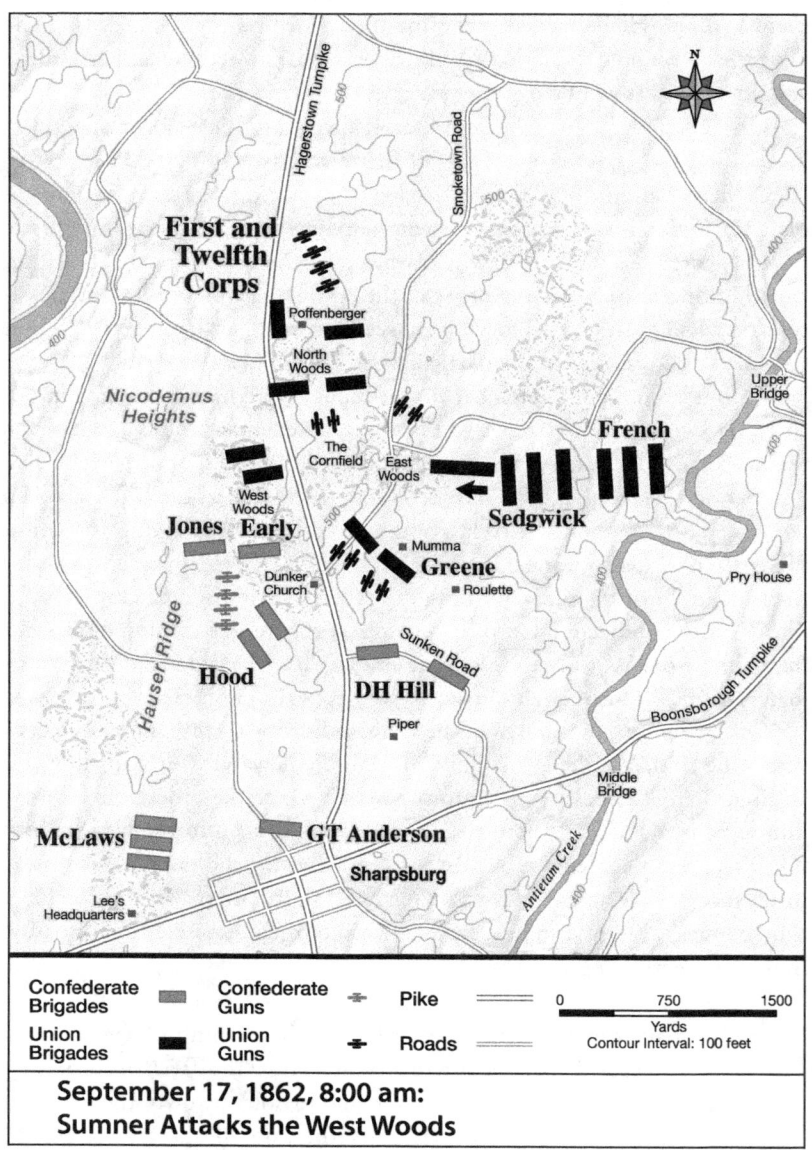

September 17, 1862, 8:00 am:
Sumner Attacks the West Woods

same direction by the commanding general about an hour later. On arriving at the place where Hooker had been engaged, I found him wounded, and his corps, after a severe contest, had been repulsed. Banks' corps, under the immediate command of General Mansfield, had gone into battle on Hooker's left, and was engaged when I came upon the field.[29]

After crossing the ford, Sumner, with Sedgwick's division in the lead, reached the vicinity of the East Woods and halted to assess the overall situation. The time was between 8:00 and 8:30 a.m., and the three-hour opening chapter of the battle was over. Accounts conflict as to precisely whom Sumner spoke with. According to one report, he encountered a wounded and somewhat incoherent Hooker, who was being carried from the field. Another account describes Sumner speaking with First Corps division commander Brig. Gen. James B. Ricketts and then new Twelfth Corps commander Brig. Gen. Alpheus Williams. Reports also differ as to whether Williams or a member of his staff attempted to apprise Sumner of the ground and the general situation. Williams had taken over the Twelfth Corps from the mortally wounded Mansfield. According to Williams, Sumner dismissed this information and made his own assessment of the overall situation before him. After his reconnaissance, Sumner deemed both the First and Twelfth Corps used up and unfit for further service. The units' respective commanders were wounded, leaving Sumner the most senior officer on this end of the field. Brig. Gen. George G. Meade of the First Corps' Third Division had assumed command in place of the wounded Hooker.

Sumner was no doubt stunned at what he was witnessing, as the remains of a fearsome struggle now lay before him. Broken caissons, dead horses, and assorted military equipment of all types littered the ground. Many of the nearly eight thousand casualties resulting from the early morning struggle were also strewn across the battlefield. In addition, Sumner observed some artillery units still in action and a Union infantry force of some size near the Dunker Church. Although he might not have known it, this was Brig. Gen. George S. Greene's Twelfth Corps division and the brand-new 125th Pennsylvania from Crawford's Twelfth Corps division. Sumner could also detect from the smoke and the sounds of battle that a struggle of some degree was going on at the northern edge of the West Woods.[30]

Additionally, and perhaps most importantly, Sumner detected no organized Confederate forces east of the Hagerstown Pike. Rebels who had participated in the morning's engagement were lying dead or wounded on the field, or they had fallen back beyond the West Woods and the church and into the Sunken Road. Sumner was unaware that a force of some seven thousand Rebel infantry was now on a collision course with the Federals. The Confederate brigade of Col. George T. Anderson, along with McLaws's and Walker's Divisions, was on the march north and would soon be in the vicinity of the Dunker Church.[31]

Options

With the battlefield now unusually quiet, Edwin Vose Sumner had three options to choose from and a critical decision to make. First, he could take command of the northern part of the field. Alternatively, he could see to the disposition of his own corps. Finally, he could attack immediately with what he had on hand.

Option 1

Sumner could immediately take command of all the Union forces on the northern end of the field. It should have been apparent to him that he was the most senior officer on this part of the field, and that someone had to take over and direct the battle if any semblance of order was to be reclaimed. Hooker had been given that responsibility initially, and with his wounding, a command vacuum now existed. Sumner could assume that his own role as wing commander was still intact, and he still had authority over two of the three corps now on the field. As late as September 16, he had issued orders to the Twelfth Corps at McClellan's behest. With regard to a later decision, we will discuss how Sumner ordered William Franklin's advance to stop; thus it seems he took control of the northern sector at some point.[32] McClellan was a mile away, and it was neither his habit nor his job to direct operations at the front. As army commander, he was responsible for bringing the soldiers to the field, providing for the overall tactical plan, and ensuring the army had whatever it need to execute that plan.

After witnessing the state of those units still on the field, Sumner could assume command over all Union forces north of the Boonsboro Turnpike and position himself in the most effective way to carry out that responsibility and direct the appropriate troops into battle. On the other hand, where the First and Twelfth Corps too severely beaten up as a result of the morning's fighting, no real advantage was to be gained by asserting command over them.

Option 2

Sumner could simply see to his own corps, at that moment split in essentially three parts, with each element in no position to immediately support another.

Sedgwick's Third Division was the only one entirely across the creek. French's Second Division was in the process of crossing and would not be situated to attack for some time. Meanwhile, McClellan was holding Richardson's First Division in the tactical reserve and out of Sumner's immediate reach. Sumner had roughly sixteen thousand mostly veteran men in his corps—a formidable force three times as large as the organized Confederate forces Lee currently had north of the Boonsboro Turnpike. Although Sumner was no doubt unaware of this numerical advantage, if he could quickly consolidate these soldiers in whole on the field, the Confederates would have a difficult task in countering a combined attack by all three of his divisions. Even if Sumner simply waited for French to be on the field to directly support Sedgwick, the advantage could still be in his favor. Sumner could work toward this end to bring the most men he could to this critical point of attack.

However, any delay on Sumner's part would allow enemy troops to reinforce their position and better prepare for an attack. As a matter of fact, Lee and Jackson were at that very moment rushing reserves north.[33]

Option 3

Sumner could reason that his best option was acting immediately and advancing Sedgwick's 5,600-man division directly into the fight to exploit what he saw as the vulnerable Confederate left in the West Woods. As an experienced commander, Sumner would have known that battle was extremely fluid by nature. He would also have known that every moment of delay would allow the situation to alter and perhaps allow the enemy to organize better, reinforce itself, and attack him. Reports of Sumner's state of mind and observations are at odds with one another. However, it is not hard to assume he saw not only that the Union offensive was in shambles, but also that he had an opportunity to attack the West Woods, which he assumed was the Confederate left flank. Sumner could quickly assess the available information and act based on his feeling that the West Woods represented a key position on the field.[34]

Decision

Sumner choose to attack (Option 3). The Second Corps commander decided not to wait or to take command of the northern end of the field, but to immediately lead Sedgwick's division into an ill-fated attack at what he assumed was Lee's flank in the West Woods. Sumner ordered Sedgwick to move his three-brigade division west. Once the soldiers were beyond the woods, he intended to wheel them to the left, occupy the West Woods, advance, and overwhelm the enemy's position to the south.

Results/Impact

Sumner's advance with Sedgwick's division into the infamous West Woods turned out to be a complete disaster, one of the most ill-famed episodes in the history of the Union army. As Sedgwick became mired in the woods, a mixed bag of five Confederate brigades hit him in the front and flank. The brigades of Brig. Gen. Joseph Kershaw, Brig. Gen. Paul Semmes, and Brig. Gen. William Barksdale of McLaws's Division, combined with Col. George T. Anderson's and Brig. Gen. Jubal A. Early's Brigades, routed Sedgwick's three Union brigades out of the woods and all but decimated his division. The attack by Sedgwick's division accomplished little besides marking an end to the early morning phase of the battle, adding nearly 2,500 more names to the ever-growing casualty list.[35]

Sumner provided the following account of events in his after-action report:

> My First Division (Sedgwick's) went into battle in three lines. After his first line had opened fire for some time, the enemy made a most determined rush to turn our left, and so far succeeded as to break through the line between Banks' corps and my own until they began to appear in our rear. In order to repel this attack from the rear, I immediately faced Sedgwick's third line about, but the fire at that moment became so severe from the left flank that this line moved off in a body to the right, in spite of all the efforts that could be made to stop it. The first and second lines after some time followed this movement, but the whole division was promptly rallied, took a strong position, and maintained it to the close of the battle.

Sumner's decision is critical because it both led to the disastrous engagement in the West Woods and shifted the axis of the battle from one that was primarily north to south to one that was mainly east to west. As we will see in discussion of a coming decision, the advance also led directly to the struggle's shift to the Sunken Road?[36]

Historians like Stephen Sears and James Murfin are highly critical of Sumner's actions and decisions on September 17. These scholars describe a corps commander who did not fully comprehend the current situation on the field, and who went bumbling off into the West Woods as a result. Also, with no cohesive plan, Sumner left French to figure things out on his own. Historians argue that this lack of guidance caused the West Woods disaster and also prompted French, for lack of any instructions to the contrary, to order his division south to attack the Sunken Road.[37]

More recent scholarship by Marion Armstrong argues the exact opposite. Armstrong writes that Sumner conducted a complete reconnaissance of the ground and quite purposely ordered French to attack the Sunken Road to guard against a potential assault in his rear. Armstrong also asserts that Sumner's plan to attack the woods was tactically sound, made disastrous only by the timely or untimely arrival of McLaws's and Walker's Confederate divisions. Basically, Sumner was a victim of unfortunate timing, not poor generalship.[38]

Whether you believe Edwin Vose Sumner was tactically obtuse on September 17 or just a victim of his own bad timing, the outcome of the engagement is unchanged. In less than an hour of fighting, Sedgwick's division was routed and devastated, suffering a casualty rate of almost 40 percent. A total of 2,200 killed, wounded, and missing.

Alternate Decision/Scenario

Had Sumner waited to launch his attack until French was up and directly on Sedgwick's left flank, we might have seen a dramatically different outcome. By advancing with French directly guarding his flank, Sedgwick might have employed a formidable ten thousand soldiers in a coordinated attack on Lee's now-vulnerable left flank. Such a force included nearly twice as many men as Lee could bring to stop it. The combined forces of Sedgwick, French, and Greene and the remnants of the First and Twelfth Corps could have made any number of scenarios possible.

It is important to remember that battles of this kind are often a matter of timing. The engagement of Sedgwick's division in the West Woods clearly demonstrates this fact. Had Sumner attacked twenty or thirty minutes later along the same axis of advance, the Confederate reserves advancing on the woods might not have been in a position to hit the Federals in their flank. Union troops could have hit the Rebels either head on or in their flank. Also, with French up and ready to directly support Sedgwick on his left, French would not have deployed farther south and attacked the Sunken Road, thus dramatically changing the next phase of the battle.

Lee Commits His Reserves

Situation

Cemetery Hill, so named for a small Lutheran cemetery located there, is a piece of high ground just east of Sharpsburg that straddles the Boonsboro Pike, or modern-day Maryland Route 34. As a critical piece of terrain, the hill

The West Woods, Antietam National Battlefield, modern image. Author.

served as a position for Longstreet's reserve artillery during most of September 17, and as the center of the Confederate line held by Brig. Gen. David R. Jones's division and Brig. Gen. Nathan G. Evans's brigade. Robert E. Lee also spent some time here observing the battle during those desperate early morning hours. This location was one of the few places from which could he see almost every other critical position on the field.[39]

By 7:30 a.m. the situation for Lee and his Army of Northern Virginia was dire indeed. Since first light, the battle had raged back and forth across the area around the Cornfield and the East and West Woods multiple times. In a little over two hours of almost continuous combat, twelve of the thirteen Confederate infantry brigades on the northern end of the field were effectively out of action. Over 30 percent of the ten thousand Confederates engaged up until this point were now casualties. J. R. Jones's and Alexander Lawton's divisions had each suffered over 30 percent casualties, and John Bell Hood's division had suffered a casualty rate approaching 50 percent. All four regimental commanders in Law's Brigade of Hood's Division were wounded.

Moreover, Jackson's two divisions were decimated at the command level, and Alexander Lawton and J. R. Jones were both wounded. Jones's replacement, Brig. Gen. William E. Starke, was killed, leaving a colonel to lead the division. Out of the eight brigades in these two divisions, only one brigade commander was not dead or wounded.

By 8:30 a.m., of all of the Confederate forces initially deployed north of the Boonsboro Turnpike, only Jubal Early's brigade and two of D. H. Hill's five brigades holding the Sunken Road had not been committed. D. H. Hill's counterattack with three of his five brigades was now falling back after running headlong into the Union Twelfth Corps.[40]

In his autobiography, Longstreet summed up the morning's engagement:

> As Jackson withdrew, General Hooker's corps retired to a point on the Hagerstown road about three-quarters of a mile north of the battle-ground, where General Doubleday established his thirty-gun battery. Jackson's and Hooker's men had fought to exhaustion, and the battle of the Twelfth Corps, taken up and continued by Mansfield, had taken defensive relations, its chief mortally wounded. Generals Lawton, Ripley, and J. R. Jones were severely wounded, and Colonel Douglas, commanding Lawton's brigade, killed. A third of the men of Lawton's, Hays's, and Trimble's brigades were reported killed or wounded. Four of the field officers of Colquitt's brigade were killed, five were wounded, the tenth and last contused by a shell. All of Jackson's and D. H. Hill's troops engaged suffered proportionally. Hood's, Walker's, and G. T. Anderson's, though longer engaged, did not lose so severely.[41]

The Union forces they had battled fared little better. The seventeen thousand men that made up the fifteen brigades in the two attacking Federal corps had suffered over four thousand casualties. The Union command structure was also significantly impacted by casualties, though not as great as those among the Confederate command. Both Federal corps commanders were now wounded, and while Hooker survived his injuries, Mansfield perished the following day.[42]

By 8:30 a.m., the Federals, now had a tenuous hold on the ground east of the Hagerstown Turnpike and north of the West Woods. This terrain included the critical high ground east of the church that was the objective of Hooker's initial advance. As the battlefield became uncharacteristically quiet, the lead elements of Sedgwick's division were at this moment entering the East Woods and would be engaged shortly. Lee might or might not have been aware of this fact, but it is reasonable to assume that he considered a Union reinforcement on his left a foregone conclusion. In the meantime, the sector south of the Boonsboro Turnpike had seen very little if any offensive action by the Federals to this point.[43]

Confederate brigadier general John R. Jones outlined the situation in his after-action report:

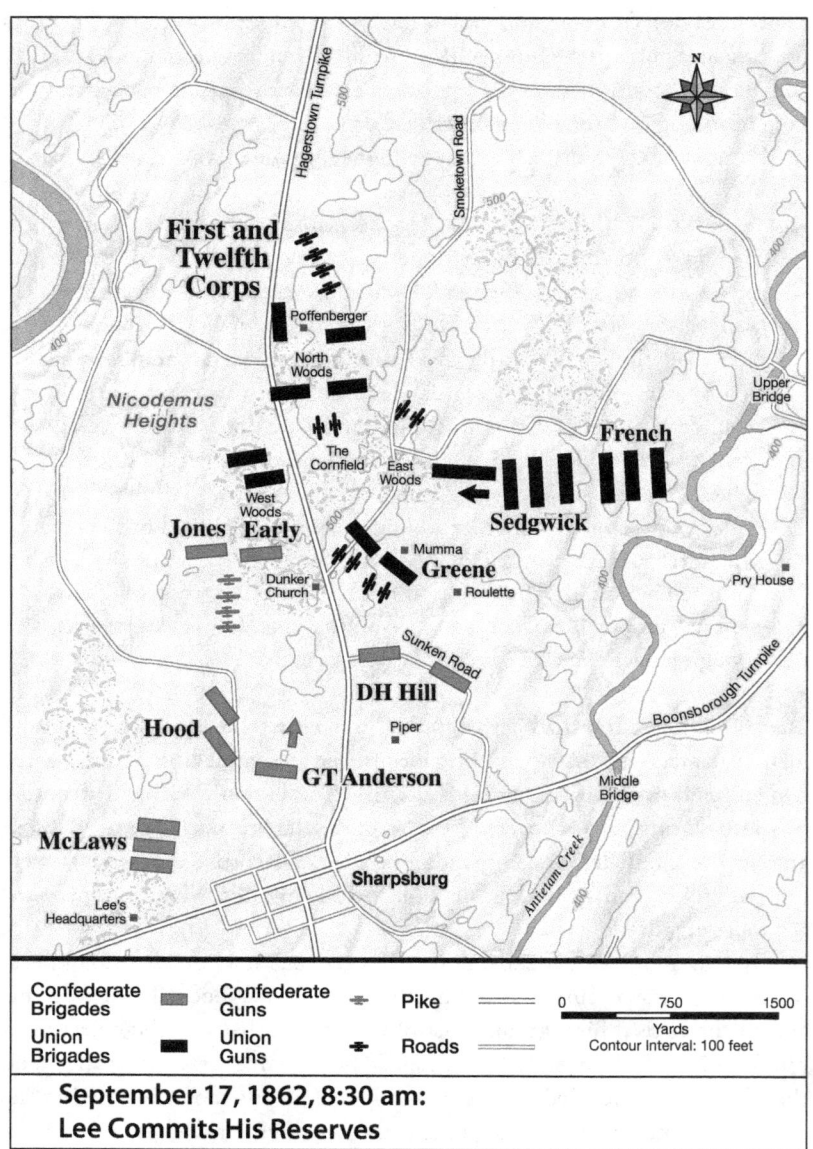

September 17, 1862

The infantry became at once engaged, and the gallant and generous Starke fell, pierced by three balls, and survived but a few moments. His fall cast a gloom over the troops. They never for a moment faltered, but rushed upon the enemy and drove him back. The struggle continued for several hours, the enemy all the while receiving reenforcements, and the division, not numbering over 1,600 men at the beginning of the fight, having no support, was finally compelled to fall back to its original line.[44]

It was near the Cemetery Hill, sometime before 8:00 a.m., that two urgent messages found the Confederate commander. Earlier that morning, D. H. Hill had requested permission to send his division to the support of the embattled Confederate left. Now, however, Hill's latest message, relayed by his adjutant, sought support for his own position as fresh Union forces were massing in his front. The second message was from Jackson, who conveyed John Bell Hood's dire prediction of the imminent collapse of the Confederate left.[45]

Options

With the outcome of the battle now seriously in doubt, the always calm and calculating Robert E. Lee had three options to choose from: consolidate his lines, fall back, or reinforce his left.

Option 1

Lee could contract and consolidate his lines. He understood the terrain well and could order his lieutenants to shorten the left side of his line by pulling it back to the outskirts of town, thereby protecting his route of retreat to the

Confederate generals—Maj. Gen. Lafayette McLaws, Col. George T. Anderson, and Maj. Gen. Richard H. Anderson. Unknown, *The Life of Lieutenant General Richard Heron Anderson*, Library of Congress / National Archives.

Potomac. Lee could also order D. H. Hill to fall back, and then he could place McLaws's and R. H. Anderson's uncommitted divisions on a line refused west that connected them with Longstreet. This option did have several disadvantages, including leaving the cavalry to cover a considerable amount of real estate between a potential new line and the Potomac. This course of action also gave up all of the high ground north of the town that the Union artillery could use as an effective firing position. Lastly, Lee would potentially make his forces more vulnerable as they fell back.

Option 2

Lee could have decided to end the battle, fall back and retreat to the Potomac River, and cross at Shepherdstown. The general had suffered plenty of casualties in those first few hours of the morning battle; the somewhat disjointed Union attacks were nonetheless effective in punching a hole in his left. Lee no doubt assumed more uncommitted Federal infantry were at McClellan's disposal, and he might also have believed that a lack of movement on his right meant that more Union corps would be committed to the assault on the other end of the field.

A small lull in the fighting could provide an opportunity to depart and cross the river. Although withdrawal was humiliating and disheartening, Lee could deem it a viable option. On the other hand, a retreat amid a major battle was a difficult and hazardous maneuver in the best of circumstances.

Option 3

Lee could determine that his best option was reinforcing his left with his reserves and forces from his right. At that moment, Lee quite possibly believed the position on his left was too important to abandon. Drawing the Union army into a decisive battle was key to the rest of his operational objectives for the campaign. McClellan was now providing that opportunity, and there was no certainty that it would present itself again if Lee disengaged.

However, there was also no guarantee that sending all of his available reserves into line on the left would stop the Union onslaught and save Lee's beleaguered line. Like the rest of Lee's army, the reserves had been actively campaigning for the last two weeks, and exhaustion was taking a real toll on his men's fighting effectiveness. The Confederate general still had almost seven thousand men in the two reserve divisions of Lafayette McLaws and Robert H. Anderson. Yet both of these exhausted divisions had arrived just that morning, having marched from Maryland Heights via Harpers Ferry, Charlestown, and Shepherdstown. Also, Lee had no real idea as to when A. P. Hill would arrive from Harpers Ferry, and his reserve forces were limited.[46]

Significantly—and this is essential to note—Lee had felt little or no pressure from the Union forces on his right up until this point in the battle. While he was undoubtedly concerned about threats to his vulnerable center and right from the Union Fifth and Ninth Corps, only artillery fire and some preliminary infantry movement had been detected in these sectors. This might have convinced Lee that there was minimal risk in shifting forces from these locations to support his left.[47]

Lee might also have seen an opportunity for a massive counterattack at McClellan's right that would deliver the fatal blow he was seeking. We do know he considered such a move later on that afternoon, and perhaps the idea was in his head at this moment. Giving up the ground on the left would make that maneuver almost impossible to execute. Lee selected this ground partly for its interior lines and network of roads and farm lanes he could use to efficiently move elements of his army from one point to another.[48]

Decision

Borne either from his innate aggressiveness or his belief that he simply had limited options, Lee decided to bolster his imperiled left by sending every available man he could into the fight north of the Boonsboro Pike (Option 3).

Results/Impact

By 9:30 a.m. Robert E. Lee had committed roughly nine thousand men from Walker's, McLaws's, and R. H. Anderson's divisions and Col. George T. Anderson's brigade into the maelstrom on the left. The result was the complete routing of Sedgwick's division in the West Woods and the escalation of the combat in the Sunken Road. Fighting at both locations was dramatically affected by the infusion of the Confederate units.[49]

In his after-action report, Lee highlighted the impact of reinforcing his left: "Upon the arrival of the re-enforcements under General McLaws, General Early attacked with great resolution the large force opposed to him. McLaws advanced at the same time, and the enemy were driven back in confusion, closely followed by our troops beyond the position occupied at the beginning of the engagement. The enemy renewed the assault on our left several times, but was repulsed with loss. He finally ceased to advance his infantry, and for several hours kept up a furious fire from his numerous batteries, under which our troops held their position with great coolness and courage."[50]

This decision was critical because it provided just enough manpower to help blunt the final Union assaults on Lee's left. McLaws and G. T. Anderson struck Sumner in the West Woods, while Walker attacked south of the Dunker Church. R. H. Anderson's division was sent to reinforce D. H. Hill's

The West Woods, Antietam National Battlefield, modern image. Author.

two brigades at the Sunken Road. This action ultimately forced a stalemate on the Confederate left, and it went a long way in convincing the Union command not to make any significant assaults on Lee's left once the fight at the Sunken Road was over. The savage fighting on this end of the field was thus brought to an end.

However, perhaps none of the results of Lee's decision were more significant than the choice to pull John Walker's division away from its position defending Snavely's Ford downstream of the Lower Bridge. The ford provided a direct line for any Union force that could cross it to potentially block the road to Shepherdstown, Lee's only line of retreat. As we will discuss later, it took McClellan's army another four hours to take advantage of this opportunity. At around 1:00 p.m., the Union Ninth Corps division of Brig. Gen. Isaac P. Rodman crossed the ford virtually unopposed to support the collapse of the Confederate position defending the Lower Bridge. This crossing would have been impossible or much more difficult had Walker's Division still defended this ground.[51]

Alternate Decision/Scenario

Indeed, Lee's withdrawal at this point in the battle might have yielded a dramatically different outcome than the one we now know. Had Lee somehow disengaged from McClellan and fallen back to the Potomac, several things could have happened. The desperate and bloody fighting, hallmarks of the West Woods and the Sunken Road, would surely not have taken place. There would likely have been no hours-long struggle for possession of the Lower Bridge and no dramatic counterattack late in the afternoon by A. P. Hill's division marching from Harpers Ferry. However, we might possibly have seen a more significant and more dramatic contest at or near Shepherdstown than the one that took place on September 19 and 20. Alternatively, we might have seen nothing at all. Seeing Lee retreat, McClellan could have been quite content to let him go unmolested, thus ending the battle then and there.

Jubal Early Deploys in the West Woods

Situation

Born in Franklin County, Virginia, Jubal Anderson Early was the third of ten children and a member one of the most well-connected old Virginian families. He graduated from West Point in 1837, ranking eighteenth in a class of fifty, and he personally stated that he was neither a good student nor a good soldier. When the Army of Northern Virginia eventually surrendered in April 1865, Jubal Early had fought in nearly all of its battles during the war.[52]

In September 1862, Brigadier General Early's brigade was in Brig. Gen. Alexander Lawton's (Ewell's) division, which had been part of the Confederate task force to eliminate the Harpers Ferry garrison. Early's troops subsequently arrived on the field at Antietam on the morning of September 16

Brig. Gen. Jubal A. Early, CSA, commander, Lawton's Division, Early's Brigade. Library of Congress / National Archives.

and went into bivouac north of Sharpsburg. By the time the battle had begun, Early and his brigade were ordered to Nicodemus Heights to support the horse artillery battery of Capt. John Pelham.

At approximately 7:00 a.m., the crisis on the Confederate left was approaching a new critical stage. To fill the holes left by his two shattered divisions, Stonewall Jackson ordered Early to leave one regiment (the Thirteenth Virginia) to continue supporting the artillery on Nicodemus Heights, then bring the rest of his brigade to hold the line west of the Hagerstown Pike. Jackson also directed Hood and D. H. Hill to advance and shore up the shattered position.

The other three brigades of Lawton's Division had been devastated by the opening Union attacks, and Lawton himself was severely wounded. Early was given command of what was left of the division. As Hood was advancing on the Cornfield, Early battled with Federal skirmishers west of the pike, driving them from the West Woods. By 8:00 a.m., Hood had fallen back, and D. H. Hill's three brigades engaged with the Union Twelfth Corps would also join them in retreat.

Early now formed a line with what remained of J. R. Jones's likewise crippled division. This division was now commanded by a colonel because Jones had been wounded and his replacement, Brig. Gen. William E. Starke, had been killed. What was left of Hood's Division minus three regiments was holding a position just west of the Dunker Church. D. H. Hill's three brigades sent in after Hood's attack were also severely mauled, and they fell back and were out of the action for the day. The Confederate position was supported by three batteries from Jones's Division, and one from the reserve artillery positioned farther west of the church on a piece of high ground known as Hauser's Ridge.[53]

By 8:30 a.m., the sector that Early had come into was about to become the epicenter of the ever-evolving battle. What the general could now see is up for debate, but the situation was developing quickly. The last remnants of Hood's and D. H. Hill's counterattacks had fallen back from the East Woods and the Cornfield. Early could discern two brigades of Brig. Gen. George Greene's division of the Twelfth Corps supported by Union artillery advancing on the contested plateau east of the Dunker Church. Greene's other brigade under Col. William B. Goodrich was advancing south along the Hagerstown Turnpike with the 124th Pennsylvania.

Furthermore, the seven-hundred-man 125th Pennsylvania Regiment that had become detached from Brig. Gen. Samuel W. Crawford's brigade was also advancing on the church from the northeast. This newly formed force was so disproportionately large that Federals and Rebels alike mistook it for a brigade. The balance of the Union First Corps save Marsena R. Patrick's brigade had fallen back to a position north of the Cornfield, where it was supported by assorted batteries that still had ammunition. In addition, a superbattery of some thirty guns collected from the First and Twelfth Corps began forming a line at the extreme right of the Union line. The line was three hundred yards wide when complete, and it entirely covered the area between the Hagerstown Pike and the Potomac.

Lastly, while Early probably did not know it, at that moment, Brig. Gen. Willis A. Gorman's lead brigade of Maj. Gen. John Sedgwick's Second Corps division had crossed the Antietam and was heading for the East Woods. Sedgwick's other two brigades were right behind this force.[54]

Later, in his autobiography, Early testified to the gravity of the circumstances he faced at the West Woods: "The situation was most critical and the necessity most pressing, as it was apparent that if the enemy got possession of this woods, possession of the hills in their rear would immediately follow, and then, across to our rear on the road leading back to the Potomac, would have been easy. In fact, the possession of these hills would have enabled him to take our whole line in reverse, and a disastrous defeat must have followed."[55]

Early had gone to Stonewall Jackson to request support for his position, which was held with perhaps 1,700 men. In Early's mind, this key position was in imminent danger of collapse. He was thus informed that Col. George T. Anderson's brigade and the lead brigade of McLaws's Division were arriving from the southwest in response to his entreaty.[56]

Options

Jubal Early had five tactical options to choose from: He could advance north, or he could advance east. Another choice involved splitting his forces and attacking in both directions. Finally, Early could hold his current position, or he could fall back. With roughly fifteen thousand Confederate and Union infantrymen about to converge on his position, the forty-five-year-old lawyer from Virginia had a critical decision to make.[57]

Option 1

Early could advance north to confront Goodrich's men. Had Early seen these troops as the most imminent threat to the Confederate line, he might have believed this option was the best one. All of that morning, the Union army's general axis of advance had come from the north. Early might therefore assume this was the next phase of the enemy's movement. He could surmise that the remnants of Hood's Division south and west of the Dunker Church could hold back Greene and the 125th Pennsylvania long enough for the arrival

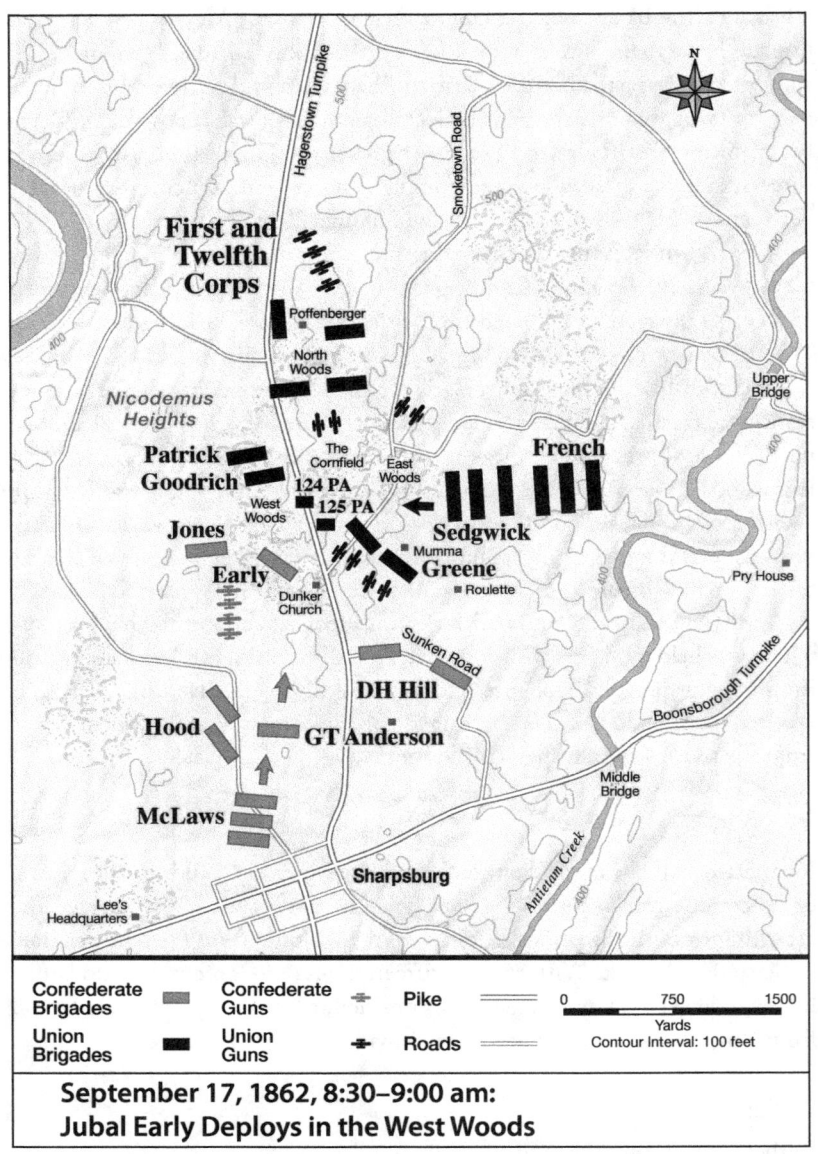

September 17, 1862, 8:30–9:00 am: Jubal Early Deploys in the West Woods

of the reinforcements he expected. However, this decision was not without risk. It could easily expose Early's right flank to attack.

Option 2

Early could determine to move east and attack the 125th Pennsylvania and/or Greene's two brigades east and north of the church. These two groups of Federals contained more numbers than did Goodrich's brigade advancing from the north; therefore, they could be perceived as the greatest threat. Yet moving east also created a problem for Early. He might feel that traveling in that direction would block the momentum and path of reinforcements advancing on the double-quick from the south. There was a good chance the units might become entangled and create mass confusion in the woods. Again, this course of action created the problem of an exposed left flank to the north.

Option 3

Early could split the combined force of his division and of Jones's. While dividing his relatively smaller force in the face of an enemy numerically superior to his own was risky, it may have presented the best choice for Early. He would not have to defeat the Union forces confronting him; he only needed to delay them long enough for help to arrive.

Option 4

Early could decide to hold his current position in the West Woods with the forces he had. The woods offered good cover, and he could attempt to position his soldiers for a defensive stand. The Rebel general could believe that holding the current position long enough might allow the reinforcements to deploy. This decision would allow any forces not attacking his position, such as the 125th Pennsylvania, to continue moving south and becoming a potential threat to the advancing Confederate reinforcements.

Option 5

Lastly, Early could fall back and allow the advancing support troops to take position in the woods. As one of the highest-ranking Confederate officers on the field, Early was probably best situated to decide how to deploy the arriving reinforcements. Several threats were now converging from two sides. Early could determine that his best option was retreating and allowing a clear path for the Confederate reinforcements to attack the Union forces head on. One disadvantage to this option was that it would permit the Union forces converging on this position to maneuver without any Confederates to impede them.

Decision

Early ultimately chose an aggressive stance, deciding to split his forces and attack (Option 3). The general moved north just enough to slow the advance of Goodrich and the 124th Pennsylvania. He then left the remnants of Jones's Division to hold off that Union threat and move by his own right flank to confront the 125th Pennsylvania. By then, the 125th had crossed the Hagerstown Turnpike and was moving into the woods just north of the church. As he was pushing the inexperienced Pennsylvanians back, Early saw troops from Col. George T. Anderson's brigade coming in on his right with McLaws's Division right behind them. These soldiers' arrival allowed the Confederate reinforcements to assemble, align themselves, and stabilize the line and the eventual counterattack on Sedgwick in the West Woods.

In his after-action report, Early outlined his decision:

> My condition, however, was exceedingly critical, as another column was advancing in my front and had reached the woods in which I was. I saw the vast importance of maintaining my ground, for, had the enemy gotten possession of this woods, the heights immediately in rear, which commanded the rear of our whole line, would have fallen into his hands. I determined to wait for the re-enforcements promised by Gen. Jackson, hoping that they would arrive in time to meet the columns on my right. I, however, threw my right flank back quietly under cover of the woods, so as not to have my rear exposed in the event of being discovered. I kept an anxious eye on the column on my right, as well as on the one moving up in my front, and very soon I saw the column on my right move into the woods in the direction of the church. I looked to the rear for the re-enforcements, and could not see them coming. I was thus cut off from the main body of our army on the right, and a column was moving against me from the left. There was no time to be lost, and I immediately ordered my brigade to move by the right flank parallel, to the enemy, and directed Col. Grigsby, who commanded the body of troops he and Col. Stafford had rallied, to move his command back in line, so as to present front to the enemy, who were coming up on the flank. I moved back along the rear of the woods until I caught up with the enemy, who had the start of me. I was, however, concealed from his view, and it was evident that my presence where I was was not suspected. Passing from behind a ridge that concealed my brigade from the enemy, we came in full view of his flankers, who, however, were made aware of my presence by a fire which I

directed the leading regiment to pour into them. They immediately ran into the main body, which halted, and I continued to move by the flank until my whole force was disclosed.[58]

Results/Impact

While a number of factors led to the clash in the West Woods, Early's decision to split his force and attack was critical for two reasons. This choice held off the Union forces converging on the woods from two directions long enough for the Confederate combined infantry to attack in force and stop them in their tracks. However, Early's course of action also set Sedgwick up for his disastrous flank encounter in the West Woods.

Early stated, "Just as I reformed my line, Semmes', Anderson's, and part of Barksdale's brigades, of McLaws' division, came up, and the whole, including Grigsby's command, advanced upon this body of the enemy, driving it with great slaughter entirely from and beyond the woods, and leaving us in possession of my former position. As soon as this was accomplished, I caused the regiments of the brigade to be reformed and placed in position as before."[59] In his after-action report, Robert E. Lee identified Early as a critical participant in the defense of the West Woods: "Upon the arrival of the re-enforcements under General McLaws, General Early attacked with great resolution the large force opposed to him."[60]

Stonewall Jackson confirmed these assertions about Early in his battle report:

> (Early) Finding here Colonels Grigsby and Stafford, with a portion of Jackson's division, which formed on his left, he determined to maintain his position there if re-enforcements could be sent to his support, of which he was promptly assured. Colonel Grigsby, with his small command, kept in check the advance of the enemy on the left flank, while General Early attacked with great vigor and gallantry the column on his right and front. The force in front was giving way under this attack when another heavy column of Federal troops were seen moving across the plateau on his left flank. By this time the expected re-enforcements (consisting of Semmes' and Anderson's brigades and a part of Barksdale's, of McLaws' division) arrived, and the whole, including Grigsby's command, now united, charged upon the enemy, checking his advance, then driving him back with great slaughter entirely from and beyond the wood, and gaining possession of our original position.[61]

The West Woods, Antietam National Battlefield, modern image. Author.

Alternate Decision/Scenario

If Early had fallen back and waited for the reinforcements to arrive, this fighting might have concluded very differently. If Early had held his position, and if the 125th Pennsylvania and Greene's two brigades had somehow been able push past the church and occupy the woods beyond sooner than they did, those troops, not Sedgwick's, might have endured a Confederate counterattack to their flank. It is difficult to tell what the outcome of this event would have had on the battle. Yet it might very well have provided Sedgwick the time needed to get his entire division west of the woods and wheel left to face the Confederates as Sumner had intended all along. Sedgwick might have been able to meet this attack head on.[62]

The Battle Shifts to the Sunken Road

Situation

Born in Baltimore in 1815, William Henry French was the grandson of Revolutionary War private Ephraim French. William and four of his fellow members of the West Point class of 1837 were at Antietam on September 17. One of these graduates, Jubal Early, was fighting in the West Woods less than a mile away as French's division took the field. Called "Old Blinky" by his men French had an unfortunate habit of continually blinking when speaking.[63]

September 17, 1862

As discussed regarding Sumner's decision to attack the West Woods, this is one of the more controversial moments in the history of the Battle of Antietam. Two widely divergent views have emerged of what exactly happened next and who the actual decision-maker was. The traditional account asserts that in his haste to attack the West Woods with Sedgwick's division, Sumner left no officer to direct French to the desired position on the field. French was left to his own devices as to where to launch his attack, and it was therefore French who was the decision-maker. More modern scholarship, however, cites evidence that French was acting on specific orders from Sumner, meaning that Sumner was the decision-maker. While the traditional account is not without merit, the latter version of events will take precedence for this decision.[64]

William French's Third Brigade was a recent and mostly untested addition to the Union Second Corps. The unit was officially organized on September 10 and not wholly assembled until the sixteenth, the day before the battle. Many of its regiments consisted of ninety-day men who had only seen garrison duty before the battle. While French was an experienced brigade commander, this was his first division-level leadership position.[65]

As dawn broke on September 17, the Second Corps and its commander were waiting for orders to cross Antietam Creek and join the fight. Once those orders came down at 7:20 a.m., French's and Sedgwick's divisions were ordered across the creek at Pry's Ford. Sedgwick's division was in the lead, and French's followed once the way was clear. General Sumner, who was

Brig. Gen. William H. French, USA, commander, Second Corps, Third Division. Library of Congress / National Archives.

with Sedgwick's lead division, had no direct communication with French, but once he understood the state of affairs on the field, he would presumably let French know what he expected from his division. After he made a reconnaissance of the field, Sumner formulated his plan on how best to continue the Union attacks that had initially launched almost three hours before.[66]

During his initial survey of the ground, Sumner not only came away with a decent understanding of the situation of the Union forces north of his position, but he also observed those Union forces engaged east of the Dunker Church and in the West Woods. This was Brig. Gen. George S. Greene's Twelfth Corps division and the 125th Pennsylvania from Crawford's Twelfth Corps division. Reports also indicate that Sumner could see Confederate forces deployed in the Sunken Road farther to their south. These were Rodes's and G. B. Anderson's uncommitted brigades from D. H. Hill's division and what remained of Colquitt's and McRae's shattered brigades.[67]

Once Sumner determined to use Sedgwick's division as his spearhead to seize the West Woods directly in his front, the Second Corps commander also had to decide how best to use French's division as support for this attack.

Options

With the attack on the West Woods about to begin and the battle at a critical stage, Sumner had two options to choose from. He could have French directly support Sedgwick's attack, or he could send him farther south.

Option 1

Sumner could decide that the best use for French's division was to have it move on a line directly on Sedgwick's left. As he planned his attack, Sumner might have considered a single-division assault too great of a risk. If he combined the two divisions he then had on hand with French's force advancing directly to Sedgwick's left and protecting his flank, Sumner would have an assault force of over ten thousand men—an intimidating number by anyone's measure. While Sumner did conduct a reconnaissance of the ground, he had no idea what Confederate forces might lie just beyond his sight south and west of the West Woods. Having French's units nearby might provide additional manpower with which he could respond to unforeseen circumstances. On the other hand, having all of his soldiers bunched together would deprive Sumner of a reserve force to respond to contingencies elsewhere. This circumstance would also leave Richardson, who would soon be arriving, to deal with any situation on his own. Lastly, advancing the six brigades that made up these two divisions in the narrow space open to them might prove too unwieldy a maneuver for the Second Corps commander even to attempt.

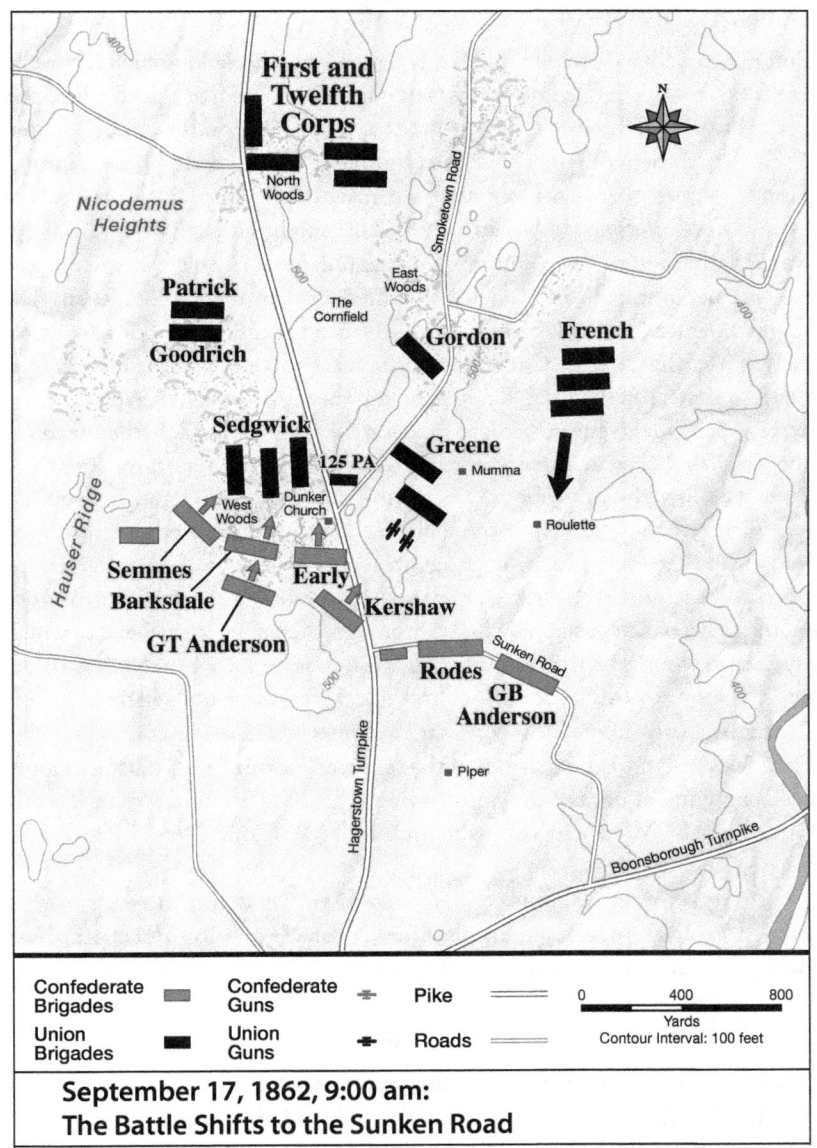

Option 2

Sumner could have decided that it made more sense to send French farther to the south to support Sedgwick's attack. It would take some time for French's three-brigade division to cross the creek and assemble on the opposite bank. Even though he was only about thirty minutes behind Sedgwick's columns, French's 5,700-man division would not reach the eastern edge of the East Woods until approximately 9:20 a.m. Sumner might have felt that waiting for French's division to be up and ready would unnecessarily delay his advance.[68]

Sumner also had to consider the Confederates in the Sunken Road; they might threaten his flank or rear as he advanced if they were not adequately dealt with. The Twelfth Corps units near the Dunker Church might be utilized to protect Sedgwick's flank as he advanced to the West Woods. Conversely, Sedgwick's advance might threaten the flank of the Confederate forces the Twelfth Corps infantry were engaged with. With no need for French to protect Sedgwick's immediate left, that division could be sent farther south.

Furthermore, just before Sumner reached the western edge of the East Woods, he received a dispatch from army headquarters: "Gen. Hooker appears to be driving the enemy rapidly. If he does not require your assistance on his right, please push up on his left through the ravine at the head of which the house was burned this morning, getting possession of the woods to the right as soon as possible & push on towards Sharpsburg and a little to its rear as rapidly as possible." Sumner might have interpreted this message as orders from McClellan to attack south of the previous morning's assaults, including on the ground at or near the Sunken Road. The house referred to in the dispatch was the Mumma Farm, which D. H. Hill's Confederate infantry had burned that morning.[69]

On the other hand, Sumner had to consider whether it was wise to send French so far south, placing his most inexperienced division and commander beyond his immediate control.

Decision

Sumner chose to send French southwest to attack the Sunken Road (Option 2). Shortly after reaching the ground just east of the East Woods, French wheeled his division to the southwest toward the Roulette Farm, driving away the Confederate pickets who were occupying it. Once he and his lead brigade reached the farm, French's men began receiving fire from D. H. Hill's forces now holding the Sunken Road. At almost the exact moment he started his attack, a courier from Sumner found French and ordered him into the battle. French had deployed his division already and was moving on the Confederates in the road, eight hundred yards south of Sedgwick's line of advance.[70]

French described the situation in his after-action report:

> When my left flank had cleared the ford a mile, the division faced to the left, forming three lines of battle adjacent to and contiguous with Sedgwick's, and immediately moved to the front.
>
> The enemy, who was in position in advance, opened his batteries, under which fire my lines steadily moved until the first line, encountering the enemy's skirmishers, charged them briskly, and, entering a group of houses on Roulette's farm, drove back the force, which had taken a strong position for defense. Whilst Max Weber was clearing his front and driving before him the enemy's first line, a sudden and terrible fire was opened upon his right by the troops, which had succeeded in breaking the center division of the line of battle. At the same time a heavy column endeavored to turn my left and rear.
>
> At this moment Captain Sumner communicated to me, from the general commanding the corps, that his right divisions were being severely handled, and directed me to press the enemy with all my force.[71]

Results/Impact

This decision is critical because it shifted the now five-hour-old battle from the West Woods south to the infamous Sunken Road or the Bloody Lane, as it came to be known. On the Union side, Israel B. Richardson's Second Corps division followed French into the desperate fight for the Sunken Road. On the Confederate side, R. H. Anderson's division was sent in to stop Richardson's and French's men, inaugurating this next phase of the constantly evolving battle. The horrendous struggle for this simple piece of dirt road lasted for the better part of three hours. The net result was almost 5,500 combined casualties, one-fifth of the casualties for the entire day.

The Bloody Lane at Antietam joined an ever-growing list of seemingly ordinary American places that became infamous for the sanguinary fighting that happened there. Sumner's decision determined this simple country lane would be recalled in the same breath as places like the Wheatfield at Gettysburg, the Hornet's Nest at Shiloh, the Stone Wall at Fredericksburg, and the Muleshoe at Spotsylvania.

Alternate Decision/Scenario

It is unclear how the battle would have changed had Sumner brought French directly to Sedgwick's left at the West Woods or even directly to the left of Greene's men east of the Dunker Church instead of sending him to the Sunken Road. While the course of the fighting would certainly have changed, to what extent can only be speculated. There also is no guarantee having Sumner's two divisions attacking together would have changed the outcome of the fight in the West Woods. French might have even been routed out of the woods along with Sedgwick.[72]

Had Sumner decided on the aforementioned course, the fight at the Sunken Road might not have taken place at all. Led by Israel B. Richardson, Sumner's last division had been ordered to French's support, and it crossed Antietam Creek at approximately 9:30 a.m. Would Richardson still have attacked the road in the event of this alternate decision, or would he have attacked farther north? Would the Sunken Road have remained untouched and not a part of the battle? In this case, Lee would have had no reason to send R. H. Anderson into the road later on to support D. H. Hill. The fight at the West Woods would have dramatically altered the shape of the battle. At approximately 10:00 to 10:30 a.m., Brig. Gen. George S. Greene's Twelfth Corps division had advanced into the woods. What might this force have done with more direct support from the two divisions of the Second Corps?[73]

Confederate Crisis in the Sunken Road

Situation

In the process of writing this manuscript, no single part of the battle proved more challenging to understand than the struggle for the Sunken Road. Pinning down the single decision that most determined the outcome was more difficult than I had initially imagined. The fighting here was a confusing morass of smoke, noise, and humanity, and several important decisions were made within moments of one another. As attacks and counterattacks rolled back and forth over the fields, farms, and woods of Antietam, the battle became a quagmire of Union and Confederate units. It is often challenging to keep track of the mixed bag of brigades and divisions involved, and the fight for the now-infamous Sunken Road is possibly the most glaring example of this fact. Before this element of the battle ended, all or part of eight separate Confederate brigades were sent into this sector. In total, some 6,700 Rebels were deployed at a section of ground that was roughly a half a mile long and perhaps two hundred yards deep.

Losses among the Confederate command no doubt also contributed to the confusion. Mounting casualties among the ranks of Rebel officers meant that more and more junior officers with little or no experience were forced to take their place. Sometimes these officers performed well, and other times not

September 17, 1862

The Sunken Road, view to the southeast, Antietam National Battlefield, modern image. Author.

so much. R. H. Anderson's four brigades most heavily engaged at the Sunken Road were composed of seventeen regiments that sustained a command loss of 82 percent. The brigade command loss rate was 75 percent. Rodes's and Anderson's Brigades of D. H. Hill's division included nine regiments whose command loss rate was over 155 percent. Rodes and G. B. Anderson were also casualties, equaling a 100 percent loss rate.[74]

As I contemplated the myriad of elements that made up this complicated and terrible struggle, again and again, one decision seemed to stand out above them all.

Roger Atkinson Pryor was born near Petersburg, Virginia, in 1828, and he could trace his family's lineage to some of the very first Virginia colonists. Pryor graduated from Hampden-Sydney College in 1845 and from the University of Virginia's law school in 1848. Before the Civil War, he worked in journalism before moving into politics.

After Virginia seceded, the Southern firebrand secured an appointment as colonel of the Third Virginia Infantry Regiment. Pryor was eventually promoted to the rank of brigadier general in April 1862, although his relative skills as a combat commander had often been called into question. His brigade fought in the Peninsula Campaign and at Second Bull Run. In addition, as part of Richard H. Anderson's division, the so-called Florida Brigade had the distinction of containing the only Florida regiments serving in the Army of Northern Virginia. This brigade and Anderson's Division participated in the capture of Harpers Ferry, although they were not significantly engaged.[75]

Brig. Gen. Roger A. Pryor, CSA, commander, Anderson's Division, Pryor's Brigade. Library of Congress / National Archives.

After falling back from South Mountain and crossing over Antietam Creek on September 15, D. H. Hill's battered division was deployed in line north of the Boonsboro Turnpike near an old, worn-down farm line that connected it with Hagerstown Pike. Eroded by years of heavy wagon traffic, a good portion of the Sunken Road was several feet below ground level, making it a ready-made fighting position.

During the morning phase of the battle, the brigade of Brig. Gen. Roswell Ripley of Hill's Division was sent north to support Hood's disintegrating counterattack. Subsequently, the brigades of Col. Alfred H. Colquitt and Col. Duncan K. McRae were also sent in to support Ripley. All these forces were eventually defeated, and they fell back south and west.[76] That left the brigades of Brig. Gen. Robert Rodes and Brig. Gen. George B. Anderson to cover the position in the Sunken Road. Rodes was posted on the left and Anderson on the right. They were eventually joined by some of the survivors of Col. Alfred H. Colquitt's and Col. Duncan McRae's shattered brigades and the brigade of Howell Cobb commanded by Lieut. Col. William MacRae. Cobb's men represented what was left of the survivors from the defense of Crampton's Gap. Altogether, this force totaled about 2,700 infantrymen supported by two batteries of artillery located near the Piper Farm, as well as batteries west of the Hagerstown Turnpike and on Cemetery Hill.

Either by necessity or by design, Lee and his commanders chose not to strengthen their defensive positions at Antietam with constructed field fortifications. Other than a few places where the Confederates took advantage of terrain features already in place, both armies for the most part fought out in the open. The Sunken Road was one of the few locations that offered significant protection for the Confederate defenders. Rebels strengthened their position by knocking down fence rails to construct makeshift breastworks along the road.[77]

On the Union side, the two Second Corps divisions of French and Richardson assaulted the road with roughly ten thousand men. This force included six infantry brigades supported by several batteries of artillery, including the long-range Parrott rifles east of the Antietam Creek. French launched his first attack at approximately 9:00 a.m. For ninety minutes, he threw three successive waves of brigade-sized attacks directly at Rodes and Anderson, losing over 1,700 of his own infantrymen in the process. Following French's assaults, Maj. Gen. Israel B. Richardson's division repeated the same tactics farther to French's left. Richardson's 4,200 veterans also attacked the road, basically one brigade at a time.[78]

As the fight dragged on for hours, both sides suffered a considerable number of casualties. But on the Confederate side, the losses were compounded by the dead and wounded tangling the bottom of the road and the toll the battle was taking on the officers.

At roughly 10:15 a.m., about the time Richardson's First Division was moving to attack the Confederate position, Maj. Gen. Richard H. Anderson's reserve division was ordered to support D. H. Hill. Like McLaws's soldiers, Anderson's troops had marched all night from Harpers Ferry. Anderson led his six brigades to the support of the embattled Confederate line, and he was wounded just as his four thousand men were positioning themselves for the attack near the Piper Farm. Command of the division now fell to Brig. Gen. Roger A. Pryor. Shortly after that, a besieged Rodes found Pryor and pleaded for help to save the Confederate position.[79]

Options

Pryor's two options were sending the division directly to the Sunken Road or attacking one or both of the Union flanks. As the crisis in what came to be known as "Bloody Lane" was reaching a decisive point, Pryor was surrounded by smoke, noise, and chaos. The political general who had never before commanded a division in combat had a critical decision to make.

Option 1

To support the road, Pryor could send his brigades in at what he deemed the most salient point of crisis. As the division approached the road, its soldiers

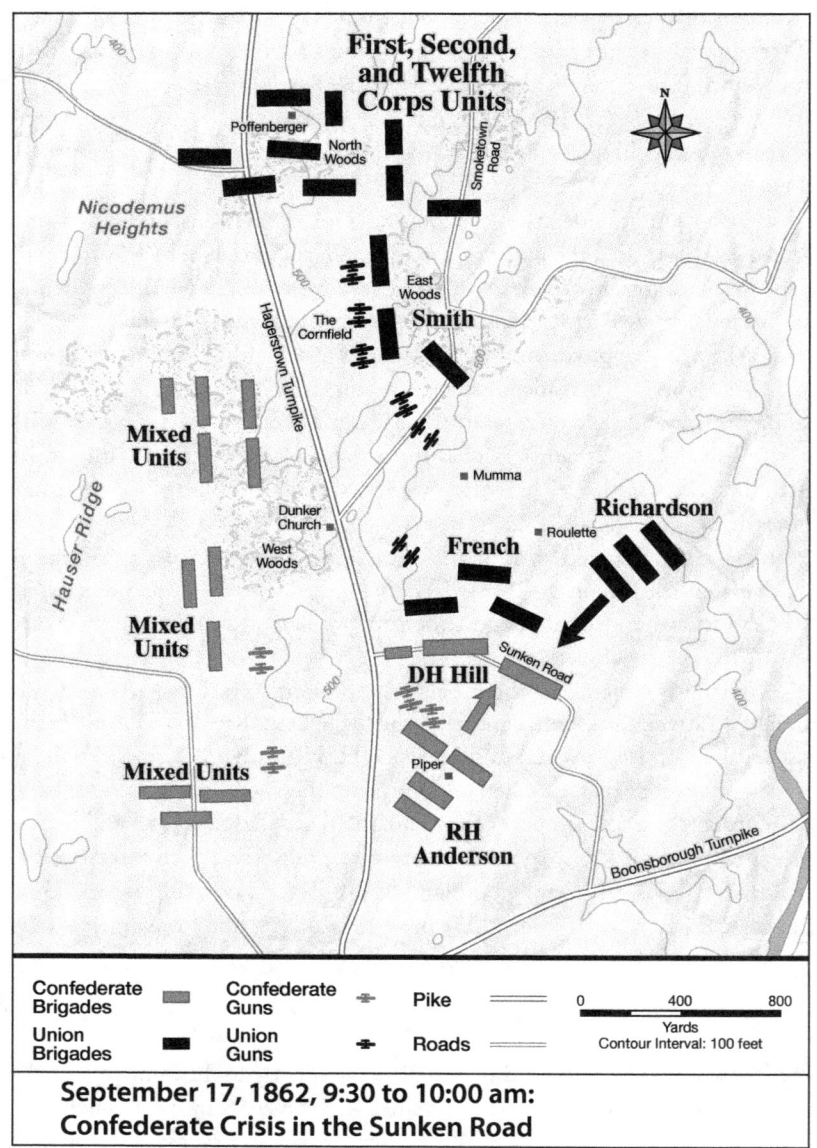

September 17, 1862, 9:30 to 10:00 am:
Confederate Crisis in the Sunken Road

could see Richardson's Union division heavily engaged with the right of the Confederate line. The lane was now drawing both sides to it as if it possessed some kind gravitational force. Because of the deadly fire of the Union infantry, the Confederates dared not venture too far from the road. Those that did were quickly pushed back. Additionally, any Rebels who loitered too long on the high ground behind the road became easy targets for Capt. John A. Tompkins's Union battery, the long-range artillery east of Antietam Creek, and the Union infantry. Naturally, many the officers and men of Anderson's Division were more than eager to seek the relative shelter of the road. Sending in the division to support the road might have seemed the most logical option for a man suddenly thrust into his first divisional command during a major battle.

Also, once Pryor took command of the division, the situation was no doubt overwhelming. He might have felt that the momentum and direction of the assault were predetermined. In addition, he might have believed that taking the force in a new direction would be too complicated a maneuver to execute given the current circumstances.[80]

Option 2

Pryor could reason that his best option was sending the division around either end of the Confederate line to threaten the one or both of the open Union flanks. As Richardson's division attacked, they slowly worked their way south and east of the Confederates in the road. Meanwhile, French's Third Division, which had suffered over 30 percent casualties, had fallen back and was holding positions just out of range of the deadly Confederate fire. Both ends of the Union line were open, and nothing guarded the troops' flanks save Tompkins's battery on the ridge where the modern-day visitor center sits. Pryor could surmise that an attack on either flank would push back the Union advance.[81]

Later on, as the Confederate line in the road was collapsing and the fighting was falling back to the Piper Farm, James Longstreet ordered an assault on the exposed flank of Kimball's Union brigade at the extreme right of French's line. About 250 men from the Twenty-Seventh North Carolina and the Third Arkansas advanced over the Dunker Church plateau and into a cornfield and the right of Kimball's brigade. Even though this advance was beaten back, it demonstrated that someone in the Confederate high command recognized vulnerability in the Union position at the road.[82]

Decision

John C. Waugh, Pryor's biographer, describes a man perhaps in over his head: "Roger found himself confronting what looked like Armageddon. . . .

Nothing in his career in law journalism and politics prepared him for this."[83] Pryor decided to send the bulk of the division piecemeal into the cauldron of humanity that was the Sunken Road (Option 1). The brigades of Brig. Gen. Ambrose R. Wright, Col. John C. Hately (Pryor), Col. Carnot Posey, and Col. Alfred Cumming were all sent to the right side of the line one after another. Two of the four brigades actually made it into the road at G. B. Anderson's position, while the other two took a position largely behind it.

Results/Impact

As it turns out, Pryor's inexperience was exposed. Ezra Carman described the situation, suggesting confusion on Pryor's part and unstated orders issued to Anderson: "R. H. Anderson had been wounded very soon after coming upon the field and Pryor, who succeeded to the command, was unaware of the orders under which Anderson was acting and did not rise to the occasion. The consequent movement of his command was disjointed and without proper direction, but when apprised by Rodes of the condition of affairs he ordered his own brigade forward."[84] An officer in the Fourth North Carolina shed further light on the situation: "I think Featherston (Posey) was started to the right, but instead of getting there came up behind us, where he was not needed, for we could have held our position indefinitely. He sustained significant loss in killed and wounded and I have always thought was the cause of the line breaking, for when he found he was not needed there he gave an order to fall back, which was mistaken for a general order and all that could walk went back with him, which caused a general break in the line."[85]

Pryor's decision pushed the division ahead piecemeal, and several of Anderson's four supporting brigades were soon crammed into the crowded road or just to its rear. This helped add to a quagmire of the living and the dead. As units became mixed, the chaos and confusion multiplied exponentially. Adding to the mayhem was the fact that no one Confederate officer was exercising overall command and control over the position. As commands fell into disarray, the confusion and casualties in the road mounted. In the span of a few moments, G. B. Anderson was mortally wounded; his successor, Col. Charles C. Tew, was killed by a bullet to the head; and Tew's successor, Col. Risden T. Bennett, was wounded as well. Between Rodes's and G. B. Anderson's brigades and R. H. Anderson's division, more than thirty command level officers were killed or wounded in this chaotic and violent struggle.[86]

At approximately 11:00 a.m., Richardson's Union division was executing one last push. Caldwell's Union brigade on the right flank of the Confederate position had extended its line beyond the end of the enemy's. This end of the Confederate line then began to collapse in great confusion. At almost that same moment, a mix-up in instructions at Rodes's position caused his portion of the line to disintegrate as well. Lieut. Col. James N. Lightfoot, whose Sixth Alabama was holding the center of the Confederate line, told Rodes that the right wing of his regiment was exposed to enfilade fire. Rodes ordered Lightfoot to throw his right wing back and out of the Sunken Road. Instead of executing the order, the lieutenant colonel moved to the rear of his regiment and gave the command "Sixth Alabama, about-face; forward march."

Seeing this, Major Hobson of the neighboring Fifth Alabama asked Lightfoot whether the order was intended for the whole brigade. Lightfoot answered in the affirmative, and the Fifth and the troops on its left thereupon withdrew. Within a matter of moments, this entire section of the line was falling back in confusion, and many Confederates did not stop running until they reached the Hagerstown Turnpike. Only a desperate last-minute stand by Confederate artillery and what infantrymen could be rallied at the Piper Farm stopped the Union deluge from completely splitting the Army of Northern Virginia in two. As the Federals were now low on ammunition, they began to fall back to the Sunken Road.[87]

Pryor's decision was critical not only because it added to a confused and chaotic situation and prevented any command and control within the Confederate units holding the road. In addition, his choice contributed to the collapse of the position. This breakdown exposed Lee's army and made it vulnerable to being split in two by any concerted Union thrust into that same area. As it turns out, that was precisely what Maj. Gen. William B. Franklin of the Union Sixth Corps was hoping would happen.

Alternate Decision/Scenario

Had Pryor sent all or part of the division around the road to attack the Union right, the outcome might have changed. A substantial gap existed between Greene's and French's positions. Other than Greene's Twelfth Corps division, Tompkins's battery, and the reserve artillery across the creek, virtually nothing guarded French's right flank. Had Pryor gotten two or three brigades on that flank, French, whose men were close to being fought out, might not have been able to stop him. In that scenario and forced to fight in two directions, the Union forces might very well have been forced to retire as their position became untenable.

The Sunken Road, circa 1862. Alexander Gardner, Library of Congress / National Archives.

Sumner Holds Back the Sixth Corps

Situation

One of the most often-repeated myths about the Battle of Antietam is that George McClellan had tens of thousands of reserves available to him on September 17. The work of recent historians like Steven Stotelmyer reveals that this is only partially true. McClellan himself noted in his 1863 after-action report that he had 87,000 men in his army while Lee had over 97,000. While the aggregate of the Union force present for duty in his army on September 17 was just over 85,000 men, McClellan never had all of those men in one place at the same time. Best estimates indicate that he had in aggregate of about 79,000 men physically at Sharpsburg, and that and of those, only 70,000 were combat effectives. In total, McClellan got about 56,000 troops engaged on that day. This was due to a number of factors: straggling, casualties suffered at South Mountain, and the absence of the better part of two corps and a division of McClellan's army at the moment the opening shots were fired at Antietam.[88]

The Union Sixth Corps and Darrius Couch's Fourth Corps division that was attached were among those absent from the Union side of the creek that morning. William B. Franklin and the seventeen thousand men that made up his wing had spent the previous two days camped five miles away near Rohrersville in Pleasant Valley. Their job was to cover the flank of the main

September 17, 1862

The Dunker Church, circa 1862. Alexander Gardner, Library of Congress / National Archives.

Union army at Sharpsburg from a potential attack up the valley from Harpers Ferry. On the evening of September 16, McClellan ordered Franklin to leave Couch's 6,400-man division in the valley and move his other two divisions under Maj. Gen. Henry W. Slocum and Maj. Gen. William F. "Baldy" Smith to Sharpsburg. On September 17, Franklin started his march to the battlefield at 5:00 a.m., about thirty minutes before Hooker was preparing to launch his initial assault on Lee's left. Franklin arrived at army headquarters at Keedysville around 11:00 a.m., when the struggle for the Sunken Road was reaching its climax.[89]

At the outset, McClellan had planned for the Sixth Corps to remain in reserve east of Antietam Creek once it arrived. Yet the morning's calamitous situation west of the creek changed his thinking. As Sedgwick was being driven from the West Woods and the state of affairs seemed headed for disaster, Sumner asked that the Sixth be sent into the battle for immediate support. In his August 1863 report McClellan detailed his thinking:

> Between 12 and 1 p.m. General Franklin's corps arrived on the field of battle, having left their camp near Crampton's Pass at 6 a.m., leaving General Couch with orders to move with his division to occupy Maryland Heights. General Smith's division lead the column followed by General Slocum's.

It was first intended to keep this corps in reserve on the east side of the Antietam, to operate on either flank or on the center, as circumstances might require, but on nearing Keedysville the strong opposition on the right, developed by the attacks of Hooker and Sumner, rendered it necessary at once to send this corps to the assistance of the right wing.[90]

Because McClellan expected that his right might again be counterattacked and because he lacked uncommitted forces west of Antietam Creek, Smith's division was immediately sent across the creek at Pry's Ford to support Sumner. Slocum crossed at the Upper Bridge and took the field shortly thereafter. Franklin then advanced a small force into the West Woods. Two regiments of Brig. Gen. Winfield S. Hancock's First Brigade of Smith's division were among the troops engaged in this first move by Franklin.[91]

By this time, the brutal fighting on the north end of the battlefield was winding down, but the battle was reaching a critical stage. For the last seven hours, 34,000 Union troops had engaged 25,000 Confederates for a roughly six-square mile piece of land. Of the 23,000 total Union and Confederate casualties resulting from the Battle of Antietam, over 80 percent occurred on the fields, farms, and woodlots north of the Boonsboro Turnpike. In the dreadful struggle for the Cornfield, the West Woods, and the Sunken Road, both armies had nearly crippled each other. The Union army, however, had one more card to play. While Lee had no more reserves to commit to this end of the field, McClellan did. The Federal commander now had the 11,000 men of the Sixth Corps available and ready to renew the attack.[92]

Meanwhile, south of the Boonsboro Turnpike, the Union Ninth Corps was now launching its third assault on the Lower Bridge just as Rodman's division was finally approaching Snavely's Ford beyond the Confederate right flank. Within the hour, this Confederate position itself collapsed under the weight of the Union attacks. At this same time, Alfred Pleasonton had sent the better part of two cavalry brigades supported by four batteries of horse artillery and an infantry regiment across the Middle Bridge. These units became engaged with the Confederates in and near the Sunken Road. The troops Pleasonton dispatched also fought with Brig. Gen. Nathan G. Evans's brigade and portions of the three brigades of D. R. Jones's division positioned on the high ground near Cemetery Hill.[93]

Except for those Confederates still battling at or near the Sunken Road, Lee's left had been completely driven west of the Hagerstown Turnpike and south to a point about two hundred yards north of the Dunker Church. While several commands held these positions, including Jones, Walker, McLaws, and Hood, it is not clear how many combat effectives the Confederates could

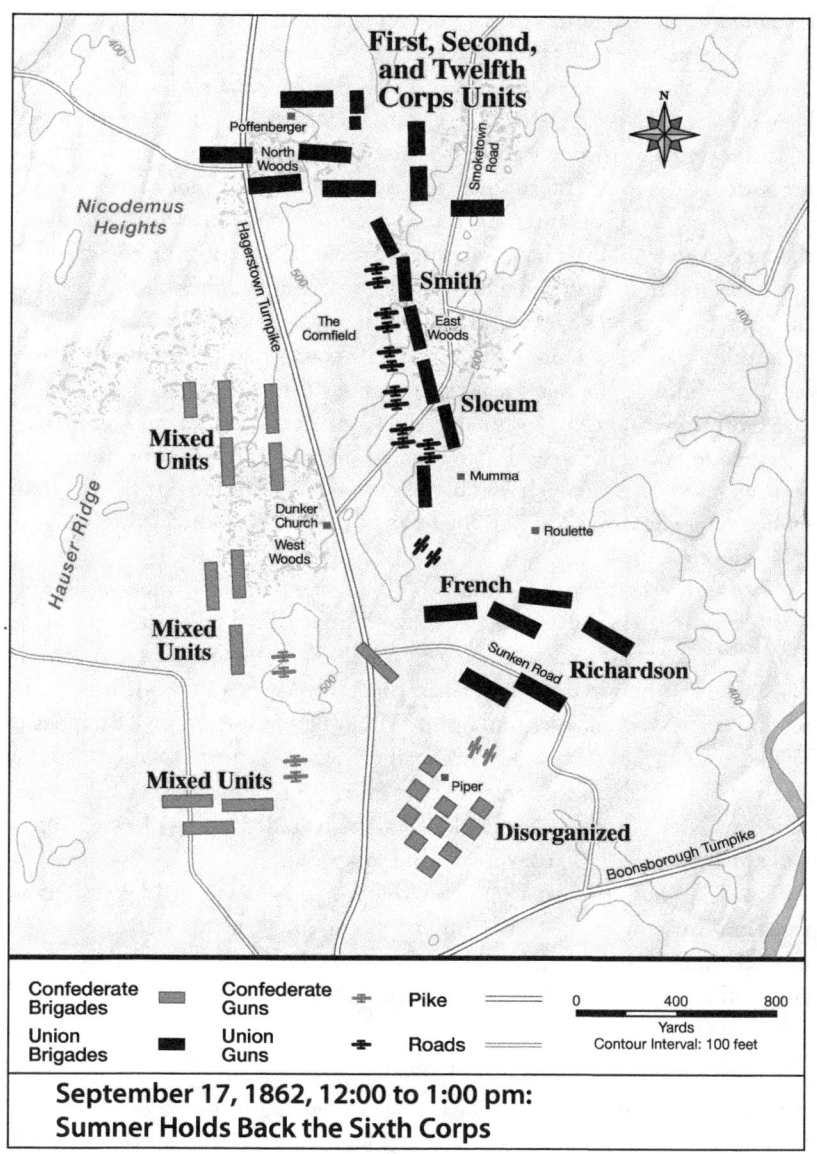

September 17, 1862, 12:00 to 1:00 pm:
Sumner Holds Back the Sixth Corps

actually muster to defend against another Union assault here. My estimate is somewhere between four thousand and six thousand troops supported by perhaps five batteries of artillery on Hauser's Ridge, but that number might have been far lower. Even in the best-case scenario for the Confederates, they were outnumbered almost two to one. It is also safe to assume that many of these units were exhausted and running low on ammunition if not completely out of it. Overall, Confederate command and control undoubtedly suffered due to the 50 percent casualty rate among the regimental and brigade commanders in this sector. It is uncertain whether the Union high command was aware of this fact, but safe money would say the officers were not.[94]

Additionally, by noon, the Confederate forces had been entirely driven out of the Sunken Road in great confusion. As the men of Richardson's Second Corps division were advancing, the Confederate command was making a desperate stand near the Piper Farm. Longstreet's staff were themselves manning two guns from Miller's battery of the Washington Artillery. All the while, the general was holding the reins of their horses, directing the fire of this makeshift crew.[95]

While the battle for the Sunken Road was going on, intense fighting was taking place in the area between the Sunken Road and just north of the Dunker Church. At 10:00 a.m., George Greene's Twelfth Corps division had driven several hundred yards west in the West Woods beyond the church, only to be pushed back by units from Manning's and Ransom's Brigades of Walker's Division. Manning's units, the Twenty-Seventh North Carolina and the Third Arkansas, were also part of a counterattack James Longstreet ordered against French's left flank. This assault failed just as the fighting in and around the Piper Farm was coming to an end.

The time was now just after noon. Supported by his fresh artillery batteries, Franklin now readied his entire corps for a new advance at the Dunker Church and the surrounding woods. However, he needed General Sumner's approval before moving forward with his attack.[96]

Options

Edwin Vose Sumner might still have been smarting from the destruction of Sedgwick's division, but he remained the ranking general on the field. He had two options to choose from at this point in the fighting: attacking or standing on the defensive.

Option 1

Sumner could launch an assault with the Sixth Corps supported by as many of the units currently on the field as he could muster. Whether he knew it or not, there might have been no better time for Sumner to order the available Union reserves to drive at Lee's embattled left one more time. Though at significant cost to the Army of the Potomac, the relentless attacks had driven the Confederates back south and west of the much-coveted high ground east of the Dunker Church. The Union offensives also forced Lee to commit all of the reserves he then had on hand.

Additionally, the Confederate forces that had been engaged on the north end of the field were mostly exhausted, fought out, disorganized, and low on ammunition. They had been fighting for almost seven straight hours, and for many of the Rebel units, this was their second major battle in three days. Moreover, all of the Confederates had done considerable marching in the past several days.

Moreover, at the Middle and Lower Bridges and the Sunken Road, the tide was beginning to shift. The conditions George McClellan had envisioned at the outset of the battle were finally coalescing after a long and bitterly contested struggle. The Union army had fought all day for this exact situation, and one could argue that McClellan had been hoping for precisely these circumstances.

Lastly, military doctrine dictates that when employing offensive tactics, one of the principal functions of a reserve force—and arguably its most important one—is to exploit any opportunities that develop during a battle. From the time of the ancient Greeks, armies have utilized the concept of a tactical reserve. However, it must be emphasized that a reserve force is useful only if the commander in question actually deploys it. The opportunity could have arrived. For all the Union high command knew, it was the only one that would present itself that day. As none other than Napoleon famously said, "A general who retains fresh troops for the day after a battle is almost always beaten."[97]

Option 2

Sumner could determine not to attack and hold Franklin on the defensive. Sumner had good reason to feel that some tactical discretion was called for at this moment. The Army of the Potomac had also been fighting for seven straight hours, and the men were not in much better shape than the Confederates they were facing. The Union First, Second, and Twelfth Corps had attacked this relatively small piece of ground relentlessly and were all but out of action. Additionally, two corps commanders and four division commanders had been wounded and were out of action. While some First and Twelfth Corps units were undoubtedly able to fight in a defensive posture, it was debatable whether they were suitable for additional offensive activities. Franklin and his two divisions might very well have to make the attack all on their own.

At this moment, an unknown number of Confederates occupied the West Woods in front of Sumner. The overwhelming Union attacks had driven the Rebels beyond the turnpike, and the West Woods, the terrain, and the woods now concealed them from Franklin's sight. Additionally, no one in the Union leadership had any idea of the Confederates' orientation or condition. If Sumner allowed Franklin to go bumbling off into the West Woods, he might just find himself in a repeat of the calamity that had befallen Sedgwick earlier that morning. One wrecked division under Sumner's command might have been enough for one day. Were the possible advantages of an attack worth the political and military cost if the last of the Union forces north of the Boonsboro Turnpike were to be defeated?

Additionally, Sumner had to consider that any offensive operations he launched had to comport with the overall plans of the commanding general. He could not undertake actions that conflicted with what McClellan was expecting him to do.

Decision

Sumner chose not to attack and hold Franklin on the defensive (Option 2). As Franklin was preparing to begin his offensive, Sumner stopped him, declaring that "if he were defeated the right would be entirely routed, his being the only troops left on the right that had any life in them." An incensed Franklin would appeal directly to McClellan. The commanding general had made his way to Sumner's headquarters to see for himself the state of affairs. After witnessing the devastation and casualties, and after consulting with his lieutenants, McClellan eventually agreed that no attack by the Sixth Corps should be launched.[98]

Results/Impact

It is not entirely clear whether Sumner was still shaken from the disaster in the West Woods, or whether he shared the commanding general's fear of a Confederate counterattack. Perhaps both men felt the condition of the army made an offensive operation too risky. Perhaps McClellan wanted to see what came of Burnside's attack at the Lower Bridge before he committed to course of action. Whatever the reason, the attack would not occur, and Franklin and his corps would essentially stand in place until the next day. This decision was critical because it ended one of the last opportunities to deal the Confederate left one final and possibly fatal blow. Furthermore, it unofficially marked the end of the fighting north of the Boonsboro Turnpike and allowed all eyes to look exclusively to the Lower Bridge and the ongoing struggle there. Lee was able to focus almost all of his attention to his right, including sending A. P. Hill, his last reserve, at Burnside, because no more pressure came from his left.

Alternate Decision/Scenario

It is impossible to say what would have resulted had Sumner allowed Franklin to launch a new attack with the Sixth Corps. However, the combat that was inaugurated that morning would undoubtedly have continued. Any number of scenarios could have resulted in a renewal of the Union attacks. Perhaps a new fight would have broken out in the West Woods or at the Dunker Church, or a struggle could have commenced closer to the town of Sharpsburg itself. Even by the most optimistic calculations the Confederates were outnumbered almost two to one. A renewed attack by Sumner might have driven them back even farther. As we will discuss in regard to the next decision, an assault by Sumner coupled with a potential advance by the Union Fifth Corps at Lee's center might have been decisive. Lee might also have been forced to use A. P. Hill's men in an entirely different way. Possibly unable to send Hill's Division in whole into the flank of the Ninth Corps, Lee might instead of split the unit in two or three to defend against attacks from several directions.

Another noteworthy outcome might have resulted from the Sixth Corps being allowed to attack. Lee, seeing that the situation was becoming more and desperate, was beginning to consider what options were open to him. While there is no evidence the Confederate commander was at that moment

Tompkins's Union Battery A, 1st Rhode Island Light Artillery and the visitor center, Antietam National Battlefield, modern image. Author.

considering a withdrawal, he was contemplating a movement beyond the Union right with his cavalry and whatever infantry and artillery he could scrape up. Lee and Jackson would spend the better part of the afternoon working to put such a plan in place. This idea was eventually scrapped when the futility of such a move became apparent. It has been argued that it was a desperate plan borne of a desperate Confederate commander who was thinking of any way, even foolhardy aggressiveness, to save his army from destruction. The only reason Lee could even think of such a move was that despite the situation becoming more perilous on his right, by 1:00 p.m. the Union assaults on his left had virtually ended.[99]

The Fifth Corps Does Not Advance

Situation

Maj. Gen. Fitz John Porter, the son of Capt. John Porter, was born in 1822 in New Hampshire. Porter's family was literally a who's who of prominent Union naval officers—his uncle was the flamboyant Cmdre. David Porter, and his cousins were William D. Porter, David Dixon Porter, and David G. Farragut. Fitz, however, pursued an army career.[100]

The unit known as the Fifth Corps was established within the Army of the Potomac on May 18, 1862, as the Fifth Corps Provisional and subsequently engaged in the Peninsula Campaign. The corps was created by merging then Brig. Gen. Fitz John Porter's Third Division of the Third Corps with Brig. Gen. George Sykes's division of US Regular troops. Porter became corps commander, and on July 22, 1862, "provisional" was dropped from the unit's name. Its formal designation was now the Fifth Corps of the Army of the Potomac. After the Seven Days' Battles, Porter was promoted to major general of volunteers on July 4, 1862.[101]

At Second Bull Run (August 28–30, 1862), Porter's corps was sent to reinforce Maj. Gen. John Pope in the Northern Virginia Campaign. Porter openly challenged this reassignment, criticizing it and Pope. As the soldiers of the Fifth Corps attacked on August 30, they were stopped by Jackson's troops in the railroad cut and by artillery on their left flank. Longstreet launched his attack against the lightly held Union position south of the Warrenton Turnpike during the Fifth's retreat. An infuriated Pope charged Porter with disobeying a lawful order and misbehaving in front of the enemy for his actions before and during the battle.[102] On September 5, Porter was relieved of his command until the charges could be answered. McClellan needed all the experienced commanders he could muster, so he asked Halleck to temporarily set aside the charges until the current crisis was concluded.[103]

September 17, 1862

Maj. Gen. Fitz John Porter, USA, commander, Union Fifth Corps. Library of Congress / National Archives

As the Army of the Potomac departed Washington, DC, Porter's Fifth Corps marched in three separate parts. Brig. Gen. George Sykes's Second Division left on September 5 with the main force of the army. Maj. Gen. George Morell's First Division accompanied by Porter did not leave its camp until September 12, and Brig. Gen. Andrew A. Humphreys's Third Division would not depart the capital until the fourteenth. As a result, Porter had only two divisions present (Morell's and Sykes's) when the battle began on the seventeenth. Humphreys's division would not join the army until the morning of September 18. After arriving on the field east of Antietam Creek with the rest of the army on September 15, Sykes and eventually Morell were positioned just east of the Middle Bridge straddling the Boonsboro Turnpike.[104]

By 2:00 p.m., the next phase of the Battle of Antietam was in full swing. The fighting by now had shifted south; until sunset, the lion's share of the conflict would take place south of the Boonsboro Pike. Sometime before noon, Pleasonton was ordered forward with a combined force with artillery to support the attack at the Sunken Road. By 12:15 p.m. this advance, aided at times by the Union guns in position east of the creek, had secured the bridge and was driving the thin Confederate line west toward the town. Sykes began feeding in several infantry units to support the Federals as this engagement progressed. By 1:00 p.m., these Fifth Corps units had all but replaced Pleasonton's cavalry west of the creek, allowing the horsemen to retire to Middle Bridge.

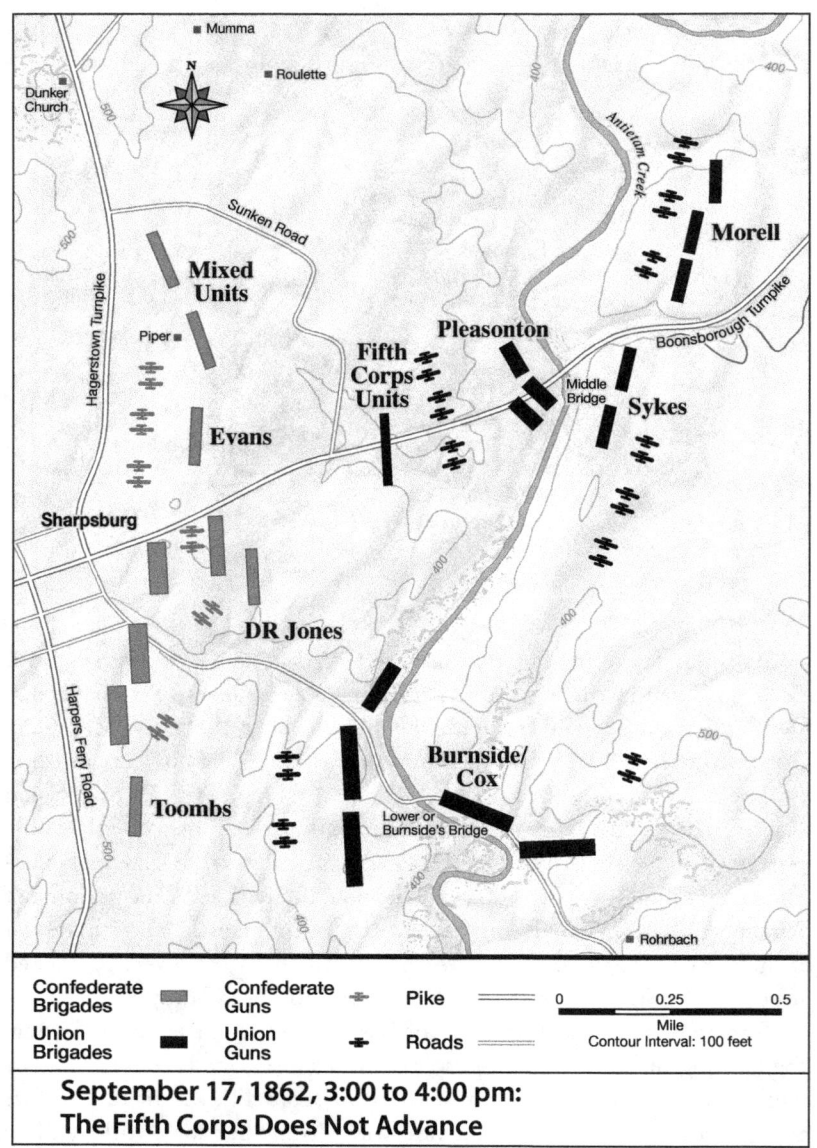

September 17, 1862, 3:00 to 4:00 pm:
The Fifth Corps Does Not Advance

By 3:00 p.m., part of Lieut. Col. Robert C. Buchanan's brigade and a part of Maj. Charles S. Lovell's brigade of Sykes's division had advanced some six hundred yards west of Antietam Creek. There, they became engaged with the thinly held Confederate position on high ground just east of the town of Sharpsburg. The Fifth Corps' advance across the creek was now about 1,640 men strong, directly supported by three batteries of artillery.[105]

South of the Middle Bridge, the Ninth Corps soldiers had established their bridgehead and were almost entirely across the bridge they had battled for three hours to seize. They would be advancing en masse on Lee's right within the hour. Meanwhile, all of the fighting at the Sunken Road and north of it had essentially come to an end. With the exception of the high ground at Cemetery Hill and in and around Piper Farm, the Army of the Potomac had secured all the terrain north of the Boonsboro Turnpike and east of the Hagerstown Turnpike.[106]

To defend his center, Lee had perhaps three thousand infantrymen in Brig. Gen. David R. Jones's division and Brig. Gen. Nathan G. Evans's brigade. These were supported by Col. Thomas A. Munford's cavalry brigade and five artillery batteries. After getting urgent messages from Lee, A. P. Hill was prodding his division forward from Harpers Ferry at a staggering pace. However, his ever-dwindling force was still two hours away.[107]

By 4:30 p.m., the Union troops in the center had advanced and were now pushing the Confederate defenders up the eastern face of Cemetery Hill. On their left, the Ninth Corps had launched its assault on the high ground south of town. Convinced that the time had come for a stronger advance, Pleasonton sent an urgent request to Porter to dispatch the balance of his corps across the creek and attack in force at the disintegrating Confederate position. He also asked Porter to place enfilading batteries on the high ground. Pleasonton would recount events in his after-action report: "It was now 4 o'clock in the afternoon. Burnside's corps had driven the enemy back upon the hill upon which his batteries were placed, and, in conjunction with the repulse of the enemy in front of Hancock, left the field open to the Sharpsburg Ridge, to which point I desired to forward my batteries, to obtain an enfilading fire upon the enemy in front of Burnside, and enable Sumner to advance to Sharpsburg. I was so satisfied that this could be done at that moment, that I sent a request to Major General Fitz John Porter, asking for the assistance of some infantry to support my advance to the Sharpsburg Ridge."[108]

Options

With the outcome of the battle still in doubt, McClellan could support the advance with Porter's corps or have those troops stand on the defensive.

Option 1

McClellan could send every available unit from Porter's corps across Antietam Creek to attack the Confederate center in force. Right now, Morell's division and the balance of Sykes's division were available to Porter. Conservatively, these forces represented perhaps four thousand infantrymen to add to those already across the creek. If McClellan felt it expedient to take advantage of the general momentum, he could commit Porter's men to the fight and continue advancing up the Boonsboro Pike. Based on McClellan's October 1862 after-action report, he had intended to "attack [the Confederate] center with any reserve... then have on hand," provided his flank attacks were successful. If the Union commander felt this was indeed that moment, an attack at Lee's center might be a sound decision.[109]

Option 2

McClellan could decide to hold the balance of Porter's corps back to reinforce this middle sector of his line. If the commander believed that Lee's army still posed a threat in the form of a flank or cavalry attack, he might have think it best to keep the rest of his force east of Antietam Creek to guard his rear. Other than the cavalry, Porter's were the only forces on hand and east of the creek, and they represented the last of McClellan's available infantry. No other uncommitted units would be available to McClellan until the following morning.

Additionally, McClellan very likely still believed that Robert E. Lee had a significant force at his disposal. If the prospect of a Confederate counterattack still preoccupied McClellan's thoughts, an advance by Porter might be too risky a venture. This possibility is particularly revealing when you consider that the specter of the recent defeat at Second Bull Run was still fresh in everyone's mind. The pressure on the Union high command not to repeat such a disaster might have been so palpable that it overwhelmingly influenced decision-making at several points during the battle.

Decision

While accounts differ as to the exact timing and who said what and when, McClellan, either independently or on Porter's advice, declined to send the rest of Fifth Corps in an advance west of Antietam Creek (Option 2). Porter mentioned this critical moment in his after-action report:

> Still later in the afternoon, I received from General Pleasonton a call for a division to press the success obtained by this small band of regulars, accompanied by the statement that Burnside and Sumner

were driving the enemy. Between the dispatching and receiving of that call the tide of battle had changed. Our troops on the left under Burnside had been driven from the heights which they had so gallantly crowned, while those on the immediate right, under Sumner, were held in check. The army was at a stand. I had not the force asked for, and could not, under my orders, risk the safety of the artillery and center of the line, and perhaps imperil the success of the day by further diminishing my small command, not then 4,000 strong—then in the front line and unsupported, and protecting all our trains.[110]

Results/Impact

With no additional forces to support them, the Fifth Corps men west of the creek only advanced to within a few hundred yards of the town before they were forced to fall back. No additional Fifth Corps units were sent across the creek that day. Burnside's advancing divisions subsequently attacked unsupported. At approximately 4:30 p.m., Burnside's three divisions were steadily advancing at the Harpers Ferry Road to the west, only to have their left collapse after A. P. Hill's Confederate division hit it in the flank. After a desperate struggle, the Ninth Corps attack lost momentum and was forced to withdraw to the Antietam Creek. The Battle of Antietam slowly flickered out along with the fading light of the setting sun.

One famous and often-disputed account tells of a reluctant McClellan prepared to advance his reserves into the fray once again, only to be ominously informed by his confidant Porter, "Remember, General I command the last reserve of the last Army of the Republic." Whether fact or fiction, for the second or possibly even the third time that day, the high command of the Union Army of the Potomac did not commit its reserve forces at a possible critical point of the battle.[111]

Alternate Decision/Scenario

Had McClellan decided that the best option was sending the whole of the Fifth Corps across the creek, we might have seen a very different outcome. Even if Sumner had not attacked on the right, as Pleasonton stated, having infantry and artillery lodged on the high ground just east of Sharpsburg could have created no end of problems for the Confederate command. There is no guarantee that this advance would have been decisive. Yet a Union force with artillery on Cemetery Hill could have used that ground to throw enfilading fire up and down Lee's line. In turn, Lee and his commanders might have been forced to deal with this threat or fall back out of range. If they had indeed fallen back, this artillery might have been able to break up or delay

Middle Bridge, circa 1862. Alexander Gardner, Library of Congress / National Archives.

Hill's counterattack. Any number of interesting possibilities can be imagined from only a slightly more aggressive Union command at Lee's center.

Locating Snavely's Ford

Situation

In the compendium of Antietam mythology, few events inspire more conversation and speculation than those at the bridge named for a long-misunderstood Union general—a general whose reputation is irrevocably linked to this simple structure of stone and mortar. In fact, Burnside Bridge is one of the few examples in Civil War history of a significant landmark connected to a major battle and officially named for an individual. Even for those with scant knowledge of the war, merely uttering the name Burnside Bridge manifests very distinct and dramatic imagery in the mind's eye. However, very little of that imagery sheds any positive light on Ambrose E. Burnside.

Ambrose Everett Burnside, the son of a former South Carolina slave owner, was born in Indiana. He graduated eighteenth in his West Point class of 1847 that ironically included a cadet by the name of Ambrose Powell Hill. It was probably here that Burnside first met and became friends with a young George McClellan.

Burnside then commanded the Coast Division or North Carolina Ex-

September 17, 1862

Maj. Gen. Ambrose E. Burnside.
Library of Congress / National Archives.

peditionary Force from September 1861 until July 1862. This unit was formed from three brigades that would eventually be the nucleus for the future Ninth Corps. While leading these servicemen, Burnside conducted a successful amphibious campaign that closed more than 80 percent of the North Carolina seacoast to Confederate shipping for the remainder of the war.

Burnside was subsequently promoted to major general of volunteers on March 18, 1862, and by July, his forces were transported to Virginia to become the Ninth Corps of the Army of the Potomac. He twice declined Lincoln's offer to command the army, partly due to his loyalty to McClellan and partly due to doubt in his own command abilities. At the outset of the Maryland Campaign, McClellan made Burnside a wing commander leading the Ninth and First Corps. By this time, the two had been close friends since their academy days, and they often referred to each other as "Burn" and "Mac," respectively.

Like McClellan, Burnside has become somewhat of a historical scapegoat over the past 150 years, with books and manuscripts often portraying him as little more than an affable buffoon. Biographer William Marvel writes that "Ambrose Burnside may be the most maligned figure of the war." I once heard a National Park Service ranger describe Burnside as a general who, when faced with several bad options, had the unfortunate knack for always choosing the worst possible one.[112]

Ambrose Burnside found himself in a somewhat ill-defined and awkward role on September 17. With the First Corps on the opposite side of the

Antietam Battlefield, he was a wing commander with no wing to command. Jesse Reno's death at Fox's Gap on September 14 meant that Jacob Cox now commanded the Ninth Corps, but Burnside was in many ways acting like a corps commander, passing orders back and forth between army headquarters and the Ninth. Cox offered to return to his divisional command and allow Burnside to lead the corps, complaining in part that his staff was not equipped to manage a corps. Burnside would not consent to this arrangement because he considered it a demotion.[113]

On September 15, as the Ninth Corps moved into line on the Union left, McClellan's plans for the corps and the entire army began to take shape. As noted concerning an earlier decision, McClellan expected the Ninth Corps to play a critical role in his overall tactical strategy in one form or another: "My plan for the impending general engagement was to attack the enemy's left with the corps of Hooker and Mansfield, supported by Sumner's and, if necessary, by Franklin's, and, as soon as matters looked favorably there, to move the corps of Burnside against the enemy's extreme right, upon the ridge running to the south and rear of Sharpsburg, and, having carried their position, to press along the crest toward our right, and, whenever either of these flank movements should be successful, to advance our center with all the forces then disposable."[114]

Antietam Creek stood in between the enemy's extreme right and the Ninth Corps, with the Lower Bridge as the most efficient way to traverse it. It is important to remember that neither the bridge nor the creek was ever Burnside's objective. As McClellan indicated, the Ninth Corps was focused on the high ground and the road to Shepherdstown beyond it on Lee's line of retreat. The creek was now an obstacle to that objective, and the bridge was but one of several ways to surmount it. As it turns out, most significant among these was Snavely's Ford about a mile downstream of the bridge.[115]

On September 16, McClellan and his staff rode to the Ninth Corps headquarters to realign the placement of the unit's four divisions. The Union commander wanted to ensure they were positioned to defend any potential attack from the direction of Harpers Ferry. He also gave Burnside an overview of his general plan and what was expected of the Ninth Corps in the coming battle. In addition, McClellan brought along two of his engineers who informed Burnside and Cox of a usable ford located about half a mile downstream. No specific location for the crossing was given, but the ford was touted as a suitable place to move infantry across to possibly threaten the Confederate position in flank and rear. About 3,200 men were selected for the operation, including Brig. Gen. Isaac P. Rodman's division with Col. Hugh Ewing's brigade from the Kanawha Division. This force was then placed on

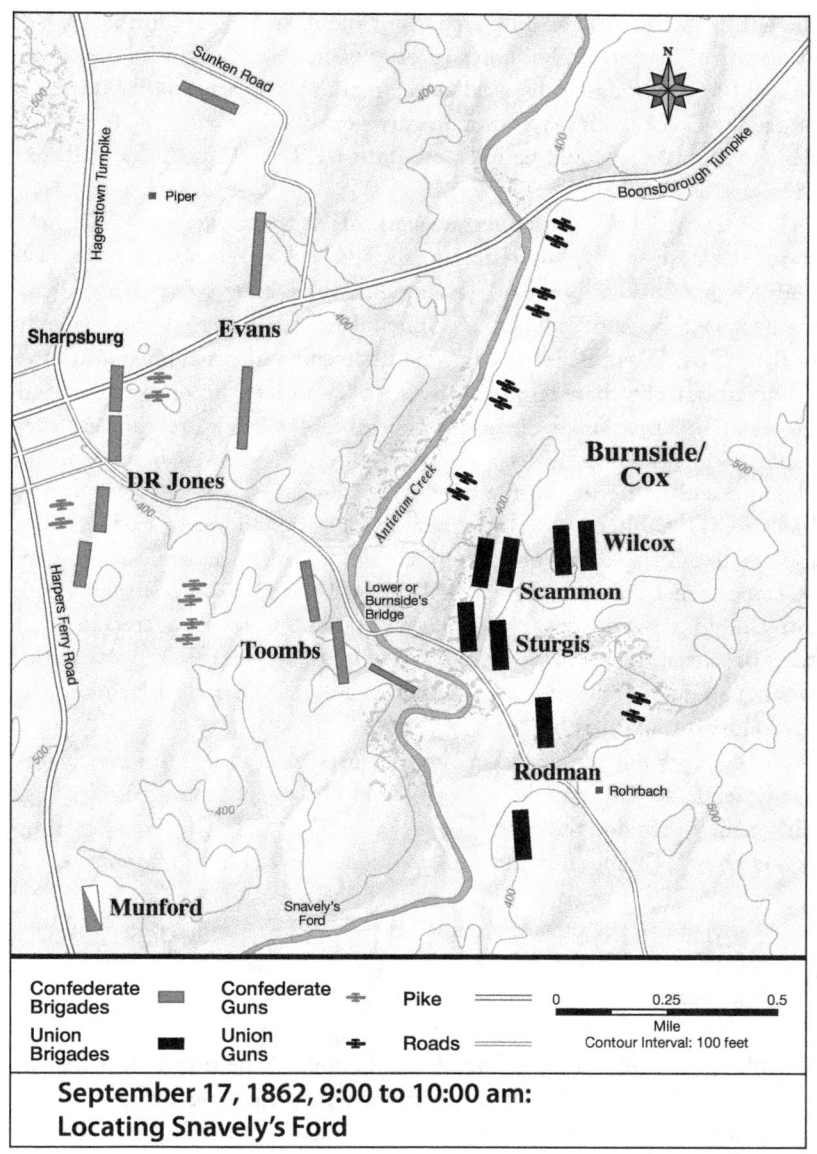

September 17, 1862, 9:00 to 10:00 am:
Locating Snavely's Ford

the left end of the line in preparation for the next day's assault. Burnside's other three divisions, numbering roughly 9,800 men, would be positioned adjacent to the bridge to be used as the main force assaulting it. The other brigade of Col. Eliakim P. Scammon's division and the division of Brig. Gen. Samuel D. Sturgis would be in front, and Brig. Gen. Orlando B. Willcox's division was in reserve.[116]

The Confederate position on the west side of the bridge was thinly held, to say the least. Walker's Division was pulled back to reinforce Lee's embattled left shortly after 9:00 a.m., leaving only three undersized Georgia regiments (about five hundred men)[117] commanded by Brig. Gen. Robert Toombs of Brig. Gen. David R. Jones's division to defend a line roughly a mile long. From left to right, these regiments were the Twentieth, Second, and Fiftieth Georgia. This tiny force's defense was aided by the creek itself and its steep banks. While not terribly deep, the creek provided a genuine obstacle to any Union assault. Arriving on the field on September 15, Toombs and his men had almost two full days to strengthen their position. Some of the Georgians took shelter in an old rock quarry directly above the bridge, while others piled up stones, fence rails, and logs as defilade. Still other Confederates took position behind trees adjacent to the bridge, and some dug shallow trenches with their bayonets. Supported by several batteries of artillery, Toombs's position was not a Gibraltar, but it was as strong as he could make it. As it turned out, it was just strong enough.[118]

While the Union infantry could wade the creek at several different places, the Federals needed something more substantial to get their artillery across. This made the bridge the critical objective for the Ninth Corps. In his after-action report, Toombs described his position at that point:

> The Antietam River runs comparatively straight from a point about 100 paces above the bridge to a point about 300 paces below the bridge, and then curves suddenly around a hill to a ford on a neighborhood road. About 600 yards to my right and rear the road from Sharpsburg to Harper's Ferry from the foot of the bridge over the Antietam turns suddenly down the river, and runs nearly upon its margin for about 300 paces; then leaves the river nearly at right angles. Upon examining the position, I found a narrow wood upon the margin of the river just above the bridge (an important and commanding position) occupied by a company of Texans from Brigadier-General Hood's command. I then ordered the Twentieth to take position, with its left near the foot of the bridge, on the Sharpsburg side, extending down the river near its margin, and the Second Georgia on its right, prolonging the line down to the point where

the road on the other side from the mountain approached the river. This required a more open order than was desirable, on account of the smallness of the regiments, both together numbering but a little over 400 muskets.[119]

At 7:00 a.m. on the morning of September 17, Burnside received an order from army headquarters to ready his infantry for the attack on the bridge. However, the order for him to attack would not reach him until three hours later, at 10:00 a.m. Burnside now had all the pieces in place, or so he thought. Whether he knew it or not, the location for the crossing for Rodman's force would be critical to the impending struggle.[120]

Options

Ambrose Burnside had two options to choose from: he could confirm the location of the critical crossing or rely on existing intelligence. With McClellan's plan unfolding, General Burnside now had a critical decision to make.

Option 1

Burnside could confirm the location of the ford and place Rodman in a better position to advance on it immediately once the order for the attack came.

Without leveling too much criticism at Burnside, it is reasonable to assume that he should have realized the difficulty of the task before him. Even though he and McClellan had ridden the lines several times, nothing prevented him from doing additional reconnaissance on his own. Burnside was still a wing commander with a staff and two companies of cavalry at his disposal. If counting the units of the Sixth New York Cavalry attached to the Kanawha Division, ten companies were available to him. McClellan, Burnside, and Cox all characterized the position at the bridge as a very strong one, and they must have had some idea how difficult it would be to overcome. In his after-action report, Burnside quoted Cox in describing the Confederates' disposition: "The turns of the roadway were covered by rifle-pits and breastworks made of rails and stone, all of which defenses, as well as the woods which covered the slope, were filled with the enemy's infantry and sharpshooters. Besides the infantry defenses, batteries were placed to enfilade the bridge and all its approaches. The crest of the first hill above the bridge is curved toward the stream at the extremes, forming a sort of natural tete-de-pont [French, meaning strategically important area of ground around the end of a bridge]."[121]

In his *Battles and Leaders* article, Jacob D. Cox, perhaps with a backward glance, bemoaned the assignment facing the Ninth Corps and the logic of the overall plan: "It is hardly disputable that this would have been a better plan than the one actually carried out. Certainly the assumption that the Ninth Corps could cross the Antietam alone at the only place on the field where the Confederates had their line immediately upon the stream which must be crossed under fire by two narrow heads of column, and could then turn to the right along the high ground occupied by the hostile army before that army had been broken or seriously shaken elsewhere, is one which would hardly be made till time had dimmed the remembrance of the actual positions of Lee's divisions upon the field."[122]

Knowing that he could not attack the flank of the Confederate army until he got his forces across the bridge, Burnside needed to do so as quickly as possible. Any frontal assaults on the Confederate position would no doubt be contested and take some time to execute. Ensuring that Rodman's flanking force reached a better position to execute a movement on the ford and confirming that location would be critical to the day's success. An adequate place for this force to cross would seem too important a detail to leave unconfirmed.

On the other hand, Burnside might feel that affirming a crossing point was not his job. On paper at least, Jacob Cox was now the leader of the Ninth Corps after Reno's death. Every time Burnside received an order from army headquarters, he immediately handed it to Cox to execute. Burnside might believe that additional reconnaissance of the field to be the responsibility of Cox as corps commander.

Option 2

Burnside could forego further reconnaissance and rely on the information he received from McClellan's engineers. Burnside and the staff of the Ninth Corps could assume that McClellan's engineers knew what they were talking about and that the ford would be easily identifiable. There would be no reason to confirm its location; the corps need only follow the instructions given to them. Burnside might also have considered Rodman's force a mere supporting player in the main assault on the bridge and therefore devoted the majority of his attention to that attack. Additionally, despite his recent communication issues with McClellan, Burnside must have retained a level of trust in his old friend. Think of Burnside's point of view regarding this situation. His boss gave him a task to perform and provided him with some details on how to better carry out that task, would he have any reason to dismiss those details out of hand unless he had absolutely no faith in McClellan's judgment?

Burnside might also believe that his force was large and powerful enough to quickly take the Confederate position at the bridge with a straightforward frontal assault. If Burnside believed he could swiftly overwhelm the bridge's defenders, why would he give any thought to Rodman if he was not foremost in his mind? Lastly, the Confederates might observe any attempt to move Rodman closer to his objective or a scouting party moving along the east bank of the creek. If this happened before Walker's men were pulled from the position, Lee might not order them to move after all.

Past historians have described a sulking and petulant Burnside at Antietam, citing his perceived demotion from wing commander and recent rebukes from McClellan as causes for his delays and poor decision-making. While still questioning his decision-making, more recent scholarship, paints a very different and slightly more positive picture of Ambrose Burnside.[123]

Decision

Burnside decided to send the attack forward on September 17 with the information he had at hand (Option 2). Rodman's force was directed to move to the ford that McClellan's engineers had indicated the day before.

Results/Impact

The ford that Rodman found initially was unusable, as the banks were far too rocky and steep for his men and artillery to cross. Thus he was forced to search for a different crossing point much farther downstream (Snavely's Ford).[124] Losing valuable time in the process, Rodman did not get his division across the creek until approximately 1:00 p.m., three hours after the main attack on the bridge had begun. The rest of the Ninth Corps had by that time launched three successive bloody assaults at the bridge. By the last assault, the Confederate defenders were extremely low on ammunition and forced to retreat. The Ninth Corps suffered over five hundred casualties taking the bridge.[125]

This decision is critical because the hours Burnside spent overcoming the obstacles to crossing had a definite and observable outcome on the battle. Nearly five hours had passed by the time Burnside was able to attack and overcome the Confederate defenders, finally ford the creek, then get his corps rearmed, reorganized, and ready to move forward. When Burnside's objective was within his grasp, A. P. Hill's division arrived from Harpers Ferry just in time to stop him, thus ending the Union attacks for the day.

Alternate Decision/Scenario

Had Burnside had some foresight, ordered reconnaissance, and better understood the task and the ground before him, the end result might very well have been different. Once the attack order was given—and there is some

Burnside's Bridge, Antietam National Battlefield, modern image. Author.

dispute as to when the order arrived, Rodman could have moved directly to the ford and forced his way across. Assuming the order arrived at 10:00 a.m., Rodman's force could reasonably have been across the creek by 11:00 a.m. This feat would immediately have made the Confederate position untenable, and Toombs's Georgians would have been forced to fall back. The rest of the Ninth Corps could then have taken the bridge much sooner than they did, and with far fewer losses if any. Had Burnside realized that the ford and not the bridge was the key to the position and confirmed the location, his forces could have crossed the creek without having to assault the well-defended position at the bridge at all. Imagine a scenario where Burnside attacked the Confederates on the high ground beyond the bridge at noon instead of 3:00 p.m. or 4:00 p.m. In turn, would this not have made it possible to attack Lee's right long before A. P. Hill could arrive, and to do so just as the Sunken Road position was collapsing, making Lee vulnerable from two directions? While this scenario rests on several assumptions, there is little doubt a different decision on the part of Burnside would have seen this third climactic act of the battle take a decidedly different turn.

CHAPTER 3

AFTER THE BATTLE, SEPTEMBER 18–20, 1862

The fighting that had commenced before the sun rose on September 17 slowly died as dusk gave way to darkness. The night provided a much-needed respite for Reb and Yank alike. While they exchanged some sporadic small-arms fire during the night, both armies' combatants were for the most part far too exhausted for added fighting. As soldiers slept on their arms in the drizzling rain, the pitiful cries of the scores of wounded men kept up a dreadful chorus throughout the night. Dawn cast light on this latest example of the terrible cost of war and brought with it the prospect of more killing to come.[1] As author and veteran Francis Palfrey wrote, "The corn and trees, so fresh and green in the morning, were reddened with blood and torn by bullet and shell, and the very earth was furrowed by the incessant impact of lead and iron."[2]

The final two decisions took place on September 18, the day after the Battle of Antietam.

McClellan Does Not Attack

Situation

On September 18, 1862, the cool and foggy dawn broke on the fields and farms around Sharpsburg, Maryland. The mist slowly cleared, revealing the death and devastation the previous day's struggle had brought.

On the Confederate side of the line, Robert E. Lee and his battered Army of Northern Virginia braced themselves for renewed fighting. On the Union side, McClellan and his army spent that morning waiting for reinforcements to arrive. In the meantime, McClellan busied himself by sending telegrams to the War Department and letters to his wife, Mary Ellen. While his communication with Halleck was somewhat reserved, the message to his wife took a decidedly different tone, extolling his performance of the day before.[3]

To Halleck, McClellan wrote as follows: "The battle of yesterday continued for fourteen hours, and until after dark. We held all we gained, except a portion of the extreme left; that was obliged to abandon a part of what it had gained. Our losses very heavy, especially in general officers. The battle will probably be renewed to-day. Send all the troops you can by the most expeditious route."[4] In contrast, he sent this message to Mary Ellen:

> We fought yesterday a terrible battle against the entire rebel Army. The battle continued 14 hours & was terrific—the fighting on both sides was superb. The general result was in our favor, that is to say we gained a great deal of ground & held it. It was a success, but whether a decided victory depends on what occurs today. I hope that God has given us a great success. It is all in his hands, where I am content to leave it. The spectacle yesterday was the grandest I could conceive of; nothing could be more sublime. Those in whose judgement I rely on tell me I fought the battle splendidly & and that it was a masterpiece of art.[5]

Both sides began the onerous task of caring for the almost twenty thousand wounded men now scattered across the field. The recovery and care of the wounded was made more difficult by the fact that no official truce had been called and stretcher-bearers risked their lives collecting the fallen. Every structure in the area capable of harboring men now became a hospital; many other soldiers awaiting treatment lay in makeshift shelters.

George McClellan's view across the lines told him that the Confederates, while more concentrated than the day before, were still there. Meanwhile, the soldiers in the Army of the Potomac anxiously awaited a battle they, too, presumed would very soon recommence. The Union commander could only speculate about the damage he had inflicted on his opponent, but he was no doubt getting preliminary returns on the losses his own forces had suffered. In twelve hours of fighting, over twelve thousand Union men became casualties, or just over 21 percent of those engaged. Among McClellan's corps and division commanders, losses were also over 33 percent.[6]

By that morning, McClellan had the whole of his army on the west side

September 18–20, 1862

Confederate dead, circa 1862. Alexander Gardner, Library of Congress / National Archives.

of Antietam Creek save the reserve artillery, the cavalry, and some units of the Fifth Corps. These troops could cross the creek uncontested whenever they wished. On the right, the Federal line now started at a point about half a mile north of Joseph Poffenberger's farm and a few hundred yards east of the Hagerstown Pike. The formation then meandered southward toward the Mumma Farm, along the Sunken Road to a point just east of and below the Lower Bridge.[7]

By noon that day, McClellan received what amounted to a brand-new corps. An additional twelve thousand men now reinforced the Union army, including Brig. Gen. Darius Couch's Fourth Corps division attached to Franklin's Sixth Corps and Brig. Gen. Andrew A. Humphreys's Fifth Corps division. These men almost entirely replaced the Union losses from the previous day's fighting. McClellan now had somewhere between fifty thousand and sixty thousand men of all arms with whom he could renew the attack if he so desired.[8]

Across the field, the injured Rebel army stood defiantly. Robert E. Lee's contracted line started on his left, just west of the Hagerstown Pike at the north end of the West Woods. It followed the pike into the town and along the heights of the Harpers Ferry Road south of Sharpsburg. Then it ended at roughly the same point the Union army's line did, only several hundred yards farther west. J. E. B. Stuart's cavalry still held positions on each flank. Over the next several days, Lee's army managed to gather up roughly six thousand stragglers to add to his various commands. In so doing, he covered nearly half

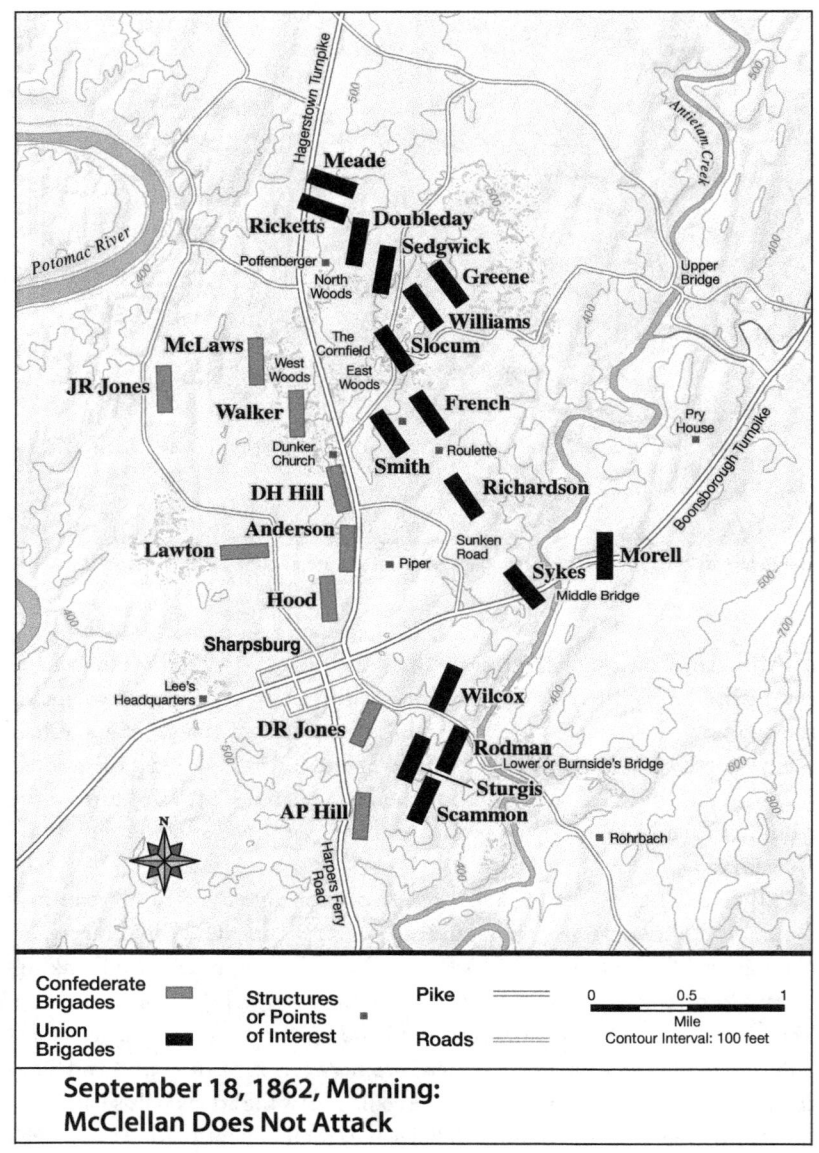

September 18, 1862, Morning: McClellan Does Not Attack

of his losses from the battle on September 17. While it is unclear how many of the stragglers arrived on the eighteenth, Lee could now field an army with an estimated strength of between twenty-five thousand and thirty thousand men. However, it is safe to say that these stragglers were probably not in prime fighting condition. Lee's men as a whole were exhausted and worn out. While the aforementioned details were significant, McClellan and his staff were no doubt unaware of the state of Lee's army.[9]

Options

In his 1863 after-action report, McClellan stated, "The night, however, brought with it grave responsibilities. Whether to renew the attack on the 18th or to defer it, even with the risk of the enemy's retirement, was the question before me."[10] With the specter of the previous day's carnage hanging over him, the general could attack immediately or wait. Choosing either option would be a critical decision.

Option 1

McClellan could continue the attacks from the day before. While it is debatable how seriously he considered renewing the battle on the eighteenth, he least thought about it. Several factors indicated that this option might be his best one. McClellan now had thousands of fresh troops to make use of, including the Sixth and Fifth Corps, which had been only lightly engaged the day before. These units were augmented by the divisions of Couch and Humphreys. By some estimates, then, McClellan now had thirty thousand fresh infantrymen at his disposal. This number constituted only one-third fewer men than the entire force he had committed to battle the day before. While he presumably did not realize it, McClellan now outnumbered his opponent by two to one. If he did not believe that those corps that had attacked on Wednesday were able to participate in new assaults, he could count on them to at least hold the ground already gained.

Although we don't know precisely what McClellan's perception of Lee's army was on September 18, he needed only to look at the casualties on the field to know his enemy had taken a real beating at the hand of his own army. There was a good chance the Confederates were in no shape to defend themselves. The fact that Lee's anticipated counterattack never materialized might have also been a telling clue as to the state of the Confederate army.[11]

The Union commander also had most of his forces positioned west of Antietam Creek, and he held all the critical crossing points. As a result, Lee could no longer count on the creek posing a significant obstacle to the Union army. It seems that some of McClellan's corps and division commanders were in favor of continuing the offensive. William B. Franklin, for example, was still eager to lead his Sixth Corps back into the fray, or so he later wrote:

> Later in the day General McClellan came again to my headquarters, and there was pointed out to him a hill on the right, commanding the wood, and it was proposed that the hill should be occupied by our artillery early the next morning, and that after shelling the wood, the attack should be made by the whole corps from the position then held by it. He assented to this, and it was understood that the attack was to be made. During the night, however, the order was countermanded. I met him about 9 o'clock on the morning of the 18th. He informed me that he countermanded the order because fifteen thousand Pennsylvania troops would soon arrive, and that upon their arrival the attack would be ordered.[12]

Additionally, the Army of Northern Virginia was still north of the Potomac at this moment. One of McClellan's campaign objectives was driving the Rebels from the state of Maryland; so long as Lee remained in the North, that part of the operational objective was not realized. As there was no guarantee that Lee would retreat on his own, additional combat might be required to persuade him to do so.[13]

Option 2

McClellan could determine to wait and see what, if anything, his opponent might do first. While it is easy to criticize McClellan's inaction, he had good reasons to be cautious. In the fight for the ground at Antietam, over 21 percent of the Army of the Potomac were now casualties. This is not an insignificant figure. Two of McClellan's six corps commanders had been wounded and/or killed, and that total increased to three if counting Reno's death at South Mountain. He had also lost five of sixteen division commanders. Most devastating of all, however, was the Union command's loss of 52 of the 165 brigade and regimental commanders—almost 32 percent—along with an untold number of company-grade and noncommissioned officers. Casualties in the officer and noncommissioned officer ranks dramatically compromised McClellan's ability to exercise command and control. Nineteenth-century armies relied heavily on the experience and knowledge of the brigade- and regimental-level commissioned and noncommissioned officers to effectively maneuver and deploy their forces in combat.[14]

While he did indeed have some fresh infantry, the four corps that had been most heavily engaged the day before were in deplorable shape. While some reports contradict, indications are that the First Corps had suffered

2,590 total casualties, or 27 percent of its men; the Second Corps suffered 5,138 total losses, or 32 percent; the Ninth Corps suffered 2,349 total casualties, or 19 percent; and the Twelfth Corps suffered 1,746 total losses, or 23 percent. McClellan had also expected Brig. Gen. John Reynolds to come from Pennsylvania with 15,000 militia; however, those troops refused to cross the border into Maryland.

It should also be noted that Humphreys's division of Pennsylvanians of the Fifth Corps, arriving before noon, consisted entirely of green regiments. To reach Antietam Creek on September 18 from Washington, DC, Humphreys had marched his division for four straight days, and McClellan believed the troops were fatigued. While Humphreys disputed this claim, he could not dispute these men's glaring lack of combat experience. Many of the rookie regiments that had fought on the seventeenth suffered immeasurably due to their inexperience.

The Union men were also reaching the end of their endurance. The previous day, McClellan's army had fought continuously from dawn until dusk. Collectively, the Army of the Potomac had been marching and/or fighting since leaving the defenses of Washington, DC, thirteen days before. Many units, like the First Corps, had fought on both September 17 and September 14. On the fourteenth, the corps had been heavily engaged in the struggle for South Mountain, a significant battle in its own right.[15]

Furthermore, while damaged and somewhat disorganized, most of the Union army's artillery had enough ammunition for another engagement. Yet the long-range twenty-pound Parrott rifles, so essential to counter-battery fire the day before, had mostly empty caissons. The promised ammunition was miles away, and replenishment would take some time.[16]

Based on the evidence, McClellan had good reason to believe that Robert E. Lee still outnumbered him and that the long-expected Confederate counterattack was inevitable. If McClellan exposed himself too much, he might be playing right into Lee's hands. In any case, it appears that Lee expected another day of battle and was waiting for it, as illustrated by his unwillingness to retreat after the fighting on the seventeenth.[17]

On a personal level, and adding to McClellan's tactical and logistical dilemmas, the dysentery that had afflicted him since his time in Mexico flared up yet again. The general was ill for the next several days.[18]

Decision

McClellan wrote on September 18, "After a night of anxious deliberation and a full and careful survey of the situation and condition of our army, the strength and position of the enemy, I concluded that the success of an attack on the 18th was not certain."[19] The Union commander decided not to renew the attack on the eighteenth (Option 2). He outlined his reasoning in his 1863 after-action report:

> The troops were greatly overcome by the fatigue and exhaustion attendant upon the long continued and severely contested battle of the 17th, together with the long day and night marches to which they had been subjected during the previous three days. The supply trains were in the rear, and many of the troops had suffered from hunger. They required rest and refreshment. One division of Sumner's and all of Hooker's corps on the right had, after fighting most valiantly for several hours, been overpowered by numbers, driven back in great disorder, and much scattered, so that they were for the time somewhat demoralized. In Hooker's corps, according to the return made by General Meade, commanding, there were but 6,729 men present on the 18th, whereas on the morning of the 22nd there were 13,093 men present for duty in the same corps, showing that previous to and during the battle 6,364 men were separated from their command.[20]

McClellan did give orders that night to prepare for an assault on the nineteenth, but when the Federals stirred to life the following morning, they discovered the Confederates were gone.

Results/Impact

While circumspect, this decision is critical because it helped conclude this battle and ensure that no additional Union assaults would be made at Sharpsburg. Soldiers on both sides observed one another warily as September 18 came and went. The Battle of Antietam was technically over, but the decision was not absolute. The end of the engagement and the overall campaign now hinged on the outcome of the next and final decision facing Robert E. Lee.

Alternate Decision/Scenario

Had McClellan decided that he was indeed in an excellent position to launch one more attack, the history of the Battle of Antietam would undoubtedly be different. There is certainly no guarantee that any attacks on the eighteenth would have been more successful than those on the seventeenth. Yet based on the results from the day before, Lee would likely have had to retreat to save his army. As we will see in discussion of the next decision, Lee did so in spite of any new assault; however, withdrawing your army under cover of darkness and doing so while under attack are two very different things.

Lee had essentially no more reserves to commit to a renewed fight other than the unknown number of stragglers that joined the army. His men were desperately tired and just as worn down as their opponents, if not more so. This fact alone, however, would not have made a more decisive victory by McClellan a certainty. Nor would it have guaranteed the destruction of Lee's army. Additionally, it is certain that both armies would have suffered more casualties in fighting on September 18, and recovery from this action would indeed have taken more time than it did.

After the war, Longstreet summed up the Confederate position this way: *"We were so badly crushed that at the close of the day ten thousand fresh troops could have come in and taken Lee's army and everything it had."*[21] We will never know if he was correct in this assessment or merely adding to a narrative.

Lee Withdraws to Virginia

Situation

As George McClellan struggled with the decisions and challenges the previous day had laid before him, Robert E. Lee faced an abundance of his own dilemmas. Dawn on September 18 began to reveal the substantial damage his army had suffered. John Bell Hood witnessed the sight and described his recollections of that dreadful September morning after the battle: "The following morning I arose before dawn and rode to the front where, just after

Capt. John Thompson's Independent Battery C, Pennsylvania Light Artillery, Antietam National Battlefield, modern image. Author.

daybreak, General Jackson came pacing up on his horse, and instantly asked, 'Hood, have they gone?' When I answered in the negative, he replied 'I hoped they had,' and then passed on to look after his brave but greatly exhausted command."[22]

Confederate stragglers scattered all over the Maryland and Virginia countryside slowly began to rejoin the Army of Northern Virginia. In small numbers, they continued to trickle in for the next week and beyond. Lee ordered the commissary and ammunition trains brought up, and he was able to feed his men and replenish his army with ammunition. Lee also concentrated his lines, bracing for a new attack.[23]

Although still ready to fight, the Confederate commander's army had suffered immeasurably. An estimated 25,000 to 30,000 Rebel's were ready for battle, although these numbers might be wildly optimistic. Lee's total casualties from the day before were between 25 and 28 percent. While his overall casualties were devastating, the losses among his leadership ranks were more catastrophic—death and/or wounding claimed 3 of Lee's 9 division commanders, 19 of his 39 brigade commanders, and 86 of his 173 regimental commanders. This is a casualty rate of nearly 50 percent at the command level. Maintaining command and control on Civil War battlefields was trying on the best days, but losses such as these among the leadership ranks increased the difficulty exponentially. It is hard to imagine any army suffering such destruction of its core command and still retaining the same level of authority and control as it had before the battle.

Confederate dead, circa 1862. Alexander Gardner, Library of Congress / National Archives.

Additionally, Lee's army had to overcome the significant problem of gathering the dead and caring for the wounded. Henry Kyd Douglas of Jackson's staff gave a grim description of the Army of Northern Virginia's state the night after Antietam: "The night after the battle of Sharpsburg was a fearful one. Not a soldier, I venture to say, slept half an hour. Nearly all of them were wandering over the field, looking for their wounded comrades, and some of them, doubtless, plundering the dead bodies of the enemy left on the field. Half of Lee's army were hunting the other half."[24]

In his after-action report, Lee spoke at length of the condition of his army:

> The arduous service in which our troops had been engaged, their great privations of rest and food, and the long marches without shoes over mountain roads, had greatly reduced our ranks before the action began. These causes had compelled thousands of brave men to absent themselves, and many more had done so from unworthy motives. This great battle was fought by less than 40,000 men on our side, all of whom had undergone the greatest labors and hardships in the field and on the march. Nothing could surpass the determined valor with which they met the large army of the enemy, fully supplied and equipped, and the result reflects the highest credit on the officers and men engaged.
>
> Our artillery, though much inferior to that of the enemy in the number of guns and weight of metal, rendered most efficient and gallant service throughout the day, and contributed greatly to the repulse of the attacks on every part of the line. General Stuart, with the cavalry and horse artillery, performed the duty entrusted to him of guarding our left wing with great energy and courage, and rendered valuable assistance in defeating the attack on that part of our line.
>
> On the 18th we occupied the position of the preceding day, except in the center, where our line was drawn in about 200 yards. Our ranks were increased by the arrival of a number of troops, who had not been engaged the day before, and, though still too weak to assume the offensive, we awaited without apprehension the renewal of the attack.[25]

It is not an overstatement to say that even the unflappable Robert E. Lee now had cause for concern. In his treatment of the campaign, noted author Joseph Harsh deftly and accurately describes the state of affairs the morning after the fighting at Antietam: "The Confederate soldiers awoke fully expecting another battle. Their brief war experience taught them that when unentrenched armies remained within several hundred yards of one another, the fighting was irresistibly renewed. Along the Chickahominy and at Second Manassas the two forces had clawed at each other day after day until one had yielded and reached safe haven. But Antietam had been a different kind of battle. Its concentrated fury knocked the wind from both armies."[26]

Perhaps Lee was finally realizing that the opportunity he sought with the calculated risk of invading the North had slipped from his fingers and was drifting farther and farther from his grasp.

Options

With the fate of his campaign and possibly that of the Army of Northern Virginia hanging in the balance, Lee had three options to choose from and one last critical decision to make. He could stand on the defensive, attack, or withdraw.

Option 1

Lee could continue on the defensive and wait for McClellan to attack again. The Rebel general's plan upon entering Maryland had been relatively basic. From the outset of the campaign, Lee wanted to advance into Maryland or possibly Pennsylvania, turn the Federals out of their Washington defenses, and compel the Union army to pursue him far from its base of supply and support. On ground of his choosing, he would then deliver the enemy a fatal blow. Other than the mission to capture Harpers Ferry, Lee had followed this script for two weeks, endeavoring to keep his campaign on course.

Given that Lee envisioned his campaign in this manner, it could reasonably be assumed that he would continue to do so on September 18. The casualties he suffered no doubt gave him pause. But Lee evidently considered allowing the Federals to continue their assaults, and this might be his best tactical option. While his army had given up a significant swath of ground during the previous day's fighting, Union soldiers had gained that ground at great cost. The Army of Northern Virginia was wounded but still able to fight. Several questions remained: How badly had the Army of the Potomac itself been wounded? Would it attack again? Could the Confederates prevail in another battle similar to the one fought the day before?

Option 2

Lee could decide to attack. If one thing can be accurately stated of Robert E. Lee, it is that he seemed to favor aggressive action. And while it might be

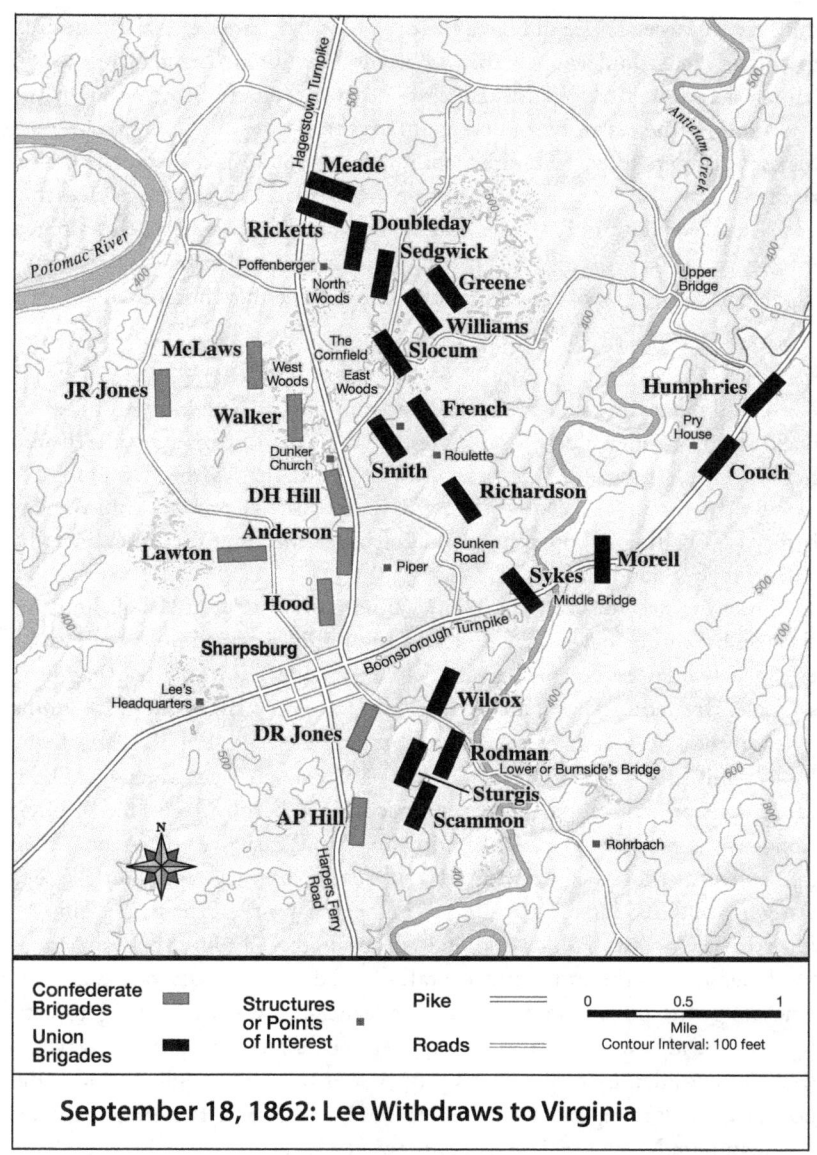

September 18, 1862: Lee Withdraws to Virginia

unlikely to succeed, Lee did have the option of an offensive. He still desired to deliver that counterpunch that we know he desired. Lee had wanted to launch a counterattack at the Federals on two separate occasions. On the afternoon of the seventeenth and again on the eighteenth, Lee had ordered his commanders to evaluate the viability of a counteroffensive on the Union right. In both cases, reconnaissance on McClellan's right determined that both endeavors would be futile. Lastly, because Lee had invested so much into the campaign up until this point, he likely hoped that his army was still capable of some kind of aggressive action to salvage that investment.[27]

Option 3
Lee could determine that withdrawal was his best option and pull his army back to the Virginia side of the Potomac. The general perhaps realized that his army was in no condition to continue the fight. As the day unfolded, he surely continued receiving more and more casualty reports from the day before. While it is unknown how much Lee realized it at the time, his army was severely wounded.

Only the brigades of Brig. Gen. William D. Pender and Col. John M. Brockenbrough (Field's) of A. P. Hill's Light Division had not been heavily engaged the day before, and most of the men collected in the rear had been stragglers from the forced marches from Harpers Ferry. Every one of Lee's nine divisions had been engaged on September 17, all save A. P. Hill's, and D. R. Jones's unit had a casualty rate in excess of 28 percent. McLaws's and D. H. Hill's divisions had casualty rates approaching 40 percent, and Hood's Division was the most devastated, suffering an overall casualty rate of more than 44 percent of those engaged. Twenty of the 173 infantry regiments in Lee's army had suffered losses exceeding 50 percent. Twenty of the thirty-nine infantry brigades now had fewer than four hundred men to fill their ranks.

Insomuch as the 25 percent overall Confederate casualty rate was overwhelming, the price paid by the army's leadership was devastating to contemplate. Only twenty-two of the 173 regiments Lee brought to Maryland were now headed by colonels. Twenty-two of his thirty-eight brigades did not have a single regiment led by a colonel, and five of these had captains commanding. Moreover, Lee had only twenty-seven general officers on hand to lead this ravaged force that day. As was the case nine months later in Pennsylvania, Lee also had thousands of severely wounded men to care for. His choice was to either leave them on Northern soil or figure how to transport this multitude back to Virginia.[28]

From a purely tactical perspective, Lee's position was precarious at best. While he could still fight, his only escape route on the Potomac was now more vulnerable. One more determined push from McClellan might very well cut off the Confederates' only line of retreat. Saving his army to fight another day might have been a prudent choice but a bitter pill for Lee to swallow. Following this course of action, would absolutely relinquish the strategic initiative Lee and his ragged army had fought so hard to gain.

Decision

Brig. Gen. John Walker later recalled, "We had fought an indecisive battle, and although we were, perhaps, in as good a condition to renew the struggle as the enemy were, General Lee recognized the fact that his ulterior plans had been thwarted by this premature engagement, and after a consultation with his corps commanders he determined to withdraw from Maryland."[29]

Lee selected Option 3, withdrawing his army on the evening of September 18. Under the cover of darkness, the Confederates slipped out of line and moved to the Potomac crossing at Shepherdstown and back to Virginia.[30]

Results/Impact

On September 19. McClellan wired Halleck this proclamation: "I have the honor to report that Maryland is entirely freed from the presence of the enemy, who have been driven across the Potomac. No fears need now be entertained for the safety of Pennsylvania. I shall at once occupy Harper's Ferry."[31] Conversely, Lee sent the following in a dispatch to Davis: "During the night of the 18th the army was accordingly withdrawn to the south side of the Potomac, crossing near Shepherdstown, without loss or molestation."[32]

One could certainly argue that the Maryland Campaign was not concluded at this point, but only the Battle of Antietam. As Lee departed Sharpsburg on the evening of the eighteenth, he intended to cross back over the Potomac at Williamsport and continue on to Pennsylvania. The general was, in fact, moving his army in that direction when his rear guard at Boteler's Ford was attacked and subsequently collapsed on the evening of the nineteenth. Lee was forced to turn his army around to address this threat.

However, once Lee traversed the Potomac on the evening of the eighteenth, for all intents and purposes, his campaign was over. Even if Lee himself did not come to this realization until five days later, there was no coming back once his army crossed the river. The Confederate commander ended the first great campaign into the North having achieved none of his operational objectives, with the exception of a few supplies and some artillery, wagons, and small arms. Lee's final critical decision ended the battle and effectively ended the 1862 Maryland Campaign.[33]

The Sunken Road, Antietam National Battlefield, modern image. Author.

Alternate Decision/Scenario

Had Lee decided to stand and fight one more day, history would indeed have been irrevocably altered. McClellan would still have been under pressure to attack had the Confederates remained on September 19. So long as Lee's army was on Union soil, he was obligated to take some kind of action. By now, McClellan's reinforcements were up and with him, and all indications pointed to his decision to launch some sort of attack. While we can only speculate how that attack might have manifested or what the outcome of new fighting on September 19 would have been, several things are certain. The carnage from the seventeenth surely portended thousands more names on the rolls of Union and Confederate killed, wounded, and missing. We can only conjecture what further devastation would have befallen Lee's already battered army, but further blows by McClellan would have had only adverse effects. The Battle of Shepherdstown would have been different, perhaps even culminating in a fighting retreat all the way to the Potomac. In the end one thing is certain: the Battle of Antietam would not now be known as the bloodiest single day in American history. It might instead have earned some other unfortunate cognomen that history would record.

CONCLUSION

SEPTEMBER 21–NOVEMBER 5, 1862

On the morning of September 19, 1862, as the head of the withdrawing Army of Northern Virginia was several miles southwest of the Potomac, its tail was crossing the river at Boteler's (Packhorse) Ford back into Virginia. This column was spotted by Brig. Gen. Alfred Pleasonton's Union cavalry, who were themselves advancing from Sharpsburg. A Confederate force commanded by Brig. Gen. William Pendleton was shielding the Potomac crossing. Posted here by Lee on September 15, this rear guard now consisted of forty-four guns from the reserve artillery and two understrength infantry brigades that included about six hundred men. Pleasonton's Union troopers lacked the strength to do anything but watch the Rebels go and report the same to McClellan.[1]

To support Pleasonton, McClellan ordered a reconnaissance in force directed at the area near Shepherdstown and the retreating Confederate army. Elements of Maj. Gen. Fitz John Porter's Fifth Corps supported by artillery advanced from Sharpsburg to the banks of the Potomac River at Boteler's Ford, a mile downstream of Shepherdstown. The Twelfth Corps was ordered to seize Maryland Heights to prevent the Confederates' reoccupation of Harpers Ferry. Meanwhile, Darius Couch's Fourth Corps division was sent to Williamsport to deal with a Rebel force reported to be there. These troops were members of J. E. B. Stuart's Confederate cavalry, and they were securing a point by which the Rebels could recross the Potomac back into Maryland. Robert E. Lee's exhausted army was now on the Virginia side of

Boteler's Ford, modern image. Author.

the Potomac and headed upstream toward Williamsport in an effort to somehow salvage his campaign.[2]

Porter's Union infantry pushed across the ford later that same afternoon. As darkness fell, the Federals chased off the small contingent of Rebel infantry- and artillerymen, captured several guns, and established a bridgehead. Pendleton fell back once his position was overrun. In response, Lee issued orders for Jackson's Command to return to Boteler's Ford at first light.[3]

The next morning, September 20, McClellan ordered Porter to press the enemy south of the river. Porter then sent four brigades across the Potomac to strengthen his position at Boteler's. By 9:00 a.m. the Union forces held a line almost a mile wide on the south side of the Potomac. Advanced pickets soon informed the Union command that a large Confederate force was bearing down on them from the south.

At just after 8:00 a.m., two Confederate divisions under Jubal Early and A. P. Hill attacked the Union force moving up from the Potomac. Jackson's counterattack stopped the Federals in their tracks, driving them back across the Potomac.

By noon the fight was over. The Battle of Shepherdstown resulted in an additional seven hundred names on the combined list of casualties, equal to 3 percent of the total losses from the fight three days earlier.[4] Thus, with renewed confidence and perhaps breathing a sigh of relief, McClellan sent two dispatches to Halleck on September 19:

But little occurred yesterday except skirmishing, being fully occupied in replenishing ammunition, taking care of wounded, &c. Last night the enemy abandoned his position, leaving his dead and wounded on the field. We are again in pursuit. I do not yet know whether he is falling back to an interior position or crossing the river. We may safely claim a complete victory.

Pleasonton is driving the enemy across the river. Our victory was complete. The enemy is driven back into Virginia. Maryland and Pennsylvania are now safe.[5]

Once Lee turned his army back to the Potomac to protect his rear at Shepherdstown, the Confederates remained in the vicinity for five more days. During this time, the general contemplated continuing his campaign by recrossing the Potomac at Williamsport and moving on Hagerstown. As the days passed, however, Robert E. Lee came to realize that his army was in no physical shape to continue the campaign. On September 25, a discouraged Lee wrote President Davis, stating, "In a military point of view, the best move, in my opinion, the army could make would be to advance upon Hagerstown and endeavor to defeat the enemy at that point. I would not hesitate to make it even with our diminished number, did the army exhibit its former temper and condition; but, as far as I am able to judge, the hazard would be great and a reverse disastrous. I am, therefore, led to pause."[6]

On September 26, orders were issued from Lee's headquarters to have the army begin moving to the relative safety of the Shenandoah Valley near Winchester. There Lee would rest, refit, and reinforce until mid-November, when the Army of the Potomac, then commanded by Ambrose Burnside, began advancing toward the Rappahannock River and Fredericksburg.[7] George McClellan paused as well once it became clear that Maryland was fully liberated from the Confederate menace. The Federal general remained north of the Potomac until October 26, 1862.

On October 1, Abraham Lincoln traveled to McClellan's headquarters near Sharpsburg to assess the state of the army and meet with its commander. Despite giving what Lincoln considered a promise to advance at once, McClellan resumed arguing why he should not as soon as the president returned to Washington, DC. Then on October 6, Henry Halleck sent a dispatch to McClellan indicating that the president was directing him to cross the Potomac, move south, and give battle to the enemy.

On October 26, 1862, forty days after the Battle of Antietam had ended, McClellan finally sent his army across the Potomac River in force. After twelve days, the Army of the Potomac progressed just over forty miles to Warrenton, Virginia, although no significant battle resulted from this advance.[8]

Lee was able to move Longstreet's Corps more quickly than McClellan, and the unit interposed itself between the Army of the Potomac and Richmond. An increasingly frustrated Lincoln was once again under a great deal of pressure to make a change. According to John Hay, Lincoln's private secretary, the president told him, "Delaying on little pretexts of wanting this and that, I began to fear that he was playing false–that he did not want to hurt the enemy." Lincoln also described what he would do if McClellan delayed again, giving Lee the advantage: "I determined to . . . remove him [McClellan]. He did so & I relieved him."[9]

On November 5, 1862, he ordered Halleck to relieve McClellan of command of the Army of the Potomac for good. For the third time, Lincoln turned to the affable Maj. Gen. Ambrose E. Burnside with an offer of command. This time Burnside reluctantly accepted.

By no coincidence, McClellan's dismissal came one day after the 1862 midterm elections in which the Republican Party saw a fifty-seat swing to the Democrats in the House of Representatives. In spite of this, the party of Lincoln still held a plurality in the House and increased its majority in the Senate.[10]

The sum total of all Union and Confederate casualties during the Maryland Campaign was around forty-one thousand men. This number includes the losses incurred in the five major battles that made up the campaign, as well

Lincoln and McClellan, circa 1862. Alexander Gardner, Library of Congress / National Archives.

September 21–November 5, 1862

Antietam National Battlefield, modern image. Author.

as the twelve thousand Union men captured at Harpers Ferry.[11] What this figure does not include, however, is the untold number of soldiers both armies lost due to straggling. While it is safe to assume many of these men eventually rejoined their respective units, noncombat losses due to straggling had an enormous and lasting effect on both armies' fighting ability during the campaign. Yet it cannot be overstated that Lee felt this negative effect more keenly and found that it severely hampered his ability to manage his campaign.

Recent estimates by historians like D. Scott Hartwig put Lee's total noncombat losses for the entire Maryland Campaign at 45 percent, or just shy of forty-four thousand men. If this number is correct, it is hard to underestimate its negative impact on Lee's ability to conduct his campaign. The degree to which it did so can only be speculated.[12]

On September 22, 1862, in direct response to the Union victory at Antietam, Abraham Lincoln issued the Preliminary Emancipation Proclamation. He stated therein that the proclamation would take effect on January 1, 1863, forever altering the nature of the Civil War and the trajectory of the country's history.[13]

Nine months after the Maryland Campaign, no doubt having learned from the events of 1862, Robert E. Lee led his army onto Northern soil once again. In early July 1863, this campaign culminated in the small Pennsylvania town of Gettysburg.

APPENDIX I

BATTLEFIELD GUIDE TO THE CRITICAL DECISIONS AT ANTIETAM

This portion of the book is designed as a guide through the geography of the Battle of Antietam as it relates to the critical decisions discussed. A navigation device or smartphone will come in handy to quickly and efficiently find the stops. I also recommend using a compass or a compass mobile app to help you better orient yourself at the various tour stops. Part of the tour will involve some light hiking, so plan accordingly.

With each stop, an address is included if one exists and/or GPS coordinates. For example: 18906 Shepherdstown Pike, Keedysville, Maryland 21756 (39.475900, -77.714034).

Each decision will be recapped in chronological order. There, are exceptions where I have grouped some decisions together to avoid excessive backtracking. Lastly, this tour is not an exact blow-by-blow account of the Battle of Antietam, but a tour that aligns with the critical decisions covered in this book. Therefore, some aspects of the battle will not be included. As a result, a basic understanding of the events surrounding the campaign and battle is essential to comprehending this book and the Antietam tour.

A necessary part of the critical decision process is recognizing how location frequently influenced decision-makers. Knowing what these individuals saw or could not see often provides context that may not otherwise be apparent.

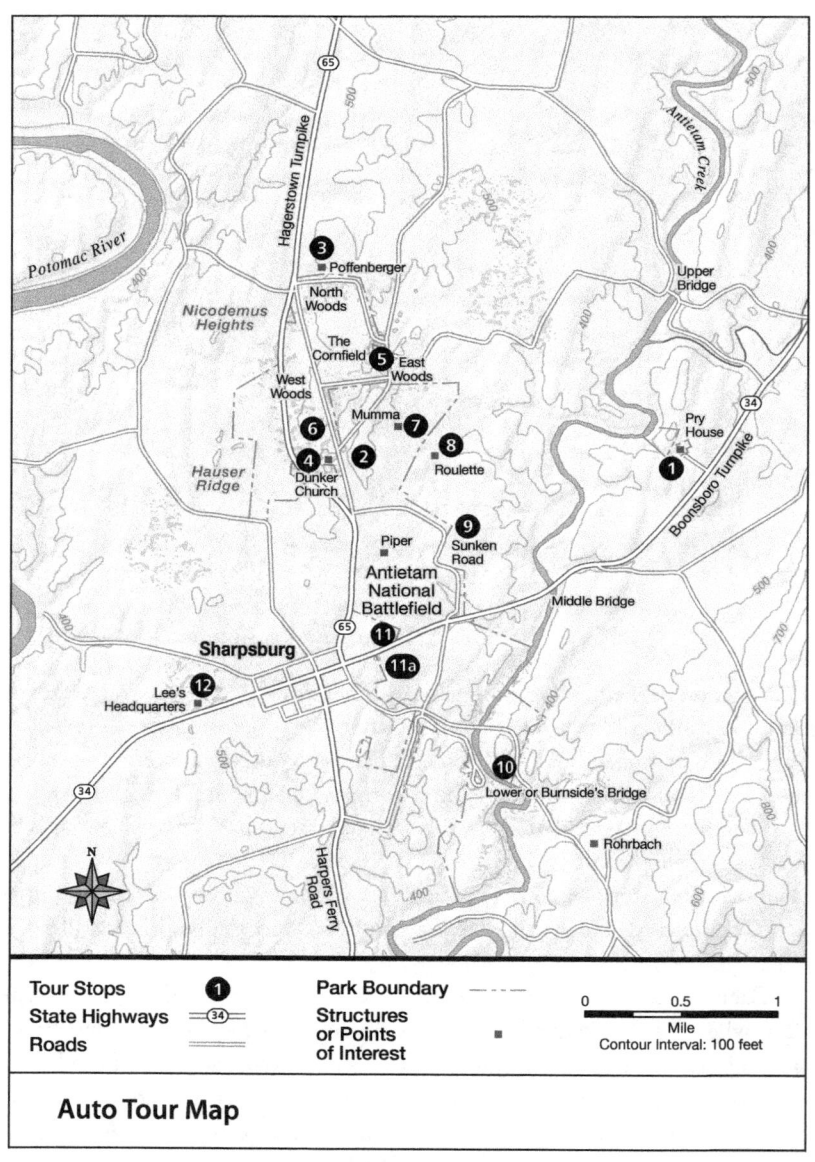

Auto Tour Map

History does not always record the precise locations where specific decisions were made, and in these cases, I supply my best guess as to the site. In other instances, the location is known, but changes in the landscape make the view less than ideal and keep it from providing proper context. In this situation, the stop will be moved to a location that affords a better understanding of the ground. In either case, I will let you know.

Our tour begins at the Antietam National Battlefield, we will be confined primarily to the property owned by the National Park Service and requires an entrance fee. We will be visiting sites that are close to private property, so please be respectful of those boundaries. Today the relatively quiet town of Sharpsburg has a population of just over seven hundred residents.[1]

Stop 1—Pry House Field Hospital Museum

18906 Shepherdstown Pike, Keedysville, Maryland 21756
(39.475900, -77.714034)

Our tour will begin here. From Sharpsburg go east on the Shepherdstown Pike (MD 34 E). In 1860 this road was more commonly referred to as the Boonsboro Pike. From the eastern edge of town drive 2.3 miles, and your destination (Pry House Field Hospital Museum) will be on the left. Turn left, and follow the driveway to the parking lot on the right. A good observation point west of the house faces west and the field at Antietam. The Pry House is open Thursday to Sunday from May through November, 11:00 a.m. to 5:00 p.m., but you can walk about the grounds during regular park hours. Our next two critical decisions occurred at this location.

Stand on the high ground west of the house with the house at your back, and look west. Depending on the time of the year and the leaves on the trees, you should be able to see the New York and Maryland Monuments near the Antietam National Battlefield Visitor Center. This high ground was the objective of Hooker's opening assault (see photo). Directly behind you is the town of Keedysville. Boonsboro, is about four miles beyond it to the northeast.

The Pry House and the high ground it occupies served not only as a place where Lee could evaluate the ground prior to the battle, but also as McClellan's forward headquarters during the fighting. Standing here affords you the view each commander had in 1862.

Decision—Lee Offers Battle at Sharpsburg

From the moment Robert E. Lee decided to divide his army on September 9, the operational clock was ticking. His calculated risk was beginning to come apart, and very little had gone according to plan. Moreover, Lee faced a

Appendix I

Pry House, circa 1862. Alexander Gardner, Library of Congress / National Archives.

daunting situation on the morning of September 15. The garrison at Harpers Ferry did not evacuate in response to his move west, and the operation to eliminate this obstacle was now three days behind schedule. McClellan had suddenly and inexplicably taken a more aggressive posture in Lee's direct front at South Mountain. By the evening of September 14, the military scales had tipped in favor of the Union.

The fighting at South Mountain on September 14 resulted in a Union victory, and the setting sun was the only thing that prevented a Union rout. After a discussion with his lieutenants, Lee determined that Longstreet's and D. H. Hill's men could not hold Turner's Gap once dawn came, and the position was abandoned. The Confederate forces defending Crampton's Gap also fell back to Pleasant Valley and south to Maryland Heights. Although Lee was unaware of the full extent of the Crampton's Gap defeat, he knew McLaws's and Anderson's combined force at Maryland Heights was the most vulnerable. The geography of the Pleasant Valley proved a real obstacle to the Confederate army. If the Union could get a sizeable force into the valley, McLaws and Anderson would have no direct line back to the main force if it remained north of the Potomac. The Rebels would then be between the proverbial rock of the Union Sixth Corps and hard place of the Harpers Ferry garrison.

On the evening of the fourteenth, Lee sent dispatches to his widely scattered commands. Longstreet and D. H. Hill were to silently withdraw from South Mountain and to fall back to Keedysville. Brig. Gen. William N. Pendleton, his chief of artillery, was ordered to position batteries three miles

Pry House, Antietam National Battlefield, modern image. Author.

west of Boonsboro and to send the remainder of the reserve artillery to a position at Boteler's/Blackburn's Ford. Supported by infantry, this artillery defended the critical Potomac crossing should the army need to continue the retreat. With the aforementioned artillery, cavalry under Brig. Gen. Fitzhugh Lee and Brig. Gen. John B. Hood's division were ordered to act as the rear guard during the retreat. Lee also sent a dispatch to Jackson asking for an estimated completion date for the Harpers Ferry operation.

Later that night, as the desperate situation began to reveal itself, Lee sent two telling messages. The first message ordered Jackson to abandon the Harpers Ferry operation and fall back to Shepherdstown and cover the army's retreat. The second message ordered McLaws to abandon Maryland Heights. His division and Anderson's would then make their way back to the relative safety of Virginia however they could. Robert E. Lee's great invasion into the North was about to come to a sudden and inglorious end.

This dispatch from Lee's headquarters to McLaws illustrates the general's dilemma and intentions:

> The day has gone assistant us and this army will go by Sharpsburg and cross the river. It is necessary for you to abandon your position to-night. Send your trains not required on the road to cross the river. Your troops you must have well in hand to unite with this command,

> which will retire by Sharpsburg. Send forward officers to explore the way, ascertain the best crossing of the Potomac, and if you can find any between you and Shepherdstown leave Shepherdstown Ford for this command.[2]

Early on Monday, September 15, Lee was scanning the countryside from a high meadow just east of the village of Sharpsburg. He mulled over his next move while he absorbed all the details of the landscape with his military engineer's eye. While initially wanting to consolidate his force at Keedysville, Lee changed his mind, seeing a better defensive position farther west beyond Antietam Creek.

Lee was probably partial to the terrain due west of the Creek for a number of reasons. First, he wanted more favorable ground on which to conduct a fighting retreat should McClellan continue his aggressive movements. Lee also sought an advantageous position to concentrate his army north of the Potomac River should he be able to continue the campaign. Additionally, because Franklin's corps was now in between McLaws's and Anderson's Divisions and the main body of Lee's army, Lee needed to be west of Elk Ridge to give the divisions a feasible route to rejoin him. Antietam Creek also provided a natural barrier to position his army behind, and the undulating ground allowed Lee to mask his real strength. The terrain west of the creek at Sharpsburg met all of these requirements. Its only drawback was its proximity to the Potomac River.

Near to where you are standing, a Confederate courier found Robert E. Lee at about 8:00 a.m., enjoying a hot cup of coffee gifted to him by a local citizen. This courier carried a dispatch from Stonewall Jackson that predicted the surrender of Harpers Ferry.[3]

The capitulation of Harpers Ferry was now imminent, and Lee finally had the opportunity he had been seeking. Upon receiving Jackson's message, the Confederate commander decided to make a stand and attempt to reunite his army at Sharpsburg. He ordered all of his forces to converge on the town, save those left to guard his escape route at Boteler's/Blackford's Ford. The twelve thousand men Lee then had on hand continued marching west, crossed the Antietam, and occupied defensive positions. Lee counted on the bottleneck of South Mountain to slow the Union army's advance for several days, thus giving him the valuable time he needed.[4]

Lee outlined his approach in a letter to Davis on September 16:

> Learning later in the evening that Crampton's Gap on the direct road from Fredericktown to Sharpsburg had been forced, and McLaws' rear thus threatened, and believing from a report from Genl Jackson that Harper's Ferry would fall next morning, I determined to withdraw Longstreet and D. H. Hill from their positions and retire to the vicinity of Sharpsburg, where the army could be more readily united. Before abandoning the position, indications led me to believe that the enemy was withdrawing, but learning from a prisoner that Sumner's corps, which had not been engaged, was being put in position to relieve their wearied troops while the most of ours were exhausted by a fatiguing march and a hard conflict and I feared would be unable to renew the fight successfully in the morning, confirmed me in my determination.[5]

This excerpt from Lee's after-action report also reveals his thinking:

> Under these circumstances, it was determined to retire to Sharpsburg, where we would be upon the flank and rear of the enemy should he move against McLaws, and where we could more readily unite with the rest of the army. This movement was efficiently and skillfully covered by the cavalry brigade of General Fitzhugh Lee, and was accomplished without interruption by the enemy, who did not appear on the west side of the pass at Boonsborough until about 8 a.m. on the following morning.
>
> The commands of Longstreet and D. H. Hill, on their arrival at Sharpsburg, were placed in position along the range of hills between the town and the Antietam, nearly parallel to the course of that stream, Longstreet on the right of the road to Boonsborough and Hill on the left.[6]

This critical decision not only determined the location for the upcoming battle but also became the next step in actually bringing the fighting on. Additionally, Lee's decision also made McClellan pause to wonder why. On September 15 and 16, the Confederate commander's aggressive stance on the west bank of Antietam Creek was almost entirely bluff. But it was a good enough bluff to make McClellan contemplate what the Rebels were up to and why they were choosing to fight here and now. There is good reason to believe that

McClellan took Lee's defiance as a sign that the enemy did indeed possess vast numbers of men. The Union commander had held this belief from the outset of the campaign. In addition, the Rebels' position offered the relatively small force natural strength.

Decision—McClellan Launches His Attack

At dawn on September 15, it became evident to the Union troops advancing on the now-abandoned Confederate positions at South Mountain that they had struck the critical first blow of the Maryland Campaign. McClellan had Lee's operational plans and had used them to drive the Confederate forces off South Mountain. By all indications, the Confederates were falling back, possibly as far as the Potomac. For the briefest of moments, McClellan had stolen the initiative from his opponent.

From his headquarters at Bolivar, George McClellan sensed there was still an opportunity to follow up on the previous night's success and to continue pressuring the retreating Rebel army. It is safe to say McClellan was still somewhat in the dark about the total number of enemy troops in his front. However, in those early morning hours he did know that a significant portion of the Confederate army was still at Harpers Ferry. For the moment, though, the odds were still in McClellan's favor.

The Union commander sent the following to Halleck on September 15:

> After a very severe engagement, the corps of Hooker and Reno have carried the heights commanding the Hagerstown road. The troops behaved magnificently. They never fought better. Franklin has been hotly engaged on the extreme left. I do not yet know the result, except that the firing indicated progress on his part. The action continued until after dark, and terminated leaving us in possession of the entire crest. It has been a glorious victory. I cannot yet tell whether the enemy will retreat during the night or appear in increased force in the morning. I am hurrying up everything from the rear, to be prepared for any eventuality.[7]

By 8:00 a.m. on September 15, McClellan and his staff shot off several dispatches to his commands indicating his intention to pursue the Confederates and attack. The commander perhaps believed Lee was falling back all the way to the Potomac. Even before that, at 7:00 a.m., Hooker had ordered Maj. Gen. Israel B. Richardson's Second Corps division that had been attached to his own corps to move out and pursue the retreating enemy. McClellan also sent two somewhat premature messages to Halleck that seem like a combination of rumor and speculation sprinkled with a few facts:

> I have just learned from General Hooker, in the advance, who states that the information is perfectly reliable that the enemy is making for Shepherdstown in a perfect panic; and General Lee last night stated publicly that he must admit they had been shockingly whipped. I am hurling everything forward to endeavor to press their retreat to the utmost.

Later that morning, McClellan sent the following to Halleck:

> Information this moment received completely confirms the rout and demoralization of the rebel army. General Lee is reported wounded and Garland killed. Hooker alone has over 1,000 more prisoners. It is stated that Lee gives his loss as 15,000. We are following as rapidly as the men can move.[8]

View of the Antietam National Battlefield from the Pry House, modern image. Author.

Appendix I

Alfred Pleasonton's cavalry was also on the move at first light, following orders to pursue the fleeing Rebels. The balance of the Union infantry corps was dispatched to follow. Learning of Franklin's success at Crampton's Gap, McClellan ordered him to advance as well. After that, however, very little went right for the Union army commander. Burnside delayed getting the Ninth Corps moving from Fox's Gap, shoddy staff work congested all the roads, and McClellan himself did not cross over South Mountain until noon. To add to McClellan's bad luck, he received two messages from Franklin as he was moving west into Pleasant Valley. The first arrived at 11:00 a.m. and indicated that Franklin's advance on Maryland Heights had stalled. The message sent at 3:15 p.m. stated that Harpers Ferry had fallen to the Confederates.

Just after noon, Richardson, accompanied by Col. John F. Farnsworth's cavalry brigade, had advanced to the east bank of Antietam Creek. The Union troops had been pressing Lee's rear guard (Brig. Gen. Fitzhugh Lee) since leaving Boonsboro. Upon reaching a point near where you are now standing, this force discovered that the Army of Northern Virginia was drawn up in line of battle west of Antietam Creek. Joined by Hooker at 2:00 p.m. and by Sumner an hour later, the generals quickly determined they lacked the manpower to attack the Confederate position that Hooker assumed was held by fifty thousand men. Rather than deploying, the Federal officers halted the advance. The resulting traffic jam clogged the roads all the way back to Turner's Gap.

McClellan himself arrived here at approximately 4:00 p.m., and he, too, determined it was impossible to attack that day. The rest of the Army of the Potomac was now spread out in a nine-mile-long column from Keedysville back to Turner's Gap. As darkness fell, McClellan ordered the army deployed, but he did not issue any orders to prepare for an attack the next day. Perhaps the commander wondered whether the Confederates would still be there once the sun came up.

By the morning of September 16, McClellan had all his forces except Franklin's corps and Couch's and Humphreys' divisions within a few miles of his forward headquarters at the Pry House. Although he did not know it, McClellan held the numerical advantage over his enemy. That soon changed as the roughly ten thousand men that made up Jackson's Command were now arriving at Sharpsburg.

A dense fog blanketing the valley that morning. Once it lifted at about 10:00 a.m., McClellan spent the next several hours assigning bivouacs, placing batteries, and riding his positions on the east side of the creek. The Union commander no doubt remained unsure of his opponent's strength. Yet McClellan might have felt that the longer he waited, the longer his odds would be as those forces at Harpers Ferry continued to make their way to

Lee. The Army of the Potomac now had fifty thousand men of all arms assembled east of the creek, and Abraham Lincoln issued the following mandate: "God bless you and all with you. Destroy the rebel army if possible."[9]

In his after-action report, McClellan bemoaned the advantages of his opponent's position: "On all favorable points the enemy's artillery was posted, and their reserves, hidden from view by the hills on which their line of battle was formed, could manoeuvre unobserved by our army, and from the shortness of their line could rapidly reinforce any point threatened by our attack. Their position, stretching across the angle formed by the Potomac and Antietam, their flanks and rear protected by these streams, was one of the strongest to be found in this region of country, which is well adapted to defensive warfare."[10]

McClellan chose to attack, and on the afternoon of the sixteenth, he issued orders for the First Corps to advance across Antietam Creek. While it is difficult to say precisely when he decided to attack, the commander did not issue those orders to Hooker until 2:00 p.m. By then, more than twenty-four hours had passed since the Army of the Potomac's arrival on the field. Unpacking McClellan's ultimate plan for the battle is challenging to be sure, as McClellan seemed to contradict himself in postwar accounts.[11]

While we can argue that he might have created unnecessary delays and that he could have attacked on September 15 or 16, McClellan in fact made the ultimate decision to attack, and he did so despite some lingering doubts about his chances for success. The most obvious and direct result of the general's decision was that it inaugurated the Battle of Antietam. Secondarily, the choice to attack ensured that the battle would be fought at the location and day that history now records. This decision also allowed Lee to fight a defensive battle on ground of his own choosing possessing good interior lines.

Stop 2—Antietam National Battlefield Visitor Center and Observation Deck

5831 Dunker Church Rd, Sharpsburg, Maryland 21782 (39.473919, -77.744968)

From the Pry House, return to your car, go back down the driveway, and turn right onto MD 34 W (Shepherdstown Pike). Then drive 2.3 miles, and turn right onto Church Street (MD 65 N). This road is also referred to as the Sharpsburg Pike and was the Hagerstown Pike in 1862. Continue on MD 65 N for 0.9 mile, and turn right onto Dunker Church Road at the entrance to the battlefield. Then turn into the parking lot of the Antietam National Battlefield Visitor Center. I recommend a slight diversion from the tour at

Appendix I

View of the Antietam National Battlefield from the Visitor Center, modern image. Author.

this point to see all the visitor center has to offer, including a film on the battle, a museum, a bookstore, and an observation deck that presents excellent views of the battlefield. It is open 7 days a week 9:00 a.m. to 5:00 p.m., excluding major holidays. The Visitor Center also provides information on hikes, guided tours, monuments, and other details about the park that are not covered in this book. Additionally, the Antietam Battlefield is a fee site with no entrance station, so the Visitor Center is where you will have to pay that fee. The observation deck at the eastern end of the Visitor Center is a great place to read this next section.

Located in a mostly rural corner of Washington County, Maryland, the Antietam Battlefield is neatly nestled in several great curves of the Potomac River. Antietam Creek generally flows north to south before emptying into the Potomac several miles below Shepherdstown. While gently sloping in some spots, the banks of the creek are incredibly steep in others. Four triple-arch stone bridges spanned the creek at the time of the battle, starting at the intersection of the Keedysville Road in the north to just above its confluence with the Potomac in the south. The three bridges closest to Sharpsburg became of interest to both armies as they represented critical potential crossing points. North to south, they are the Upper, Middle, and Lower Bridges, respectively. Several fords also intersected Antietam Creek at vital points.

The Hagerstown Turnpike (now called the Sharpsburg Pike / Maryland Route 65) goes north from Sharpsburg to Hagerstown. West of the turnpike is a series of low ridges that begin in the north at a bend in the Potomac and run south through Sharpsburg and along the Harpers Ferry Road.

Splitting the battlefield along its north–south axis, the Boonsboro Turnpike (Maryland Route 34) crossed Antietam Creek at the Middle Bridge, then entered the eastern end of Sharpsburg. Now called the Shepherdstown Pike, the route connects Sharpsburg to the Potomac and beyond. The Middle Bridge has been replaced by a modern structure.

The deceivingly uneven ground of this field can hide entire brigades from view while exposing others to deadly fire. In 1862 the area was mostly agricultural; farmhouses, country lanes, fields, and woodlots dotted this pastoral landscape at the time of the battle, much as they do today.

Note the fifty-eight-foot-tall New York State Monument just north of the visitor center. As the tallest structure on this part of the battlefield, it is visible from several other points, and seeing it is an excellent way to get your bearings.

As you face due east, South Mountain is 6.5 miles in that direction. The Pry House is roughly 1.5 miles away in the same direction, and the meandering Antietam Creek is 1.0 mile away. The Joseph Poffenberger Farm is 1.5 miles north (to your left). Between you and the Poffenberger property are the David Miller Farm, the Cornfield, and Smoketown Road. About 0.5 mile southwest of you (on your right), you will see the sixty-foot Observation Tower at a bend in the Sunken Road. More or less in that same direction about 1.75 miles away is the Burnside Bridge. The Potomac River is located about 2.75 miles west of you (directly behind you). The southern extension of the West Woods and Hauser's Ridge are situated between here and there.

The next four stops—the Joseph Poffenberger Farm, the Dunker Church, the East Woods, and the West Woods—can all be a walking tour if you choose. Typically, there is not a lot of traffic on the battlefield, so walking on the roads is relatively safe, but please be mindful of vehicles at all times. Additionally, walking the field yields a very different perspective of the ground and this opening phase of the battle. Making the stops slightly out of order, you will travel in an approximately three-mile-long circle starting from the visitor center. However, you can drive to each stop if this suits you.

To walk the tour, from the visitor center, travel north on Dunker Church Road, and stop at the Dunker Church (Stop 4). Then walk north to Mansfield Avenue and the Joseph Poffenberger Farm (Stop 3). At this point, continue east and south until Mansfield Avenue connects to Smoketown Road. Go right on Smoketown Road, following it until you reach Cornfield Avenue, and turn right here, and you will be at the East Woods (Stop 5). Then go west on Cornfield Ave. and turn left at Dunker Church Road. Turn right at the entrance to the West Woods (Stop 6), then proceed south to return to the visitor center. Many of these roads were not here at the time of the battle, but our map lists them as they exist today. To understand how they looked at the time of the battle, please refer to the maps provided in chapters 1 and 2.

Stop 3—Antietam National Battlefield, Joseph Poffenberger Farm

(39.488870, -77.747188)

Decision—Hooker Opens the Battle

From the visitor center turn right onto Dunker Church Road, and head north for 1.0 mile. Turn right on Mansfield Avenue, and drive about 0.2 mile until you reach the parking area on your left. Park your car here. You will see monuments for Clara Barton and for the Eighth and Fourth Pennsylvania Reserves.

Walk south across the road to the Cornfield Trail. Walk 250 feet farther south through the trees to the southern edge of the North Woods to get a better view. Facing south in the direction of the visitor center, you will see the field as Hooker saw it on the morning of September 17. About a mile to the south, you should be able to see the high ground that the visitor center now occupies. (Look for the New York State Monument.)

Depending on the day and time of year, you can also see the Dunker Church nestled in the West Woods along Dunker Church Road. This high ground was the objective of Hooker's opening attack.

Joe Hooker spent the night of the sixteenth in the barn of Joseph Poffenberger, whose farm is just behind you. In 1862 Dunker Church Road was part of Hagerstown Pike. The Potomac River is just short of 1,800 yards west of you (to your right), and Antietam Creek is about 3,000 yards east of you (to your left). The northern edge of the East Woods is about 430 yards away (in your front and to the right), and the northern edge of the West Woods is 800 yards away (in your front and to the left). Between you and the visitor center are the Miller Farm and the northern edge of the Cornfield, 570 yards away. The Sunken Road is 1.17 miles from you, and the town of Sharpsburg is roughly 1.0 mile beyond that.

By the morning of September 17, Hooker's First Corps had been right in the thick of the action of the previous three days. As part of Burnside's wing, the corps was heavily engaged on September 14 at Turner's Gap, suffering roughly one thousand casualties. After pursuing the retreating Confederates from Turner's Gap, the First Corps was among the first Union elements to arrive east of Antietam Creek on the afternoon of September 15. Hooker's

View looking south from the Poffenberger Farm, Antietam National Battlefield, modern image. Author.

men then discovered a Confederate army that had turned to challenge its Federal pursuers. On the afternoon of September 16, McClellan ordered the three divisions of Hooker's 9,400-man corps west of Antietam Creek to open the offensive on Lee's left the next day. The Union commanding general gave Hooker authority over that end of the field and empowered the First Corps commander to ask for necessary reinforcements. Hooker also assumed that any reinforcements sent to aid him would fall under his control. This gave him license to determine how this initial effort of the battle would manifest itself.[12]

The topography west of the creek was a key to Lee's position here, and he set his forces accordingly. As indicated in discussion of a previous decision, the Army of Northern Virginia occupied a 3.5-mile line that extended from just south of the Rohrbach Bridge, north across the Boonsboro Turnpike, and along the high ground that ran more or less parallel to the Hagerstown Pike. The northern end of the line bent to the west, where it was anchored at a bend in the Potomac. The high ground directly east of a little whitewashed church next to the pike, where the visitor center is today, was the prominent feature of this end of the field. Lee massed his infantry and artillery here. He also positioned units to contest any attempted crossing of both the Lower and Middle Bridges, but he took no such precautions for the Upper Bridge. This compelled Lee to place the bulk of his forces on the more vulnerable left side of his line. Jackson, who commanded this end of the field, had about fourteen thousand men in line and in immediate support.[13]

A mixed bag of forces made up Jackson's wing, including the better part of the divisions of Brig. Gen. John R. Jones and Brig. Gen. Alexander Lawton. These soldiers were positioned in and around the plateau of ground near the Dunker Church, and in the West Woods. Brig. Gen. John B. Hood's two-brigade division was in immediate reserve west of the church, with D. H. Hill's division nearby in the Sunken Road. These units were supported by no fewer than eight batteries of artillery. Brig. Gen. Fitzhugh Lee's cavalry brigade and three batteries of horse artillery commanded by Capt. John Pelham formed the extreme left of the line. Pelham's artillery defended the half-mile gap between the Hagerstown Turnpike and the Potomac River. The position on Nicodemus Heights, sometimes referred to as Nicodemus Hill, was also supported throughout the morning by Brig. Gen. Jubal A. Early's brigade of Lawton's Division. This high ground is about 0.6 mile west of your position (to your right). Look to the line of trees on the high ground just beyond the Dunker Church Road and the Sharpsburg Pike (Maryland Route 65).

At 2:00 p.m. on September 16, McClellan ordered Hooker to cross the Antietam by the Upper Bridge and the ford below, to attack and, if possible, crush Lee's left. Maj. Gen. George G. Meade's and Brig. Gen. James Ricketts's First Corps divisions crossed at the bridge, and the division of Brig. Gen. Abner Doubleday crossed at the ford. By 4:00 p.m., Hooker had put his troops in motion. As the sun was setting, Hooker was fully across and had advanced Meade's division into the East Woods to probe the Confederate position.

Pickets belonging to Brig. Gen. Truman Seymour's brigade made contact with Hood's Division that was occupying a position near the East Woods, and a small but sharp engagement ensued. The fighting died down as darkness fell. Not wanting to face the Rebels with his corps alone, Hooker had earlier asked McClellan for additional support. The Union commanding general responded by sending the 7,600 men of Mansfield's Twelfth Corps across the creek later that night. The Twelfth took position about a mile to Hooker's left and rear just west of the Upper Bridge crossing. McClellan also made Sumner's Second Corps available as his reserve force.

From his headquarters on the Joseph Poffenberger Farm, Hooker could just see a little whitewashed building on some high ground to the south. The Dunker Church was a mile or so in that direction, and open high ground lay just to its east. Sometimes referred to as a schoolhouse in after-action reports, the church made an easily identifiable objective for Hooker's men to converge on. Hooker also saw this high ground as key terrain, as he believed he was on Lee's left flank. If he could take this area, he could imperil the Confederate position, In addition, he could place his own artillery there to enfilade the Confederates occupying the Sunken Road and the town beyond. Hooker deployed his corps in and around the Poffenberger Farm with the intent of launching his attack at dawn. The stage was now set for the opening phase of the battle, and the question Joe Hooker faced was how exactly he would strike the first blow.

In his after-action report written on November 8, 1862, Hooker indicated his intentions:

> At daylight Gibbon's and Hartsuff's brigades were thrown forward, supported with the brigades of their respective divisions, while Meade followed them up in the center, instructed to spring to the assistance of either, as circumstances might require. Seymour continued to hold the advance, with the utmost firmness and resolution, until our troops had passed him. With these dispositions completed, the battle was soon renewed on the morning of the 17th. My object was to gain the high ground nearly three-quarters of a mile in advance of me, and which commanded the position taken by the enemy on his retreat from South Mountain; to prevent which he had been re-enforced by Jackson's corps during the night and at the same time had planted field batteries on high ground on our right and rear, to enfilade our lines when exposed during the advance.[14]

Hooker opened the battle between 5:30 a.m. and 5:45 a.m. with only his corps, and he eventually committed all three of his divisions in an effort to drive the Confederates from the high ground before him. Doubleday, Ricketts, and Meade battled with Jackson's two divisions for the quarter-square-mile area that made up the East Woods, the West Woods, and the space surrounding the Dunker Church. Ordered in at 5:30, Mansfield's Twelfth Corps joined the battle at 7:15 a.m. The Second Corps would not cross Antietam Creek until 7:20 a.m. that morning. The unit joined the battle at 8:30 a.m. Additionally, only the Second Corps divisions of Maj. Gen. John Sedgwick and Brig. Gen. William French were in this initial movement. McClellan held back Maj. Gen. Israel B. Richardson's division until a division from the Fifth Corps could replace it in the tactical reserve. Richardson did not cross the creek until almost two hours later.

Despite fearing that the Confederates would overwhelm his single unit, Hooker primarily fought the opening phase of the battle (almost two hours) with the First Corps alone. Mansfield's Twelfth Corps did not join the battle until approximately 7:15 a.m. By the time Mansfield was in action, the First was essentially rendered combat ineffective. Additionally, Hooker never explained why he did not bring Mansfield's corps closer to his own that morning, or why he waited so long before ordering the force in. Perhaps Mansfield's position gave Hooker some deployment flexibility that only he understood. Additionally, based on reports, confusion and ignorance of the enemy's position prevailed in the Union army that day. Hooker possibly felt that attacking with the whole force at his disposal was far too risky.[15]

Hooker also erroneously believed that he was on the enemy's flank. While he did not realize it, the piecemeal attacks at the opening of the battle played right into Lee's hands. Committing at most two divisions at a time enabled Lee and Jackson to deploy their reserves at one point of attack on the field and then another to counter Hooker. At least three or four times during the morning phase of the battle, Confederates described the desperate nature of their position as the weight of the Union attacks pushed them near the breaking point. In each case, the Rebels were able to resist the Union tide.[16]

Hooker's attacks flowed along the line of the Hagerstown Turnpike from the Cornfield, the West Woods, and toward the Sunken Road with the Twelfth and Second, each coming in on the right one at a time. Consequently, each of the three Union corps involved in the morning phase of the battle was used up one by one. The Confederates were able to counter one unsupported attack after the other. Hooker and Mansfield both became casualties, and any semblance of command and control was lost. In his after-action report, Hooker conveyed his impressions of the situation:

Brig. Gen. George G. Meade, who took over the corps after Hooker was wounded, described his division's performance in his after-action report:

> At early daylight on the 17th the contest was warmly renewed by Seymour, the enemy attacking him with vigor. The general commanding the corps had sent Ricketts' division to Seymour's support, and had advanced Doubleday's division along the woods occupied by Magilton's and Anderson's brigades. These brigades were formed in column of battalions in mass, and were moved forward in rear of Doubleday. Seymour and Ricketts advancing through one piece of woods, and Doubleday, on their right, advancing along the Hagerstown pike, left an open space between, in which was a plowed field and an orchard; beyond this was a cornfield, the possession of which the enemy warmly disputed.
>
> Ransom's battery was advanced into the open ground between the two advancing columns, and played with great effect on the ene-

> my's infantry and batteries. The brigades of Anderson and Magilton on reaching the cornfield were massed in a ravine extending up to the pike. Soon after forming, I saw the enemy were driving our men from the cornfield. I immediately deployed both brigades, and formed line of battle along the fence bordering the corn-field, for the purpose of covering the withdrawal of our people and resisting the farther advance of the enemy.[17]

This decision was critical because it kicked off a battle that was a series of largely uncoordinated frontal assaults and counterattacks on both sides. While inflicting severe losses on the enemy and driving them from the high ground, the Union could not break the Confederate line. Additionally, Hooker's decision determined the course of the fighting. A number of choices made the battle on the Union right flow back and forth across the Cornfield and the East Woods, into the West Woods, and finally into the Sunken Road, but Hooker's decision set all of those events in motion.

Stop 4—Antietam National Battlefield, Dunker Church
(39.475400, -77.746608)

Decision—Hood Counterattacks at the Cornfield

Return to your car, and drive west on Mansfield Avenue. Continue for 0.2 mile, then turn left on Dunker Church Road. Drive south for 1.0 mile, pull over to the right, and park in front of the Dunker Church. With your back to the church, you are looking east. The Pry House is located about 1.7 miles in that direction, just across Antietam Creek. The J. Poffenberger Farm is a mile north (to your left), and the town of Sharpsburg is about a mile south (to your right). The West Woods is situated behind you and to your left. If you walk about five hundred feet to the northeast, just past the massive Maryland Monument, and turn to the north, you will see the field as Hood saw it on the morning of September 17.

By the time of the opening shots of the Battle of Antietam, Hood's Division had been one of the most active in Longstreet's Command. Its soldiers had marched to Hagerstown to counter a nonexistent threat and then back to bolster D. H. Hill's line at South Mountain. They were also part of Lee's rear guard as the army fell back to Sharpsburg. Once they crossed the creek on September 15, Hood's soldiers were eventually placed near the church with Jackson's divisions on the left of Lee's line.

View looking north to the Cornfield from the Smoketown Road, Antietam National Battlefield, modern image. Author.

On the night of September 16, Hood's two brigades were holding position north of the Mumma Farm straddling Smoketown Road. As Meade's division advanced south on the road, Truman Seymour's Union brigade skirmished with the center of Hood's line just as darkness was falling. Once the fighting ceased and he had conversed with Stonewall Jackson, Hood was able to get his exhausted and hungry division relieved at the front by the brigades of Col. Marcellus Douglass and Col. James A. Walker of Lawton's Division. These reinforcements were arranged with the proviso that Hood would come at once if called for. Hood's two-thousand-man division then fell back to a position west of the Dunker Church to finally rest and eat.[18]

At 6:45 a.m. on September 17, with the battle now ninety minutes old, the Army of Northern Virginia faced its first real crisis of the morning. Hooker's first two attacking divisions, were almost wholly wrecked themselves. Yet they had driven Lawton's and J. R. Jones's divisions south of the Cornfield to Smoketown Road and had all but rendered the Confederates combat ineffective. Only Brig. Gen. Roswell S. Ripley's brigade of D. H. Hill's division held a position near the Mumma Farm. Thirty-two percent of the soldiers engaged on both sides were now casualties. Jackson later described the situation in his after-action report: "General Lawton, commanding division, and Colonel Walker, commanding brigade, were severely wounded. More than half of the brigades of Lawton and Hays were either killed or wounded, and more than a third of Trimble's, and all the regimental commanders in those brigades, except two, were killed or wounded. Thinned in their ranks, and exhausted of their ammunition, Jackson's Division and the brigades of Lawton, Trimble and Hays retired to the rear, and Hood, of Longstreet's command, again took the position from which he had been before relieved."[19]

Jackson, who was busily shoring up his battered line, little knew that the balance of George Meade's division was now entering the fight for the Cornfield while the van of Mansfield's Twelfth Corps was approaching the J. Poffenberger Farm. John B. Hood's division had been ready almost soon as they heard the first sounds of battle. At approximately 7:00 a.m. Hood received word to come at once with his division to support Lawton's shattered line. Hood marched his men across the Hagerstown Turnpike and wheeled them to the left about where you are now. He was just in time to see a brigade of Lawton's Division commanded by Col. Marcellus Douglass falling back in disarray.

Directly in front of Hood, to the north, the better part of four Union brigades held a line beginning west of the Hagerstown Turnpike and running past the southern edge of the Cornfield and beyond the eastern edge of the East Woods. Hood could also see the brigades of Brig. Gen. Marsena R. Patrick and Brig. Gen. John Gibbon of Doubleday's First Corps division advancing on the Confederate position from the northwest along the Hagerstown Pike.

True to form, the aggressive Hood ordered his division's nine regiments forward into the maelstrom that was the Cornfield and the East Woods. His two thousand men drove headlong into the Union brigades, catching the enemy completely off guard with their boldness. The Rebels ultimately knocked the Union line back to the Miller Farm, almost where it had started two hours ago. John Bell Hood described his decision in his after-action report:

> On the morning of the 17th instant, about 3 o'clock, the firing commenced along the line occupied by General Lawton. At 6 o'clock I received notice from him that he would require all the assistance I could give him. A few minutes after, a member of his staff reported to me that he was wounded and wished me to come forward as soon as possible. Being in readiness I at once marched out on the field in line of battle and soon became engaged with an immense force of the enemy, consisting of not less than two corps of their army. It was here that I witnessed the most terrible clash of arms, by far, that has occurred during the war. The two little giant brigades of this division

> wrestled with this mighty force, losing hundreds of their gallant officers and men but driving the enemy from his position and forcing him to abandon his guns on our left. The battle raged with the greatest fury until about 9 o'clock, the enemy being driven from 400 to 500 yards. Fighting, as we were, at right angles with the general line of battle, and General Ripley's brigade being the extreme left of General D. H. Hill's forces and continuing to hold their ground, caused the enemy to pour in a heavy fire upon the rear and right flank of Colonel Law's brigade, rendering it necessary to move the division to the left and rear into the woods near the Saint Mumma church.[20]

Hood's Division was decimated in the process, suffering over one thousand casualties, or 50 percent of those who had stepped off to fight that morning. The First Texas of Wofford's Brigade lost its flag, eight color-bearers, and 182 of its 211 men in the assault. That is a loss rate of nearly 87 percent—one of the highest casualty figures suffered by any regiment in a single battle during the Civil War.[21] Col. William T. Wofford, who commanded a brigade in Hood's wrecked division, later wrote, "This brigade went into the action numbering 854, and lost, in killed, wounded, and missing, 560—over one-half. . . . These brave officers all fell while gallantly leading their small bands on an enemy five times their number. They deserved a better fate than to have been, as they were, sacrificed for the want of proper support."[22]

In spite of this, Hood's decision was critical for a number of reasons. First of all, it drove the last of Hooker's corps from the area north of Smoketown Road and the Cornfield, stopping the momentum of the Federals' initial morning assaults. These attacks had come within an inch of collapsing Lee's left. Moreover, the assault all but knocked the First Corps out of the action for the day. Secondly, the offensive forced Hooker to call on Mansfield's Twelfth Corps for support to shore up his shattered divisions. Lastly, Hood's assault staved off Confederate disaster by allowing Lee and Jackson time to move critical reinforcements to the sector and prop up the devastated Confederate left.

Additionally, Hood's attack drew additional Union infantry and artillery into the seesaw fight for the Cornfield to stop him. Thus engaged, the Federal troops could not go elsewhere on the field. More specifically, they were prevented from supporting any more significant attack on Hood's left. Also, Hood's decision and the subsequent attacks by D.H. Hill's division might have had a more substantial effect than anyone at the time realized. Across Antietam Creek, McClellan was at that moment contemplating where to send the Second Corps. Sumner had been chomping at the bit since before dawn while waiting for orders, and at 7:20 a.m. McClellan ordered him to cross the creek and join the battle. Hooker was sweeping the field with his early morning attack, only to be violently knocked back by Hood's devastating assault. Perhaps feeling his right was now on the verge of collapse and receiving Hooker's requests for support, McClellan ordered Sumner across of Antietam Creek to reinforce Hooker.[23]

Stop 5—Antietam National Battlefield, East Woods
(39.481311, -77.742244)

Decision—Sumner Attacks the West Woods

Return to your car, turn around, and head back north on Dunker Church Road. After 150 feet, turn right on Smoketown Road. Drive approximately 0.5 mile, and then turn left on the Cornfield Avenue. You will see a parking area immediately on your right; pull in here and park. You are now standing in the East Woods, which had a much larger footprint in 1862, extending south well beyond the Smoketown Road.

Looking west down Cornfield Avenue, you will see the northernmost extension of the West Woods about 0.50 mile from your current location. The Cornfield is also just west down this road as well, about 0.025 mile and on the right, and the Sunken Road is about 0.60 mile due south (on your left). You are now seeing the field as Sumner saw when his Second Corps entered the fight at approximately 8:30 a.m.

At the Battle of Antietam, Edwin Vose Sumner was the most senior corps commander in the Army of the Potomac. He also commanded the largest corps in the army, counting some sixteen thousand men of all arms. Sumner's three divisions were commanded by Maj. Gen. Israel B. Richardson, Maj. Gen. John Sedgwick, and Brig. Gen. William H. French. By the time the battle was over, Richardson and Sedgwick were both wounded. While Sedgwick soon recovered, Richardson succumbed to his wound eight weeks later.[24]

Bivouacked just north of the Pry House, the Second was tasked with being part of the opening attack on September 16. McClellan's plan called for the corps to operate as reinforcements exploiting any Union breakthrough. While he ordered Sumner to have his corps ready before dawn, the commanding general did not release the unit for action until after the opening phase of the battle was almost over. It is possible that McClellan wanted to wait and see how the battle developed before he committed the Second to any particular part of the field.

Appendix I

Once Hooker had his First Corps in position on Lee's left on September 16, he asked McClellan for support, fearing that the Confederates could quickly overrun him. McClellan then ordered Sumner to make the Twelfth Corps available to Hooker. The corps was sent across Antietam Creek and eventually bivouacked behind and to the left of Hooker's men. Still in the position of wing commander, Sumner assumed his Second Corps soon followed, but McClellan had ordered the unit to wait. The Twelfth and Second Corps had made up the middle column during the march out from Washington, so Sumner considered including the Second a logical move. Unfortunately, he had to wait for orders.

Once Hood's Division could be observed driving the First Corps back across the Cornfield, McClellan assumed his flank was collapsing, and ordered Sumner in. Once the directive came down, Sumner crossed at Pry's Ford with Sedgwick's division in the lead. French followed shortly thereafter, but Richardson's division did not get permission to advance until almost an hour later, when Maj. Gen. George W. Morell's Fifth Corps division replaced it in the tactical reserve. Sumner described this situation in his after-action report:

> SIR: I have the honor to report that, on the evening of the 16th ultimo, I received an order at Keedysville to send the Twelfth Corps

View of the West Woods from the East Woods, Antietam National Battlefield, modern image. Author.

> (Banks') to support General Hooker, and to hold my own, the Second Corps, in readiness to march for the same purpose an hour before daylight. Banks' corps, under General Mansfield, marched at 11.30 p.m., and my own corps was ready to move at the time ordered, but did not receive from headquarters the order to march till 7.20 a.m. on the 17th. I moved Sedgwick's division immediately in three columns on the receipt of the order, followed by French's division in the same order. Richardson was ordered to move in the same direction by the commanding general about an hour later. On arriving at the place where Hooker had been engaged, I found him wounded, and his corps, after a severe contest, had been repulsed. Banks' corps, under the immediate command of General Mansfield, had gone into battle on Hooker's left, and was engaged when I came upon the field. General Mansfield, a worthy and gallant veteran, was unfortunately mortally wounded while leading his corps into action.[25]

After crossing the ford, Sumner reached the East Woods with Sedgwick's division, and very near where you are now, he halted to assess the overall situation. The time was approximately 9:00 a.m., and the three-hour opening chapter of the battle was now over. Sumner interacted with a number of officers from whom he gleaned information on the general state of the fighting to this point. Accounts are inconsistent as to whom exactly Sumner spoke with. According to one report, he encountered a wounded and somewhat incoherent Hooker being carried from the field. Sumner would then speak with First Corps division commander Brig. Gen. James B. Ricketts, and with new Twelfth Corps commander Brig. Gen. Alpheus Williams.

It was Williams or a member of his staff who attempted to apprise Sumner of the ground and the general situation. Williams had taken over the Twelfth Corps from the mortally wounded Mansfield. According to Williams, Sumner dismissed his information, made his own assessment of the overall situation, and declared both the First and Twelfth Corps were used up and unfit for further service. Both corps' commanders were wounded, leaving Sumner the most senior officer on the field. Brig. Gen. George G. Meade of the First Corps' Third Division had assumed command in place of the wounded Hooker.

Sumner could now see the carnage of the opening battle before him. Many of the nearly eight thousand casualties that resulted from the opening struggle were no doubt strewn across the battlefield. Sumner also observed some artillery units still in action and a Union infantry force of some size near the Dunker Church. Although he might not have known it, these troops were Brig. Gen. George S. Greene's Twelfth Corps division and the brand-new 125th Pennsylvania from Crawford's Twelfth Corps division.

Additionally, and perhaps most importantly, Sumner could detect no organized Confederate forces east of the Hagerstown Pike. Of the Rebels who had participated in the morning's engagement, those who were not lying dead or wounded on the field had fallen back beyond the West Woods and the church and to the Sunken Road. Sumner was unaware that Col. George T. Anderson's brigade and McLaws's Division were now on the march north and would soon be in the vicinity of the Dunker Church. As a result, Sumner led Sedgwick's division immediately into an ill-fated attack at what he assumed was Lee's flank at or near the West Woods.

Sumner's advance with Sedgwick's division into the infamous West Woods turned out to be a complete disaster, one of the most ill-famed incidents in the history of the Union army during the Civil War. As Sedgwick became mired in the woods, a mixed bag of five Confederate brigades hit him in the front and flank. The brigades of Brig. Gen. Joseph Kershaw, Brig. Gen. Paul Semmes, and Brig. Gen. William Barksdale of McLaws's Division combined with Col. George T. Anderson's and Brig. Gen. Jubal A. Early's brigades to rout Sedgwick's three Union brigades out of the woods and all but decimate his division. The attack by Sedgwick's force accomplished but marking an end to the early morning phase of the battle, not to mention adding nearly 2,500 more names to the ever-growing casualty list.[26]

Sumner described these events in his after-action report:

> My First Division (Sedgwick's) went into battle in three lines. After his first line had opened fire for some time, the enemy made a most determined rush to turn our left, and so far succeeded as to break through the line between Banks' corps and my own until they began to appear in our rear. In order to repel this attack from the rear, I immediately faced Sedgwick's third line about, but the fire at that moment became so severe from the left flank that this line moved off in a body to the right, in spite of all the efforts that could be made to stop it. The first and second lines after some time followed this movement, but the whole division was promptly rallied, took a strong position, and maintained it to the close of the battle.[27]

Brig. Gen. Oliver O. Howard, who was deployed in the rear of the attacking force, described the moment his brigade came under attack in the woods:

> Nearly the whole of the first line in good order stood and fired some 30 or 40 rounds per man, when word came that the left of our division had been completely turned by the enemy, and the order was given by General Sumner in person to change the position of the third line. He afterward indicated to me the point where the stand was to be made, where he wished to repel a force of the enemy already in our rear. The noise of musketry and artillery was so great that I judged more by the gestures of the general as to the disposition he wished me to make than by the orders that reached my ears.
>
> The troops were hastily faced about, and moved toward the rear and right in considerable confusion, but at about 100 yards from the right of where the first line was engaged, and nearly perpendicular to the turnpike, a portion of General Gorman's brigade, with one regiment of Dana's brigade, was first halted in line, and by a sharp fire repulsed the enemy advancing at that point. On the left of the turnpike regiments of the second and third lines were rallied, facing in the same direction toward Sharpsburg, and here they fired.[28]

Sumner's decision to attack is critical because it not only led to the disastrous engagement in the West Woods, but also shifted the axis of the battle from one that was primarily north to south to one that was mainly east to west. This choice also directly caused the struggle to shift to the Sunken Road?

Some historians are highly critical of Sumner's actions and decisions on September 17. They describe a corps commander who did not fully comprehend the current situation on the field and went bumbling off into the West Woods as a result. Also, with no cohesive plan, Sumner left French to figure things out on his own. Such scholars argue that this circumstance caused the West Woods disaster, and that it also resulted in French, for lack of instructions to the contrary, directing his division south to attack the Sunken Road.[29]

More recent scholarship argues the exact opposite. It proposes that Sumner conducted a complete reconnaissance of the ground and quite purposely ordered French to attack the Sunken Road to guard against a potential strike in his rear, and that Sumner's plan to attack the woods was tactically sound, disastrous only due to the timely or untimely arrival of McLaws's and Walker's Confederate divisions.[30]

Whether you believe Edwin Vose Sumner was tactically obtuse or just a victim of his own bad timing on September 17, the outcome of the fighting is unchanged. Sedgwick's division was routed and devastated in less than an hour of action. The force suffered a casualty rate of 40 percent, and division commander John Sedgwick was among the 2,200 killed, wounded, and missing.

Stop 6—Antietam National Battlefield, West Woods
(39.478269, -77.749252)

Decision—Jubal Early Deploys In the West Woods

Return to your car, and head west on Cornfield Avenue toward Dunker Church Road. After 0.35 mile, turn left at Dunker Church Road, go south for another 0.15 mile, and turn right at the entrance to the West Woods parking lot located four hundred feet west of Dunker Church Road. Park near the large Philadelphia Brigade Monument at the center of the parking lot.

Once you exit your car, look back down the driveway you just traveled. You are now facing east. The East Woods, about 0.5 mile away, is slightly northeast of your position. The southwest corner of the Cornfield is 300 yards away from you (to your left and front), and the Poffenberger Farm beyond that is about 0.75 mile away. The Dunker Church is about 425 yards south (on your right). In 1862, the woods behind you continued on for several hundred yards almost to Hauser's Ridge.

This spot witnessed the Confederates' devastating counterattack that hammered Sedgwick's Second Corps division in the flank and eventually drove them north, as well as Jubal Early's successful efforts to buy critical time for that attack to happen. In September 1862, Brig. Gen. Jubal Early's brigade was in Brig. Gen. Alexander Lawton's division (Ewell's Division) as a part of the Confederate task force to eliminate the Harpers Ferry garrison. The troops subsequently arrived on the field at Antietam on the morning of the sixteenth and went into bivouac north of Sharpsburg. By the time the battle began, Early and his brigade had been ordered to Nicodemus Heights to support Capt. John Pelham's horse artillery battery.

At approximately 7:00 a.m., the crisis on the Confederate left was approaching a new critical point. To fill the holes left by his two shattered divisions, Stonewall Jackson ordered Early to leave one regiment (the Thirteenth Virginia) to continue supporting the artillery on Nicodemus Heights and come with the rest of his brigade to hold the line west of the Hagerstown Pike. Jackson also ordered Hood and D. H. Hill to advance and shore up the shattered position.

The opening Union attacks had devastated the other three brigades of Lawton's Division, and Lawton himself was severely wounded. Early was

Brockenbrough's Maryland battery (2nd Baltimore) in the West Woods, Antietam National Battlefield, modern image. Author.

ordered to take command of what was left of the division. As Hood was advancing on the Cornfield, Early battled with Federal skirmishers west of the pike, driving them from the West Woods. By 8:00 a.m., Hood had fallen back, and D. H. Hill's three brigades engaged with the Union Twelfth Corps would soon join them in retreat.

Early now formed a line with what remained of J. R. Jones's likewise crippled division. As Jones had been wounded and his replacement, Brig. Gen. William E. Starke, had been killed, the unit was now commanded by a colonel. What was left of Hood's Division minus three regiments held a position just west of the Dunker Church. D. H. Hill's three brigades sent in after Hood's attack were also severely mauled, and they fell back, taken out of action for the day. The Confederate position was supported by three batteries from Jones's Division, as well as one from the reserve artillery positioned farther west of the church on a piece of high ground known as Hauser's Ridge.[31]

By 8:30 a.m., the sector that Early had come into was about to become the epicenter of the battle. What Early could now see is up for debate, but the situation was evolving constantly and quickly. The last remnants of Hood's and D. H. Hill's counterattacks had fallen back from the East Woods and the Cornfield. Additionally, Early could see two brigades of Brig. Gen. George Greene's division of the Twelfth Corps supported by Union artillery advancing on the contested plateau east of the Dunker Church. Greene's other brigade under Col. William B. Goodrich was advancing south along the Hagerstown Turnpike with the 124th Pennsylvania of Crawford's brigade. Furthermore, the seven-hundred-man 125th Pennsylvania Regiment also became detached from Brig. Gen. Samuel W. Crawford's brigade and was advancing on the church from the northeast. This newly formed regiment was so disproportionately large that Union and Confederate soldiers alike mistook it for a brigade.

Save Marsena R. Patrick's brigade, the balance of the Union First Corps had fallen back to a position north of the Cornfield. The Federals' locations were supported by an assortment of those batteries that still had ammunition. In addition, a superbattery of some thirty guns collected from the First and Twelfth Corps began forming a line at the extreme right of the Union line. The superbattery's line was three hundred yards wide when complete, and it completely covered the area between the Hagerstown Pike and the Potomac River.

Lastly, while Early probably did not know it, Maj. Gen. John Sedgwick's Second Corps division had crossed Antietam Creek and was at that moment heading for the East Woods.[32]

In his autobiography, Early testified to the gravity of the circumstances he had faced: "The situation was most critical and the necessity most pressing, as it was apparent that if the enemy got possession of this woods, possession of the hills in their rear would immediately follow, and then, across to our rear on the road leading back to the Potomac, would have been easy. In fact, the possession of these hills would have enabled him to take our whole line in reverse, and a disastrous defeat must have followed."[33]

Early had gone to Stonewall Jackson to request support for his position that he held with perhaps 1,700 men and feared was in imminent danger of collapse. He was informed that Col. George T. Anderson's brigade and the lead brigade of McLaws's Division were, in fact, en route from the southwest in to reinforce his men.

Early then acted decisively and split his forces. He advanced just far enough north to slow the advance of Goodrich and the 124th Pennsylvania, and he then left what remained of Jones's Division to hold off that Union threat, move by his right flank, and confront the 125th Pennsylvania. By then, the 125th had crossed the Hagerstown Turnpike and was moving into the woods just north of the church. As he was pushing the rookie Pennsylvanians back, Early saw Col. George T. Anderson's brigade coming in on his right and McLaws's Division right behind it. This development allowed the Confederate reinforcements to assemble, align themselves, and stabilize the line, and it also led to the eventual counterattack on Sedgwick in the West Woods.

In his after-action report, Early outlined his decision:

> My condition, however, was exceedingly critical, as another column was advancing in my front and had reached the woods in which I was. I saw the vast importance of maintaining my ground, for, had the enemy gotten possession of this woods, the heights immediately in rear, which commanded the rear of our whole line, would have fallen into his hands. I determined to wait for the re-enforcements promised by Gen. Jackson, hoping that they would arrive in time to meet the columns on my right. I, however, threw my right flank back quietly under cover of the woods, so as not to have my rear exposed in the event of being discovered. I kept an anxious eye on the column on my right, as well as on the one moving up in my front, and very soon I saw the column on my right move into the woods in the direction of the church. I looked to the rear for the re-enforcements, and could not see them coming. I was thus cut off from the main body of our army on the right, and a column was moving against me from the left. There was no time to be lost, and I immediately ordered my brigade to move by the right flank parallel, to the enemy, and directed Col. Grigsby, who commanded the body of troops he and Col. Stafford had rallied, to move his command back in line, so as to present front to the enemy, who were coming up on the flank. I moved back along the rear of the woods until I caught up with the enemy, who had the start of me. I was, however, concealed from his view, and it was evident that my presence where I was was not suspected. Passing from behind a ridge that concealed my brigade from the enemy, we came in full view of his flankers, who, however, were made aware of my presence by a fire which I directed the leading regiment to pour into them. They immediately ran into the main body, which halted, and I continued to move by the flank until my whole force was disclosed.[34]

While a number of factors lead to the clash in the West Woods, Early's decision was critical for two reasons. First, it held off the Union forces converging on the woods from two directions long enough for the Confederate combined infantry to attack in force and stop this new threat in its tracks. In addition, Early's choice set up Sedgwick for his flank encounter with the Rebels in the West Woods. Early went go on to state, "Just as I reformed my line, Semmes', Anderson's, and part of Barksdale's brigades, of McLaws'

Appendix I

division, came up, and the whole, including Grigsby's command, advanced upon this body of the enemy, driving it with great slaughter entirely from and beyond the woods, and leaving us in possession of my former position. As soon as this was accomplished, I caused the regiments of the brigade to be reformed and placed in position as before."[35]

The next three destinations, Mumma Farm (Stop 7), the Sunken Road (Stop 8), and the Roulette Farm (Stop 9), are best toured on foot. A great National Park Service trail will accommodate your journey. The route is mostly flat, and it covers approximately 1.5 miles.

Stop 7—Antietam National Battlefield, Mumma Farm

(39.477297, -77.740818)

Decision—Sumner Holds Back the Sixth Corps

Return to your car, leave the West Woods parking lot, and return to the visitor center. From the West Woods lot turn right on Dunker Church Road. After 0.25 mile, turn left into the visitor center parking lot.

On the southeast side of the visitor center, you will see two cannon (First Rhode Island Light, Battery A, Capt. John A. Tompkins) and a paved road running northeast (Mumma Lane) just beyond it. Walk to the road, and turn left heading northeast. After 0.25 mile, you will reach the Mumma Farm.

Mumma Farm, Antietam National Battlefield, modern image. Author.

Turn around, and look back toward the direction of the visitor center (southwest). While it is unclear where Sumner was at the time of the decision, he was probably situated someplace between Antietam Creek and the Hagerstown Turnpike.

William B. Franklin and the seventeen thousand men that made up his wing had spent the previous two days camped five miles away near Rohrersville in Pleasant Valley. Their job was to cover the flank of the main Union army at Sharpsburg from a potential attack up the valley from Harpers Ferry. On the evening of September 16, McClellan ordered Franklin to leave Couch's 6,400-man division in the valley and move his other two divisions under Maj. Gen. Henry W. Slocum and Maj. Gen. William F. "Baldy" Smith to Keedysville. On the seventeenth, Franklin started his march at 5:00 a.m., roughly the time Hooker was getting ready to launch his initial assault on Lee's left. Franklin arrived at army headquarters around 11:00 a.m., at about the same time the struggle for the Sunken Road was reaching its climax.

At the outset McClellan had planned for the Sixth Corps, when it arrived, to remain in reserve east of Antietam Creek; however, the morning's calamitous situation west of the creek changed his thinking. As Sedgwick was being driven from the West Woods and the state of affairs looked as if it might result in disaster, Sumner asked that the Sixth be sent into the battle for immediate support. In his August 1863 report McClellan detailed his thinking:

> Between 12 and 1 p.m. General Franklin's corps arrived on the field of battle, having left their camp near Crampton's Pass at 6 a.m., leaving General Couch with orders to move with his division to occupy Maryland Heights. General Smith's division lead the column followed by General Slocum's.
>
> It was first intended to keep this corps in reserve on the east side of the Antietam, to operate on either flank or on the center, as circumstances might require, but on nearing Keedysville the strong opposition on the right, developed by the attacks of Hooker and Sumner, rendered it necessary at once to send this corps to the assistance of the right wing.[36]

Because McClellan expected that his right might again be counterattacked, Smith's division was immediately sent across the creek at Pry's Ford, to support Sumner. Slocum crossed at the Upper Bridge and would be on the field shortly thereafter. Franklin initially advanced a small force into the West

Woods. Among the forces he engaged in this first move were two regiments of Brig. Gen. Winfield S. Hancock's First Brigade of Smith's division. Pry's Ford is about 1.25 miles east of here (behind you and to your right), and the Upper Bridge is about 1.75 miles to the northeast (behind you and to your right).

By this time, the brutal fighting on the north end of the battlefield was winding down. The battle, however, was reaching a critical stage. For the last seven hours, approximately 34,000 Union troops had engaged roughly 25,000 Confederates for a five-square-mile piece of land. Of the nearly 22,000 total casualties of the Battle of Antietam, over 80 percent were incurred on the fields, farms, and woodlots north of the Boonsboro Turnpike. In the bloody struggle for the Cornfield, the West Woods, and the Sunken Road, both armies had almost crippled each other. The Union army, however, had one more card to play. While Lee had no more reserves to commit to this end of the field, McClellan did. The Union commander now had the 11,000 men of the Sixth Corps available and ready to renew the attack.[37]

Meanwhile, south of the Boonsboro Turnpike, the Union Ninth Corps was now launching its third assault on the Lower Bridge just as Rodman's division was finally nearing Snavely's Ford beyond the Confederate right flank. Within the hour, this Confederate position collapsed under the weight of the Union attacks. At this same time, Alfred Pleasonton had sent the better part of two cavalry brigades supported by four batteries of horse artillery and an infantry regiment across the Middle Bridge. These units became engaged with not only the Confederates in and near the Sunken Road but also Brig. Gen. Nathan G. Evans's and Brig. Gen. James L. Kemper's men positioned on the high ground near Cemetery Hill.

Except for those Confederates still battling at or near the Sunken Road, Lee's entire left had been driven west of the Hagerstown Turnpike and south to a point about two hundred yards north of the Dunker Church. While several commands held these positions, including those of Jones, Walker, McLaws, and Hood, it is not clear how many combat effectives the Confederates could actually muster to defend against another Union assault here. My guess is somewhere between four thousand and six thousand men supported by perhaps five batteries of artillery on Hauser's Ridge. In the best-case scenario for the Confederates, they were still outnumbered almost two to one. It is also safe to assume that many of these units were exhausted and low on ammunition if not completely lacking it. Moreover, while it is uncertain whether the Union high command was aware of this fact, safe money would say they were not.

Additionally, the Confederate forces had been entirely driven out of the Sunken Road in great confusion by 12:00 noon. As the men of Richardson's

Second Corps division were advancing, the Confederate command was desperately making a stand near the Piper Farm.

It was now just after noon. Supported by his own fresh artillery batteries, Franklin readied his entire corps for a possible new advance at the Dunker Church and the surrounding woods. The forest lay to the west just beyond your vision on the other side of the ridge where the visitor center is located.

At this moment, an unknown number of Confederates occupied the West Woods in front of Sumner. The overwhelming Union attacks had driven the Confederates beyond the turnpike, and the West Woods, the terrain, and the woods now concealed them from Franklin's sight. Additionally, no one in the Union leadership had any idea of the Rebels' orientation or condition. If Sumner allowed Franklin to go bumbling off into the woods again, he just might just find himself in a calamity like the one that had befallen Sedgwick earlier that morning. One wrecked division under Sumner's command should have been enough for one day.

Just as Franklin was preparing to begin his attack, Sumner stopped him, saying that "if he were defeated the right would be entirely routed, his being the only troops left on the right that had any life in them."[38] An incensed Franklin then took his appeal to McClellan directly. The Union commander at first approved the plan, but he eventually sided with Sumner.

It is not entirely clear whether Sumner was still shaken from the disaster in the West Woods or whether he shared the commanding general's fear of a counterattack. But the attack would not take place; Sumner and his corps would mainly stand in place until the next day. This decision was critical because it ended one of the last possible opportunities to deal the Confederate left one final and possibly fatal blow. Also, Sumner's choice unofficially marked the end of the fighting north of the Boonsboro Turnpike, allowing all eyes to look exclusively to the Lower Bridge and the ongoing struggle there.

Stop 8—Antietam National Battlefield, Roulette Farm

(39.477297, -77.740818)

Decision—The Battle Shifts to the Sunken Road

From the Mumma Farm, follow the Bloody Lane Trail to the southeast. After about five hundred yards, you will reach the Roulette Farm and our next stop. Walk a few feet to the high ground south of the farm. From this position, you should be able to see the Observation Tower at the southeast end of the Sunken Road, which is about six hundred yards southwest of your current location. You should also see a farm lane that runs from the left of your current

Appendix I

View of the Sunken Road from the Roulette Farm, Antietam National Battlefield, modern image. Author.

position to the right of the tower. The West Woods is roughly 0.5 mile to the northwest (on your right), and the East Woods is roughly 0.5 mile to the north (behind you and to the right). The Antietam Creek is just over 0.5 mile behind you.

William French's Third Division was a recent and mostly untested addition to the Union Second Corps. It was officially organized on September 10, 1862, and not wholly assembled until the sixteenth, the day before the battle. Many of its regiments were filled with ninety-day men or those who had only seen garrison duty before this engagement. While French was an experienced brigade commander, this was his first division-level command.[39]

As dawn broke on September 17, the Second Corps and its commander were waiting for orders to cross Antietam Creek and join the fight. Once those orders came down at 7:20 a.m., French's and Sedgwick's divisions were ordered across the creek at Pry's Ford. Sedgwick's division was in the lead, and French followed once the way was clear. General Sumner, who was with Sedgwick's lead division, had no direct communication with French, but once he understood the state of affairs on the field, he would presumably let French know what he expected from this division. Once Sumner completed his reconnaissance of the field, he formulated his plan on how best to continue the Union attacks that had begun almost three hours before.[40]

During his initial survey of the ground, Sumner not only came away with a decent understanding of the situation of the Union forces north of his position, but he also observed those Union forces engaged east of the Dunker Church and in the West Woods. These troops were Brig. Gen. George S. Greene's Twelfth Corps Division and the 125th Pennsylvania from Crawford's Twelfth Corps division. Reports also indicate that Sumner could see Confederates deployed in the Sunken Road farther south; these were Rodes's and G. B. Anderson's uncommitted brigades from D. H. Hill's division and what remained of Colquitt's and McRae's shattered brigades.[41]

Once Sumner determined to use Sedgwick's division as his spearhead to seize the West Woods directly in his front, he also had to decide how best to use French's division as support for this attack. Just before the Second Corps commander reached the western edge of the East Woods, he received a dispatch from army headquarters: "Gen. Hooker appears to be driving the enemy rapidly. If he does not require your assistance on his right, please push up on his left through the ravine at the head of which the house was burned this morning, getting possession of the woods to the right as soon as possible & push on toward Sharpsburg and a little to its rear as rapidly as possible. Use your artillery freely." Sumner might have interpreted this message as McClellan's directions to attack south of the previous morning's assaults, including on ground at or near the Sunken Road. The house references in the dispatch was the Muma Farm, burned that morning by D.H. Hill's Confederate infantry.[42]

Sumner chose to send French southwest to the Sunken Road. Shortly after reaching the ground just east of the East Woods, French wheeled his division to the southwest toward the Roulette Farm, driving away the Confederate pickets who were occupying it. Once French and his lead brigade reached the Roulette Farm, his men began receiving fire from D. H. Hill's forces now holding the Sunken Road. At almost the exact moment he started his attack, French was ordered into battle by a courier from Sumner. French had deployed his division already and was moving on the Confederates in the road, eight hundred yards south of Sedgwick's line of advance.[43]

French described the situation in his after-action report:

> My division, composed of Brig. Gen. Max Weber's and Kimball's brigades, and three regiments of new levies under the command of Col. Dwight Morris (Fourteenth Connecticut), having been in readiness since daybreak on the 17th instant, was put in motion by orders of the general commanding the corps at about 7.30 o'clock a.m. The Antietam Creek was forded by the division, marching in three columns of brigades, Max Weber on the left, the new regiments in the

> center, and Kimball's brigade on the right. When my left flank had cleared the ford a mile, the division faced to the left, forming three lines of battle adjacent to and contiguous with Sedgwick's, and immediately moved to the front.
>
> The enemy, who was in position in advance, opened his batteries, under which fire my lines steadily moved until the first line, encountering the enemy's skirmishers, charged them briskly, and, entering a group of houses on Roulette's farm, drove back the force, which had taken a strong position for defense. Whilst Max Weber was clearing his front and driving before him the enemy's first line, a sudden and terrible fire was opened upon his right by the troops, which had succeeded in breaking the center division of the line of battle. At the same time a heavy column endeavored to turn my left and rear.
>
> At this moment Captain Sumner communicated to me, from the general commanding the corps, that his right divisions were being severely handled, and directed me to press the enemy with all my force.[44]

This decision is critical because it shifted the now five-hour-old battle from the West Woods south to the infamous Sunken Road or the Bloody Lane, as it came to be known. On the Union side, Israel B. Richardson's Second Corps division followed French into the desperate fight for the Sunken Road. R. H. Anderson's division was sent in to stop the Federals, inaugurating this next phase of the ever-evolving battle. The horrendous struggle for this nondescript piece of dirt road lasted for the better part of three hours and produced almost 5,500 combined casualties, or one-fifth of the casualties for the entire day.

Brig. Gen. Nathan Kimball in French's trailing brigade described the fighting in the Sunken Road:

> Directly on my front, in a narrow road running parallel with my line, and, being washed by water, forming a natural rifle-pit between my line and a large corn-field, I found the enemy in great force, as also in the corn-field in rear of the ditch. As my line advanced to the crest of the hill, a murderous fire was opened upon it from the entire force in front. My advance farther was opened upon it from the entire force in front. My advance farther was checked, and for three hours and thirty minutes the battle raged incessantly, without either

> party giving way. The enemy, having been re-enforced, made an attempt to turn my left flank by throwing three regiments forward entirely to the left of my line, which I met and repulsed, with loss, by extending my left wing, Seventh Virginia and One hundred and thirty-second Pennsylvania, in that direction. Being foiled in this, he made a heavy charge on my center, thinking to break my line, but was met by my command and repulsed with great slaughter. I then, in turn, ordered a charge, which was promptly responded to, and which resulted in driving the enemy entirely from the ditches, &c., and some distance into the corn-field beyond. In this charge my command captured about 300 prisoners, the enemy in his flight leaving on the field several stand of colors, which were taken by some parties outside of my brigade whilst we were pursuing him.[45]

Stop 9—Antietam National Battlefield, Sunken Road

(39.470725, -77.739850)

Decision—Confederate Crisis in the Sunken Road

From the Roulette Farm, follow the trail to Roulette Lane 0.025 mile to the southwest and to the Sunken Road, where one of the most dramatic events of the war took place. The best place to view the terrain relating to this decision is from the Observation Tower.

Facing east, the Pry House is about 1.25 miles in that direction and just to your left. The Dunker Church is about 0.6 mile to the northwest (behind you and to the left), and the center of the town of Sharpsburg is to your southwest (behind you and to the right). The Burnside Bridge is about 1.25 miles south (on your right).

As attack and counterattack rolled back and forth over the fields, farms, and woods of Antietam, the battle became a quagmire of Union and Confederate units. Such a mixed bag of brigades and divisions participated in the fighting that it was challenging to keep track of them all. The fight for the now infamous Sunken Road is possibly the most glaring example of this chaos. Before this portion of the battle was over, all or part of eight separate Confederate brigades were sent into the action in this sector. In total, some 6,700 Rebels were deployed at a section of ground that was roughly a half mile long and perhaps two hundred yards deep. In many cases, the Confederate units were quite literally on top of one another.

Appendix I

Confederate command losses no doubt added to the confusion. As casualties among the officer ranks mounted, more and more junior officers with little or no experience were forced to step in and lead units. In many cases, the next man in line was also killed or wounded shortly after taking command. Sometimes these officers performed well, and other times not so much.

Among the seventeen regiments in R. H. Anderson's four brigades that were the most heavily engaged at the Sunken Road, the regimental command loss rate was 82 percent. The brigade command loss rate was 75 percent. Rodes's and G. B. Anderson's Brigades of D. H. Hill's division included nine regiments that suffered a command loss rate of over 155 percent. Rodes and G. B. Anderson were also casualties, equaling a 100 percent loss rate.[46]

After falling back from South Mountain and crossing over Antietam Creek on September 15, D. H. Hill's battered division was deployed in line north of the Boonsboro Turnpike near an old worn-down farm line connecting it with Hagerstown Pike. This Sunken Road had been eroded by years of heavy wagon traffic. As a good portion of the route was several feet below ground level, it was a ready-made fighting position.

During the morning phase of the battle, Brig. Gen. Roswell Ripley's brigade of Hill's Division was sent north to support Hood's disintegrating counterattack. Subsequently, the brigades of Col. Alfred H. Colquitt and Col. Duncan K. McRae were dispatched to support Ripley. All the brigades were eventually defeated, at which point they fell back south and west.[47]

This development left the brigades of Brig. Gen. Robert Rodes and

The Sunken Road, Antietam National Battlefield, modern image. Author.

Brig. Gen. George B. Anderson to cover the position in the Sunken Road. Rodes was posted on the left and Anderson on the right. They were eventually joined by some of the survivors of Col. Alfred H. Colquitt's and Col. Duncan McRae's shattered brigades, Howell Cobb's brigade commanded by Lieut. Col. William MacRae, and the remaining survivors from the defense of Crampton's Gap. Altogether, this force totaled about 2,700 infantrymen supported by two batteries of artillery near the Piper Farm and batteries west of the Hagerstown Turnpike and on Cemetery Hill. These troops benefited from the fact that the Sunken Road was one of the few places that offered significant protection for the Confederate defenders. Rebels strengthened this position by knocking down fence rails to construct makeshift breastworks along the road.[48]

On the Union side, the two Second Corps divisions of French and Richardson assaulted the road with roughly ten thousand men in six infantry brigades supported by several batteries of artillery, including the long-range Parrott rifles east of Antietam Creek. French launched his first attack at approximately 9:00 a.m. For ninety minutes, French threw three successive waves of brigade-sized assaults directly at Rodes and Anderson. French's 5,700 infantry were decimated in the process. Following these assaults, Maj. Gen. Israel B. Richardson's division repeated the same tactics farther to French's left. Richardson's 4,200 veterans also attacked the road, basically one brigade at a time.[49]

As the fight dragged on for hours, both sides suffered a considerable number of casualties. On the Confederate side, the losses were compounded by the dead and wounded tangling the bottom of the road and the toll the battle was taking on the officers. At roughly 10:15 a.m., about the time Richardson's First Division was moving to attack the Confederate position, the last reserve division of Maj. Gen. Richard H. Anderson was ordered in to support D. H. Hill. Anderson's men, like McLaws's, had marched all night from Harpers Ferry. Just as the four thousand men in his six brigades were positioning themselves for the attack near Piper Farm, Anderson was wounded. The command of the division now fell to Brig. Gen. Roger A. Pryor. Shortly after that, a besieged Rodes found Pryor and pleaded for help to save the Confederate position.[50]

Pryor, the political general who had never commanded a division before in combat, had a critical decision to make. Biographer John C. Waugh describes the officer as a man perhaps a bit in over his head: "Roger found himself confronting what looked like Armageddon. . . . Nothing in his career in law journalism and politics prepared him for this."[51] Even so, Pryor decided to send the bulk of the division piecemeal into the cauldron of humanity that was the Sunken Road. The brigades of Brig. Gen. Ambrose R. Wright, Col. John C. Hately (Pryor), Col. Carnot Posey, and Col. Alfred Cumming were all sent to the right side of the line one after another. Two of the four brigades actually made it into the road at G. B. Anderson's position, while the other two took a position largely behind it.

As it turns out, Pryor's decision exposed his inexperience. Ezra Carman, who was no fan of the general, described a situation including confusion on Pryor's part and some unstated orders issued to Anderson: "R. H. Anderson had been wounded very soon after coming upon the field and Pryor, who succeeded to the command, was unaware of the orders under which Anderson was acting and did not rise to the occasion. The consequent movement of his command was disjointed and without proper direction, but when apprised by Rodes of the condition of affairs he ordered his own brigade forward."[52]

An officer in the Fourth North Carolina wrote, "I think Featherston (Posey) was started to the right, but instead of getting there came up behind us, where he was not needed, for we could have held our position indefinitely. He sustained significant loss in killed and wounded and I have always thought was the cause of the line breaking, for when he found he was not needed there he gave an order to fall back, which was mistaken for a general order and all that could walk went back with him, which caused a general break in the line."[53]

Pryor's decision pushed the division ahead piecemeal, and several of Anderson's four supporting brigades were soon crammed into the crowded road or just to the rear of it. This helped add to a quagmire of the living and the dead. Units intermixed, exponentially multiplying the chaos and confusion. The fact that no one Confederate officer was exercising overall command and control over the position only added the mayhem. As commands mixed, the confusion and casualties in the road mounted. In the span of a few moments, G. B. Anderson was mortally wounded; his successor, Col. Charles C. Tew, was killed by a bullet to the head; and Tew's successor, Col. Risden T. Bennett, was wounded as well. Between Rodes's and G. B. Anderson's brigades and R. H. Anderson's division, more than thirty command-level officers were killed or wounded in this chaotic and violent struggle.[54]

At approximately 11:00 a.m., Richardson's Union division was executing one last push. Caldwell's Union brigade on the right flank of the Confederate position had extended its line beyond the end of the enemy's. This end of the Confederate line then began to collapse "in great confusion." At almost that same moment, a mix-up in instructions at Rodes's position caused his portion of the line to disintegrate as well. Lieut. Col. James N. Lightfoot, whose Sixth Alabama was holding the center of the Confederate line, told

Rodes that the right wing of his regiment was exposed to enfilade fire. In response, Rodes ordered him to throw his right wing back and out of the Sunken Road. Instead of executing the order, the lieutenant colonel moved to the rear of his regiment and gave the command "Sixth Alabama, about-face; forward march." Seeing this, Major Hobson of the neighboring Fifth Alabama asked Lightfoot whether the order was intended for the whole brigade. Lightfoot answered in the affirmative, whereupon the Fifth and troops on its left withdrew. Within a matter of moments, this entire section of the line was falling back in confusion. Many Confederates did not stop running until they reached the Hagerstown Turnpike.

As the Confederate line in the road was collapsing and the fighting was falling back to the Piper Farm, James Longstreet ordered an assault on the exposed flank of Kimball's Union brigade at the extreme right of French's line. About 250 men from the Twenty-Seventh North Carolina and the Third Arkansas advanced over the Dunker Church plateau and into a cornfield and the right of Kimball's brigade. Only a desperate last-minute stand by Confederate artillery and what infantrymen could be rallied at the Piper Farm stopped the Union deluge from completely splitting the Army of Northern Virginia in two. As the Union men were now low on ammunition, they began to retreat to the Sunken Road.[55]

Rodes bore witness to the chaos and confusion that accompanied the abandonment of the Confederate position in the Sunken Road:

> Just as I was moving on after Lightfoot, I heard a shot strike Lieutenant Birney, who was immediately behind me. Wheeling, I found him falling, and found that he had been struck in the face. He found that he could walk after I raised him, though he thought a shot or piece of shell had penetrated his head just under the eye. I followed him a few paces, and watched him until he had reached a barn, a short distance to the rear, where he first encountered someone to help him in case he needed it. As I turned toward the brigade, I was struck heavily by a piece of shell on my thigh. At first I thought the wound was serious, but, finding, upon examination, that it was slight, I again turned toward the brigade, when I discovered it, without visible cause to me, retreating in confusion. I hastened to intercept it at the Hagerstown road. I found, though, that, with the exception of a few men from the Twenty-sixth, Twelfth, and Third, and a few under Major Hobson, not more than 40 in all, the brigade had completely disappeared from this portion of the field.[56]

The decision by Pryor was critical not only because it exacerbated a confused and chaotic situation, prevented any command and control within the Confederate units holding the road, and contributed to the collapse of the position. This breakdown exposed Lee's army and made it vulnerable to being split in two by any concerted Union thrust into that same area. As it turns out, that is was precisely what Maj. Gen. William B. Franklin of the Union Sixth Corps, was hoping would happen.

From the tower walk northwest about one thousand feet, and you will pick up the trail just past the 130th Pennsylvania Monument. This trail will take you back to the visitor center.

Stop 10—Antietam National Battlefield, Burnside Bridge

(39.469449, -77.736036)

Decision—Locating Snavely's Ford

Return to your car, and from the visitor center turn left on Dunker Church Road. After 338 feet, turn left onto Maryland Route 65. Drive for 0.9 mile, turn left onto East Main Street, drive 0.6 mile to Rodman Avenue, and turn right. After 0.5 mile, turn left onto Old Burnside Bridge Road, follow the road for 0.5 mile to the Burnside Bridge parking lot, and park your vehicle here.

Take the path to the bridge itself, and cross over to the Union side of Antietam Creek. Continue walking east to the tree line, and turn around to face the bridge. This is the ground that part of the Ninth Corps charged over to assault the bridge. During the battle, Burnside was actually much farther east (behind you), but you cannot see the bridge from that location. The town of Sharpsburg is about 1,500 yards to the northwest (to your right and in front). Harpers Ferry Road is about 1,400 yards to the west (straight ahead). Snavely's Ford is about 1,500 yards southwest (to your right and in front), and McClellan's headquarters at the Pry House is about 2.0 miles to the northeast (behind you and to the right).

Even for those with scant knowledge of the war, merely uttering the name Burnside Bridge manifests very distinct and dramatic imagery in the mind's eye. However, very little of that imagery sheds positive light on Ambrose E. Burnside.

Like McClellan, Burnside has become somewhat of a historical scapegoat over the past 150 years, with books and manuscripts often potraying him as little more than an affable buffoon. [57]

Unlike McClellan, Burnside now found himself in a somewhat ill-defined and awkward role on September 17. With the First Corps on the

Burnside's Bridge, Antietam National Battlefield, modern image. Author.

opposite side of the Antietam Battlefield, he was a wing commander with no wing to command. With Jesse Reno's death at Fox's Gap on the fourteenth, Jacob Cox now commanded the Ninth Corps. Burnside was acting like a corps commander in many ways, passing orders back and forth between army headquarters and the Ninth Corps. Cox offered to return to his divisional command and allow Burnside to lead the corps, complaining in part that his staff was not equipped to manage a corps. However, Burnside considered this arrangement a demotion and would not permit it.[58]

As the Ninth Corps moved into line on September 15 on the Union left, McClellan's plans for it and the entire army began to take shape. As noted in discussion of an earlier decision, McClellan intended the Ninth Corps to be a critical part of his overall tactical plan in one form or another. The Union commander stated, "My plan for the impending general engagement was to attack the enemy's left with the corps of Hooker and Mansfield, supported by Sumner's and, if necessary, by Franklin's, and, as soon as matters looked favorably there, to move the corps of Burnside against the enemy's extreme right, upon the ridge running to the south and rear of Sharpsburg, and, having carried their position, to press along the crest toward our right, and, whenever either of these flank movements should be successful, to advance our center with all the forces then disposable."[59]

Appendix I

Antietam Creek stood in between the enemy's extreme right and the Ninth Corps, with the Lower Bridge as the most efficient way to traverse it. It is important to remember that neither the bridge nor the creek was ever Burnside's objective. As McClellan indicated, the Ninth Corps was focused on the high ground and road to Shepherdstown beyond it on Lee's line of retreat. The creek was now an obstacle to that objective, and the bridge was but one of several ways to surmount it. As it turns out, most significant among these was Snavely's Ford about a mile downstream of the bridge.[60]

On September 16, McClellan and his staff rode to the Ninth Corps headquarters to realign the placement of the unit's four divisions. The Union commander wanted to ensure that they were positioned to defend any potential attack from the direction of Harpers Ferry. He also gave Burnside an overview of his general plan and of what he expected from the Ninth Corps in the coming battle. In addition, McClellan brought along two of his engineers who informed Burnside and Cox of a usable ford located about half a mile downstream. No specific location for the crossing was given, but it was touted as a suitable place to move infantry across to threaten the Confederate position in flank and rear. About 3,200 men were selected for the operation, including Brig. Gen. Isaac P. Rodman's division with Col. Hugh Ewing's brigade from the Kanawha Division. This force was then placed on the left end of the line in preparation for the next day's assault. Burnside's other three divisions, totaling roughly 9,800, would be positioned adjacent to the bridge to be used as the main force assaulting it. The other brigade of Col. Eliakim P. Scammon's and Brig. Gen. Samuel D. Sturgis's divisions would be in front, and Brig. Gen. Orlando B. Wilcox's division was in reserve.[61]

The Confederate position on the west side of the bridge was thinly held to say the least. Once Walker's Division was pulled back to reinforce Lee's embattled left shortly after 9:00 a.m., only three undersized Georgia regiments (about five hundred men)[62] commanded by Brig. Gen. Robert Toombs of Brig. Gen. David R. Jones's division were left to defend a line roughly a mile long. From left to right, they were the Twentieth, Second, and Fiftieth Georgia. This tiny force's defense was aided by the creek itself and its steep banks. While not terribly deep, the creek provided a genuine obstacle to any Union assault. Arriving on the field on September 15, Toombs and his men had almost two full days to strengthen their position. Some of the Georgians took shelter in an old rock quarry directly above the bridge, while others piled up stones, fence rail, and logs as defilade. Still other Confederates took position behind trees adjacent to the bridge, and some dug shallow trenches with their bayonets. Supported by several batteries of artillery, Toombs's position was not a Gibraltar, but it was as strong as he could make it.[63]

While the Union infantry could wade the creek at several different places, the Federals needed something more substantial to get their artillery across. This made the bridge the critical objective for the Ninth Corps. In his after-action report, Toombs described his position at that point:

> The Antietam River runs comparatively straight from a point about 100 paces above the bridge to a point about 300 paces below the bridge, and then curves suddenly around a hill to a ford on a neighborhood road. About 600 yards to my right and rear the road from Sharpsburg to Harper's Ferry from the foot of the bridge over the Antietam turns suddenly down the river, and runs nearly upon its margin for about 300 paces; then leaves the river nearly at right angles. Upon examining the position, I found a narrow wood upon the margin of the river just above the bridge (an important and commanding position) occupied by a company of Texans from Brigadier-General Hood's command. I then ordered the Twentieth to take position, with its left near the foot of the bridge, on the Sharpsburg side, extending down the river near its margin, and the Second Georgia on its right, prolonging the line down to the point where the road on the other side from the mountain approached the river. This required a more open order than was desirable, on account of the smallness of the regiments, both together numbering but a little over 400 muskets.[64]

At 7:00 a.m. on the morning of September 17, Burnside received an order from army headquarters to ready his infantry for the attack on the bridge. However, the order for him to attack would not reach him until three hours later, at 10:00 a.m. Burnside now had all the pieces in place, or so he thought. Whether he knew it or not, the location for the crossing for Rodman's force would be critical to the impending struggle.[65]

In his after-action report, Burnside quoted Cox's description of the Confederate position: "The turns of the roadway were covered by rifle-pits and breastworks made of rails and stone, all of which defenses, as well as the woods which covered the slope, were filled with the enemy's infantry and sharpshooters. Besides the infantry defenses, batteries were placed to enfilade the bridge and all its approaches. The crest of the first hill above the bridge is curved toward the stream at the extremes, forming a sort of natural tete-de-pont [French, meaning strategically important area of ground around the end of a bridge]."[66]

In his *Battles and Leaders* article, Jacob D. Cox, perhaps with a backward glance, bemoaned the assignment facing the Ninth Corps and the logic of the overall plan: "It is hardly disputable that this would have been a better plan than the one actually carried out. Certainly the assumption that the Ninth Corps could cross the Antietam alone at the only place on the field where the Confederates had their line immediately upon the stream which must be crossed under fire by two narrow heads of column, and could then turn to the right along the high ground occupied by the hostile army before that army had been broken or seriously shaken elsewhere, is one which would hardly be made till time had dimmed the remembrance of the actual positions of Lee's divisions upon the field."[67]

Knowing that he could not launch an attack on the flank of the Confederate army until he got his forces across the bridge, Burnside needed to do so as quickly as he possibly could. Any frontal assaults on the Confederate position would no doubt be contested and take some time to execute. Ensuring that Rodman's flanking force reached a better position to execute the movement on the ford and confirming that location would be critical to the day's success. An adequate place for this force to cross would seem too important a detail to leave unconfirmed.

On the other hand, Burnside might feel that affirming a crossing place was not his job. On paper at least, Jacob Cox was now the commander of the Ninth Corps after Reno's death. Every time Burnside received an order from army headquarters, he immediately gave it to Cox to execute. Burnside might have believed any additional reconnaissance of the field to be Cox's responsibility as corps commander.

Burnside and the staff of the Ninth Corps might also assume that McClellan's engineers knew what they were talking about, and that the ford would be easily identifiable. There would be no reason to confirm its location, as they needed to simply follow the instructions given to them. Burnside might also see Rodman's force as merely a supporting role to the main assault on the bridge and therefore devote the majority of his attention to that task. Additionally, despite his recent communication issues with McClellan, Burnside must have retained a level of trust in his old friend.

Moreover, Burnside might have believed that his force was large and powerful enough to quickly take the Confederate position at the bridge with a straightforward frontal assault. If Burnside felt he could overwhelm the bridge's defenders swiftly, why he give any thought to Rodman if he was not foremost in his mind? Lastly, the Confederates might observe any attempt to move Rodman closer to his position or send a scouting party along the east bank of the creek. If that happened before Walker's men were pulled from the position, Lee might not order them to move after all.

Past historians have described a sulking and petulant Burnside at Antietam, citing his perceived demotion from wing commander and recent rebukes from McClellan as causes for his delays and poor decision-making. While more recent scholarship still questions his decision-making, it paints a very different and slightly more positive picture of Ambrose Burnside.[68]

Burnside decided to send the attack forward on September 17 with the information he had at hand. Rodman's force was directed to move to the ford that McClellan's engineers had indicated the day before. However, the ford that Rodman found was initially unusable; the banks were far too rocky and steep for his men and artillery to cross. Forced to search for a different crossing point much farther downstream (Snavely's Ford), he lost valuable time in the process. Rodman did not get his division across the creek until approximately 1:00 p.m., three hours after the main attack on the bridge had begun. By that time, the rest of the Ninth Corps had launched three successive bloody assaults at the bridge. By the last assault, the Confederate defenders were extremely low on ammunition and forced to retreat. The Ninth Corps suffered over five hundred casualties taking the bridge.[69]

Burnside's decision is critical because the hours it took to overcome obstacles had a definite and observable outcome on the battle. Nearly five hours had passed by the time he was able to attack and overcome the Confederate defenders, finally get his corps across the creek, and then get his men re-armed, reorganized, and ready to move forward. Just as Burnside's objective was within his grasp, A. P. Hill's division arrived from Harpers Ferry just in time to stop him, thus ending the final Union attacks for the day.

Stop 11—Antietam National Cemetery / Cemetery Hill

302 East Main Street, Sharpsburg, Maryland 21782 (39.460307, -77.741752)

This location will concern out next three critical decisions.

From the Burnside Bridge parking lot, head north on Old Burnside Bridge Road for 0.5 mile. This road turns into Branch Avenue. Follow Branch Avenue for 0.9 mile, and turn right onto Harpers Ferry Road. After 0.6 mile, this road turns into South Mechanic Street as you enter the town. Go 0.2 mile farther, and turn right onto East Main Street. Stay on Main (Maryland Route 34) for 0.4 mile, and the destination will be on the right. The National Cemetery is open from 9:00 a.m. to 5:00 p.m. seven days a week. You can park on the street or in the parking lot just east of the cemetery on the north side of the road. In 1862, this piece of high ground just east of Sharpsburg and straddling the Boonsboro Pike (modern Maryland Route 34), was referred to as Cemetery Hill because of the old Lutheran cemetery located just east of the town.

Appendix I

First, enter the private Mountain View Cemetery on the north side of the road, and follow the footpath about two hundred feet to the north until you reach high ground. If you face due north, you will see more high ground and the visitor center just short of one mile away. The Cornfield is about 0.5 mile beyond that position. You can also see the Observation Tower at the Sunken Road to the northeast (in front and to your right). The Antietam Creek is about 0.93 miles east of you (on your right), and the Potomac River is about 1.75 miles due west of you (on your left). Burnside Bridge is located about 0.88 mile to your southeast (behind you and to the right).

It is possible that Lee observed some of the morning phases of the battle near this spot. Our next decision will be discussed at this location.

Decision—Lee Commits His Reserves

As a critical piece of terrain, this location served as a position for Longstreet's reserve artillery during most of September 17 and as the center of the Confederate line held by Brig. Gen. David R. Jones's division and Brig. Gen. Nathan G. Evans's brigade. Robert E. Lee also spent some time here observing the battle during those desperate early morning hours. This location was one of the few places from which Lee could see almost every other critical position on the field.[70]

By 7:30 a.m., the situation for Lee and his Army of Northern Virginia was dire indeed. Since first light, the battle had raged back and forth across the area around the Cornfield and the East and West Woods multiple times. In a little over two hours of almost continuous combat, twelve of the thirteen Confederate infantry brigades on the northern end of the field were effectively taken out of action. Of the ten thousand Confederates engaged up until this point, over 30 percent were now casualties. In addition, over 30 percent of J. R. Jones's and Alexander Lawton's divisions had become casualties, and John Bell Hood's division had suffered a casualty rate approaching 50 percent. Every one of the four regimental commanders in Law's Brigade of Hood's Division was wounded.

Jackson's two divisions were also decimated at the command level. Alexander Lawton and J. R. Jones were both wounded. Jones's replacement, Brig. Gen. William E. Starke, was killed, leaving a colonel to lead the division. All but one of the commanders of the eight brigades in these two divisions were now dead or wounded.

By 8:30 a.m., out of all of the Confederate forces initially deployed north of the Boonsboro Turnpike, only Jubal Early's brigade and two of D. H. Hill's five brigades holding the Sunken Road had not been committed. D. H. Hill's counterattack with three of his five brigades was now falling back after running headlong into the Union Twelfth Corps.[71]

In his autobiography, Longstreet summed up the morning's engagement:

> As Jackson withdrew, General Hooker's corps retired to a point on the Hagerstown road about three-quarters of a mile north of the battleground, where General Doubleday established his thirty-gun battery. Jackson's and Hooker's men had fought to exhaustion, and the battle of the Twelfth Corps, taken up and continued by Mansfield, had taken defensive relations, its chief mortally wounded. Generals Lawton, Ripley, and J. R. Jones were severely wounded, and Colonel Douglas, commanding Lawton's brigade, killed. A third of the men of Lawton's, Hays's, and Trimble's brigades were reported killed or wounded. Four of the field officers of Colquitt's brigade were killed, five were wounded, the tenth and last contused by a shell. All of Jackson's and D. H. Hill's troops engaged suffered proportionally. Hood's, Walker's, and G. T. Anderson's, though longer engaged, did not lose so severely.[72]

The Union had fared little better. The seventeen thousand men that made up the fifteen brigades in the two attacking Union corps had suffered over four thousand casualties. Though to a lesser extent than the Rebel command, the Union command structure was also significantly impacted by casualties. Both of the Federal corps commanders were now wounded, and while Hooker survived his injury, Mansfield perished the following day.[73]

By 8:30 a.m., the Federals had established a tenuous hold on the ground east of the Hagerstown Turnpike and north of the West Woods. This terrain included the critical high ground east of the church that was the objective of Hooker's initial advance. As the battlefield became uncharacteristically quiet, the lead elements of Sedgwick's division were at this moment entering the East Woods. They would be engaged shortly. It is unclear whether Lee was aware of this fact, but it is reasonable to assume that he considered a Union reinforcement on his left a foregone conclusion. In the meantime, the sector south of the Boonsboro Turnpike had seen very little if any offensive action by the Federals to this point.[74]

John R. Jones outlined the situation in an excerpt from his after-action report:

> The infantry became at once engaged, and the gallant and generous Starke fell, pierced by three balls, and survived but a few moments.

Appendix I

View looking north from Cemetery Hill, Antietam National Battlefield, modern image. Author.

> His fall cast a gloom over the troops. They never for a moment faltered, but rushed upon the enemy and drove him back. The struggle continued for several hours, the enemy all the while receiving re-enforcements, and the division, not numbering over 1,600 men at the beginning of the fight, having no support, was finally compelled to fall back to its original line. Early's brigade coming up at this opportune moment, Colonel Grigsby, commanding the division, rallied its shattered columns and joined General Early, and drove the enemy half a mile from the field, capturing many prisoners and covering the field with the dead and wounded of the enemy.[75]

Sometime before 8:00 a.m., two urgent messages found the Confederate commander near Cemetery Hill. Earlier that morning, D. H. Hill had requested permission to send his division to the support of the embattled Confederate left. In his latest message, relayed by his adjutant, Hill was seeking support for his own position as fresh Union forces were now massing in his front. The second communication Lee received was from Jackson, and it conveyed John Bell Hood's dire prediction of the imminent collapse of the Confederate left.[76]

With the outcome of the battle now seriously in doubt, Lee had yet another critical decision to make. The general still had almost seven thousand men in the two reserve divisions of Lafayette McLaws and Robert H. Anderson. However, both of these exhausted divisions had arrived just that morning, having marched from Maryland Heights via Harpers Ferry, Charlestown, and Shepherdstown. Moreover, Lee had no real idea as to when A. P. Hill would arrive from Harpers Ferry, and his reserve forces were limited.[77]

Significantly and essentially, Lee had felt little or no pressure from the Union forces on his right prior to this point in the battle. While he was undoubtedly concerned about attacks on his vulnerable center and right from the Union Fifth and Ninth Corps, only artillery fire and some preliminary infantry movement had been detected in these sectors. This might have persuaded Lee that there was minimal risk in shifting forces from here to support his left.[78]

It is also possible that Lee saw an opportunity to launch a massive counterattack at McClellan's right or to slip around the Union army and escape north. We do know he would consider such a move later on that afternoon, and perhaps the idea was in his head at this moment. Giving up the ground on the left would make that move impossible to execute. Lee selected this ground partly because its interior lines and network of roads and farm lanes would allow him to efficiently move elements of his army from one point to another.[79]

Borne either from his innate aggressiveness or his belief that he simply had no choice, Lee bolstered his imperiled left by sending every available man he could into the fight north of the Boonsboro Pike. By 9:30 a.m., Lee had committed roughly nine thousand men from Walker's, McLaws's, and R. H. Anderson's divisions and Col. George T. Anderson's brigade into the maelstrom on the left. The result was the complete routing of Sedgwick's division in the West Woods and the escalation of the combat in the Sunken Road. Fighting at both locations was dramatically affected by the infusion of the Confederate units.[80]

Lee highlighted this fact in his after-action report: "Upon the arrival of the re-enforcements under General McLaws, General Early attacked with great resolution the large force opposed to him. McLaws advanced at the same time, and the enemy were driven back in confusion, closely followed by our troops beyond the position occupied at the beginning of the engagement. The enemy renewed the assault on our left several times, but was repulsed with loss. He finally ceased to advance his infantry, and for several hours kept up a furious fire from his numerous batteries, under which our troops held their position with great coolness and courage."[81]

Lee's decision is critical because it provided just enough manpower to help blunt the final Union assaults on his left. McLaws and G. T. Anderson struck Sumner in the West Woods, while Walker attacked south of the Dunker Church. R. H. Anderson's division was sent to reinforce D. H. Hill's two brigades at the Sunken Road, ultimately forcing a stalemate on the Confederate left. This action went a long way toward convincing Union commanders not to launch any significant assaults on Lee's left after the fight at Sunken Road, thus bringing the savage battle on this end of the field to an end.

Pulling John Walker's division away from its position defending Snavely's Ford downstream of the Lower Bridge was perhaps the most significant result of Lee's decision to reinforce his left. The ford provided a direct line for any Union force that could cross it to potentially block the road to Shepherdstown, Lee's only line of retreat. As we will discuss later on, it took McClellan's army several hours to take advantage of this opportunity.[82]

Stop 11A—Antietam National Cemetery

Cross to the south side of Main Street (Maryland Route 34), and enter the National Cemetery. Just inside the wall on your left as you enter the cemetery, you will see a cannon that represents Squires's Battery, First Company, Washington Artillery of New Orleans commanded by Capt. Charles W. Squires. Walk to the easternmost wall of the cemetery. This is considered hallowed ground, so please be respectful.

Because this location provides the best view of this part of the battlefield, we will review the next two decisions here.

Decision—The Fifth Corps Does Not Advance

Fitz John Porter's Fifth Corps had only two divisions present (Morell's and Sykes's) at the time the battle began on the seventeenth. Humphreys's division would not join the army until the morning of September 18. After arriving on the field east of Antietam Creek with the rest of the army on September 15, Sykes and eventually Morell were positioned just east of the Middle Bridge straddling the Boonsboro Turnpike.[83]

By 2:00 p.m., the next phase of the Battle of Antietam was in full swing. The fighting by now had shifted south, and until sunset, the lion's share of the conflict would take place south of the Boonsboro Pike.

Sometime before noon, Pleasonton was ordered forward with a combined force and artillery to support the attack at the Sunken Road. By 12:15 p.m. this advance, aided at times by the Union guns in position east of the creek, had secured the bridge and was driving the thin Confederate line west toward the town. Sykes began to feed in several infantry units to support this engagement as it progressed. By 1:00 p.m. these Fifth Corps units had all but replaced Pleasonton's cavalry west of the creek, and the cavalrymen had retired to Middle Bridge.

View Looking east from the National Cemetery, Antietam National Battlefield, modern image. Author.

By 3:00 p.m., part of Lieut. Col. Robert C. Buchanan's brigade and part of Maj. Charles S. Lovell's brigade of Sykes's division had advanced some six hundred yards west of the creek and become engaged with the thinly held Confederate position on high ground just east of Sharpsburg. The Fifth Corps' advance across the creek was now about 1,640 men strong and directly supported by three batteries of artillery.[84]

South of the Middle Bridge, the Ninth Corps had established its bridgehead and was almost entirely across the bridge the troops had battled for three hours to seize. Within the hour, they would be advancing en masse on Lee's right. Meanwhile, all of the fighting at the Sunken Road and north of it had come to an end. With the exception of the high ground at Cemetery Hill and in and around the Piper Farm, the Army of the Potomac had secured all the terrain north of the Boonsboro Turnpike and east of the Hagerstown Turnpike.[85]

To defend his center, Lee had perhaps three thousand infantrymen in Brig. Gen. David R. Jones's division and Brig. Gen. Nathan G. Evans's brigade. These were supported by Col. Thomas A. Munford's cavalry brigade and five artillery batteries. After getting urgent messages from Lee, A. P. Hill was driving his division forward from Harpers Ferry at a staggering pace. However, his ever-dwindling force was still two hours away.[86]

By 4:30 p.m., the Union troops in the center had advanced and were now pushing the Confederate defenders up the eastern face of Cemetery Hill.

On their left, the Ninth Corps had launched its assault on the high ground south of town. Convinced that the time had come for a stronger advance, Pleasonton sent an urgent request to Porter to send the balance of his corps across the creek, attack in force at the disintegrating Confederate position, and place enfilading batteries on the high ground.

Pleasonton wrote in his after-action report:

> It was now 4 o'clock in the afternoon. Burnside's corps had driven the enemy back upon the hill upon which his batteries were placed, and, in conjunction with the repulse of the enemy in front of Hancock, left the field open to the Sharpsburg Ridge, to which point I desired to forward my batteries, to obtain an enfilading fire upon the enemy in front of Burnside, and enable Sumner to advance to Sharpsburg. I was so satisfied that this could be done at that moment, that I sent a request to Major General Fitz John Porter, asking for the assistance of some infantry to support my advance to the Sharpsburg Ridge."[87]

With the outcome of the battle still in doubt, McClellan had yet one more critical decision to make. McClellan in all likelihood still believed Robert E. Lee had a significant force at his disposal. If McClellan remained preoccupied with the prospect of a Confederate counterattack, an advance by Porter might be too risky a venture. This situation is particularly revealing when you consider that the specter of the recent defeat at Second Bull Run lingered in everyone's mind. The pressure on the Union high command not to repeat such a disaster might have been so palpable that it overwhelmingly influenced decision-making at several points during the campaign.

While accounts differ as to the exact timing and who said what and when, McClellan, either independently or on Porter's advice, declined to send the rest of Fifth Corps in an advance west of Antietam Creek. Porter mentioned this critical moment in his after-action report:

> Still later in the afternoon, I received from General Pleasonton a call for a division to press the success obtained by this small band of regulars, accompanied by the statement that Burnside and Sumner were driving the enemy. Between the dispatching and receiving of that call the tide of battle had changed. Our troops on the left under Burnside had been driven from the heights which they had so gallantly crowned, while those on the immediate right, under Sumner,

> were held in check. The army was at a stand. I had not the force asked for, and could not, under my orders, risk the safety of the artillery and center of the line, and perhaps imperil the success of the day by further diminishing my small command, not then 4,000 strong—then in the front line and unsupported, and protecting all our trains. Before dark General Sykes had ordered Lieutenant Miller to report with his battery to General Burnside. Colonel Warren, with his brigade, had been sent earlier in the day.[88]

With no additional forces to support them, the Fifth Corps men west of Antietam Creek only advanced to within a few hundred yards of the town before they were forced to fall back. No additional Fifth Corps units were sent across the creek that day, so Burnside's advancing divisions subsequently attacked unsupported. At approximately 4:00 p.m., Burnside's three divisions were steadily advancing at Harpers Ferry Road to the west, only to have their left collapse after A. P. Hill's Confederate division hit it in the flank. After a desperate struggle, the Ninth Corps attack lost momentum and was forced to fall back to the creek. The Battle of Antietam slowly flickered out along with the fading light of the setting sun.

One famous and often-disputed account tells of a reluctant McClellan prepared to advance his reserves into the fray once again, only to be ominously informed by his confidant Porter, *"Remember, General I command the last reserve of the last Army of the Republic."* Whether this incident is fact or fiction, for the second or possibly even the third time that day, the high command of the Union Army of the Potomac did not commit its reserve forces at a possible critical point of the battle.[89]

Decision—McClellan Does Not Attack

On September 18, 1862, the cool and foggy dawn broke on the fields and farms around Sharpsburg, Maryland. As the mist slowly cleared, it revealed the death and devastation that the previous day's struggle had brought. On the Confederate side of the line, Robert E. Lee and his battered Army of Northern Virginia braced themselves for renewed fighting. On the Union side, McClellan and his army spent that morning waiting for reinforcements to arrive. In the meantime, the Federal commander busied himself by sending telegrams to the War Department and letters to his wife. While his communication with Maj. Gen. H. W. Halleck was somewhat reserved, McClellan's letter to his wife, Mary Ellen, took a decidedly different tone, extolling his performance of the day before.[90]

Appendix I

To Halleck, McClellan wrote as follows: "The battle of yesterday continued for fourteen hours, and until after dark. We held all we gained, except a portion of the extreme left; that was obliged to abandon a part of what it had gained. Our losses very heavy, especially in general officers. The battle will probably be renewed to-day. Send all the troops you can by the most expeditious route."[91] In contrast, he sent this message to Mary Ellen:

> We fought yesterday a terrible battle against the entire rebel Army. The battle continued 14 hours & was terrific—the fighting on both sides was superb. The general result was in our favor, that is to say we gained a great deal of ground & held it. It was a success, but whether a decided victory depends on what occurs today. I hope that God has given us a great success. It is all in his hands, where I am content to leave it. The spectacle yesterday was the grandest I could conceive of; nothing could be more sublime. Those in whose judgement I rely on tell me I fought the battle splendidly & and that it was a masterpiece of art.[92]

Both sides began the onerous task of caring for the almost twenty thousand wounded men now scattered across the field. The difficulty of recovering and caring for the wounded was compounded by the fact that no official truce had been called.

George McClellan's view across the lines told him that the Confederates, while more concentrated than the day before, were still there. Meanwhile, the soldiers in the Army of the Potomac anxiously awaited a battle they, too, presumed would very soon recommence. The Union commander could only speculate about the damage he had inflicted on his opponent, but he was no doubt getting preliminary returns on the losses his own forces had suffered. In twelve hours of fighting, over twelve thousand Union men became casualties, or just over 21 percent of those engaged. Among McClellan's corps and division commanders, losses were over 30 percent.[93]

By that morning, McClellan had the whole of his army on the west side of Antietam Creek save the reserve artillery, the cavalry, and some units of the Fifth Corps. These troops could cross the creek uncontested whenever they wished. On the right, the Federal line now started at a point about half a mile north of the Joseph Poffenberger Farm and a few hundred yards east of the Hagerstown Pike. It then meandered southward along the Mumma Farm, along the Sunken Road to a point just east of and just below the Lower Bridge.[94]

Each commander's clouded view of his opponent's strength remained; neither man knew precisely what numbers he was facing. By noon that day, McClellan received what amounted to a brand-new corps. An additional twelve thousand men now reinforced the Union army, including Brig. Gen. Darius Couch's Fourth Corps division attached to Franklin's Sixth Corps and Brig. Gen. Andrew A. Humphreys's Fifth Corps division. These men almost entirely replaced the Union losses from the previous day's fighting. McClellan now had somewhere between fifty thousand and sixty thousand men of all arms to use in a potential renewed attack.[95]

Across the field, the injured Rebel army stood defiantly. Robert E. Lee's contracted line started on his left, just west of the Hagerstown Pike at the north end of the West Woods. The formation followed the pike into the town and along the heights of Harpers Ferry Road south of Sharpsburg. It ended at roughly the same point the Union army's line did, only several hundred yards farther west. J. E. B. Stuart's cavalry still held positions on each flank. Over the next several days, Lee's army managed to gather up roughly six thousand stragglers to add to his various commands, thereby covering nearly half of his losses from the battle on September 17. While it is unclear how many stragglers arrived on the eighteenth, it is estimated that Lee could now field an army of between twenty-five thousand and thirty thousand men. However, it is safe to say that these men probably were not in prime fighting condition. Lee's troops as a whole were exhausted and worn out. While the

Antietam National Cemetery, modern image. Author.

aforementioned details were significant, the state of Lee's army was no doubt unknown to McClellan and his staff.[96]

In his 1863 after-action report, McClellan stated, "The night, however, brought with it grave responsibilities. Whether to renew the attack on the 18th or to defer it, even with the risk of the enemy's retirement, was the question before me."[97] On the day after the bloodiest one-day battle of the war, George B. McClellan had one more critical decision to make.

The Union commander now had thousands of fresh troops that he could make use of. Both the Sixth and Fifth Corps had been only lightly engaged the day before, and these units were augmented by Couch's and Humphreys's divisions. By some estimates, McClellan now had thirty thousand fresh infantrymen at his disposal, only one-third fewer men than he had committed to battle the day before. While he presumably did not realize it, the general now outnumbered his opponent by two to one. If he did not believe that corps that had launched offensives on Wednesday were able to participate in new attacks, he could count on them to at least hold the ground already gained.

Although we don't know precisely what McClellan's perception of Lee's army was on September 18, he needed only to look at the casualties on the field to know that his army had given the enemy a real beating. There was a good chance the Rebels were in no shape to defend themselves. The fact that Lee's anticipated counterattack never materialized might also have been a telling clue as to the state of the Confederate army.[98]

The Federal commander also had most of his forces west of Antietam Creek, and he held all the critical crossing points. As a result, Lee could no longer count on the creek on being a significant obstacle to the Union army. It seems that some of McClellan's corps and division commanders were in favor of continuing the offensive. William B. Franklin, for example, was still eager to lead his Sixth Corps back into the fray, or so he later wrote:

> Later in the day General McClellan came again to my headquarters, and there was pointed out to him a hill on the right, commanding the wood, and it was proposed that the hill should be occupied by our artillery early the next morning, and that after shelling the wood, the attack should be made by the whole corps from the position then held by it. He assented to this, and it was understood that the attack was to be made. During the night, however, the order was countermanded. I met him about 9 o'clock on the morning of the 18th. He informed me that he countermanded the order because fifteen thousand Pennsylvania troops would soon arrive, and that upon their arrival the attack would be ordered.[99]

Additionally, the Army of Northern Virginia was at this moment still north of the Potomac River. One of McClellan's objectives in the campaign was driving the Rebels from the state of Maryland, and so long as Lee remained in the North, that part of his operational objective was not realized. There was at that moment no guarantee that Lee would retreat on his own. Additional combat might be required to persuade him to do so.[100]

In the fight for the ground at Antietam, the Army of the Potomac had suffered over 21 percent casualties—not an insignificant number. From wounding and/or death, McClellan had lost two of his six corps commanders, and if counting Reno's death at South Mountain, he had lost three corps commanders. McClellan had also lost five of sixteen division commanders. Most devastating of all, however, was the Union command's loss of 52 of its 165 brigade and regimental commanders—a casualty rate of almost 32 percent—along with an untold number of company-grade and noncommissioned officers. Casualties in the officer and noncommissioned officer ranks dramatically compromised McClellan's ability to exercise command and control. To effectively maneuver and deploy their forces in combat, nineteenth-century armies relied heavily on the experience and knowledge of brigade- and regimental-level commissioned and noncommissioned officers.[101]

While McClellan did indeed have some fresh infantry, the four corps most heavily engaged the day before were in deplorable shape. While reports contradict, indications are that the First Corps had suffered 2,590 total casualties, or 27 percent of its men; the Second Corps suffered 5,138 total losses, or 32 percent; the Ninth Corps suffered 2,349 total casualties, or 19 percent; and the Twelfth Corps suffered 1,746 total losses, or 23 percent. McClellan had also expected Brig. Gen. John Reynolds to come from Pennsylvania with 15,000 militia; however, those troops refused to cross the border into Maryland.

It should also be noted that Humphreys's division of Pennsylvanians of the Fifth Corps, arriving before noon, was made up entirely of green regiments. To get to Antietam Creek on September 18 from Washington, DC, Humphreys had marched his division for four straight days, and McClellan deemed the troops fatigued. While Humphreys disputed this claim, he could not dispute the men's glaring lack of combat experience. Many of the rookie regiments who had fought on the seventeenth suffered immeasurably due to their inexperience.

The Union men were also reaching the end of their endurance. The previous day, McClellan's army had fought continuously from dawn until dusk. Collectively, the Army of the Potomac had been marching and/or fighting since it left the defenses of Washington, DC, thirteen days before. Many units, like the First Corps, had not only fought on the seventeenth but also been heavily engaged in the struggle for South Mountain on the fourteenth, a significant battle in its own right.[102]

Additionally, while damaged and somewhat disorganized, most of the Union army's artillery had enough ammunition for another engagement. However, the long-range twenty-pound Parrott rifles, so essential to counter-battery fire the day before, had mostly empty caissons. The promised ammunition was miles away, and replenishment would take some time.[103]

Based on the evidence, McClellan had good reason to believe that Robert E. Lee still outnumbered him and that the long-expected Confederate counterattack was inevitable. If McClellan exposed himself too much, he might be playing right into Lee's hands. In any case, it appears that Lee expected another day of battle and was waiting for it, as illustrated by his unwillingness to retreat after the fighting on September 17.[104]

Lastly, adding to McClellan's tactical and logistical dilemmas was the fact that the dysentery that had afflicted him since his time in Mexico flared up yet again. The commander was ill for the next several days.[105]

McClellan wrote on September 18, "After a night of anxious deliberation and a full and careful survey of the situation and condition of our army, the strength and position of the enemy, I concluded that the success of an attack on the 18th was not certain.[106] In his 1863 after-action report, The Union commander outlined the reasoning behind his decision not to renew the assault:

> The troops were greatly overcome by the fatigue and exhaustion attendant upon the long continued and severely contested battle of the 17th, together with the long day and night marches to which they had been subjected during the previous three days. The supply trains were in the rear, and many of the troops had suffered from hunger. They required rest and refreshment. One division of Sumner's and all of Hooker's corps on the right had, after fighting most valiantly for several hours, been overpowered by numbers, driven back in great disorder, and much scattered, so that they were for the time somewhat demoralized. In Hooker's corps, according to the return made by General Meade, commanding, there were but 6,729 men present on the 18th, whereas on the morning of the 22nd there were 13,093 men present for duty in the same corps, showing that previous to and during the battle 6,364 men were separated from their command.[107]

McClellan did give orders that night to prepare for an assault on September 19, but when the Federals stirred to life the following morning, they discovered the Confederates were gone.

While circumspect, McClellan's decision is critical because it helped mark the conclusion of this battle. The commander's choice also ensured that no additional Union assaults would be made at Sharpsburg. Rebels and Federals observed one another warily as September 18 came and went. The Battle of Antietam was technically over, but the decision was not absolute. The end of the fighting and the overall campaign now hinged on the outcome of Robert E. Lee's next and final decision.

Other than the unknown number of stragglers that joined the army, Lee had essentially no more reserves to commit to a renewed fight. His men were desperately tired and just as worn down as their opponents, if not more so. This fact alone, however, would not have made a more decisive victory by McClellan a certainty. Nor would it have guaranteed the destruction of Lee's army. Additionally, both armies would inevitably have suffered additional casualties in renewed fighting on the eighteenth, and recovery from this would have indeed taken more time than it did.

After the war, Longstreet summed up the Confederate position this way: "We were so badly crushed that at the close of the day ten thousand fresh troops could have come in and taken Lee's army and everything it had."[108] We will never know if he was correct in this assessment or merely adding to a narrative.

Stop 12—Lee's Headquarters, Sharpsburg, Maryland

17424 Shepherdstown Pike, Sharpsburg, Maryland 21782
(39.455190, -77.760081)

Return to your car, and head southwest on the Shepherdstown Pike (Maryland Route 34 / Main Street). After 1.0 mile, just beyond the town of Sharpsburg on the right, you will see a grove of trees in what looks like a park. There, Lee's headquarters site during the battle is marked with a sign and stone marker. Park on the right, and walk to the marker at the center of the field. As you face the marker, you are looking almost due north. Antietam Creek is 2.0 miles to the east (on your right). Shepherdstown is about 2.0 miles down the road to the southwest (on your left). As the crow flies, you are about 1.7 miles from the Dunker Church to the northeast (in front and to your right) and 1.5 miles from Burnside Bridge to the southeast (behind you and to the right).

Appendix I

Decision—Lee Withdraws to Virginia

Just as McClellan was struggling with his decisions and the challenges that the previous day had laid before him, Robert E. Lee was facing an abundance of his own dilemmas. On September 18, dawn began to reveal the substantial damage his army had suffered. After the war, John Bell Hood described that dreadful morning after the battle: "The following morning I arose before dawn and rode to the front where, just after daybreak, General Jackson came pacing up on his horse, and instantly asked, "Hood, have they gone?" When I answered in the negative, he replied "I hoped they had," and then passed on to look after his brave but greatly exhausted command."[109]

Confederate stragglers now scattered all over the Maryland and Virginia countryside slowly began to rejoin the Army of Northern Virginia. trickling in in small numbers for the next week and beyond. Lee ordered the commissary and ammunition trains brought up to feed his men and replenish his army with ammunition. He also concentrated his lines and braced for a new attack.[110]

Although still ready to fight, Lee's army had suffered much. That morning the Confederate commander had between 25,000 and 30,000 men present for duty, although these numbers might have been wildly optimistic. Lee's total casualties from the day before were between 25 and 28 percent. While his overall losses were devastating, the depletion of his leadership ranks was even more catastrophic. Lee had lost to death and/or wounding 3 of his 9 division commanders, 19 of his 39 brigade commanders, and 86 of his 173 regimental

Lee's headquarters in Sharpsburg, Maryland, modern image. Author.

commanders. This is an overall casualty rate of nearly 50 percent. Of the 173 regiments Lee brought to Maryland, only 22 were now headed by colonels. Twenty-two of his 38 brigades did not have a single regiment led by a colonel, and 5 of these had captains commanding. To lead this devastated force that day, Lee had only 27 general officers on hand. Maintaining command and control on Civil War battlefields was trying on the best days, and losses like these would have made the task even more difficult. It is hard to imagine any army with such a diminished core command, retaining the same level of authority as it did before the battle.

As was the case nine months later in Pennsylvania, Lee had now thousands of severely wounded men to care for. He could either leave them on Northern soil or figure how to transport this multitude back to Virginia.[111]

In his after-action report, Lee described the condition of his army at length:

> The arduous service in which our troops had been engaged, their great privations of rest and food, and the long marches without shoes over mountain roads, had greatly reduced our ranks before the action began. These causes had compelled thousands of brave men to absent themselves, and many more had done so from unworthy motives. This great battle was fought by less than 40,000 men on our side, all of whom had undergone the greatest labors and hardships in the field and on the march. Nothing could surpass the determined valor with which they met the large army of the enemy, fully supplied and equipped, and the result reflects the highest credit on the officers and men engaged.
>
> Our artillery, though much inferior to that of the enemy in the number of guns and weight of metal, rendered most efficient and gallant service throughout the day, and contributed greatly to the repulse of the attacks on every part of the line. General Stuart, with the cavalry and horse artillery, performed the duty entrusted to him of guarding our left wing with great energy and courage, and rendered valuable assistance in defeating the attack on that part of our line.
>
> On the 18th we occupied the position of the preceding day, except in the center, where our line was drawn in about 200 yards. Our ranks were increased by the arrival of a number of troops, who had not been engaged the day before, and, though still too weak to assume the offensive, we awaited without apprehension the renewal of the attack. The day passed without any demonstration on the part of the enemy, who, from the reports received, was expecting the arrival

> of re-enforcements. As we could not look for a material increase in strength, and the enemy's force could be largely and rapidly augmented, it was not thought prudent to wait until he should be ready again to offer battle.[112]

It is not an overstatement to say that even the unflappable Robert E. Lee now had cause for concern. In his treatment of the campaign, noted author Joseph Harsh deftly and accurately describes the state of affairs the morning after the fighting: "The Confederate soldiers awoke fully expecting another battle. Their brief war experience taught them that when unentrenched armies remained within several hundred yards of one another, the fighting was irresistibly renewed. Along the Chickahominy and at Second Manassas the two forces had clawed at each other day after day until one had yielded and reached safe haven. But Antietam had been a different kind of battle. Its concentrated fury knocked the wind from both armies."[113]

Perhaps Lee was finally realizing that the opportunity he sought with the calculated risk of invading the North had slipped from his fingers and was drifting farther and farther from his grasp. With the fate of his campaign and possibly of the Army of Northern Virginia hanging in the balance, the Confederate commander could stand on the defensive, attack, or withdraw.

During the battle on the seventeenth, only the brigades of Brig. Gen. William D. Pender and Col. John M. Brockenbrough (Field's) of A. P. Hill's Light Division had not been heavily engaged. Most of the men now being collected in the rear were stragglers from the forced marches from Harpers Ferry. Every one of Lee's nine divisions had been engaged on the seventeenth, and all save A. P. Hill's and D. R. Jones's experienced a casualty rate in excess of 28 percent. McLaws's and D. H. Hill's divisions had casualty rates approaching 40 percent, and Hood's Division was the most devastated, suffering an overall casualty rate of more than 44 percent of those engaged. Twenty of the 173 infantry regiments in Lee's army had suffered losses exceeding 50 percent. Moreover, twenty of the 39 infantry brigades now had fewer than 400 men to fill their ranks.

From a purely tactical perspective, Lee's position was precarious at best. While he could still fight, his escape route was now more vulnerable. One more determined push from McClellan might very well cut off his only line of retreat. Brig. Gen. John Walker later recalled the Confederate commander's decision to abandon the field: "We had fought an indecisive battle, and although we were, perhaps, in as good a condition to renew the struggle as the enemy were, General Lee recognized the fact that his ulterior plans had been thwarted by this premature engagement, and after a consultation with

Potomac River at Boteler's Ford, modern image. Author.

his corps commanders he determined to withdraw from Maryland."[114] On the evening of September 18, under the cover of darkness, the Confederate army slipped out of line. The Rebels fell back to the Potomac River crossing at Shepherdstown to Virginia.[115]

The final battle of the campaign, Shepherdstown, began the next day. McClellan wired Halleck this proclamation: "I have the honor to report that Maryland is entirely freed from the presence of the enemy, who have been driven across the Potomac. No fears need now be entertained for the safety of Pennsylvania. I shall at once occupy Harper's Ferry."[116] Conversely, Lee sent the following in a dispatch to Davis: "During the night of the 18th the army was accordingly withdrawn to the south side of the Potomac, crossing near Shepherdstown, without loss or molestation."[117]

One could certainly argue that the Maryland Campaign was not concluded at this point, but only the Battle of Antietam. As Lee departed Sharpsburg on the evening of September 18, he intended to cross back over the Potomac at Williamsport and continue on to Pennsylvania. Lee was, in fact, moving his army in that direction when his rear guard at Boteler's Ford was attacked and subsequently collapsed on the evening of the nineteenth. Lee was forced to turn his army around to address this threat.

However, once Lee crossed over the Potomac on the evening of the eighteenth, for all intents and purposes, the campaign was over. This was the case even if the Confederate commander did not reach this conclusion until five days later.

APPENDIX II

UNION ORDER OF BATTLE

Casualty statuses are listed from September 1, 1862, to September 20, 1862.

Abbreviations

k—killed, c—captured, mw–mortally wounded, w—wounded
Gen.—General
Lieut. Gen.—Lieutenant General
Maj. Gen.—Major General
Brig. Gen.—Brigadier General
Col.—Colonel
Lieut. Col.—Lieutenant Colonel
Maj.—Major
Capt.—Captain
Lieut.—Lieutenant
Surg.—Surgeon

ARMY OF THE POTOMAC
    Maj. Gen. George B. McClellan, Commanding

GENERAL STAFF
    Chief of Staff
        Brig. Gen. Randolph B. Marcy

Assistant Adjutant General
   Brig. Gen. Seth Williams
Inspector General
   Brig. Gen. Delos B. Sackett
Chief of Artillery
   Brig. Gen. Henry J. Hunt
Chief Quartermaster
   Lieut. Col. Rufus Ingalls

GENERAL HEADQUARTERS

ESCORT
   Capt. James B. McIntyre
   Independent Company Oneida (New York) Cavalry
      Capt. Daniel P. Mann
   4th United States Cavalry, Company A
      Lieut. Thomas H. McCormick
   4th United States Cavalry, Company E
      Capt. James B. McIntyre
REGULAR ENGINEER BATTALION
   Capt. James C. Duane
PROVOST GUARD
   Maj. William H. Wood
   2nd United States Cavalry, Companies E, F, H, and K
      Capt. George A. Gordon
   8th United States, Companies A, D, F, and G
      Capt. Royal T. Frank
   19th United States, Company G
      Capt. Edmund L. Smith
   19th United States, Company H
      Capt. Henry S. Welton
HEADQUARTERS GUARD
   Maj. Granville O. Haller
   93rd New York
      Lieut. Col. Benjamin C. Butler
QUARTERMASTER'S GUARD
1st United States Cavalry, Companies B, C, H, and I
   Capt. Marcus A. Reno

FIRST CORPS
  (1) Maj. Gen. Joseph Hooker (w 9/17)
  (2) Brig. Gen. George G. Meade

ESCORT
  2nd New York Cavalry, Companies A, B, I, and K
    Capt. John E. Naylor

FIRST DIVISION
  (1) Brig. Gen. Rufus King (relieved 9/14)
  (2) Brig. Gen. John P. Hatch (w 9/14)
  (3) Brig. Gen. Abner Doubleday

First Brigade
  Col. Walter Phelps Jr.
  22nd New York
    Lieut. Col. John McKie Jr.
  24th New York
    Capt. John D. O'Brian (w 9/17)
  30th New York
    Col. William M. Searing
  84th New York (14th Brooklyn)
    Maj. William H. deBevoise
  2nd United States Sharpshooters
    Col. Henry A. V. Post (w 9/17)

Second Brigade
  (1) Brig. Gen. Abner Doubleday
  (2) Col. William Wainwright (w 9/14)
  (3) Lieut. Col. J. William Hofmann
  7th Indiana
    Maj. Ira G. Grover
  76th New York
    (1) Col. William Wainwright
    (2) Capt. John W. Young
  95th New York
    Maj. Edward Pye
  56th Pennsylvania
    (1) Lieut. Col. J. William Hofmann
    (2) Capt. Frederick William

THIRD BRIGADE
  Brig. Gen. Marsena R. Patrick
  21st New York
    Col. William F. Rogers
  23rd New York
    Col. Henry C. Hoffman
  35th New York
    Col. Newton B. Lord
  80th New York (20th Militia)
    Lieut. Col. Theodore B. Gates
FOURTH BRIGADE (IRON BRIGADE)
  Brig. Gen. John Gibbon
  19th Indiana
    (1) Col. Solomon Meredith
    (2) Lieut. Col. Alois O. Bachman (k 9/17)
    (3) Capt. William W. Dudley
  2nd Wisconsin
    (1) Col. Lucius Fairchild (w 9/14)
    (2) Lieut. Col. Thomas S. Allen (w 9/17)
    (3) Capt. George B. Ely
  6th Wisconsin
    (1) Lieut. Col. Edward S. Bragg (w 9/17)
    (2) Maj. Rufus R. Dawes
  7th Wisconsin
    Capt. John B. Callis
ARTILLERY
  Capt. J. Albert Monroe
  New Hampshire Light, 1st Battery
    Lieut. Frederick M. Edgell
  1st Rhode Island Light, Battery D
    Capt. J. Albert Monroe
  1st New York Light, Battery L
    Capt. John A. Reynolds
  4th United States, Battery B
    (1) Capt. Joseph B. Campbell (w 9/17)
    (2) Lieut. James Stewart

SECOND DIVISION
  Brig. Gen. James B. Ricketts (w 9/17)

First Brigade
  Brig. Gen. Abram Duryée
  97th New York
    Maj. Charles B. Northrup
  104th New York
    Maj. Lewis C. Skinner
  105th New York
    (1) Col. Howard Carroll (mw 9/17)
    (2) Capt. John C. Whiteside
  107th Pennsylvania
    Capt. James McThomson
Second Brigade
  (1) Col. William A. Christian
  (2) Col. Peter Lyle
  26th New York
    Lieut. Col. Richard H. Richardson
  94th New York
    Lieut. Col. Calvin Littlefield
  88th Pennsylvania
    (1) Lieut. Col. George W. Gile (w 9/17)
    (2) Capt. Henry B. Myers
  90th Pennsylvania
    (1) Col. Peter Lyle
    (2) Lieut. Col. William A. Leech
Third Brigade
  (1) Brig. Gen. George L. Hartsuff (w 9/17)
  (2) Col. Richard Coulter
  12th Massachusetts
    (1) Maj. Elisha Burbank (mw 9/17)
    (2) Capt. Benjamin F. Cook
  13th Massachusetts
    Maj. J. Parker Gould
  83rd New York (9th Militia)
    Lieut. Col. William Atterbury
  11th Pennsylvania
    (1) Col. Richard Coulter
    (2) Capt. David M. Cook
  16th Maine (not present)
    Col. A. W. Wildes

ARTILLERY
    1st Pennsylvania Light, Battery F
        Capt. Ezra W. Matthews
    Pennsylvania Light, Battery C
        Capt. James Thompson

THIRD DIVISION
    (1) Brig. Gen. John F. Reynolds
    (2) Brig. Gen. George G. Meade
    (3) Brig. Gen. Truman Seymour

FIRST BRIGADE
    (1) Brig. Gen. Truman Seymour
    (2) Col. Richard Biddle Roberts
    1st Pennsylvania Reserves
        (1) Col. Richard Biddle Roberts
        (2) Capt. William C. Talley
    2nd Pennsylvania Reserves
        Capt. James N. Byrnes
    5th Pennsylvania Reserves
        Col. Joseph W. Fisher
    6th Pennsylvania Reserves
        Col. William Sinclair
    13th Pennsylvania Reserves (1st Pennsylvania Rifles "Bucktails")
        (1) Col. Hugh W. McNeil (k 9/16)
        (2) Capt. Dennis McGee

SECOND BRIGADE
    Col. Albert L. Magilton
    3rd Pennsylvania Reserves
        Lieut. Col. John Clark
    4th Pennsylvania Reserves
        Maj. John Nyce
    7th Pennsylvania Reserves
        (1) Col. Henry C. Bolinger (w 9/14)
        (2) Maj. Chauncey A. Lyman
    8th Pennsylvania Reserves
        Maj. Silas M. Bailey

THIRD BRIGADE
    (1) Col. Thomas F. Gallagher (w 9/14)
    (2) Lieut. Col. Robert Anderson

9th Pennsylvania Reserves
    Capt. Samuel B. Dick
10th Pennsylvania Reserves
    (1) Lieut. Col. Adoniram J. Warner (w 9/17)
    (2) Capt. Jonathan P. Smith
11th Pennsylvania Reserves
    Lieut. Col. Samuel M. Jackson
12th Pennsylvania Reserves
    Capt. Richard Gustin

ARTILLERY
1st Pennsylvania Light, Battery A
    Lieut. John G. Simpson
1st Pennsylvania Light, Battery B
    Capt. James H. Cooper
5th United States, Battery C
    Capt. Dunbar R. Ransom

SECOND CORPS
Maj. Gen. William V. Sumner

ESCORT
6th New York Cavalry, Company D
    Capt. Henry W. Lyon
6th New York Cavalry, Company K
    Capt. Riley Johnson

FIRST DIVISION
(1) Maj. Gen. Israel B. Richardson (mw 9/17)
(2) Brig. Gen. John C. Caldwell
(3) Brig. Gen. Winfield S. Hancock

FIRST BRIGADE
Brig. Gen. John C. Caldwell
5th New Hampshire
    Col. Edward E. Cross (w 9/17)
7th New York
    Capt. Charles Brestel
61st and 64th New York
    (1) Col. Francis C. Barlow (w 9/17)
    (2) Lieut. Col. Nelson A. Miles

Appendix II

    81st Pennsylvania
        Maj. H. Boyd McKeen

SECOND BRIGADE (IRISH BRIGADE)
    (1) Brig. Gen. Thomas F. Meagher (w 9/17)
    (2) Col. John Burke
    29th Massachusetts
        Lieut. Col. Joseph H. Barnes
    63rd New York
        (1) Col. John Burke
        (2) Lieut. Col. Henry Fowler (w 9/17)
        (3) Maj. Richard C. Bentley (w 9/17)
        (4) Capt. Joseph O'Neill
    69th New York
        (1) Lieut. Col. James Kelly (w 9/17)
        (2) Maj. James Cavanagh
    88th New York
        Lieut. Col. Patrick Kelly

THIRD BRIGADE
    Col. John R. Brooke
    2nd Delaware
        Capt. David L. Stricker
    52nd New York
        Col. Paul Frank
    57th New York
        (1) Lieut. Col. Philip S. Parisen (k 9/17)
        (2) Maj. Alford B. Chapman
    66th New York
        Capt. Julius Wehle
    53rd Pennsylvania
        Lieut. Col. Richards McMichael

ARTILLERY
    1st New York Light, Battery B
        Capt. Rufus D. Pettit
    4th United States, Batteries A and C
        Lieut. Evan Thomas

SECOND DIVISION
    (1) Maj. Gen. John Sedgwick (w 9/17)
    (2) Brig. Gen. Oliver O. Howard

FIRST BRIGADE
    Brig. Gen. Willis A. Gorman
    15th Massachusetts
        Lieut. Col. John W. Kimball
    1st Minnesota
        Col. Alfred Sully
    34th New York
        Col. James A. Suitor
    82nd New York (2nd Militia)
        Col. Henry W. Hudson
    Massachusetts Sharpshooters, 1st Company
        Capt. John Saunders (k 9/17)
    Minnesota Sharpshooters, 2nd Company
        Capt. William F. Russell

SECOND BRIGADE (PHILADELPHIA BRIGADE)
    (1) Brig. Gen. Oliver O. Howard
    (2) Col. Joshua T. Owen
    (3) Col. De Witt C. Baxter
    69th Pennsylvania
        Col. Joshua T. Owen
    71st Pennsylvania
        Col. Isaac J. Wistar (w 9/17)
    72nd Pennsylvania
        Col. DeWitt C. Baxter
    106th Pennsylvania
        Col. Turner G. Morehead

THIRD BRIGADE
    (1) Brig. Gen. Napoleon J. T. Dana (w 9/17)
    (2) Col. Norman J. Hall
    19th Massachusetts
        (1) Col. Edward W. Hinks (w 9/17)
        (2) Lieut. Col. Arthur F. Devereux (w 9/17)
        (3) Capt. H. G. Weymouth
    20th Massachusetts
        Col. William R. Lee
    7th Michigan
        (1) Col. Norman J. Hall
        (2) Capt. Charles J. Hunt
    42nd New York
        (1) Lieut. Col. George N. Bomford (w 9/17)
        (2) Maj. James E. Mallon

59th New York
    Col. William L. Tidball

ARTILLERY
    1st Rhode Island Light, Battery A
        Capt. John A. Tompkins
    1st United States, Battery I
        Lieut. George A. Woodruff

THIRD DIVISION
    Brig. Gen. William B. French

FIRST BRIGADE
    Brig. Gen. Nathan Kimball
    14th Indiana
        Col. William Harrow
    8th Ohio
        Lieut. Col. Franklin Sawyer
    132nd Pennsylvania
        (1) Col. Richard A. Oakford (k 9/17)
        (2) Lieut. Col. Vincent M. Wilcox
    7th West Virginia
        Col. Joseph Snider

SECOND BRIGADE
    Col. Dwight Morris
    14th Connecticut
        Lieut. Col. Sanford H. Perkins
    108th New York
        Col. Oliver H. Palmer
    130th Pennsylvania
        Col. Henry I. Zinn

THIRD BRIGADE
    (1) Brig. Gen. Max Weber (w 9/17)
    (2) Col. John W. Andrews
    1st Delaware
        (1) Col. John W. Andrews
        (2) Lieut. Col. Oliver Hopkinson (w 9/17)
    5th Maryland
        (1) Maj. Leopold Blumenberg (w 9/17)
        (2) Capt. William W. Bamberger (w 9/17)

(3) Capt. Salome Marsh (w and c 9/17)
(4) Capt. Ernest F. M. Faehtz
4th New York
Lieut. Col. John D. MacGregor

UNATTACHED ARTILLERY
1st New York Light, Battery G
Capt. John D. Frank
1st Rhode Island Light, Battery B
Capt. John G. Hazard
1st Rhode Island Light, Battery G
Capt. Charles D. Owen

FOURTH CORPS / FIRST DIVISION (Arrived at Antietam 9/18)
Maj. Gen. Darius M. Couch

FIRST BRIGADE
Brig. Gen. Charles Devens Jr.
7th Massachusetts
Col. David A. Russell
10th Massachusetts
Col. Henry L. Eustis
36th New York
Col. William H. Browne
2nd Rhode Island
Col. Frank Wheaton

SECOND BRIGADE
Brig. Gen. Albion P. Howe
62nd New York
Col. David J. Nevin
93rd Pennsylvania
Col. James M. McCarter
98th Pennsylvania
Col. John F. Ballier
102nd Pennsylvania
Col. Thomas A. Rowley
139th Pennsylvania
Col. Frank H. Collier

THIRD BRIGADE
Brig. Gen. John Cochrane

65th New York
    Col. Alexander Shaler
67th New York
    Col. Julius W. Adams
122nd New York
    Col. Silas Titus
23rd Pennsylvania
    Col. Thomas H. Neill
31st Pennsylvania
    Col. George C. Spear
61st Pennsylvania
    Col. David H. Williams

ARTILLERY
    New York Light, 3rd Battery
        Capt. William Stuart
    1st Pennsylvania Light, Battery C
        Capt. Jeremiah McCarthy
    1st Pennsylvania Light, Battery D
        Capt. Michael Hall
    2nd United States, Battery G
        Lieut. John H. Butler

FIFTH CORPS
Maj. Gen. Fitz John Porter

ESCORT
    1st Main Cavalry (detachment)
        Capt. George J. Summat

FIRST DIVISION
    Maj. Gen. George W. Morell

FIRST BRIGADE
    Col. James Barnes
    2nd Maine
        Col. Charles W. Roberts
    18th Massachusetts
        Lieut. Col. Joseph Hayes
    22nd Massachusetts
        Lieut. Col. William S. Tilton

1st Michigan
    Capt. Emory W. Belton
13th New York
    Col. Elisha Marshall
25th New York
    Col. Charles A. Johnson
118th Pennsylvania
    (1) Col. Charles M. Prevost (w 9/20)
    (2) Lieut. Col. James Gwyn
Massachusetts Sharpshooters, 2nd Company
    Capt. Lewis E. Wentworth

SECOND BRIGADE
Brig. Gen. Charles Griffin
2nd District of Columbia
    Col. Charles M. Alexander
9th Massachusetts
    Col. Patrick R. Guiney
32nd Massachusetts
    Col. Francis J. Parker
4th Michigan
    Col. Jonathan W. Childs
14th New York
    Col. James McQuade
62nd Pennsylvania
    Col. Jacob B. Sweitzer

THIRD BRIGADE
Col. Thomas B. W. Stockton
20th Maine
    Col. Adelbert Ames
16th Michigan
    Lieut. Col. Norval E. Welch
12th New York
    Capt. William Huson
17th New York
    Lieut. Col. Nelson B. Bartram
44th New York
    Maj. Freeman Conner
83rd Pennsylvania
    Capt. Orpheus S. Woodward
Michigan Sharpshooters, Brady's Company
    Lieut. Jonas H. Titus Jr.

ARTILLERY
    Massachusetts Light, Battery C
        Capt. Augustus P. Martin
    1st Rhode Island Light, Battery C
        Capt. Richard Waterman
    5th United States, Battery D
        Lieut. Charles E. Hazlett

SHARPSHOOTERS
    1st United States
        Capt. John B. Isler

SECOND DIVISION
    Brig. Gen. George Sykes

FIRST BRIGADE
    Lieut. Col. Robert C. Buchanan
    3rd United States
        Capt. John D. Wilkins
    4th United States
        Capt. Hiram Dryer
    12th United States, 1st Battalion
        Capt. Matthew M. Blunt
    12th United States, 2nd Battalion
        Capt. Thomas M. Anderson
    14th United States, 1st Battalion
        Capt. W. Harvey Brown
    14th United States, 2nd Battalion
        Capt. David B. McKibbin

SECOND BRIGADE
    Maj. Charles S. Lovell
    1st and 6th United States
        Capt. Levi C. Bootes
    2nd and 10th United States
        Capt. John S. Poland
    11th United States
        Maj. DeLancey Floyd-Jones
    17th United States
        Maj. George L. Andrews

THIRD BRIGADE
    Col. Gouverneur K. Warren

5th New York
Capt. Cleveland Winslow
10th New York
Lieut. Col. John W. Marshall

ARTILLERY
1st United States, Batteries E and G
Lieut. Alanson M. Randol
5th United States, Battery I
Capt. Stephen H. Weed
5th United States, Battery K
Lieut. William E. Van Reed

THIRD DIVISION (Arrived at Antietam 9/18)
Brig. Gen. Andrew A. Humphreys

FIRST BRIGADE
Brig. Gen. Erastus B. Tyler
91st Pennsylvania
Col. Edgar M. Gregory
126th Pennsylvania
Col. James G. Elder
129th Pennsylvania
Col. Jacob G. Frick
134th Pennsylvania
Col. Matthew S. Quay

SECOND BRIGADE
Col. Peter H. Allabach
123rd Pennsylvania
Col. John B. Clark
131st Pennsylvania
Lieut. Col. William B. Shaut
133rd Pennsylvania
Col. Franklin B. Speakman
155th Pennsylvania
Col. Edward J. Allen

ARTILLERY
1st New York Light, Battery C
Capt. Almont Barnes
1st Ohio Light, Battery L
Capt. Lucius N. Robinson

ARTILLERY RESERVE
    Lieut. Col. William Hays
    1st Battalion New York Light, Battery A
        Lieut. Bernhard Wever
    1st Battalion New York Light, Battery B
        Lieut. Alfred von Kleiser
    1st Battalion New York Light, Battery C
        Capt. Robert Langner
    1st Battalion New York Light, Battery D
        Capt. Charles Kusserow
    New York Light, 5th Battery
        Capt. Elijah D. Taft
    1st United States, Battery K
        Capt. William M. Graham
    4th United States, Battery G
        Lieut. Marcus P. Miller

SIXTH CORPS
    Maj. Gen. William B. Franklin

ESCORT
    6th Pennsylvania Cavalry, Companies B and G
        Capt. Henry P. Muirheid

FIRST DIVISION
    Maj. Gen. Henry W. Slocum

FIRST BRIGADE
    Col. Alfred T. A. Tolbert
    1st New Jersey
        Lieut. Col. Mark W. Collet
    2nd New Jersey
        Col. Samuel L. Buck
    3rd New Jersey
        Col. Henry W. Brown
    4th New Jersey
        Col. William B. Hatch
SECOND BRIGADE
    Col. Joseph J. Bartlett

5th Maine
    Col. Nathaniel J. Jackson
16th New York
    Lieut. Col. Joel J. Seaver
27th New York
    Lieut. Col. Alexander D. Adams
96th Pennsylvania
    Col. Henry L. Cake

THIRD BRIGADE
Brig. Gen. John Newton
18th New York
    Lieut. Col. George R. Myers
31st New York
    Lieut. Col. Francis H. Pinto
32nd New York
    Col. Roderick Matheson

ARTILLERY
Capt. Emory Upton
Maryland Light, Battery A
    Capt. John W. Wolcott
Massachusetts Light, Battery A
    Capt. Josiah Porter
New Jersey Light, Battery A
    Capt. William Hexamer
2nd United States, Battery D
    Lieut. Edward B. Williston

SECOND DIVISION
Maj. Gen. William F. Smith

FIRST BRIGADE
(1) Brig. Gen. Winfield S. Hancock
(2) Col. Amasa Cobb
6th Maine
    Col. Hiram Burnham
43rd New York
    Maj. John Wilson
49th Pennsylvania
    Lieut. Col. William Brisbane

137th Pennsylvania
   Col. Henry M. Bossert
5th Wisconsin
   Col. Amasa Cobb

SECOND BRIGADE
   Brig. Gen. W. T. H. Brooks
   2nd Vermont
      Maj. James H. Walbridge
   3rd Vermont
      Col. Breed N. Hyde
   4th Vermont
      Lieut. Col. Charles B. Stoughton
   5th Vermont
      Col. Lewis A. Grant
   6th Vermont
      Maj. Oscar L. Tuttle

THIRD BRIGADE
   Col. William H. Irwin
   7th Maine
      Maj. Thomas W. Hyde
   20th New York
      Col. Ernst von Vegesack
   33rd New York
      Lieut. Col. Joseph W. Corning
   49th New York
      (1) Lieut. Col. William C. Alberger (w 9/17)
      (2) Maj. George W. Johnson
   77th New York
      Capt. Nathan S. Babcock

ARTILLERY
   Capt. Romeyn B. Ayres
   Maryland Light, Battery B
      Lieut. Theodore J. Vanneman
   New York Light, 1st Battery
      Capt. Andrew Cowan
   5th United States, Battery F
      Lieut. Leonard Martin

NINTH CORPS
   (1) Maj. Gen. Ambrose E. Burnside

(2) Maj. Gen. Jesse L. Reno (k 9/14)
(3) Brig. Gen. Jacob D. Cox

ESCORT
1st Maine, Company G
Capt. Zebulon B. Blethen

FIRST DIVISION
(1) Brig. Gen. Isaac Stevens (k 9/1)
(2) Col. Benjamin C. Christ
(3) Brig. Gen. Orlando B. Wilcox

FIRST BRIGADE
Col. Benjamin C. Christ
28th Massachusetts
Capt. Andrew P. Caraher
17th Michigan
Col. William H. Withington
79th New York
Lieut. Col. David Morrison
50th Pennsylvania
(1) Maj. Edward Overton Jr. (w 9/17)
(2) Capt. William H. Diehl

SECOND BRIGADE
Col. Thomas Welsh
8th Michigan
Lieut. Col. Frank Graves
Maj. Ralph Ely
46th New York
Lieut. Col. Joseph P. Gerhardt
45th Pennsylvania
Lieut. Col. John I. Curtin
100th Pennsylvania
Lieut. Col. David A. Leckey

ARTILLERY
Massachusetts Light, 8th Battery
Capt. Asa M. Cook
2nd United States, Battery E
Lieut. Samuel N. Benjamin

SECOND DIVISION
Brig. Gen. Samuel D. Sturgis

First Brigade
Brig. Gen. James Nagle
2nd Maryland
Lieut. Col. J. Eugene Duryée
6th New Hampshire
Col. Simon G. Griffin
9th New Hampshire
Col. Enoch Q. Fellows
48th Pennsylvania
Lieut. Col. Joshua K. Sigfried

Second Brigade
Brig. Gen. Edward Ferrero
21st Massachusetts
Col. William S. Clark
35th Massachusetts
(1) Col. Edward A. Wild (w 9/14)
(2) Maj. Sumner Carruth (w 9/17)
51st New York
Col. Robert B. Potter
51st Pennsylvania
Col. John F. Hartranft

Artillery
Pennsylvania Light, Battery D
Capt. George W. Durell
4th United States, Battery E
(1) Capt. Joseph C. Clark Jr. (w 9/17)
(2) Lieut. George Dickenson
(3) 1ST Sgt. C. F. Merkle

THIRD DIVISION
(1) Brig. Gen. Isaac P. Rodman (mw 9/17)
(2) Col. Edward Harland

First Brigade
Col. Harrison S. Fairchild
9th New York
Lieut. Col. Edgar A. Kimball

89th New York
    Maj. Edward Jardine
103rd New York
    Maj. Benjamin Ringold

SECOND BRIGADE
    Col. Edward Harland
    8th Connecticut
        (1) Lieut. Col. Hiram Appelman (w 9/17)
        (2) Maj. John H. Ward
    11th Connecticut
        (1) Col. Henry W. Kingsbury (mw 9/17)
        (2) Lieut. Col. G. A. Steadman
    16th Connecticut
        Col. Francis Beach
    4th Rhode Island
        (1) Col. William H. P. Steere (w 9/17)
        (2) Lieut. Col. Joseph B. Curtis

ARTILLERY
    5th United States, Battery A
        Lieut. Charles P. Muhlenberg

KANAWHA DIVISION
    (1) Brig. Gen. Jacob D. Cox
    (2) Col. Eliakim P. Scammon

FIRST BRIGADE
    (1) Col. Eliakim P. Scammon
    (2) Col. Hugh Ewing
    12th Ohio
        Col. Carr B. White
    23rd Ohio
        (1) Lieut. Col. Rutherford B. Hayes (w 9/14)
        (2) Maj. James M. Comly
    30th Ohio
        (1) Col. Hugh Ewing
        (2) Lieut. Col. Theodore Jones (w and c 9/17)
        (3) Maj. George H. Hildt
    Ohio Light Artillery, 1st Battery
        Capt. James R. McMullin

Gilmore's Company, West Virginia Cavalry
   Lieut. James Abraham
Harrison's Company, West Virginia Cavalry
   Lieut. Dennis Delaney

SECOND BRIGADE
  (1) Col. Augustus Moor (c 9/12)
  (2) Col. George Crook
  11th Ohio
     (1) Lieut. Col. Augustus H. Coleman (k 9/17)
     (2) Maj. Lyman J. Jackson
  28th Ohio
     Lieut. Col. Gottfried Becker
  36th Ohio
     (1) Col. George Crook
     (2) Lieut. Col. Melvin Clarke (k 9/17)
     (3) Maj. Ebenezer B. Andrews
  Schambeck's Company/Chicago Dragoons
     Capt. Frederick Schambeck
  Kentucky Light Artillery, Simmonds's Battery
     Capt. Seth J. Simmonds

UNATTACHED
  6th New York Cavalry (8 companies)
     Col. Thomas C. Devin
  Ohio Cavalry, 3rd Independent Company
     Lieut. Jonas Seamen
  3rd United States, Batteries L and M
     Capt. John Edwards Jr.
  2nd New York Artillery, Battery L
     Capt. Jacob Roemer

TWELFTH CORPS
  (1) Maj. Gen. Joseph K. F. Mansfield (mw 9/17)
  (2) Brig. Gen. Alpheus S. Williams

ESCORT
  1st Michigan Cavalry, Company L
     Capt. Melvin Brewer

FIRST DIVISION
  (1) Brig. Gen. Alpheus S. Williams

(2) Brig. Gen. Samuel W. Crawford (w 9/17)
   (3) Brig. Gen. George H. Gordon

First Brigade
   (1) Brig. Gen. Samuel W. Crawford (w 9/17)
   (2) Col. Joseph F. Knipe
   5th Connecticut
      Capt. Henry W. Daboll
   10th Maine
      Col. George L. Beal (w 9/17)
   28th New York
      Capt. William H. H. Mapes
   46th Pennsylvania
      (1) Col. Joseph F. Knipe
      (2) Lieut. Col. James L. Selfridge
   124th Pennsylvania
      (1) Col. Joseph W. Hawley (w 9/17)
      (2) Maj. Isaac L. Haldeman
   125th Pennsylvania
      Col. Jacob Higgins
   128th Pennsylvania
      (1) Col. Samuel Croasdale (k 9/17)
      (2) Lieut. Col. William W. Hammersly (w 9/17)
      (3) Maj. Joel B. Wanner
Third Brigade
   (1) Brig. Gen. George H. Gordon
   (2) Col. Thomas H. Ruger
   27th Indiana
      Col. Silas Colgrove
   2nd Massachusetts
      Col. George L. Andrews
   13th New Jersey
      Col. Ezra A. Carman
   107th New York
      Col. Robert B. Van Valkenburg
   Pennsylvania Zouaves d'Afrique
      (Unknown)
   3rd Wisconsin
      Col. Thomas H. Ruger

SECOND DIVISION
Brig. Gen. George S. Greene

First Brigade
(1) Lieut. Col. Hector Tyndale (w 9/17)
(2) Maj. Orrin J. Crane
5th Ohio
    Maj. John Collins
7th Ohio
    (1) Maj. Orrin J. Crane
    (2) Capt. Frederick A. Seymour
66th Ohio
    Lieut. Col. Eugene Powell (w 9/17)
28th Pennsylvania
    Maj. Ario Pardee Jr.

Second Brigade
Col. Henry J. Stainrook
3rd Maryland
    Lieut. Col. Joseph H. Sudsburg
102nd New York
    Lieut. Col. James C. Lane
109th Pennsylvania
    Capt. George E. Seymore
111th Pennsylvania
    Maj. Thomas M. Walker (w 9/17)

Third Brigade
(1) Col. William B. Goodrich (k 9/17)
(2) Lieut. Col. Jonathan Austin
3rd Delaware
    (1) Maj. Arthur Maginnis (w 9/17)
    (2) Capt. William J. McKaig
Purnell (Maryland) Legion
    Lieut. Col. Benjamin L. Simpson
60th New York
    Lieut. Col. Charles R. Brundage
78th New York
    (1) Lieut. Col. Jonathan Austin
    (2) Capt. Henry R. Stagg

Artillery
Capt. Clermont L. Best

Maine Light, 4th Battery
    Capt. O'Neill W. Robinson Jr.
Maine Light, 6th Battery
    Capt. Freeman McGilvery
1st New York Light, Battery M
    Capt. George W. Cothran
New York Light, 10th Battery
    Capt. John T. Bruen
Pennsylvania Light, Battery E
    Capt. Joseph M. Knap
Pennsylvania Light, Battery F
    Capt. Robert B. Hampton
4th United States, Battery F
    Lieut. Edward D. Muhlenberg

CAVALRY DIVISION
Brig. Gen. Alfred Pleasonton

First Brigade
Maj. Charles J. Whiting
5th United States
    Capt. Joseph H. McArthur
6th United States
    Capt. William P. Sanders

Second Brigade
Col. John F. Farnsworth
8th Illinois
    Maj. William H. Medill
3rd Indiana
    Maj. George H. Chapman
1st Massachusetts
    Capt. Caspar Crowninshield
8th Pennsylvania
    Capt. Peter Keenan

Third Brigade
Col. Richard H. Rush
4th Pennsylvania
    (1) Col. James H. Childs (k 9/17)
    (2) Lieut. Col. James K. Kerr

6th Pennsylvania
    Lieut. Col. C. Ross Smith
FOURTH BRIGADE
  Col. Andrew T. McReynolds
  1st New York
    Maj. Alonzo W. Adams
  12th Pennsylvania
    Maj. James A. Congdon
FIFTH BRIGADE
  Col. Benjamin F. Davis
  8th New York
    Col. Benjamin F. Davis
  3rd Pennsylvania
    Lieut. Col. Samuel W. Owen
HORSE ARTILLERY
  2nd United States, Battery A
    Capt. John C. Tidball
  2nd United States, Batteries B and L
    Capt. James M. Robertson
  2nd United States, Battery M
    Lieut. Peter C. Hains
  3rd United States, Batteries C and G
    Capt. Horatio G. Gibson
UNATTACHED
  1st Maine Cavalry
    Col. Samuel H. Allen
  15th Pennsylvania Cavalry (detachment)
    Col. William J. Palmer

APPENDIX III

CONFEDERATE ORDER OF BATTLE

Casualty statuses are listed from September 1, 1862, to September 20, 1862.

Abbreviations

k—killed, c—captured, mw–mortally wounded, w—wounded

ARMY OF NORTHERN VIRGINIA
  Gen. Robert E. Lee, Commanding

LEE'S HEADQUARTERS STAFF
  Chief of Staff / Adjutant Gen.
    Lieut. Col. Robert H. Chilton
  Assistant Adjutant Gen. / Aide-de-Camp
    Maj. Walter H. Taylor
  Assistant Adjutant Gen. / Aide-de-Camp
    Maj. Charles S. Venable
  Assistant Adjutant Gen.
    Capt. Arthur P. Mason
  Aide-de-Camp
    Maj. Charles Marshall
  Aide-de-Camp / Chief Engineer
    Maj. Thomas M. R. Talcott

Aide-de-Camp
    Capt. Lathom Woodville
Chief of Ordnance
    Col. E. P. Alexander
Chief Surgeon / Medical Director
    Surg. LaFayette Guild, MD
Secretary
    Col. Armistead L. Long

LONGSTREET'S COMMAND/WING
Maj. Gen. James Longstreet

ESCORT
Independent Company, South Carolina Cavalry
    Capt. James Doby

ANDERSON'S DIVISION
(1) Maj. Gen. Richard H. Anderson (w 9/17)
(2) Brig. Gen. Roger A. Pryor

Wilcox's Brigade
(1) Brig. Gen. Cadmus M. Wilcox
(2) Col. Alfred Cumming (w 9/17)
(3) Maj. Hilary Abner Herbert
(4) Capt. James M. Crow
8th Alabama
    Maj. Hilary A. Herbert
9th Alabama
    (1) Maj. Jeremiah H. Johnston (w 9/17)
    (2) Capt. James M. Crow
    (3) Lieut. A. C. Chisholm
10th Alabama
    Capt. George C. Whatley (k 9/17)
11th Alabama
    Maj. John Christopher C. Sanders

Mahone's Brigade
Col. William A. Parham
6th Virginia
    Capt. John R. Ludlow

12th Virginia
    Capt. John R. Lewellen (w 9/14)
16th Virginia
    Maj. Francis D. Holliday (c 9/14)
41st Virginia
    Lieut. Col. Joseph Minetree
61st Virginia
    Unknown

FEATHERSTON'S BRIGADE
(1) Brig. Gen. Winfield Scott Featherston
(2) Col. Carnot Posey
12th Mississippi
    Col. William H. Taylor
16th Mississippi
    Capt. Abram M. Feltus
19th Mississippi
    Col. Nathaniel H. Harris (w 9/17)
2nd Mississippi Battalion (6 companies)
    Maj. William S. Wilson (mw 9/17)

ARMISTEAD'S BRIGADE
(1) Brig. Gen. Lewis A. Armistead (w 9/17)
(2) Col. James G. Hodges
9th Virginia
    Capt. William J. Richardson
14th Virginia
    Col. James G. Hodges
38th Virginia
    Col. Edward C. Edmonds
53rd Virginia
    (1) Capt. William G. Pollard (k 9/17)
    (2) Capt. Joseph C. Harwood
57th Virginia
    Col. David Dyer
5th Virginia Battalion
    Unknown

PRYOR'S BRIGADE (FLORIDA BRIGADE)
(1) Brig. Gen. Roger A. Pryor
(2) Col. John C. Hately (w 9/17)

14th Alabama
    Maj. James A. Broome
2nd Florida
    (1) Col. William D. Ballantine (w 9/17)
    (2) Lieut. Henry C. Geiger
5th Florida
    (1) Col. John C. Hately (w 9/17)
    (2) Lieut. Col. Thomas B. Lamar (w 9/17)
    (3) Maj. Benjamin F. Davis
8th Florida
    (1) Lieut. Col. Georges A. G. De Coppens (k 9/17)
    (2) Capt. Richard A. Waller (k 9/17)
    (3) Capt. William Baya
3rd Virginia
    (1) Col. Joseph Mayo Jr. (w 9/17)
    (2) Lieut. Col. Alexander D. Callcote

WRIGHT'S BRIGADE
    (1) Brig. Gen. Ambrose R. Wright (w 9/17)
    (2) Col. Robert H. Jones (w 9/17)
    (3) Col. William Gibson
44th Alabama
    (1) Lieut. Col. Charles A. Derby (k 9/17)
    (2) Maj. William F. Perry
3rd Georgia
    (1) Capt. Reuben B. Nisbit (w and c 9/17)
    (2) Capt. John T. Jones
22nd Georgia
    (1) Col. Robert H. Jones (w 9/17)
    (2) Capt. Lawrence D. Lallerstedt (w 9/17)
48th Georgia
    Col. William Gibson

ARTILLERY
    Maj. John S. Saunders
    Donaldsonville (Louisiana) Artillery
        Capt. Victor Maurin
    Norfolk (Virginia) Artillery (Huger's Battery)
        Lieut. Charles R. Phelps
    Moorman's (Virginia) Battery
        Capt. Marcellus N. Moorman

Portsmouth (Virginia) Artillery
    (1) Capt. Cary F. Grimes (k 9/17)
    (2) Lieut. John H. Thompson
Dixie (Virginia) Artillery
    Capt. William H. Chapman

JONES'S DIVISION
  Brig. Gen. David R. Jones

TOOMBS'S BRIGADE
    (1) Brig. Gen. Robert A. Toombs (w 9/17)
    (2) Col. Henry L. Benning
  2nd Georgia
    (1) Lieut. Col. William R. Holmes (k 9/17)
    (2) Maj. Skidmore Harris (w 9/17)
    (3) Capt. Abner M. Lewis
  15th Georgia
    (1) Col. William T. Millican (mw 9/17)
    (2) Capt. Thomas H. Jackson
  17th Georgia
    Capt. John A. McGregor
  20th Georgia
    Col. John B. Cumming

DRAYTON'S BRIGADE
  Brig. Gen. Thomas F. Drayton
  50th Georgia
    Lieut. Col. Francis Kearse
  51st Georgia
    Unknown
  Philips's "Georgia" Legion (9 companies)
    Lieut. Col. Robert Thomas Cook
  15th South Carolina
    Col. William D. DeSaussure
  3rd South Carolina Battalion (7 companies)
    (1) Lieut. Col. George S. James (k 9/14)
    (2) Maj. William G. W. Rice (w 9/14)
    (3) Capt. George M. Gunnels

KEMPER'S BRIGADE
  Brig. Gen. James L. Kemper

1st Virginia
    (1) Capt. George F. Newton (w 9/17)
    (2) Maj. William H. Palmer
7th Virginia
    Maj. Arthur Herbert
11th Virginia
    (1) Maj. Adam Clement (w 9/14)
    (2) Capt. Phillip S. Ashby
17th Virginia
    Col. Montgomery D. Corse (w 9/17)
24th Virginia
    Col. William R. Terry

PICKETT'S / GARNETT'S BRIGADE
  Brig. Gen. Richard B. Garnett
  8th Virginia
    Col. Eppa Hunton
  18th Virginia
    Maj. George C. Cabell
  19th Virginia
    (1) Col. John B. Strange (k 9/14)
    (2) Lieut. William N. Wood
    (3) Capt. J. L. Cochran
    (4) Capt. Benjamin J. Brown
  28th Virginia
    Capt. William L. Wingfield
  56th Virginia
    (1) Col. William D. Stuart
    (2) Capt. John B. McPhail Jr. (w 9/14)

JENKINS'S BRIGADE
  Col. Joseph Walker
  1st South Carolina (Volunteers)
    Lieut. Col. Daniel Livingston (w 9/17)
  2nd South Carolina Rifles
    Col. Robert A. Thompson
  5th South Carolina
    Capt. Thomas C. Beckham
  6th South Carolina
    Capt. Edward B. Cantey (w 9/17)
  4th South Carolina Battalion (5 companies)
    Lieut. W. T. Field

Palmetto (South Carolina) Sharpshooters (12 companies)
   (1) Capt. Alfred H. Foster (w 9/17)
   (2) Capt. Franklin W. Kirkpatrick
Jones's / G. T. Anderson's Brigade
   Col. George T. Anderson
   1st Georgia (Regulars)
      (1) Col. William J. Magill (w 9/17)
      (2) Capt. Richard A. Wayne
   7th Georgia
      Col. George H. Carmical
   8th Georgia
      Col. John R. Towers
   9th Georgia
      Lieut. Col. John C. L. Mounger (w 9/17)
   11th Georgia– (Five Companies)
      Maj. Francis H. Little
Artillery
   Wise (Virginia) Artillery
      Capt. James S. Brown

HOOD'S DIVISION
   Brig. Gen. John B. Hood

Hood's "Texas" / Wofford's Brigade
   Col. William T. Wofford
   18th Georgia
      Lieut. Col. Solon Z. Ruff
   Hampton's (South Carolina) Legion
      Lieut. Col. Martin W. Gary
   1st Texas
      Lieut. Col. Philip A. Work
   4th Texas
      Lieut. Col. Benjamin F. Carter
   5th Texas
      Capt. Ike N. M. Turner
Law's Brigade
   Col. Evander M. Law
   4th Alabama
      (1) Lieut. Col. Owen K. McLemore (mw 9/14)

Appendix III

  (2) Capt. Lawrence H. Scruggs (w 9/17)
  (3) Capt. William M. Robbins
 2nd Mississippi
  (1) Col. John M. Stone (w 9/17)
  (2) Lieut. William C. Moody
 11th Mississippi
  (1) Col. Philip F. Lidell (mw 9/16)
  (2) Lieut. Col. Samuel F. Butler (mw 9/17)
  (3) Maj. Taliaferro S. Evans (k 9/17)
  (4) Capt. Francis M. Green
 6th North Carolina
  Maj. Robert F. Webb (w 9/17)

ARTILLERY
 Maj. Bushrod W. Frobel
 German (South Carolina) Artillery
  Capt. William K. Bachman
 Palmetto (South Carolina) Artillery
  Capt. Hugh R. Garden
 Rowan (North Carolina) Artillery
  Capt. James Reilly

EVANS'S BRIGADE
 (1) Brig. Gen. Nathan G. Evans
 (2) Col. Peter F. Stevens (w 9/17)
 17th South Carolina
  Col. Fitz W. McMaster
 18th South Carolina
  Col. William H. Wallace
 22nd South Carolina
  Maj. Miel Hilton
 23rd South Carolina
  Lieut. E. R. White
 Holcombe (South Carolina) Legion
  Col. Peter F. Stevens
 Macbeth (South Carolina) Artillery
  Capt. Robert Boyce

RESERVE ARTILLERY

WASHINGTON (LOUISIANA) ARTILLERY
 Col. James B. Walton
 1st Company
  Capt. Charles W. Squires

2nd Company
 Capt. John B. Richardson
3rd Company
 Capt. Merritt B. Miller
4th Company
 Capt. Benjamin F. Eshleman

LEE'S BATTALION
 Col. Stephen D. Lee
 Ashland (Virginia) Artillery
  Capt. Pichegru Woolfolk Jr.
 Bedford (Virginia) Artillery
  Capt. Tyler C. Jordan
 Brooks (South Carolina) Artillery (Rhett's Battery)
  Lieut. William Elliott
 Eubank's (Virginia) Battery
  Capt. John L. Eubank
 Madison (Louisiana) Light Artillery
  Capt. George V. Moody
 Parker's (Virginia) Battery
  Capt. William W. Parker

JACKSON'S COMMAND/WING
 Maj. Gen. Thomas J. Jackson

ESCORT
 Company H, 4th Virginia Cavalry (Black Horse Troop)
  Capt. Robert Randolph
 White's Virginia Cavalry (3 Companies)
  Capt. Elijah V. White

EWELL'S/LAWTON'S DIVISION
 (1) Brig. Gen. Alexander Lawton (w 9/17)
 (2) Brig. Gen. Jubal A. Early

LAWTON'S BRIGADE
 (1) Col. Marcellus Douglass (k 9/17)
 (2) Maj. John H. Lowe
 (3) Col. John H. Lamar
 13th Georgia
  Capt. D. A. Kidd

26th Georgia
    Col. Edmund N. Atkinson
31st Georgia
    (1) Lieut. Col. John T. Crowder (w 9/17)
    (2) Maj. John H. Lowe
38th Georgia
    (1) Capt. William H. Battey (k 9/17)
    (2) Capt. Peter Brennan
    (3) Capt. John W. McCardy
60th Georgia
    Maj. Waters B. Jones
61st Georgia
    (1) Col. John H. Lamar
    (2) Maj. Archibald P. McRae (k 9/17)
    (3) Capt. James D. van Valkenburg

TRIMBLE'S BRIGADE
    (1) Capt. W. F. Brown (k 9/01)
    (2) Col. James A. Walker (w 9/17)
    15th Alabama
        Capt. Isaac B. Feagin (w 9/17)
    12th Georgia
        (1) Capt. James G. Rogers (k 9/17)
        (2) Capt. John T. Carson
    21st Georgia
        (1) Maj. Thomas C. Glover (w 9/17)
        (2) Capt. James C. Nisbit
    21st North Carolina
        Capt. F. P. Miller (k 9/17)
    1st North Carolina Battalion Sharpshooters

HAYS'S BRIGADE
    Brig. Gen. Harry T. Hays
    5th Louisiana
        Col. Henry Forno
    6th Louisiana
        (1) Col. Henry B. Strong (k 9/17)
        (2) Lieut. Col. Nathaniel G. Offutt
    7th Louisiana
        Col. Davison B. Penn (w 9/17)
    8th Louisiana
        Lieut. Col. Trevanion D. Lewis (w 9/17)

14th Louisiana
  Lieut. Col. David Zable (w 9/17)

Early's Brigade
  (1) Brig. Gen. Jubal A. Early
  (2) Col. William Smith (w 9/17)
  13th Virginia
    Capt. Frank V. Winston
  25th Virginia
    Capt. Robert D. Lilley
  31st Virginia
    Col. John S. Hoffman
  44th Virginia
    Capt. David W. Anderson (w 9/17)
  49th Virginia
    (1) Col. William Smith
    (2) Lieut. Col. Jonathan C. Gibson (w 9/17)
  52nd Virginia
    Col. Michael G. Harman
  58th Virginia
    Capt. H. W. Wingfield

Artillery
  Maj. Alfred R. Courtney
  Johnson's (Virginia) Battery
    Capt. John R. Johnson
  Louisiana Guard Artillery
    Capt. Louis E. D'Aquin

A. P. HILL'S LIGHT DIVISION
  Maj. Gen. Ambrose P. Hill

Branch's Brigade
  (1) Brig. Gen. Lawrence O. Branch (k 9/17)
  (2) Col. James H. Lane
  7th North Carolina
    Col. Edward G. Haywood
  18th North Carolina
    Lieut. Col. Thomas J. Purdie
  28th North Carolina
    (1) Col. James H. Lane
    (2) Maj. William J. Montgomery

33rd North Carolina
   Lieut. Col. Robert F. Hoke
37th North Carolina
   Capt. William G. Morris

GREGG'S BRIGADE
   Brig. Gen. Maxcy Gregg (w 9/17)
   1st South Carolina (Provisional Army)
      (1) Maj. Edward McCrady Jr.
      (2) Col. Daniel H. Hamilton Sr.
   1st South Carolina Rifles
      Lieut. Col. James M. Perrin (w 9/17)
   12th South Carolina
      (1) Col. Dixon Barnes (mw 9/17)
      (2) Lieut. Col. Cadwallader Jones
      (3) Maj. William H. McCorkle
   13th South Carolina
      Col. Oliver E. Edwards
   14th South Carolina
      Lieut. Col. William D. Simpson

ARCHER'S BRIGADE
   Brig. Gen. James J. Archer (ill 9/17)
   Col. Peter Turney
   5th Alabama Battalion
      Capt. Charles M. Hooper
   19th Georgia
      Maj. James H. Neal
   1st Tennessee (Provisional Army)
      Col. Peter Turney
   7th Tennessee
      (1) Maj. Samuel G. Shepard
      (2) Lieut. George A. Howard
   14th Tennessee
      (1) Col. William McComb (w 9/17)
      (2) Lieut. Col. James W. Lockert

FIELD'S BRIGADE
   Col. John M. Brockenbrough
   40th Virginia
      Lieut. Col. Fleet W. Cox
   47th Virginia
      Lieut. Col. John W. Lyell

55th Virginia
    Maj. Charles N. Lawson
22nd Virginia Battalion (6 companies)
    Maj. Edward P. Tayloe

THOMAS'S BRIGADE
  Col. Edward L. Thomas
  14th Georgia
      Col. R. W. Folsom
  35th Georgia
      Lieut. Col. Bolling H. Holt
  45th Georgia
      Maj. Washington L. Grice
  49th Georgia
      Lieut. Col. Seaborn. M. Manning

PENDER'S BRIGADE
  Brig. Gen. William Dorsey Pender
  16th North Carolina
      Lieut. Col. William A. Stowe
  22nd North Carolina
      Maj. Christopher C. Cole
  34th North Carolina
      Lieut. Col. John McDowell
  38th North Carolina
      Lieut. Col. Robert F. Armfield

ARTILLERY
  Lieut. Col. Reuben L. Walker
  Pee Dee (South Carolina) Artillery
      Capt. David G. McIntosh
  Crenshaw's (Virginia) Battery
      Capt. William G. Crenshaw
  Fredericksburg (Virginia) Artillery
      Capt. Carter M. Braxton
  Purcell (Virginia) Artillery
      Capt. William R. J. Pegram
  Lecher's (Virginia) Artillery
      Capt. Greenlee Davison

JACKSON'S/JONES'S DIVISION
  (1) Brig. Gen. John R. Jones (w 9/17)

(2) Brig. Gen. William E. Starke (k 9/17)
(3) Col. Andrew J. Grigsby

STONEWALL'S / WINDER'S BRIGADE
(1) Col. Andrew J. Grigsby
(2) Lieut. Col. Robert D. Gardner (w 9/17)
(3) Maj. Hazael J. Williams
4th Virginia
    Lieut. Col. Robert D. Gardner
5th Virginia
    (1) Maj. Hazael J. Williams
    (2) Capt. E. L. Curtis (w 9/17)
27th Virginia
    Capt. Frank C. Wilson
33rd Virginia
    (1) Capt. Jacob Golladay (w 9/17)
    (2) Lieut. David Walton

JONES'S BRIGADE
(1) Capt. John E. Penn (w 9/17)
(2) Capt. A. C. Page (w 9/17)
(3) Capt. Robert W. Withers
21st Virginia
    Capt. Archer C. Page
42nd Virginia
    (1) Capt. Robert W. Withers
    (2) Capt. D. W. Garrett
48th Virginia
    Capt. John H. Candler
1st (Irish) Virginia Battalion (5 companies)
    Lieut. Charles A. Davidson

TALIAFERRO'S BRIGADE
(1) Col. Edward T. H. Warren
(2) Col. James W. Jackson (w 9/17)
(3) Col. James L. Sheffield
47th Alabama
    (1) Col. James W. Jackson
    (2) Maj. James M. Campbell
48th Alabama
    Col. James L. Sheffield

10th Virginia
    Col. Edward T. H. Warren
23rd Virginia
    Lieut. Col. Simeon T. Walton
37th Virginia
    Lieut. Col. John F. Terry (w 9/17)

STARKE'S BRIGADE
    (1) Brig. Gen. William E. Starke (k 9/17)
    (2) Col. Jesse M. Williams (w 9/17)
    (3) Col. Leroy A. Stafford (w 9/17)
    (4) Col. Edmond Pendleton
    1st Louisiana
        (1) Lieut. Col. Michael Nolan (w 9/17)
        (2) Capt. William E. Moore
    2nd Louisiana
        Col. Jesse M. Williams
    9th Louisiana
        (1) Col. Leroy A. Stafford (w 9/17)
        (2) Lieut. Col. William R. Peck
    10th Louisiana
        Capt. Henry D. Monier
    15th Louisiana
        Col. Edmund Pendleton
    Coppens's (First Louisiana Zouaves) Battalion
        Capt. M. Alfred Coppens

ARTILLERY
    Maj. Lindsay M. Shumaker
    Alleghany (Virginia) Artillery
        Capt. Joseph Carpenter
    Baltimore (Maryland) Artillery
        Capt. John B. Brockenbrough
    Danville (Virginia) Artillery
        Capt. George Wooding
    Hampden (Virginia) Artillery
        Capt. William H. Caskie
    Lee (Virginia) Battery
        Capt. Charles I. Raine
    Rockbridge (Virginia) Artillery
        Capt. William T. Poague

UNATTACHED DIVISIONS

MCLAWS'S DIVISION
Maj. Gen. Lafayette McLaws

Kershaw's Brigade
Brig. Gen. Joseph B. Kershaw
2nd South Carolina
  (1) Col. John D. Kennedy (w 9/17)
  (2) Maj. Franklin Gaillard
3rd South Carolina
  Col. James D. Nance
7th South Carolina
  (1) Col. David W. Aiken (w 9/17)
  (2) Capt. John S. Hard
8th South Carolina
  Lieut. Col. Axalla J. Hoole

Cobb's Brigade
(1) Brig. Gen. Howell Cobb
(2) Lieut. Col. Christopher C. Sanders
(3) Lieut. Col. William MacRae
16th Georgia
  Lieut. Col. Philip Thomas
24th Georgia
  Maj. Robert E. McMillan (w 9/17)
Cobb's (Georgia) Legion
  Lieut. Col. Luther Glenn
15th North Carolina
  Lieut. Col. William MacRae

Semmes's Brigade
Brig. Gen. Paul J. Semmes
10th Georgia
  (1) Maj. Willis C. Holt (w 9/17)
  (2) Capt. William Johnston (w 9/17)
  (3) Capt. Philologus H. Loud (w 9/17)
53rd Georgia
  (1) Lieut. Col. Thomas Sloan (mw 9/17)
  (2) Capt. Samuel W. Marshborne
15th Virginia
  (1) Capt. Emmett M. Morrison (w and c 9/17)
  (2) Capt. Edward J. Willis

32nd Virginia
    Col. Edgar B. Montague

BARKSDALE'S BRIGADE
  Brig. Gen. William Barksdale
  13th Mississippi
    Lieut. Col. Kennon McElroy (w 9/15)
  17th Mississippi
    Lieut. Col. John C. Fiser
  18th Mississippi
    (1) Maj. James C. Campbell (w 9/17)
    (2) Lieut. Col. William H. Luse
  21st Mississippi
    (1) Capt. John Sims
    (2) Col. Benjamin G. Humphreys

ARTILLERY
  (1) Maj. Samuel P. Hamilton
  (2) Col. Henry C. Cabell
  Manly's Battery (1st North Carolina, Battery A)
    Capt. Basil C. Manly
  Pulaski (Georgia) Artillery
    Capt. John P. W. Read
  Richmond (Fayette) Artillery
    Capt. Miles C. Macon
  Richmond Howitzers, 1st Company
    Capt. Edward S. McCarthy
  Troup (Georgia) Artillery
    Capt. Henry H. Carlton

D. H. HILL'S DIVISION
Maj. Gen. Daniel H. Hill

RIPLEY'S BRIGADE
  (1) Brig. Gen. Roswell S. Ripley (w 9/17)
  (2) Col. George P. Doles
  4th Georgia
    (1) Col. George P. Doles
    (2) Maj. Robert S. Smith (k 9/17)
    (3) Capt. William H. Willis
  44th Georgia
    Capt. John C. Key

1st North Carolina
    Lieut. Col. Hamilton A. Brown
3rd North Carolina
    (1) Col. William L. De Rosset (w 9/17)
    (2) Maj. Stephen D. Thurston (w 9/17)

RODES'S BRIGADE
  Brig. Gen. Robert E. Rodes (w 9/17)
  3rd Alabama
    Col. Cullen A. Battle
  5th Alabama
    Maj. Edwin L. Hobson
  6th Alabama
    (1) Col. John B. Gordon (w 9/17)
    (2) Lieut. Col. James N. Lightfoot (w 9/17)
  12th Alabama
    (1) Col. Bristor B. Gayle (k 9/14)
    (2) Lieut. Col. Samuel B. Pickens (w 9/14)
    (3) Capt. Exton Tucker (k 9/17)
    (4) Capt. W. L. Maroney (w 9/17)
    (5) Capt. Adolph Proskauer (w 9/17)
  26th Alabama
    Col. Edward A. O'Neal (w 9/17)

GARLAND'S BRIGADE
  Brig. Gen. Samuel Garland Jr. (k 9/14)
  Col. Duncan K. McRae (w 9/17)
  5th North Carolina
    (1) Col. Duncan K. McRae (w 9/17)
    (2) Capt. Thomas M. Garrett
  12th North Carolina
    Capt. Shugan Snow
  13th North Carolina
    (1) Lieut. Col. Thomas Ruffin Jr. (w 9/17)
    (2) Capt. Joseph H. Hyman
  20th North Carolina
    Col. Alfred Iverson Jr.
  23rd North Carolina
    (1) Col. Daniel H. Christie
    (2) Lieut. Col. Robert D. Johnston

ANDERSON'S BRIGADE
  (1) Brig. Gen. George B. Anderson (mw 9/17)

(2) Col. Charles C. Tew (k 9/17)
(3) Col. Risden T. Bennett (w 9/17)
(4) Col. Daniel Harvey Christie
2nd North Carolina
    (1) Col. Charles C. Tew (k 9/17)
    (2) Maj. John Howard (w 9/17)
    (3) Capt. Gideon M. Roberts
4th North Carolina
    (1) Col. Bryan Grimes
    (2) Capt. William T. Marsh (k 9/17)
    (3) Capt. Edwin A. Osborn (w 9/17)
    (4) Capt. Daniel P. Latham (k 9/17)
14th North Carolina
    (1) Col. Risden T. Bennett (w 9/17)
    (2) Lieut. Col. William A. Johnson (w 9/17)
    (3) Maj. Andrew W. Sillers
30th North Carolina
    (1) Col. Francis M. Parker (w 9/17)
    (2) Maj. William W. Sillers

RAIN'S / COLQUITT'S BRIGADE
  Col. Alfred H. Colquitt
  13th Alabama
    (1) Col. Birkett D. Fry (w 9/17)
    (2) Lieut. Col. William H. Betts (w 9/17)
    (3) Maj. Algernon S. Reaves (w 9/17)
  6th Georgia
    (1) Lieut. Col. James M. Newton (k 9/17)
    (2) Maj. Philemon Tracy (k 9/17)
    (3) Lieut. Eugene P. Bennett
  23rd Georgia
    (1) Col. William P. Barclay (k 9/17)
    (2) Lieut. Col. Emory F. Best (w 9/17)
    (3) Maj. James H. Huggins (w 9/17)
  27th Georgia
    (1) Col. Levi B. Smith (k 9/17)
    (2) Lieut. Col. Charles T. Zachry (w 9/17)
    (3) Capt. William H. Rentfro
  28th Georgia
    (1) Maj. Tully Graybill (w 9/17)
    (2) Capt. Nehemiah J. Garrison (w 9/17)
    (3) Capt. George W. Warthen

ARTILLERY
    Maj. Scipio F. Pierson
    Hardaway's (Alabama) Battery
        Capt. Robert A. Hardaway
    Jefferson Davis (Alabama) Artillery
        Capt. James W. Bondurant
    Jones's (Virginia) Battery
        Capt. William B. Jones
    King William (Virginia) Artillery
        Capt. Thomas H. Carter (w 9/17)

WALKER'S DIVISION
    Brig. Gen. John G. Walker

WALKER'S BRIGADE
    (1) Col. Vannoy H. Manning (w 9/17)
    (2) Col. Edward D. Hall
    3rd Arkansas
        Capt. John W. Reedy
    27th North Carolina
        Col. John R. Cooke
    46th North Carolina
        (1) Col. Edward D. Hall
        (2) Lieut. Col. William A. Jenkins
    48th North Carolina
        (1) Col. Robert C. Hill
        (2) Lieut. Col. Samuel H. Walkup
    30th Virginia
        Lieut. Col. Robert S. Chew (w 9/17)
    French's (Virginia) Battery
        Capt. Thomas B. French
    2nd Georgia Battalion

RANSOM'S BRIGADE
    Brig. Gen. Robert Ransom Jr.
    24th North Carolina
        Lieut. Col. John L. Harris
    25th North Carolina
        Col. Henry M. Rutledge
    35th North Carolina
        Col. Matt W. Ransom

49th North Carolina
 Lieut. Col. Leroy M. McAfee
Branch's (Virginia) Battery
 Capt. James R. Branch

ARTILLERY RESERVE
 Brig. Gen. William N. Pendleton

BROWN'S BATTALION
 Col. J. Thompson Brown
 Powhatan (Virginia) Artillery
  Capt. Willis J. Dance
 Richmond (Virginia) Howitzers, 2nd Company
  Capt. David Watson
 Richmond (Virginia) Howitzers, 3rd Company
  Capt. Benjamin H. Smith Jr.
 Salem (Virginia) Artillery
  Capt. Abraham Hupp
 Williamsburg (Virginia) Artillery
  Capt. John A. Coke

CUTTS'S BATTALION
 Lieut. Col. A. S. Cutts
 Blackshear's (Georgia) Battery
  Capt. James A. Blackshear
 Irwin (Georgia) Artillery
  Capt. John Lane
 Lloyd's (North Carolina) Battery
  Capt. Whitmel P. Lloyd
 Patterson's (Georgia) Battery
  Capt. George M. Patterson
 Ross's (Georgia) Battery
  Capt. Hugh M. Ross

JONES'S BATTALION
 Maj. H. P. Jones
 Morris (Virginia) Artillery
  Capt. Richard C. M. Page
 Orange (Virginia) Artillery
  Capt. Jefferson Peyton
 Turner's (Virginia) Battery
  Capt. William H. Turner

Long Island (Virginia) Battery
    Capt. Abram Wimbish

NELSON'S BATTALION
    Maj. William Nelson
    Amherst (Virginia) Artillery
        Capt. Thomas J. Kirkpatrick
    Fluvanna (Virginia) Artillery
        Capt. John J. Ancell
    Huckstep's (Virginia) Battery
        Capt. Charles T. Huckstep
    Johnson's (Virginia) Battery
        Capt. Marmaduke Johnson
    Milledge (Georgia) Artillery
        Capt. John Milledge

MISCELLANEOUS BATTERIES
    Cutshaw's (Virginia) Battery
        Capt. Wilford A. Cutshaw
    Magruder (Virginia) Artillery
        Capt. Thomas J. Page Jr.
    Rice's (Virginia) Battery / 8th Star New Market
    (Virginia) Artillery
        Capt. William H. Rice
    Dixie (Virginia) Artillery
        Capt. G. B. Chapman

CAVALRY
Maj. Gen. James E. B. Stuart

HAMPTON'S BRIGADE
    Brig. Gen. Wade Hampton
    1st North Carolina
        Col. Laurence S. Baker
    2nd South Carolina
        Col. Matthew C. Butler
    10th Virginia
    Cobb's (Georgia) Legion
        (1) Lieut. Col. Pierce M. B. Young (w)
        (2) Maj. William G. Delony

Jeff Davis (Mississippi) Legion
   Lieut. Col. William T. Martin
LEE'S BRIGADE
   Brig. Gen. Fitzhugh Lee
   1st Virginia
      Lieut. Col. Luke T. Brien
   3rd Virginia
      (1) Lieut. Col. John T. Thornton (k 9/17)
      (2) Capt. Thomas Owens
   4th Virginia
      Col. Williams C. Wickham
   5th Virginia
      Col. Thomas L. Rosser
   9th Virginia
      Col. William Henry (Rooney) Fitzhugh Lee (w 9/15)
ROBERTSON'S / MUNFORD'S BRIGADE
   Col. Thomas T. Munford
   2nd Virginia
      Lieut. Col. Richard H. Burks
   6th Virginia
      Col. Thomas S. Flournoy
   7th Virginia
      Capt. Samuel B. Myers
   12th Virginia
      Col. Asher W. Harman
   17th Virginia Battalion
HORSE ARTILLERY
   Capt. John Pelham
   Chew's (Virginia) Battery
      Capt. R. Preston Chew
   Hart's (South Carolina) Battery
      Capt. James F. Hart
   Pelham's (Virginia) Battery
      Capt. John Pelham

APPENDIX IV

STRENGTHS AND CASUALTIES OF UNION AND CONFEDERATE FORCES

The figures contained in the tables are compiled from the following sources:

United States War Department, *The War of the Rebellion: Official Records of the Union and Confederate Armies* (hereafter cited as *OR*) (Washington, DC: United States Government Printing Office, 1887), vol. 19, pt. 1, pp. 67, 183–204, 548–49, 810–13.

D. Scott Hartwig, *To Antietam Creek: The Maryland Campaign of September 1862* (Baltimore: Johns Hopkins University Press, 2012), 542, 674–86.

Walter Herron Taylor, *Four Years with General Lee* (New York: D. Appleton, 1878), 71–75.

Ezra A. Carman, *The Maryland Campaign of 1862*, ed. Thomas G. Clemens (El Dorado Hills, CA: Savas Beatie, 2012), 1:567–620.

Daniel J. Vermilya, *Perceptions, Not Realities: The Strength, Experience, and Condition of the Army of the Potomac at Antietam - Joseph L. Harsh Scholarship Award Winner, 2012* (SHAF—Save Historic Antietam Foundation, 2012), 23.

C. W. Whitehair, *Escape Across the Potomac* (Infinity, 2009), 134–35.

Thomas A. McGrath, *Shepherdstown: Last Clash of the Antietam Campaign* (Lynchburg, VA: Schroeder, 2013), 64, 211–17.

Appendix IV

Union Army of the Potomac
Union Overview

Source →	McClellan	Hartwig		
Corps ↓	After-action report - 1863	PFD 09-02	K.W.M. -So. Mtn.	Present on 09-17
First - Hooker	14,856	16,536	923	10,903
Second - Sumner	18,813	18,282	0	17,716
Fourth - Couch (Div)	NA	6,400	0	NA
Fifth - Porter	12,930	8,639	0	9,589
Sixth - Franklin	12,300	13,841	533	11,862
Ninth - Reno - Cox\Burnside	13,819	16,621	889	14,650
Twelfth - Mansfield	10,126	13,161	0	8,861
Cav. - Pleasonton	4,320	4,812	0	4,543
Reserve Artil.	NA	950	0	950
Total	87,164	99,242	2,345	79,074

Source →	Carman\OR			Vermilya
Corps ↓	Engaged on 09-17	Casualties	%	Present on 09/17
First - Hooker	9,438	2,590	27.44%	9,438
Second - Sumner	16,065	5,138	31.98%	16,065
Fourth - Couch (Div)	NA	9	0.00%	0
Fifth - Porter	3,224	109	3.38%	8,000
Sixth - Franklin	2,585	439	16.98%	11,865
Ninth - Reno - Cox\Burnside	12,693	2,349	18.51%	12,693
Twelfth - Mansfield	7,631	1,746	22.88%	7,631
Cav. - Pleasonton	4,320	30	0.69%	4,320
Reserve Artil.	* NA	0	0.00%	NA
Total	55,956	12,410	22.18%	70,012

** Available 09-18	43,546

* Included in Fifth Corps totals
** This number does not include the more than 12,000 men in Couch's and Humphrey's Divisions

Union Detail

South Mountain - September 14

AotP Divisions	PFD	Engaged	KWM	KWM %
First Corps				
First - Doubleday	3,920	3,920	495	12.63%
Second - Ricketts	3,193	3,193	35	1.10%
Third - Mead	3,247	3,147	392	12.46%
Second Corps				
First - Richardson	4,275	NA	0	0.00%
Second - Sedgwick	5,681	NA	0	0.00%
Third - French	5,740	NA	0	0.00%
Artillery-Unatt.	369	NA	0	0.00%
Fourth Corps				
First - Couch	6,400	NA	0	0.00%
Fifth Corps				
First - Morell	6,100	NA	0	0.00%
Second - Sykes	3,489	NA	0	0.00%
Third - Humphreys	6,400	NA	0	0.00%
Artillery Res.	950	NA	0	0.00%
Sixth Corps				
First - Slocum	6,532	6,532	513	7.85%
Second - Smith	7,309	0	19	0.26%
Ninth Corps				
First - Wilcox	3,603	3,603	355	9.85%
Second - Sturgis	3,923	3,923	157	4.00%
Third - Rodman	2,934	0	20	0.68%
Kanawha - Cox	3,510	3,510	356	10.14%
Twelfth Corps				
First - Williams	4,735	NA	0	0.00%
Second - Greene	2,504	NA	0	0.00%
Artillery-Unatt.	392	NA	0	0.00%
Cavalry				
Cavalry	4544	4544	1	0.02%
General Staff			3	

Appendix IV

Antietam - September 17

AotP Divisions	PFD	Engaged	KWM	KWM %
First Corps				
First - Doubleday	3,425	3,425	812	23.71%
Second - Ricketts	3,158	3,158	1,204	38.13%
Third - Mead	2,855	2,855	573	20.07%
Second Corps				
First - Richardson	4,275	4,275	1,165	27.25%
Second - Sedgwick	5,681	5,681	2,210	38.90%
Third - French	5,740	5,740	1,750	30.49%
Artillery-Unatt.	369	369	10	2.71%
Fourth Corps				
First - Couch	6,400	0	9	0.14%
Fifth Corps				
First - Morell	6,100	0	0	0.00%
Second - Sykes	3,489	3,224	98	3.04%
Third - Humphreys	6,400	0	0	0.00%
Artillery Res.	950	950	11	1.16%
Sixth Corps				
First - Slocum	6,019	0	65	1.08%
Second - Smith	7,290	2,585	373	14.43%
Ninth Corps				
First - Wilcox	3,248	3,248	338	10.41%
Second - Sturgis	3,766	3,354	679	20.24%
Third - Rodman	2,914	2,914	1,077	36.96%
Kanawha - Scammon	3,154	3,154	255	8.08%
Twelfth Corps				
First - Williams	4,735	4,735	1,077	22.75%
Second - Greene	2,504	2,504	651	26.00%
Artillery-Unatt.	392	392	17	4.34%
Cavalry				
Cavalry	4543	4543	30	0.66%
General Staff			6	

Shepherdstown - September 19&20

AotP Divisions	PFD	Engaged	KWM	KWM %
First Corps				
First - Doubleday	2,613	NA	0	0.00%
Second - Ricketts	1,954	NA	0	0.00%
Third - Mead	2,282	NA	0	0.00%
Second Corps				
First - Richardson	3,110	NA	0	0.00%
Second - Sedgwick	3,471	NA	0	0.00%
Third - French	3,990	NA	0	0.00%
Artillery-Unatt.	359	NA	0	
Fourth Corps				
First - Couch	6,391	NA	0	0.00%
Fifth Corps				
First - Morell	6,100	6,100	349	5.72%
Second - Sykes	3,126	3,224	15	0.47%
Third - Humphreys	6,400	NA	0	0.00%
Artillery Res.	939	950	3	0.32%
Sixth Corps				
First - Slocum	5,954	NA	0	0.00%
Second - Smith	2,212	NA	0	0.00%
Ninth Corps				
First - Wilcox	2,910	NA	0	0.00%
Second - Sturgis	2,675	NA	0	0.00%
Third - Rodman	1,837	NA	0	0.00%
Kanawha - Scammon	2,899	NA	0	0.00%
Twelfth Corps				
First - Williams	3,658	NA	0	0.00%
Second - Greene	1,853	NA	0	0.00%
Artillery-Unatt.	375	NA	0	0.00%
Cavalry				
Cavalry	4,513	4513	3	0.07%

Appendix IV

Confederate Army of Northern Virginia
Confederate Overview

Source ➡	Walter Taylor	Hartwig					
Divisions ⬇	"Four Years With General Lee"	Present 09-2-62	PFD-So. Mtn. & Harpers Ferry	KWM-So. Mtn. & Harpers Ferry	PFD 09-17 (Est.)	Non Combat Losses	Non Combat Losses %
R.H. Anderson	3,500	11,024	7,601	177	4,000	6,847	62%
DR Jones	2,430	9,034	6,563	953	3,392	4,943	55%
Hood	3,852	3,839	2,970	24	2,304	1,332	35%
Evans Brig.	2,200	1,058	550	216	399	443	42%
S.D. Lee Batt.	*	*	*	*	318		
Washington Artil.	*	590	0	0	596	0	0%
Ewell (Lawton)	3,400	6,246	5,186	0	4,127	2,119	34%
A.P. Hill	3,400	8,464	5,824	69	3,014	5,481	65%
Jackson (J.R. Jones)	3,852	5,578	3,882	0	2,094	3,476	62%
McLaws	2,893	7,759	4,432	962	3,312	3,524	45%
Walker	3,200	5,159	4,555	4	3,946	1,209	23%
D.H. Hill	3,000	9,842	8,314	1,000	5,790	3,057	31%
Cav. Stuart	*	5,313	5,000	0	4,500	813	15%
Reserve Artil.	*	1,299	700	0	621	678	52%
Cav. & Artil. Est.	8,000	NA	NA	NA	NA	NA	NA
Total	39,727	75,205	55,577	3,405	38,413	33,922	45%

Source ➡	Carman		
Divisions ⬇	Engaged 09-17	KWM Antietam	%
R.H. Anderson	4,000	1,278	31.95%
D.R. Jones	3,392	758	22.35%
Hood	2,304	1,025	44.49%
Evans Brig.	399	84	21.05%
S.D. Lee Batt.	318	85	26.73%
Washington Artil.	278	34	12.23%
Ewell (Lawton)	4,127	1,338	32.42%
A.P. Hill	2,568	417	16.24%
Jackson (J.R. Jones)	2,094	648	30.95%
McLaws	2,961	1,119	37.79%
Walker	3,994	1,120	28.04%
D.H. Hill	5,795	2,310	39.86%
Cav. Stuart	4,500	49	1.09%
Reserve Artil.	621	51	8.21%
Cav. & Artil. Est.	NA	NA	NA
Total	37,351	10,316	27.62%

* Available 09-18   27,035
* This figure does not include the 6000 Confederate stragglers that reportedly joined Lee's army on the 18th.

Confederate Detail

South Mountain & Harpers Ferry - September 13 to 15

AoNV Divisions	PFD	Engaged	KWM	KWM %
Longstreet				
R.H. Anderson	7,601	7,601	177	2.33%
D.R. Jones	6,563	6,563	953	14.52%
Hood	2,970	2,970	24	0.81%
Evans Brig.	550	550	216	39.27%
S.D. Lee Batt.	*	*	*	*
Washington Artil.	0	0	0	0
Jackson				
Ewell (Lawton)	5,186	5,186	0	0.00%
A.P. Hill	5,824	5,824	69	1.18%
Jackson (J.R. Jones)	3,882	3,882	0	0.00%
Unattached				
McLaws	4,432	4,432	962	21.71%
Walker	4,555	4,555	4	0.09%
D.H. Hill	8,314	8,314	1,000	12.03%
Cav. Stuart	5,000	5,000	0	0.00%
Reserve Artil.	700	700	0	0.00%

Antietam - September 17

AoNV Divisions	PFD	Engaged	KWM	KWM %
Longstreet				
R.H. Anderson	4,000	4,000	1,278	31.95%
D.R. Jones	3,392	3,392	758	22.35%
Hood	2,304	2,304	1,025	44.49%
Evans Brig.	399	399	84	21.05%
S.D. Lee Batt.	318	318	85	26.73%
Washington Artil.	596	278	34	12.23%
Jackson				
Ewell (Lawton)	4,127	4,127	1,338	32.42%
A.P. Hill	3,014	2,568	417	16.24%
Jackson (J.R. Jones)	2,094	2,094	648	30.95%
Unattached				
McLaws	3,312	2,961	1,119	37.79%
Walker	3,946	3,994	1,120	28.04%
D.H. Hill	5,790	5,795	2,310	39.86%
Cav. Stuart	4,500	4,500	49	1.09%
Reserve Artil.	621	621	51	8.21%

Shepherdstown - September 19&20

AoNV Divisions	PFD	Engaged	KWM	KWM %
Longstreet				
R.H. Anderson *	2,722	450	5	1.11%
D.R. Jones	2,634	NA	0	0.00%
Hood	1,279	NA	0	0.00%
Evans Brig.	315	NA	0	0.00%
S.D. Lee Batt.	233	NA	0	0.00%
Washington Artil.	562	NA	0	0.00%
Jackson				
Ewell (Lawton) *	2,789	300	9	3.00%
A.P. Hill *	2,597	2,597	292	11.24%
Jackson (J.R. Jones)	1,446	NA	0	0.00%
Unattached				
McLaws	2,193	NA	0	0.00%
Walker	2,826	NA	0	0.00%
D.H. Hill *	3,480	100	0	0.00%
Cav. Stuart *	4,451	4,451	0	0.00%
Reserve Artil.	570	570	2	0.35%

* Estimated

Harpers Ferry Garrison

Harpers Ferry Overview

Unit ⬇	PFD 09/13/62	Killed or Wounded	Missing or Captured	Casualties KW %
General Staff	7	1	6	14.29%
First Brigade - D'utassy	3,454	47	3,407	1.36%
Second Brigade - Trimble	4,357	81	4,276	1.86%
Third Brigade - Ford	1,352	79	1,139	5.84%
Fourth Brigade - Ward	1,710	1	1,709	0.06%
Unattached	3,294	2	1,999	0.06%
Total	14,174	211	12,536	1.49%

Appendix IV

Harpers Ferry Detail

	Present	Killed or Wounded	Missing or Captured
General Staff	7	1	6
FIRST BRIGADE			
Col. Frederick D'utassy	1	0	1
65th Illinois - Col. Daniel Cameron	817	7	810
39th New York - Maj. Hugo Hildebrandt	545	15	530
111th New York - Col. Jesse Segoine	981	11	970
115th New York - Col. Simeon Sammon	989	11	978
15th Indiana Battery - Capt. John Von Sehlen	121	3	118
First Birgade Total	3,454	47	3,407
SECOND BRIGADE			
Col. William Trimble	1	0	1
125th New York - Col. George Willard	922	3	919
126th New York - Col. Eliakim Sherrill	1,031	55	976
60th Ohio - Lieut. Col. Noah Hixon	913	8	905
9th Vermont - Col. George Stannard	747	3	744
3rd Maryland Potomac Home Guard - Lieut. Col. Stephen Downey	546	12	534
1st Indiana Battery - Capt. Silas Rigby	113	0	113
Ohio Battery - Capt. Benjamin Potts	84	0	84
Second Birgade Total	4,357	81	4,276
THIRD BRIGADE			
Col. Thomas Ford	1	0	1
1st Maryland Potomac Home Guard (Battalion) - Maj. John Steiner	307	6	313
32nd Ohio - Col. Thomas Ford	742	68	674
5th New York Heavy Artillery, Bat. F - Capt. Eugene McGrath	133	2	131
1st Maryland Cavalry (detachment) - Capt. Charles Russell	23	3	20
7th Squadron, Rhode Island Cavalry - Maj. A. Corliss	146	0	0
Third Birgade Total	1,352	79	1,139
FOURTH BRIGADE			
Col. William Ward	1	0	1
12th New York (militia) - Col. William Ward	560	0	560
87th Ohio - Col. Henry Banning	1,015	1	1,014
5th New York Heavy Artillery, Co. A - Capt. J. Graham	134	0	134
Fourth Birgade Total	1,710	1	1,709
UNATTACHED			
1st Maryland Potomac Home Guard - Col. William P. Maulsby	478	0	478
1st Maryland Potomac Home Guard Cavalry (including Loudoun Rangers) - Maj. Henry Cole	136	0	0
12th Illinois Cavalry - Col. Hasbrouck Davis	702	2	157
8th New York Cavalry - Col. Benjamin Davis	706	0	92
2nd Illinois Artillery - Capt. John Phillips	100	0	100
Unattached - Orderlies, men in hospital and hospital staff	1172	0	1,172
Unattached Total	3294	2	1,999
Garrison Total	14,174	211	12,536

NOTES

Preface

1. Steven M. Gillon, *10 Days That Unexpectedly Changed America* (New York: Broadway Books, 2006), 98.
2. James Murfin, *The Gleam of Bayonets: The Battle of Antietam and Robert E. Lee's Maryland Campaign, September 1862* (Baton Rouge: Louisiana State University Press, 1964), 9.
3. Stephen W. Sears, *Landscape Turned Red: The Battle of Antietam* (New Haven: Ticknor and Fields, 1983), xi.
4. D. Scott Hartwig, *To Antietam Creek: The Maryland Campaign of September 1862* (Baltimore: Johns Hopkins University Press, 2012), 2.
5. Daniel J. Vermilya, *That Field of Blood: The Battle of Antietam* (El Dorado Hills: Savas Beatie 2018), xxiv.
6. Francis F. Browne, *The Every-Day Life of Abraham Lincoln* (1913; repr., New York: Diversion Books, 2014), 218.

Introduction

1. James M. McPherson, *The Illustrated Battle Cry of Freedom: The Civil War Era* (New York: Oxford University Press, 2003), 277–86.

2. Ezra J. Warner, *Generals in Blue: Lives of the Union Commanders* (Baton Rouge: Louisiana State University Press, 1964), 290–92. Technically, A. P. Hill and John Gibbon did not graduate until 1847, but they both entered the academy in 1842. Bvt. Maj. Gen. George W. Cullum, Biographical Register of the Officers and Graduates of the U.S. Military Academy at West Point N.Y. (Boston: Houghton, Mifflin, 1891), 2:249–305; Stephen W. Sears, *George B. McClellan: The Young Napoleon* (New York: De Capo, 1999), 47–48.

3. Stephen W. Sears, *Lincoln's Lieutenants: The High Command of the Army of the Potomac* (Boston: Houghton, Mifflin, Harcourt, 2017), 78–104.

4. Sears, *Landscape Turned Red*, 31; Murfin, *Gleam of Bayonets*, 52–53.

5. Murfin, *Gleam of Bayonets*, 55–60.

6. McPherson, *Battle Cry of Freedom*, 439

7. Stephen B. Oates, *With Malice Toward None* (New York: Harper and Row, 1977), 313.

8. Browne, *The Every-Day Life*, 217–18.

9. J. Cutler Andrews, *The North Reports the Civil War* (Pittsburgh: University of Pittsburgh Press, 1955), 270; Sears, *Landscape Turned Red*, 7.

10. Steven E Woodworth, *Davis & Lee at War* (Lawrence: University Press of Kansas, 1995), 130, 180.

11. United States War Department, *The War of the Rebellion: Official Records of the Union and Confederate Armies* (Washington, DC: United States Government Printing Office, 1974–1880), vol. 19, pt. 2, p. 590. Hereafter, this source will be cited in the following format: *OR*, vol. 19, pt. 2, p. 590

12. See appendix 3 for the Confederate order of battle, and see appendix 4 for details on troop strength.

13. See appendix 3 for the Confederate order of battle, and see appendix 4 for details on troop strength.

14. George Brinton, McClellan, *McClellan's Own Story: The War for the Union, the Soldiers Who Fought It, the Civilians Who Directed It and His Relations to It and to Them* (New York: C. L. Webster, 1887), 572.

15. McPherson, *Battle Cry of Freedom*, 461–463; *OR*, vol. 19, pt. 1, p. 951–55.

Chapter 1

1. Edward Clifford Gordon, "Memorandum of a Conversation With R.E. Lee." In *Lee the Soldier*, ed. Garry Gallagher, (Lincoln: University of Nebraska Press, 1996), 25; *OR*, vol. 19, pt. 1, p. 140.
2. James Longstreet, *From Manassas to Appomattox: Memoirs of the Civil War in America* (1896; repr., New York, William S. Konecky Associates, 1992), 227; *OR*, vol. 19, pt. 2, pp. 608–9; vol. 51, pt. 2, p. 618; Murfin, *Gleam of Bayonets*, 186–92; Ezra A. Carman, *The Maryland Campaign of September 1862: Ezra A. Carman's Definitive Study of the Union and Confederate Armies at Antietam*, ed. Joseph Pierro (Hoboken, NJ: Taylor and Francis, 2008), 169–73; *Taken at the Flood: Robert E. Lee and Confederate Strategy in the Maryland Campaign of 1862* (Kent, OH: Kent State University Press, 1999), 294.
3. *OR*, vol. 51, pt. 2, pp. 618–19.
4. Harsh, *Taken at the Flood*, 292.
5. Hartwig, *To Antietam Creek*, 481–84.
6. *OR*, vol. 19, pt. 1, p. 951.
7. This number is an estimate based on the men in Longstreet's and D. H. Hill's commands. See appendix 3 for the Confederate order of battle, and see appendix 4 for details on troop strength.
8. Longstreet, *From Manassas to Appomattox*, 233–34; Harsh, *Taken at the Flood*, 330.
9. Harsh, *Taken at the Flood*, 301; Sears, *Landscape Turned Red*, 167–69.
10. It seems logical that Lee was still looking to accomplish the political and military objectives he set at the beginning of the campaign. Murfin, *Gleam of Bayonets*, 63-71
11. *OR*, vol. 19, pt. 1, p. 140.
12. Recent research by Dennis Frye traces this quote by Lee to Douglas Southall Freeman, who quoted a 1911 book by William H. Morgan entitled *Personal Reminiscences of the War of 1861–5*. Morgan, who was not at Antietam during the battle, indicates he heard the quote from some of his fellow soldiers in the Eleventh Virginia. Dennis E. Frye, *Antietam Shadows: Mystery, Myth and Machination* (Sharpsburg, MD: Antietam Rest, 2018), 21–25; Douglas Southall Freeman, *R. E. Lee: A Biography* (New York: Charles Scribner's Sons, 1936), 2:378; Harsh, *Taken at the Flood*, 334, 344, 354–55.

13. Sears, *Landscape Turned Red*, 160–61.
14. McClellan, *McClellan's Own Story*, 613–15.
15. Sears, *Landscape Turned Red*, 162–64; Ethan S. Rafuse, *McClellan's War: The Failure of Moderation in the Struggle for the Union* (Bloomington: Indiana University Press, 2005), 303–8; Steven R. Stotelmyer, *Too Useful to Sacrifice: Reconsidering George B. McClellan's Generalship in the Maryland Campaign from South Mountain to Antietam* (El Dorado Hills, CA: Savas Beatie, 2019), 94, 140.
16. McClellan, *McClellan's Own Story*, 584–87.
17. *OR*, vol. 19, pt. 2, p. 289.
18. McClellan, *McClellan's Own Story*, 584
19. *OR*, vol. 19, pt. 2, p. 294.
20. This is a perfect example of information that made its way to McClellan during the campaign that combined some small bits of truth with rumor and speculation. Because of an injury to both wrists several days earlier, Lee was probably riding in his ambulance during this time. This may explain why he was reported as wounded. *OR*, vol. 19, pt. 2, pp. 295–96.
21. *OR*, vol. 19, pt. 1, p. 47, pt. 2, p. 296.
22. Murfin, *Gleam of Bayonets*, 199, 204–6; Carman, *Maryland Campaign: Ezra A. Carman's Definitive Study*, 175–80; Walter H. Hebert, *Fighting Joe Hooker* (Indianapolis: Bobbs-Merrill, 1944), 137–38.
23. See appendix 4. Hartwig, *To Antietam Creek*, 515, 582, 585–88, 594; Bradley M. Gottfried, *The Maps of Antietam: An Atlas of The Antietam (Sharpsburg) Campaign, Including the Battle of South Mountain, September 2–20*, (El Dorado Hills: Savas Beatie, 2012), 116–18.
24. *OR*, vol. 19, pt. 1, p. 52. See appendix 4 of this work for details on troop strength.
25. McClellan, *McClellan's Own Story*, 588.
26. *OR*, vol. 19, pt. 2, pp. 307–8; Hartwig, *To Antietam Creek*, 436; Carman, *Maryland Campaign*, 1:343; Rafuse, *McClellan's War*, 282.
27. Hartwig, *To Antietam Creek*, 160
28. *OR*, vol. 19, pt. 1, p. 30, 55, 217–18; Jacob D. Cox, "The Battle of Antietam" In *Battles and Leaders of the Civil War*, ed. Robert Underwood Johnson and Clarence Clough Buel (New York: Century, 1887) 2:633
29. Frye, *Antietam Shadows*, 144–47.

Chapter 2

1. Ezra J. Warner, *Generals in Blue: Lives of the Union Commanders* (Baton Rouge: Louisiana State University Press, 1964), 233–35; Stephen W. Sears, *Chancellorsville* (Boston: Houghton Mifflin Harcourt, 1996), 54–57; Bvt. Maj. Gen. George W. Cullum, *Biographical Register of the Officers and Graduates of the U.S. Military Academy at West Point N.Y.* (Boston: Houghton, Miffin, 1891), 1:660–97; Gen. Francis W. Palfrey, The Antietam and Fredericksburg Campaigns (1912; repr., Da Capo, 1996), 55; Hebert, *Fighting Joe Hooker*, 90–91.

2. *OR*, vol. 19, pt. 1, pp. 213–17. See also appendix 4 of this work for details on troop strength.

3. For positions at dawn on September 17, see United States War Department, map 1, in *Atlas of the Battlefield of Antietam, Prepared Under the Direction of the Antietam Battlefield Board, Lieut. Col. Geo. W. Davis, U.S.A., President, Gen. E. A. Carman, U.S.V., Gen. H. Heth, C.S.A. Surveyed by Lieut. Col. E. B. Cope, Engineer, H. W. Mattern, Assistant Engineer, of the Gettysburg National Park. Drawn by Charles H. Ourand. Position of Troops by Gen. E. A. Carman. Published by Authority of the Secretary of War, Under the Direction of the Chief of Engineers, U.S. Army, 1908* (Washington, DC: Government Printing Office, 1908), https://www.loc.gov/item/2008621532/. Hereafter, maps from this source are cited in the following format: US War Department, map 1, in *Atlas of the Battlefield of Antietam*. See appendix 4 of this work for details on troop strength, and see appendix 3 for the Confederate order of battle.

4. Harsh, *Taken at the Flood*, 350–52; *OR*, vol. 19, pt. 1, p. 475; McClellan, *McClellan's Own Story*, 590–91; Ezra Carman, *The Maryland Campaign of September 1862*, ed. Thomas G. Clemens, vol. 2, *Antietam* (El Dorado Hills, CA: Savas Beatie, 2012), 28–29. See also appendix 4 of this work for details on troop strength.

5. *OR*, vol. 19, pt. 1, p. 218. McClellan and Hooker met several times that day, and Hooker was reportedly at the Pry House on the morning of the sixteenth. Hartwig, *To Antietam Creek*, 589, 594, 608. Sunrise was officially at 5:53 a.m., but it was probably light enough for action by 5:30 or 5:45 a.m. Joseph L. Harsh, *Sounding the Shallows: A Confederate Companion for the Maryland Campaign of 1862* (Kent, OH: Kent State University Press, 2000), 19.

6. Ezra Carman, *The Maryland Campaign of September 1862*, ed. Thomas G. Clemens, vol. 2, *Antietam* (El Dorado Hills, CA: Savas Beatie, 2012), 21.

7. Harsh, *Taken at the Flood*, 348.
8. *OR*, vol. 19, pt. 1, p. 218.
9. Best evidence indicates that Hooker ordered the Twelfth Corps to advance to his support as soon as the battle opened. Joe Harsh asserts that the orders were given at 5:30 a.m. Alpheus Williams stated that the Twelfth Corps moved as soon as the sounds of battle were heard. Small-arms fire began as soon as there was enough light to see, perhaps as early as 5:15 a.m. Carman also recounts a dawn movement, but he also says that Mansfield stopped his corps several times. All sources indicate that the Twelfth Corps was not engaged until 7:15 a.m. Harsh, *Taken at the Flood*, 369, 372; *OR*, vol. 19, pt. 1, p. 475; Carman, *Maryland Campaign*, 2:113–15.
10. *OR*, vol. 19, pt. 1, pp. 30, 476; Cox, "The Battle of Antietam" In *Battles and Leaders*, 2:637–45.
11. Ethan S. Rafuse, *Antietam, South Mountain, & Harpers Ferry: A Battlefield Guide* (Lincoln: University of Nebraska Press. 2008, 27–28.
12. The Union command likely did not fully comprehend Lee's position on the morning of the seventeenth, having no knowledge beyond what they ascertained from Meade's probes the evening before. McClellan, *McClellan's Own Story*, 587.
13. Longstreet, *From Manassas to Appomattox*, 241–44; *OR*, vol. 19, pt. 1, p. 956.
14. *OR*, vol. 19, pt. 1, pp. 218.
15. Warner, *Generals in Gray*, 142–43; Cullum, *Biographical Register*, 2:515–71; John B. Hood, *Advance and Retreat: Personal Experiences in the United States and Confederate States Armies* (New Orleans: Published for the Hood Orphan Memorial Fund, G. T. Beauregard, 1880), 1–8, 15–20.
16. Hood is listed as having 2,304 men in his division PFD on the morning of September 17. This number includes the 300 men in his artillery. *OR*, vol. 19, pt. 1, pp. 922–23. See also appendix 4 of this manuscript for details on troop strength.
17. Harsh, *Taken at the Flood*, 373.
18. *OR*, vol. 19, pt. 1, pp. 952–58.
19. For positions at 7:00 a.m. on September 17, see US War Department, map 3, in *Atlas of the Battlefield of Antietam*; Hood, *Advance and Retreat*, 41–43; Gottfried, *Maps of Antietam*, 142–43.
20. Carman, *Maryland Campaign*, 2:88–89.

21. *OR*, vol. 19, pt. 1, pp. 923.
22. Based on the Ezra A. Carman maps, Hood's Division was engaged for forty-five to seventy-five minutes. US War Department, maps 3, 4, and 5, in *Atlas of the Battlefield of Antietam*; Carman, *Maryland Campaign*, 2:109, 605.
23. *OR*, vol. 19, pt. 1, pp. 929. See also appendix 4 of this manuscript for details on casualties.
24. Accounts conflict as to the reason Sumner was sent across the creek. According to *New York Tribune* writer George Smalley, Sumner was dispatched to follow up on Hooker's initial success. According to author Ethan Rafuse, the order was issued in response to Hood driving Hooker back. While both of these sources indicate the action could be seen from the Pry House, other scholars dispute this claim. George M. Smalley, "Battle-Field of Antietam" *New York Tribune*, September 19, 1862; Rafuse, *McClellan's War*, 315.
25. Warner, *Generals in Blue*, 489–90; Warner, *Generals in Gray*, 191; Thomas K. Tate, *General Edwin Vose Sumner, USA: A Civil War Biography* (Jefferson, NC: McFarland, 2013), 36.
26. Rafuse, *McClellan's War*, 190–91.
27. That evening, Sumner was receiving orders from McClellan for the Twelfth Corps. This fact indicates that both Sumner and McClellan believed Sumner was still acting as wing commander. *OR*, vol. 19, pt. 1, p. 275; Sears, *Landscape Turned Red*, 216–17.
28. See notation 24 above.
29. *OR*, vol. 19, pt. 1, p. 275.
30. Sears, *Landscape Turned Red*, 220–22; Tate, *General Edwin Vose Sumner*, 166–68; Carman, *Maryland Campaign*, 2:172–75; Marion V. Armstrong, *Unfurl Those Colors: McClellan, Sumner & the Second Army Corps in the Antietam Campaign* (Tuscaloosa: University of Alabama Press, 2008), 175.
31. Sears, *Landscape Turned Red*, 218–19; US War Department, maps 7 and 8, in *Atlas of the Battlefield of Antietam*. See appendix 4 of this manuscript for information on troop strength.
32. See Franklin's after-action report, *OR*, vol. 19, pt. 1, p. 377.
33. See appendix 2 for Union order of Battle and appendix 4 on strength
34. In chapter 8 of *Unfurl Those Colors*, Marion Armstrong gives a very different account of Sumner's orders and his actions before and during the struggle for the West Woods.

35. See appendix 4 for information on troop strength and casualties.
36. See Sumner's and McLaws's after-action reports, *OR*, vol. 19, pt. 1, pp. 275–76, 857–59.
37. Murfin, *Gleam of Bayonets*, 227, 233–36; Sears, *Landscape Turned Red*, 220–22.
38. Armstrong, *Unfurl Those Colors*, 173–79, 203–5.
39. See the report of Confederate colonel James B. Walton of the Washington Artillery concerning the positions at Cemetery Hill, *OR*, vol. 19, pt. 1, pp. 848–51.
40. Harsh, *Taken at the Flood*, 377–81; Sears, *Landscape Turned Red*, 213–14. See appendix 4 of this manuscript for further details concerning strength and casualties.
41. Longstreet, *From Manassas to Appomattox*, 243.
42. Reports indicate that both Hooker and Mansfield were wounded between 7:30 a.m. and 9:00 a.m. Sears, *Landscape Turned Red*, 215; Carman, *Maryland Campaign*, 2:162, 165; Murfin, *Gleam of Bayonets*, 225.
43. See appendix 2 for the Union order of battle and appendix 4 for additional information on troop strength and casualties.
44. *OR*, vol. 19, pt. 1, p. 1008.
45. *OR*, vol. 19, pt. 1, pp. 1022–23; Harsh, *Taken at the Flood*, 378–85.
46. See appendix 4 concerning troop strength.
47. For positions, see US War Department, maps 6 and 7, in *Atlas of the Battlefield of Antietam*.
48. Harsh, *Taken at the Flood*, 407–8.
49. See appendix 4 on troop strength.
50. *OR*, vol. 19, pt. 1, p. 149.
51. For positions, see US War Department, maps 7 and 8, in *Atlas of the Battlefield of Antietam*.
52. Warner, *Generals in Gray*, 79–80; Cullum, *Biographical Register*, 1:674; Jubal A. Early, *Lieutenant General Jubal A. Early, Confederate States of America* (1912; repr., Oxfordshire, UK, Acheron, 2012), 1, 5.
53. Harsh, *Taken at the Flood*, 373–74, 388; US War Department, maps 5, 6, and 7, in *Atlas of the Battlefield of Antietam*.
54. By all indications the so-called superbattery began forming between 8:00 a.m. or 8:30 a.m. and was built up as the day wore on. Marion V. Armstrong, *Opposing the Second Corps at Antietam: The Fight for the Confederate Left and Center on America's Bloodiest Day* (Tuscaloosa:

University of Alabama Press, 2016), 153; Harsh, *Taken at the Flood*, 387–90; Gottfried, *Maps of Antietam*, 166–67; *OR*, vol. 19, pt. 1, pp. 967–70; US War Department, maps 5–7, in *Atlas of the Battlefield of Antietam*.

55. Early, *Lieutenant General Jubal A. Early*, 67.
56. *OR*, vol. 19, pt. 1, p. 970.
57. This number is based on the combined numbers of the 124th and 125th Pennsylvania, Goodrich's brigade, Green's division, and Sedgwick's division. The figure also takes into account Confederates in McLaws's, Walker's, and G. T. Anderson's commands, as well as those already in the West Woods. See appendix 2 for the Union order of Battle and appendix 4 on troop strength.
58. *OR*, vol. 19, pt. 1, pp. 970–71.
59. *OR*, vol. 19, pt. 1, p. 971.
60. *OR*, vol. 19, pt. 1, p. 149.
61. *OR*, vol. 19, pt. 1, p. 956.
62. While it is difficult to know precisely what Sumner had in mind on September 17, it does seem that he intended to move into or just beyond the woods with Sedgwick and wheel left to sweep the Confederates before him. Carman, *Maryland Campaign: Ezra A. Carman's Definitive Study*, 254.
63. Warner, *Generals in Blue*, 161–62; Cullum, *Biographical Register*, 1:676–79.
64. While evidence supports both versions of what happened to French and the ultimate direction of his division, it is less confusing for the reader to commit to one. However, in each scenario the options open to the decision-maker and the results are almost identical. For details on the two competing versions of events, see the following: Francis Amasa Walker, *History of the Second Army Corps in the Army of the Potomac* (New York: C. Scribner's Sons, 1886), 41; Murfin, *Gleam of Bayonets*, 246–47; Sears, *Landscape Turned Red*, 235–36; Armstrong, *Unfurl Those Colors*, 169–71, 179.
65. Lawrence A. Kreiser Jr., *Defeating Lee: A History of the Second Corps, Army of the Potomac* (Bloomington: Indiana University Press, 2011), 47–49.
66. See Sumner's decision to attack the West Woods for discussion of what else Sumner saw and the overall situation.
67. Armstrong, *Unfurl Those Colors*, 176–79; US War Department, map 8, in *Atlas of the Battlefield of Antietam*.

68. *OR*, vol. 19, pt. 1, p. 323; Sears, *Landscape Turned Red*, 221.
69. Armstrong, *Unfurl Those Colors*, 171–72.
70. Carman, *Maryland Campaign*, 2:247, 252.
71. *OR*, vol. 19, pt. 1, pp. 323–24.
72. Joe Harsh presents an attack by French due west and on the left of Greene as a possible option, but he does not talk about how French would have dealt with Hill's men on his flank. Harsh, *Taken at the Flood*, 395.
73. See Greene's after-action report, *OR*, vol. 19, pt. 1, p. 505.
74. These are the command losses for Willcox, Featherston, Pryor, and Wright of Anderson's Division and Rodes and Anderson of Hill's Division. See appendix 3 for the Confederate order of battle.
75. John C. Waugh, *Surviving the Confederacy: Rebellion, Ruin and Recovery; Roger and Sara Pryor during the Civil War* (New York: Harcourt, 2002), 5–8, 24–25, 46, 54–55, 58–57, 82–89; Warner, *Generals in Gray*, 247–48.
76. See D. H. Hill's after-action report, *OR*, vol. 19, pt. 1, pp. 1022–23.
77. See appendix 3 of this book for the Confederate order of Battle and appendix 4 for or information on troop strength and casualties. For positions, see US War Department, maps 7, 8, and 9, in *Atlas of the Battlefield of Antietam*; Gottfried, *Maps of Antietam*, 184.
78. Gottfried, *Maps of Antietam*, 184; Harsh, *Taken at the Flood*, 395–97.
79. On paper, Anderson had six brigades. Mahon's Brigade had only eighty-two men at Antietam and was acting as a regiment attached to Pryor's Brigade. Armistead's Brigade was detached and operating in support of McLaws. Sears, *Landscape Turned Red*, 240–41; *OR*, vol. 19, pt. 1, p. 1037; Carman, *Maryland Campaign*, 2:257. See appendix 3 of this book for the Confederate order of battle.
80. *OR*, vol. 19, pt. 1, pp. 308–9.
81. For positions, see US War Department, map 9, in *Atlas of the Battlefield of Antietam*; Gottfried, *Maps of Antietam*, 188–89.
82. *OR*, vol. 19, pt. 1, pp. 915–16; US War Department, map 10, in *Atlas of the Battlefield of Antietam*.
83. Waugh, *Surviving the Confederacy*, 167.
84. Carman, *Maryland Campaign*, 2:270.
85. Carman, *Maryland Campaign*, 2:281.
86. Gottfried, *Maps of Antietam*, 192–93; *OR*, vol. 19, pt. 1, p. 1024. See also appendix 3 of this book for the Confederate order of battle.

87. Rafuse, *Antietam, South Mountain, & Harpers Ferry*, 138–43; *OR*, vol. 19, pt. 1, pp. 884, 1023; Armstrong, *Opposing the Second Corps*, 110–15.
88. *OR*, vol. 19, pt. 1, p. 67. See appendix 2 of this work for Union order of battle and appendix 4 for information on troop strength and casualties.
89. *OR*, vol. 19, pt. 1, p. 376.
90. *OR*, vol. 19, pt. 1, p. 61.
91. *OR*, vol. 19, pt. 1, pp. 376–77.
92. See appendix 4 of this book on strength and casualties. Harsh, *Taken at the Flood*, 397.
93. US War Department, maps 10 and 11, in *Atlas of the Battlefield of Antietam*.
94. It is difficult to say what the state and strength of the Confederate units were in the positions west and north of the Dunker Church. If you sum both units' manpower and subtract the recorded casualties, you get a number close to nine thousand. It is safe to assume, however, that this number is wildly optimistic. If you factor in soldiers' exhaustion and lack of ammunition, as well as the men knocked loose from their units and those who fell farther back to the rear, you might get a total of perhaps six thousand. Carman, *Maryland Campaign*, 2:352. See also the reports of Hood, McLaws, and J. R. Jones, *OR*, vol. 19, pt. 1, pp. 859, 923, 1008.
95. Harsh, *Taken at the Flood*, 397.
96. Snell, *From First to Last*, 194.
97. For details on tactical reserves, see Maj. Gregory J. Borden, *"True" Tactical Reserves in Striking Force Operations: Pilfery of Combat Power at the Line of Contact?* (Fort Leavenworth, KS: School of Advanced Military Studies, US Army Command and General Staff College, 1995).
98. Marion Armstrong describes a series of communications between Sumner and McClellan, noting that McClellan initially ordered the Sixth Corps to hold position, and that Sumner wanted permission to attack. After initially granting Sumner permission to move forward with the attack if he felt it practicable, McClellan rode to the front to see for himself. It was then that the commanding general decided no assault should be made. Armstrong, *Unfurl Those Colors*, 268–73; Franklin, "Notes On Crampton's Gap And Antietam," in *Battles and Leaders of the Civil War* (New York: Century, 1887), 2:597.
99. *OR*, vol. 19, pt. 1, pp. 956–57.
100. Warner, *Generals in Blue*, 378–80; Cullum, *Biographical Register*, 2:219–20.

101. For a history of the Fifth Corps prior to Second Bull Run, see William Henry Powell, *The Fifth Army Corps (Army of the Potomac): A Record of Operations during the Civil War in the United States of America, 1861–1865* (New York: G. P. Putnam's Sons, 1896), chapters 1–3.

102. For details on the Second Battle of Bull Run, see Matt Spruill III and Matt Spruill IV, *Decisions at Second Manassas: The Fourteen Critical Decisions That Defined the Battle* (Knoxville: University of Tennessee Press, 2018). For details on the court-martial of Porter, see Curt Anders, *Injustice on Trial: Second Bull Run, General Fitz John Porter's Court Martial, and the Schofield Board Investigation That Restored His Good Name* (New York, Curt Anders Books, 2002).

103. Longstreet, *From Manassas to Appomattox*, 185–87; Hartwig, *To Antietam Creek*, 140–41.

104. *OR*, vol. 19, pt. 1, pp. 338–41.

105. See US War Department, maps 10–13, in *Atlas of the Battlefield of Antietam*; Carman, *Maryland Campaign*, 2:358–88; *OR*, vol. 19, pt. 1, p. 356–57.

106. See US War Department, maps 11 and 12, in *Atlas of the Battlefield of Antietam*; *OR*, vol. 19, pt. 1, pp. 350–52.

107. See appendix 4 of this book for information on book strength. A. P. Hill indicated that he arrived on the field by 2:30 p.m. Harsh asserts that the hour was closer to 3:30 p.m., and that Hill's Division was still crossing the Potomac as Hill rode on ahead to meet Lee. *OR*, vol. 19, pt. 1, p. 981; Harsh, *Taken at the Flood*, 417–18.

108. *OR*, vol. 19, pt. 1, p. 212. See US War Department, maps 12 and 13, in *Atlas of the Battlefield of Antietam*.

109. These two divisions were not at full strength, as part of Morell's division was sent on other duties. *OR*, vol. 19, pt. 1, p. 339. See appendix 4 of this work for details on armies' strength. *OR*, vol. 19, pt. 1, p. 29.

110. *OR*, vol. 19, pt. 1, p. 399.

111. In detailing this incident, Steven Stotelmyer not only disputes that Porter ever made this statement, but also reevaluates the reserve forces McClellan had at hand. See Stotelmyer, *Too Useful to Sacrifice*, chapter 4. For the account published in 1886, see Thomas M. Anderson, "The Reserves at Antietam," *Century Illustrated Magazine* 32 (May 1886–October 1886): 783.

112. Warner, *Generals in Blue*, 57–58; Cullum, *Biographical Register*, 2:316,

318–20; Sears, *Lincoln's Lieutenants*, 400; William Marvel, Burnside. (Chapel Hill: University of North Carolina Press, 1991), xii, 13–16, 18–24, 31–33, 42–43, 97–100.

113. Cox, "The Battle of Antietam" In *Battles and Leaders*, 2:631–32.
114. *OR*, vol. 19, pt. 1, p. 55.
115. *OR*, vol. 19, pt. 1, pp. 31, 424. See US War Department, map 9, in *Atlas of the Battlefield of Antietam*.
116. Hartwig, *To Antietam Creek*, 590–92; *OR*, vol. 19, pt. 1, pp. 423–24. See appendix 4 of this work for additional information on armies' strength.
117. The exact number of Georgians defending this position is not clear. Toombs stated the number was four hundred, while Phillip Tucker indicates it might have been as low as three hundred. Phillip Thomas Tucker, *Burnside's Bridge: The Climactic Struggle of the 2nd and 20th Georgia at Antietam Creek* (Mechanicsburg, PA: Stackpole Books, 2000), 62.
118. *OR*, vol. 19, pt. 1, p. 914; Tucker, *Burnside's Bridge*, 47–52.
119. *OR*, vol. 19, pt. 1, pp. 888–93.
120. The question of when the order for the Ninth Corps to attack was issued remains somewhat unresolved. McClellan said in his 1862 report that Burnside was ordered to attack at 10:00 a.m. In his 1863 report, he stated that he sent the order at 8:00 a.m. He also indicated the bridge was carried at 1:00 p.m. after a three-hour delay, suggesting a time of 10:00 a.m. for the attack order. Burnside also confirmed a 10:00 a.m. order in his report. Cox asserted in his report that the initial order to get the corps ready was issued at 7:00 a.m. and received at 9:00 a.m. In his article for *Battles and Leaders* Cox indicated 10:00 a.m. as the time the order was received. *OR*, vol. 19, pt. 1, pp. 30, 63, 419, 424; Cox, "The Battle of Antietam" In *Battles and Leaders*, 2:647.
121. *OR*, vol. 19, pt. 1, p. 420.
122. Cox, "The Battle of Antietam" in *Battles and Leaders*, 2:634.
123. Sears, *Landscape Turned Red*, 257–59; Murfin, *Gleam of Bayonets*, 267–68; Hartwig, *To Antietam Creek*, 590–92; *OR*, vol. 19, pt. 1, p. 591.
124. While the bulk of Rodman's force crossed at Snavely's Ford, some Ohio units crossed at an unnamed ford several hundred yards upstream. See US War Department, map 11, in *Atlas of the Battlefield of Antietam*.
125. Sears, *Landscape Turned Red*, 263–64, 267. See US War Department, map 11, in *Atlas of the Battlefield of Antietam*.

Chapter 3

1. Sears, *Landscape Turned Red*, 293; Harsh, *Sounding the Shallows*, 21.
2. Palfrey, *Antietam and Fredericksburg Campaigns*, 124.
3. Harsh, *Sounding the Shallows*, 21; Murfin, *Gleam of Bayonets*, 295–96.
4. *OR*, vol. 19, pt. 2, p. 322.
5. McClellan, *McClellan's Own Story*, 612–13.
6. See appendices 2 and 4 for details on casualties.
7. For positions at the end of the battle, see US War Department, map 14, in *Atlas of the Battlefield of Antietam*; Gottfried, *The Maps of Antietam*, 235.
8. Carman, *Maryland Campaign: Ezra A. Carman's Definitive Study*, 365–66.
9. See appendix 4 for details on casualties.
10. *OR*, vol. 19, pt. 1, p. 65.
11. See appendix 4 for details on casualties and appendix 2 for the Union order of battle.
12. Franklin, "Notes On Crampton's Gap And Antietam," in *Battles and Leaders*, 2:597.
13. Stotelmyer, *Too Useful to Sacrifice*, 54.
14. The casualty rates are from those divisions engaged on the seventeenth. Division commanders killed or wounded include Ricketts, Richardson, Sedgwick, Rodman, and Crawford. See appendix 2 and appendix 4 for further details.
15. See Humphreys's after-action report, *OR*, vol. 19, pt. 1, pp., 368–74. See appendix 4 of this work for details on casualties and appendix 2 for the Union order of battle.
16. Kevin Pawlak, "Railroads—Tracks to the Antietam: The Railroad Supplies the Army of the Potomac, September 18, 1862," Emerging Civil War, posted October 27, 2018, https://emergingcivilwar.com/2018/10/27/railroads-tracks-to-the-antietam-the-railroad-supplies-the-army-of-the-potomac-september-18-1862; *OR*, vol. 19-1, pp. 205–7.
17. Communications in the *Official Records* provide no specific details on what numbers McClellan believed he faced on September 18. But accounts Cox and McClellan wrote after the fighting would seem to lend credence to the notion that McClellan still believed Lee had a significant force at his disposal. Cox, "The Battle of Antietam" in *Battles and Leaders*, 2:658; *OR*, vol. 19, pt. 1, pp. 65–66.
18. Harsh, *Taken at the Flood*, 440.

19. *OR*, vol. 19, pt. 1, p. 65.
20. *OR*, vol. 19, pt. 1, p. 66.
21. Longstreet, "The Invasion of Maryland" In *Battles and Leaders of the Civil War* (New York: Century, 1887) 2:670
22. Hood, *Advance and Retreat*, 45.
23. Harsh, *Taken at the Flood*, 431.
24. See appendices 3 and 4 for details on casualties. Henry Kyd Douglas, *I Rode with Stonewall, Being Chiefly the War Experiences of the Youngest Member of Jackson's Staff from the John Brown Raid to the Hanging of Mrs. Surratt* (Chapel Hill: University of North Carolina Press, 1940), 174.
25. *OR*, vol. 19, pt. 1, p. 151.
26. Harsh, *Taken at the Flood*, 430.
27. Lee's desire part to get past the Union right and attack might have also been an escape plan. Sears, *Landscape Turned Red*, 274–75; Harsh, *Taken at the Flood*, 441–43.
28. Harsh, *Taken at the Flood*, 431–33. See appendix 4 of this book for details on casualties.
29. Walker, "Sharpsburg," in *Battles and Leaders of the Civil War* (New York: Century Co., 1887), 2:682.
30. Harsh, *Taken at the Flood*, 444–47.
31. *OR*, vol. 19, pt. 1, p. 68.
32. Confederate States of America, *Reports of the Operations of the Army of Northern Virginia: From June 1862, to and Including the Battle at Fredericksburg, Dec. 13, 1862* (Richmond: R. M. Smith, public printer, 1864), 1:36.
33. The totality of men and supplies captured by Confederates at Harpers Ferry was 12,000 prisoners, 13,000 small arms, 73 cannon, 305 pairs of shoes, a number of wagons, and food and other stores. This haul no doubt greatly aided Lee's army and embarrassed the Union. Yet the cost at which it was purchased was very high, and it did not significantly impact the outcome of the war. Harsh, *Taken at the Flood*, 321; *OR*, vol. 19, pt. 1, pp. 955, 981.

Conclusion

1. *OR*, vol. 19, pt. 1, pp. 212, 339–40, 830–31.
2. *OR*, vol. 19, pt. 1, pp. 212, 479; Harsh, *Taken at the Flood*, 452–54, 462.

3. Thomas A. McGrath, *Shepherdstown: Last Clash of the Antietam Campaign* (Lynchburg, VA: Schroeder, 2013), 65–67, 83; Harsh, *Taken at the Flood*, 459–61; Douglas Southall Freeman, *Lee's Lieutenants: A Study in Command*, vol. 2: Cedar Mountain to Chancellorsville, (New York: Charles Scribner's Sons, 1942), 2:717., 2:232.

4. Carman, *Maryland Campaign: Ezra A. Carman's Definitive Study*, 371–75; *OR*, vol. 19, pt. 1, pp. 338–41, 348–49, 982.

5. *OR*, vol. 19, pt. 1, p. 330.

6. *OR*, vol. 19, pt. 2, pp. 627

7. Harsh, *Taken at the Flood*, 475–76; *OR*, vol. 19, pt. 2, pp. 626–27, 628–29.

8. *OR*, vol. 19, pt. 1, p. 72; Sears, *Lincoln's Lieutenants*, 424–25, 433–36; *OR*, vol.1 9, pt. 2, 336–545.

9. McPherson, *Battle Cry of Freedom*, 491–92; Michael Burlingame and John R. T. Ettlinger, eds., Entry for September 25, 1864, in *Inside Lincoln's White House: The Complete Civil War Diary of John Hay* (Carbondale: Southern Illinois University Press, 1997), 232.

10. *OR*, vol. 19, pt. 2, pp. 545–46; James McPherson, *Battle Cry of Freedom: Illustrated Edition* (Oxford University Press, 1988), 483

11. The five battles are Turner's and Fox's Gaps, Crampton's Gap, Harpers Ferry, Antietam, and Shepherdstown. Often, the three South Mountain battles are considered to be one. As the engagements at Turner's and Fox's Gaps were some six miles from Crampton's Gap and no units at any one location were in a position to support those at another, the battles were essentially two separate engagements. And while both engagements shared the strategic goal of splitting Lee's army, the Sixth Corps at Crampton's Gap had an exclusive objective, namely the relief of Harpers Ferry. Lastly, while the Confederate forces under the command of Lafayette McLaws fought at both Harpers Ferry and Crampton's, most accounts treat those battles as separate engagements.

12. Hartwig, *To Antietam Creek*, 686. See appendix 4 of this book for details on casualties.

13. See "Transcript of the Proclamation," National Archives: Online Exhibits, Updated May 5, 2017, https://www.archives.gov/exhibits/featured-documents/emancipation-proclamation/transcript.html.

Appendix I

1. For history on the town of Sharpsburg, see "History of Sharpsburg," *Sharpsburg, Maryland: A Town Rich in History and Heritage*, https://sharpsburgmd.com/history/.
2. *OR*, vol. 51, pt. 1, p. 618–19.
3. *OR*, vol. 19, pt. 1, p. 951.
4. See appendix 4 for details on troop strength.
5. *OR*, vol. 19, pt. 1, p. 140.
6. *OR*, vol. 19, pt. 1, pp. 147–48.
7. *OR*, vol. 19, pt. 2, p. 289.
8. *OR*, vol. 19, pt. 2, pp. 294–95.
9. *OR*, vol. 19, pt. 1, p. 53.
10. *OR*, vol. 19, pt. 1, p. 54. See appendix 4 of this book for details on troop strength.
11. *OR*, vol. 19, pt. 1, p. 30.
12. *OR*, vol. 19, pt. 1, pp. 213–17. See also appendix 4 of this book for details on troop strength.
13. See appendix 4 for details on armies' strength.
14. *OR*, vol. 19, pt. 1, p. 218.
15. The Union command likely did not comprehend Lee's position on the morning of September 17 beyond what information they had ascertained from Meade's probes the evening before. McClellan, *McClellan's Own Story*, 587.
16. Longstreet, *From Manassas to Appomattox*, 241–44; *OR*, vol. 19, pt. 1, p. 956.
17. *OR*, vol. 19, pt. 1, pp. 269–70.
18. Hood is listed as having 2,304 men in his division PFD on the morning of the seventeenth. This number includes the 300 men in his artillery. *OR*, vol. 19, pt. 1, pp. 922–23. See also appendix 4 of this manuscript for details on troop strength.
19. *OR*, vol. 19, pt. 1, p. 956.
20. *OR*, vol. 19, pt. 1, p. 923.
21. Based on Ezra Carman's maps, Hood's Division was engaged for between forty-five and seventy-five minutes. US War Department, maps 3, 4, and 5, in *Atlas of the Battlefield of Antietam*; Carman, *Maryland Campaign*, 2:109, 605.

22. *OR*, vol. 19, pt. 1, p. 929.
23. Accounts conflict as to the reason Sumner was sent across the creek. According to *New York Tribune* writer George Smalley, Sumner was to follow up Hooker's initial success. According to author Ethan Rafuse, Sumner was dispatched in response to Hood driving Hooker back. Both sources indicate the action could be seen from the Pry House; however, modern scholars dispute this claim. George M. Smalley, "Battle-Field of Antietam," *New York Tribune*, September 19, 1862; Rafuse, *McClellan's War*, 315.
24. See appendix 2 of this manuscript for the Union order of battle and appendix 4 for information on armies' strength. Kreiser, *Defeating Lee*, ix–xiii.
25. *OR*, vol. 19, pt. 1, p. 275.
26. See appendix 4 of this book concerning armies' strength and casualties. *OR*, vol. 19, pt. 1, pp. 275–76, 857–59.
27. *OR*, vol. 19, pt. 1, pp. 275–76.
28. *OR*, vol. 19, pt. 1, p. 306.
29. Murfin, *Gleam of Bayonets*, 227, 233–36; Sears, *Landscape Turned Red*, 220–22.
30. Armstrong, *Unfurl Those Colors*, 173–79, 203–5.
31. Harsh, *Taken at the Flood*, 373–74, 388; US War Department, maps 5, 6, and 7, in *Atlas of the Battlefield of Antietam*.
32. By all indications the so-called super-battery began forming about 8:00 or 8:30 a.m. and was built up as the day wore on. Armstrong, *Opposing the Second Corps*, 153; Harsh, *Taken at the Flood*, 387–90; Gottfried, *Maps of Antietam*, 166–67; *OR*, vol. 19, pt. 1, pp. 967–70; US War Department, maps 5–7, in *Atlas of the Battlefield of Antietam*.
33. Early, *Lieutenant General Jubal A. Early*, 67.
34. *OR*, vol. 19, pt. 1, pp. 970–71.
35. *OR*, vol. 19, pt. 1, p. 971.
36. *OR*, vol. 19, pt. 1, p. 61.
37. See appendix 4 for information on armies' strength and casualties.
38. Franklin, "Notes on Crampton's Gap and Antietam," In *Battles and Leaders*, 2:597, 39. Kreiser, *Defeating Lee*, 47–49.
40. See the discussion of Sumner's decision to attack the West Woods for details on what Sumner saw and the overall situation.

41. Armstrong, *Unfurl Those Colors*, 176–79, US War Department, map 8, in *Atlas of the Battlefield of Antietam*.
42. Armstrong, *Unfurl Those Colors*, 171–72.
43. Carman, *Maryland Campaign*, 2:247, 252.
44. *OR*, vol. 19, pt. 1, pp. 323–24.
45. *OR*, vol. 19, pt. 1, pp. 327.
46. These are the command losses for Wilcox, Featherston, Pryor and Wright of Anderson's Division and Rodes and Anderson of Hill's Division. See appendix 3 for the Confederate order of battle.
47. See D. H. Hill's after-action report, *OR*, vol. 19, pt. 1, pp. 1022–23.
48. See appendix 3 of this book for the Confederate order of Battle, and see appendix 4 for information on armies' strength and casualties. For positions, see US War Department, maps 8, 9, and 7, in *Atlas of the Battlefield of Antietam*; Gottfried, *Maps of Antietam*, 184.
49. Gottfried, *Maps of Antietam*, 184; Harsh, *Taken at the Flood*, 395–97.
50. On paper, Anderson had six brigades. Mahon's Brigade had only eighty-two men at Antietam and was acting as a regiment attached to Pryor's Brigade. Armistead's Brigade was detached and operating in support of McLaws. Sears, *Landscape Turned Red*, 240–41; *OR*, vol. 19, pt. 1, p. 1037; Carman, *Maryland Campaign*, 2:257; See appendix 3 of this work for the Confederate order of battle.
51. Waugh, *Surviving the Confederacy*, 167.
52. Carman, *Maryland Campaign*, 2:270.
53. Carman, *Maryland Campaign*, 2:281.
54. Gottfried, *Maps of Antietam*, 192–93; *OR*, vol. 19, pt. 1, p. 1024. See also appendix 3 of this book for the Confederate order of battle.
55. Rafuse, *Antietam, South Mountain & Harpers Ferry*, 138–43; *OR*, vol. 19, pt. 1, pp. 884, 915–16, 1023; Armstrong, *Opposing the Second Corps*, 110–15; US War Department, map 10, in *Atlas of the Battlefield of Antietam*.
56. *OR*, vol .19, pt. 1, p. 1038.
57. Warner, *Generals in Blue*, 57–58; Cullum, *Biographical Register*, 2:316, 318–20; Sears, *Lincoln's Lieutenants*, 400; Marvel, *Burnside*, xii, 13–16, 18–24, 31–33, 42–43, 97–100.
58. Cox, "The Battle of Antietam" In *Battles and Leaders*, 2:631–32. 59. *OR*, vol. 19, pt. 1, p. 55.

60. *OR*, vol. 19, pt. 1, pp. 31, 424. See US War Department, map 9, in *Atlas of the Battlefield of Antietam*.
61. Hartwig, *To Antietam Creek*, 590–92; *OR*, vol. 19, pt. 1, pp. 423–24. See appendix 4 of this work for details on armies' strength.
62. The exact number of Georgians defending this position is not clear. Toombs stated the number was 400, while Phillip Tucker indicates it may might been as low as 300. Tucker, *Burnside's Bridge*, 62.
63. *OR*, vol. 19, pt. 1, p. 914; Tucker, *Burnside's Bridge*, 47–52.
64. *OR*, vol. 19, pt. 1, p. 889.
65. The question of when the order for the Ninth Corps to attack was issued remains somewhat unresolved. McClellan said in his 1862 report that Burnside was ordered to attack at 10:00 a.m. Yet in his 1863 report the commanding general said he sent the order at 8:00 a.m. McClellan also indicated the bridge was carried at 1:00 p.m. after a three-hour delay, which indicates a time of 10:00 a.m. for the attack order. Burnside also confirmed a 10:00 a.m. order in his narrative of the fighting. Cox indicated that the initial order to get the corps ready was issued at 7:00 a.m. and received at 9:00 a.m. In his article for *Battles and Leaders*, Cox indicates 10:00 a.m. as the time the order was received. *OR*, vol. 19, pt. 1, pp. 30, 63, 419, 424; Cox, "The Battle of Antietam" In *Battles and Leaders*, 2:647. 66. *OR*, vol. 19, pt. 1, p. 420.
67. Cox, "The Battle of Antietam" In *Battles and Leaders*, 634. 68. Sears, *Landscape Turned Red*, 257–59; Murfin, *Gleam of Bayonets*, 267–68; Hartwig, *To Antietam Creek*, 590–92; *OR*, vol. 19, pt. 1, p. 591.
69. Sears, *Landscape Turned Red*, 263–64, 267. US War Department, map 11, in *Atlas of the Battlefield of Antietam*.
70. See the report of Confederate Col. James B. Walton of the Washington Artillery on the positions at Cemetery Hill, *OR*, vol. 19, pt. 1, pp. 848–51.
71. Harsh, *Taken at the Flood*, 377–81; Sears, *Landscape Turned Red*, 213–14. See appendix 4 of this book for information on troop strength and casualties.
72. Longstreet, *From Manassas to Appomattox*, 243.
73. Reports indicate that both Hooker and Mansfield were wounded between 7:30 and 9:00 am. Sears, *Landscape Turned Red*, 215; Carman, *Maryland Campaign*, 2:162, 165; Murfin, *Gleam of Bayonets*, 225.
74. See appendix 2 for the Union order of battle, and see appendix 4 for information on troop strength and casualties.

75. *OR*, vol. 19, pt. 1, p. 1008.
76. *OR*, vol. 19, pt. 1, pp. 1022–23; Harsh, *Taken at the Flood*, 378–85.
77. See appendix 4 for further details on armies' strength.
78. For positions, see US War Department, maps 6 and 7, in *Atlas of the Battlefield of Antietam*.
79. Harsh, *Taken at the Flood*, 407–8.
80. See appendix 4 for information on troop strength.
81. *OR*, vol. 19, pt. 1, p. 149.
82. For positions, see US War Department, maps 7 and 8, in *Atlas of the Battlefield of Antietam*.
83. *OR*, vol. 19, pt. 1, pp. 338–41.
84. See US War Department, maps 10–13, in *Atlas of the Battlefield of Antietam*; Carman, *Maryland Campaign*, 2:358–88.
85. See US War Department, maps 11 and 12, in *Atlas of the Battlefield of Antietam*; *OR*, vol. 19, pt. 1, pp. 350–52.
86. See appendix 4 of this work for details on armies' strength. A. P. Hill indicated that he arrived on the field by 2:30 p.m. Harsh asserts that the time was closer to 3:30 p.m., and that Hill's Division was still crossing the Potomac as Hill rode on ahead to meet Lee. *OR*, vol. 19, pt. 1, p. 981; Harsh, *Taken at the Flood*, 417–18.
87. *OR*, vol. 19, pt. 1, p. 212. See US War Department, maps 12 and 13, in *Atlas of the Battlefield of Antietam*.
88. *OR*, vol. 19, pt. 1, p. 399.
89. Steven Stotelmyer details this incident in his book, not only disputing that Porter ever made this statement but also reevaluating the reserve forces McClellan had at hand. See Stotelmyer, *Too Useful to Sacrifice*, chapter 4; For the account published in 1886, see Anderson, "Reserves at Antietam," 783.
90. Harsh, *Sounding the Shallows*, 21; Murfin, *Gleam of Bayonets*, 295–96.
91. *OR*, vol. 19, pt. 2, p. 322.
92. McClellan, *McClellan's Own Story*, 612.
93. See appendices 2 and 4 for details on casualties.
94. For positions at the end of the battle, US War Department, map 14, in *Atlas of the Battlefield of Antietam*; Gottfried, *Maps of Antietam*, 235.
95. Carman, *Maryland Campaign: Ezra A. Carman's Definitive Study*, 365–66.

96. See appendix 4 for details on casualties.
97. *OR*, vol. 19, pt. 1, p. 65.
98. See appendix 4 for details on casualties, and see appendix 2 for the Union order of battle.
99. Franklin, "Notes on Crampton's Gap And Antietam," in *Battles and Leaders*, 2:597 100. Stotelmyer, *Too Useful to Sacrifice*, 54.
101. The casualty rates are from those divisions engaged on September 17. Division commanders killed or wounded include Ricketts, Richardson, Sedgwick, Rodman, and Crawford. See appendix 2 and appendix 4 for further details.
102. See Humphreys's after-action report, *OR*, vol. 19, pt. 1, pp. 368–74. See appendix 4 of this book for details on casualties, and see appendix 2 for the Union order of battle.
103. Pawlak, "Railroads—Tracks to the Antietam"; *OR*, vol. 19-1, pp. 205–7.
104. No communications in the Official Records contain specific details about the numbers of enemy troops McClellan belielved he faced on the eighteenth. Accounts Cox and McClellan wrote afterward seem to lend credence to the idea that McClellan still believed Lee had a significant force available to him. Cox, "The Battle of Antietam" In *Battles and Leaders*, 2:658; *OR*, vol. 19, pt. 1, pp. 65–66.
105. Harsh, *Taken at the Flood*, 440.
106. *OR*, vol. 19, pt. 1, p. 65.
107. *OR*, vol. 19, pt. 1, p. 66.
108. Longstreet, "The Invasion of Maryland" In *Battles and Leaders*, 2:670.
109. Hood, *Advance and Retreat*, 45.
110. Harsh, *Taken at the Flood*, 431.
111. Harsh, *Taken at the Flood*, 431–33; See appendix 4 of this book for details on casualties
112. *OR*, vol. 19, pt. 1, p. 151.
113. Harsh, *Taken at the Flood*, 430.
114. Walker, "Antietam," in *Battles and Leaders*, 2:682. 115. Harsh, *Taken at the Flood*, 444–47.
116. *OR*, vol. 19, pt. 1, p. 68.
117. Confederate States of America, *Reports of the Operations of the Army of Northern Virginia*, 36.

BIBLIOGRAPHY

Anders, Curt. *Injustice on Trial: Second Bull Run, General Fitz John Porter's Court Court-Martial, and the Schofield Board Investigation That Restored His Good Name.* New York: Curt Anders Books, 2002.

Anderson, Thomas M. "The Reserves at Antietam." *Century Illustrated Monthly Magazine* 32 (May–October 1886).

Andrews, J. Cutler. *The North Reports the Civil War.* Pittsburgh: University of Pittsburgh Press, 1955.

Armstrong, Marion V. *Opposing the Second Corps at Antietam: The Fight for the Confederate Left and Center on America's Bloodiest Day.* Tuscaloosa: University of Alabama Press, 2016.

———. *Unfurl Those Colors: McClellan, Sumner & the Second Army Corps in the Antietam Campaign.* Tuscaloosa: University of Alabama Press, 2008.

"A Barbarian Invasion of the North." *New York Times*, September 3, 1862, p. 4. *New York Times* Archive. https://www.nytimes.com/1862/09/03/archives/a-barbarian-invasion-of-the-north.html.

Borden, Maj. Gregory J. *"True" Tactical Reserves in Striking Force Operations: Pilfery of Combat Power at the Line of Contact?* Fort Leavenworth, KS: School of Advanced Military Studies, US Army Command and General Staff College, 1995.

Browne, Francis F. *The Every-Day Life of Abraham Lincoln.* 1913. Reprint. New York: Diversion Books, 2014.

Burlingame, Michael, and John R. T. Ettlinger, eds. *Inside Lincoln's White House: The Complete Civil War Diary of John Hay*. Carbondale: Southern Illinois University Press, 1997.

Carman, Ezra A. *The Maryland Campaign of 1862*. 3 Vols. Edited by Thomas G. Clemens. El Dorado Hills, CA: Savas Beatie, 2010, 2012, and 2017.

———. *The Maryland Campaign of September 1862: Ezra A. Carman's Definitive Study of the Union and Confederate Armies at Antietam*. Edited by Joseph Pierro. Hoboken, NJ: Taylor and Francis, 2008.

Confederate States of America Army. *Reports of the Operations of the Army of Northern Virginia: From June 1862, to and Including the Battle at Fredericksburg, Dec. 13, 1862*. Vol. 1. Richmond: R. M. Smith, public printer, 1864.

Cox, Jacob D. "The Battle of Antietam," in *Battles and Leaders of the Civil War*. Vol. 2., edited by Robert Underwood Johnson and Clarence Clough Buel of the editorial staff of "The Century Magazine" New York: Century, 1887–88.

———. *Military Reminiscences of the Civil War*. Vol. 1, *April 1861–November 1863*. New York: Charles Scribner's Sons, 1900.

Cozzens, Peter. *General John Pope: A Life for the Nation*. Champaign: University of Illinois Press, 2000.

Cullum, Bvt. Maj. Gen. George W. *Biographical Register of the Officers and Graduates of the U.S. Military Academy at West Point N.Y.* Vols. 1 and 2. Boston: Houghton, Mifflin, 1891.

Douglas, Henry Kyd. *I Rode with Stonewall, Being Chiefly the War Experiences of the Youngest Member of Jackson's Staff from the John Brown Raid to the Hanging of Mrs. Surratt*. Chapel Hill: University of North Carolina Press, 1940.

Early, Jubal A. *Lieutenant General Jubal A. Early, Confederate States of America*. 1912. Reprinted, Oxfordshire, United Kingdom, Acheron, 2012.

Franklin, William B., "Notes on Crampton's Gap and Antietam," in *Battles and Leaders of the Civil War*. Vol. 2., edited by Robert Underwood Johnson and Clarence Clough Buel of the editorial staff of "The Century Magazine" New York: Century, 1887–88.

Freeman, Douglas Southall. *Lee: Abridged and Edited by Richard Harwell*. 1st Touchstone ed. New York: Simon and Schuster, 1997.

———. *Lee's Lieutenants: A Study in Command*. Vol. 2: *Cedar Mountain to Chancellorsville*. New York: Charles Scribner's Sons, 1942.

Frye, Dennis E. *Antietam Shadows: Mystery, Myth and Machination.* Sharpsburg, MD: Antietam Rest, 2018.

Gillon, Steven M. *10 Days That Unexpectedly Changed America.* New York: Broadway Books, 2006.

Gordon, Edward Clifford. "Memorandum of a Conversation With R.E. Lee." In *Lee the Soldier,* edited by Garry Gallagher (Lincoln: University of Nebraska Press, 1996), 25.

Gottfried, Bradley M., *Bradley M. Gottfried, The Maps of Antietam: An Atlas of The Antietam (Sharpsburg) Campaign, Including the Battle of South Mountain, September 2–20, (El Dorado Hills: Savas Beatie, 2012).* El Dorado Hills, CA: Savas Beatie, 2012.

Greeley, Horace. "A Prayer for Twenty Millions." *New York Tribune*, August 20, 1862.

Gwynne, S. C. *Rebel Yell: The Violence, Passion, and Redemption of Stonewall Jackson.* New York: Scribner, 2014.

Harsh, Joseph L. *Sounding the Shallows: A Confederate Companion for the Maryland Campaign of 1862.* Kent, OH: Kent State University Press, 2000.

———. *Taken at the Flood: Robert E. Lee and Confederate Strategy in the Maryland Campaign of 1862.* Kent, OH: Kent State University Press, 1999.

Hartwig, D. Scott. *To Antietam Creek: The Maryland Campaign of September 1862.* Baltimore: Johns Hopkins University Press, 2012.

Hebert, Walter H. *Fighting Joe Hooker.* Indianapolis: Bobbs-Merrill, 1944.

"History of Sharpsburg." Sharpsburg, Maryland: A Town Rich in History and Heritage. https://sharpsburgmd.com/history/.

Hood, John B. *Advance and Retreat: Personal Experiences in the United States and Confederate States Armies.* New Orleans: Published for the Hood Orphan Memorial Fund, G. T. Beauregard, 1880.

Kreiser, Lawrence A., Jr. *Defeating Lee: A History of the Second Corps, Army of the Potomac.* Bloomington: Indiana University Press, 2011.

Longstreet, James. *From Manassas to Appomattox: Memoirs of the Civil War in America.* 1896 Reprint. New York: William S. Konecaky Associates, 1992.

———. "The Invasion of Maryland" in *Battles and Leaders of the Civil War.* Vol. 2., edited by Robert Underwood Johnson and Clarence Clough Buel of the editorial staff of "The Century Magazine" New York: Century, 1887–88.

Marvel, William. *Burnside*. Chapel Hill: University of North Carolina Press, 1991.

Mattern, H. W., and E. A. Carman. *Theatre of Operations, Maryland Campaign, September 1862*. https://www.loc.gov/item/2009584566/.

McClellan, George Brinton. *McClellan's Own Story: The War for the Union, the Soldiers Who Fought It, the Civilians Who Directed It and His Relations to It and to Them*. New York, C. L. Webster, 1887.

McGrath, Thomas A. *Shepherdstown: Last Clash of the Antietam Campaign*. Lynchburg, VA: Schroeder, 2013.

McPherson, James M. *The Illustrated Battle Cry of Freedom: The Civil War Era*. New York: Oxford University Press, 2003.

Murfin, James. *The Gleam of Bayonets: The Battle of Antietam and Robert E. Lee's Maryland Campaign, September 1862*. Baton Rouge: Louisiana State University Press, 1964.

Oates, Stephen B. *With Malice Toward None*. New York: Harper and Row, 1977.

Palfrey, Gen. Francis W. *The Antietam and Fredericksburg Campaigns*. 1912. Reprint. New York: Da Capo, 1996.

Pawlak, Kevin. "Railroads—Tracks to the Antietam: The Railroad Supplies the Army of the Potomac, September 18, 1862." Emerging Civil War. Posted October 27, 2018. https://emergingcivilwar.com/2018/10/27/railroads-tracks-to-the-antietam-the-railroad-supplies-the-army-of-the-potomac-september-18-1862/?fbclid=IwAR3SRmkuuzAzDvsD_rOOrktikPTiDkLZBdswRbbccrrWiL8wxYAtFfE3QGw.

Powell, William Henry. *The Fifth Army Corps (Army of the Potomac): A Record of Operations during the Civil War in the United States of America, 1861–1865*. New York: G. P. Putnam's Sons, 1896.

Priest, John Michael. *Before Antietam: The Battle for South Mountain*. Shippensburg, PA: White Mane Books, 1992.

Rafuse, Ethan S. *Antietam, South Mountain, & Harpers Ferry: A Battlefield Guide*. Lincoln: University of Nebraska Press, 2008.

———. *McClellan's War: The Failure of Moderation in the Struggle for the Union*. Bloomington: Indiana University Press, 2005.

Sears, Stephen W., *Chancellorsville*. Boston: Houghton Mifflin Harcourt, 1996.

———. *Landscape Turned Red: The Battle of Antietam*. New Haven, CT: Ticknor and Fields, 1993.

———. *Lincoln's Lieutenants: The High Command of the Army of the Potomac.* Boston: Houghton, Mifflin, Harcourt, 2017.

Smalley, George M., "Battle-Field of Antietam" *New York Tribune,* September 19, 1862.

Spruill, Matt, III, and Matt Spruill IV. *Decisions at Second Manassas: The Fourteen Critical Decisions That Defined the Battle.* Knoxville: University of Tennessee Press, 2018.

Stotelmyer, Steven R. *Too Useful to Sacrifice: Reconsidering George B. McClellan's Generalship in the Maryland Campaign from South Mountain to Antietam.* El Dorado Hills, CA: Savas Beatie, 2019.

Tate, Thomas K. *General Edwin Vose Sumner, USA: A Civil War Biography.* Jefferson, NC: McFarland, 2013.

Taylor, Walter Herron. *Four Years with General Lee.* New York: D. Appleton, 1878.

"Transcript of the Proclamation." National Archives: Online Exhibits. May 2017. https://www.archives.gov/exhibits/featured-documents/emancipation-proclamation/transcript.html.

Tucker, Phillip Thomas. *Burnside's Bridge: The Climactic Struggle of the 2nd and 20th Georgia at Antietam Creek.* Mechanicsburg, PA: Stackpole Books, 2000.

United States War Department. *Atlas of the Battlefield of Antietam, Prepared Under the Direction of the Antietam Battlefield Board, Lieut. Col. Geo. W. Davis, U.S.A., President, Gen. E. A. Carman, U.S.V., Gen. H. Heth, C.S.A. Surveyed by Lieut. Col. E. B. Cope, Engineer, H. W. Mattern, Assistant Engineer, of the Gettysburg National Park. Drawn by Charles H. Ourand. Position of Troops by Gen. E. A. Carman. Published by Authority of the Secretary of War, Under the Direction of the Chief of Engineers, U.S. Army, 1908.* Washington, DC: Government Printing Office, 1908. https://www.loc.gov/item/2008621532/.

United States War Department. *The War of the Rebellion: Official Records of the Union and Confederate Armies.* 128 vols. Washington, DC: United States Government Printing Office, 1874–80.

Vermilya, Daniel J. Perceptions, Not Realities: *The Strength, Experience, and Condition of the Army of the Potomac at Antietam - Joseph L. Harsh Scholarship Award, 2012.* SHAF—Save Historic Antietam Foundation, 2012.

———. *That Field of Blood: The Battle of Antietam.* El Dorado Hills, CA: Savas Beatie, 2018.

Walker, Francis Amasa. *History of the Second Army Corps in the Army of the Potomac.* New York: C. Scribner's Sons, 1886.

Walker, John G. "Sharpsburg," in *Battles and Leaders of the Civil War. Vol. 2.,* edited by Robert Underwood Johnson and Clarence Clough Buel of the editorial staff of "The Century Magazine" New York: Century, 1887–88.

Warner, Ezra J. *Generals in Blue: Lives of the Union Commanders.* Baton Rouge: Louisiana State University, 1964.

———. *Generals in Gray: Lives of the Confederate Commanders.* Baton Rouge: Louisiana State University, 1959.

Waugh, John C. *Surviving the Confederacy: Rebellion, Ruin and Recovery; Roger and Sara Pryor during the Civil War.* New York: Harcourt, 2002.

Whitehair, C. W. *Escape Across the Potomac.* Infinity, 2009.

Woodworth, Steven E. *Davis & Lee at War.* Lawrence: University Press of Kansas, 1995.

INDEX

Abbreviations
AET = Army of East Tennessee
ANV = Army of Northern Virginia
AO = Army of the Ohio
AP = Army of the Potomac
AT = Army of Tennessee
AV = Army of Virginia
Adj = Adjutant
Arty = Artillery
Assist = Assistant
Bde = Brigade
Bn = Battalion
Btry = Battery
Cav = Cavalry
Cmdr = Commander
Dept = Department
Div = Division
Garr = Garrison
Reg = Regiment
Res = Reserve

Abolitionists, 5
Anderson, George B., Brig. Gen., CSA (Bde Cmdr)
  actions at the Sunken Road, 75–77
  battlefield tour, 166, 167, 168
  wounding, 80
Anderson, George T., Col., CSA (Bde Cmdr), 50, 59, 179
  photo, 57
Anderson, Richard H., Maj. Gen, CSA (Div Cmdr), 75
  actions at Harpers Ferry, 12, 13, 15, 75, 130–32
  actions at the Sunken Road, 59, 73, 74, 77–80, 164, 166–68, 179
  in reserve at Sharpsburg, 58, 74, 179
  march to Sharpsburg, 18
  photo, 57
Anderson, Robert, Lieut. Col., USA (Bde and Reg Cmdr), 145
Antietam, Battle of (Sharpsburg), xvi, 29, 39, 46
  actions after 09/17, 105, 112, 119, 120, 123, 125, 189, 193
  actions at the middle bridge, 180
  battlefield tour, 127–29
  Bloody Lane, 73, 77, 164

Index

Antietam, Battle of (Sharpsburg) (*cont.*)
  casualties, 84, 110, 111, 160, 187
  actions at the lower bridge, 91, 95, 96, 103, 171, 175
  Hood's attack, 145
  Hookers' attack, 137
  Lee offers battle, 18
  McLellan's launches his attack, 21
  quotes on, xvii, 115, 116, 192
  Second Corps actions, 69, 73, 149
  Union reserves, 82
Antietam Creek, Maryland
  battlefield tour, 140, 159, 162, 176, 187, 189
  Burnside's actions 98–104, 170–75
  D. H. Hill's Division crossing, 76, 166
  Fifth Corps actions, 91, 93–95, 180, 182–83
  Hood's actions, 39, 43–45, 145, 148, 149
  Hookers' attack, 30–36, 141, 143
  Lee's decision to stand at Sharpsburg, 13, 15–19, 132, 133
  McClellan's decision to attack, 22–25, 136–39
  Second Corps crossing, 63, 69, 74, 150, 156, 162, 163
  Twelfth Corps crossing, 47
  Union artillery east of, 77, 79, 167
  Union positions/reserves/reinforcements, 83, 84, 91, 107, 109, 111, 159, 184, 186, 187
Antietam National Battlefield, 30
  photos, 19, 27, 38, 45, 54, 60, 68, 75, 89, 104, 113, 120, 125, 131, 135, 138, 141, 146, 150, 155, 158, 162, 166, 170, 171, 178, 181
  tour, 129, 137, 140, 145, 149, 154, 158, 161, 165, 170
Antietam National Battlefield Visitor Center, 79, 129
  photos, 89, 125, 138
  tour, 137–41, 158, 159, 161, 170, 176

Antietam National Cemetery
  photos, 181, 185
  tour, 175, 180
Armstrong, Marion V., 53
Army of Northern Virginia (CSA)
  actions on 9/15, 15, 22, 136
  after Antietam, 61, 106, 110, 114, 116, 121, 183, 187, 190, 192
  before the campaign, 39
  during the Antietam battle, 31, 54, 141, 146, 169, 176
  Florida Brigade, 75
  Henry Kyd Douglas quote after the battle, 115
  Hoods counter attack, 40
  images, 8
  Sunken Road, 81
Army of Northern Virginia (CSA), commands, divisions, battalions, and brigades
  Anderson's Brigade (George B.), 70, 75, 80, 163, 166, 168
  Anderson's Brigade (George T.), 52, 59, 63, 66, 67, 152, 156, 179
  Anderson's Division (R. H.), 58:
    actions at the Sunken Road, 59, 63, 73–75, 77–80, 164, 166–68, 179;
    in reserve at Sharpsburg, 58
  Barksdale's Brigade, 67, 157
  Cobb's Brigade, 76
  Colquitt's Brigade, 76, 166
  Cumming's Brigade, 80, 168
  Early's Brigade, 33, 38, 55, 61, 142, 154, 176, 178
  Evans's Brigade, 54, 84, 93, 160, 176, 181
  Florida Brigade (*see* Pryor's Brigade)
  Grigsby's Division/Command (a.k.a. John R Jones's Division): actions in the West Woods, 62, 66, 67, 157, 158; command of Jones's Division, 54, 62, 155
  Hately's Brigade (*see* Pryor's Brigade)

Index

Hayes' Brigade, 42, 146, 147
Hill's Division (D. H.): actions at South Mountain, 12, 13, 39, 130, 145; actions at the Cornfield, 39, 40, 44, 55, 62, 146, 148, 155, 176; actions at the Sunken Road, 59, 62, 70, 72, 75, 76, 163, 166, 179; burning the Mumma Farm, 72; casualties, 192; positions before the battle, 33, 142
Hill's Division (A. P.), 118, 192; as a reserve force, 89; casualties, 192; flank attack on the Union Ninth Corps, 95, 96, 103, 175, 183
Hood's Division, 63, 148; actions at South Mountain, 13; actions at the Cornfield, 39, 42–45, 47, 55, 57, 62, 76, 148–50, 155, 166, 178; actions on 09/16, 33, 39, 40, 142, 146; before the campaign, 39, 145; casualties, 54, 118, 148, 176, 177, 192; march to Hagerstown, 39; position on 09/17 (a.m.), 142, 145, 146, 147; position after the assault, 62, 155; position at the lower bridge, 100, 173; retreat to Sharpsburg, 13, 131
Hood's "Texas" Brigade (a.k.a. Wofford's Brigade), 39, 44, 148
Jackson's Command/Wing: actions at Harpers Ferry, 132; actions at Second Bull Run, 90; actions at Shepherdstown, 122; casualties, 54, 176, 177; early morning actions on 09/17, 36, 40, 42, 55, 143, 147; march from Harpers Ferry, 24, 136; position before the battle, 31, 36, 39, 142, 143, 145
Jackson's Division (*see* Jones's Division [John R.])
Jones's Division (David R.), 54, 84, 93, 100, 172, 176, 181; casualties, 118, 192

Jones's Division (John R.) (a.k.a. Grigsby's Division or Jackson's Division): casualties, 54, 176; early morning actions on 09/17, 42, 54, 67, 146, 158; position after morning action, 62, 66, 155, 156
Kemper's Brigade, 160
Kershaw's Brigade, 52, 152
Law's Brigade, 44, 54, 147, 148, 176
Lawton's Brigade (a.k.a. Douglas's Brigade), 42, 55, 177
Lawton's Division (a.k.a. Ewell's Division): actions at Harpers Ferry, 61, 154; casualties, 54, 55, 62, 154, 176; early morning actions on 09/17, 42, 147; position on 09/16, 40, 146; positions before the battle, 33, 142
Lee's Battalion (Stephen D.), 19, 33
Longstreet's Command/Wing: actions at South Mountain, 12, 39, 130; actions at the Sunken Road, 86; after the battle, 124; before the campaign, 39; casualties, 147; positions before the battle, 54, 145, 176; reserve artillery, 54, 176
Manning's Brigade (*see* Walker's Brigade)
McLaws's Division/Command: actions at Harpers Ferry, 12, 15, 130, 132; actions in the West Woods, 50, 52, 53, 63, 66, 152, 153, 156; as a reserve force, 58, 77; casualties, 118, 192; march from Harpers Ferry, 77
McRae's Brigade (a.k.a. Garland's Brigade), 70, 76, 163, 167
Munford's Cavalry Brigade, 93, 181
Pelham's Horse Artillery Battalion, 33, 62, 63, 142, 154
Pender's Brigade, 118, 192
Posey's Brigade (*see* Featherston's Brigade)

Index

Army of Northern Virginia (CSA), commands, divisions, battalions, and brigades (*cont.*)
Pryor's Brigade (a.k.a. Florida Brigade or Hately's Brigade), 80, 168
Ransom's Brigade, 86
Ripley's Brigade, 40, 42, 43, 76, 146, 148, 166
Rodes's Brigade: actions at the Sunken Road, 70, 75–77, 80, 81, 163, 163, 167, 168; casualties, 75, 80, 166
Semmes's Brigade, 52, 67, 152, 157
Toombs's Brigade, 100, 104, 172, 173
Trimble's Brigade (a.k.a. Walker's Brigade [James A.]), xvi; casualties, 55, 147, 177; Hood's counterattack at the cornfield, 42, 43; relief of Hood's division on 09/16, 40, 146; Walker's wounding, 40, 42
Walker's Brigade (a.k.a. Manning's Brigade), xv, 86
Walker's Brigade (James A.) (*see* Trimble's Brigade)
Walker's Division: actions at Harpers Ferry, 8; actions in the West Woods, 39, 50, 53, 55, 59, 84, 86, 153, 160, 179; casualties, 177; command, xv, xvi; position at Snavely's Ford, 60, 100, 103, 172, 174, 180
Wofford's Brigade (*see* Hood's Texas Brigade)
Wright's Brigade: actions at the Sunken Road, 80, 168
Army of Northern Virginia (CSA), batteries, infantry, and cavalry regiments
Alabama: 3rd Infantry, 169; 5th Infantry, 81, 169; 6th Infantry, 81, 168, 169; 12th Infantry, 169; 26th Infantry, 169
Arkansas: 3rd Infantry, 79, 86, 169
Georgia: 2nd Infantry, 100, 104, 172, 173; 15th Infantry, 100, 104, 172; 20th Infantry, 100, 104, 172; 21st Infantry, 42
Louisiana: 1st Company—Washington (Louisiana) Artillery (Squires' Battery), 180; 3rd Company—Washington (Louisiana) Artillery (Miller's Battery), 86
Maryland: Baltimore (Maryland) Artillery (Brockenbrough's Battery), 155
North Carolina: 4th Infantry, 80, 168; 27th Infantry, 79, 86, 169
Texas: 1st Infantry, 44, 148; 4th Infantry, 39
Virginia: 3rd Infantry, 75; 13th Infantry, 62, 154
Army of the Potomac (USA), 16, 17
action at the Union center, 95
actions in the West woods, 52, 152
actions on 09/18, 109, 186
actions on the peninsula, 5, 6
advance from Washington, 9, 91
advance to Sharpsburg on 09/15, 22, 36, 136, 144
advance to the Rappahannock, 123
after Antietam, 106, 111, 116, 123, 124, 184, 187, 179
casualties, 110, 187
creation of, 3, 46, 90, 97
during the Antietam battle, 87, 93, 149, 181, 179
First Bull Run, 2, 3
Lee commits his reserves, 58
Lee divided his army, 8
Lee's operational objectives, 17, 116
McClellan launches his attack, 20, 25, 26, 93, 136, 137
McClellan's plans for Franklin's corps, 83, 84, 87, 159
reinforcements, 107, 185
reserves, 95, 183, 160, 183
Army of the Potomac (USA), Wings Burnside's Wing, 98, 101, 103, 171, 175;

actions at South Mountain, 30, 140; advance from Washington, 97
Franklin's Wing, 82, 159
Sumner's Wing, 47, 50, 150
Army of the Potomac (USA), Infantry Corps
 First Corps (Hooker/Meade): actions on 09/15/ and 09/16, 30, 140; after the battle, 111, 187; casualties, 110, 111, 187; commander, 29; counterattacked by Hood, 44, 45, 47, 147, 150; crossing the Antietam, 17, 26, 33, 42, 137, 141, 142; Hooker opens the battle, 34–36, 40, 47, 143; Meade takes command, 49, 151; out of action on the 17th, 63, 148, 156; part of Burnside's Wing, 97, 170; support by the Second, 49, 151; support by the Twelfth, 36, 150
 Fifth Corps (Porter): actions on 09/15 and 09/16, 24; as a reserve force, 36, 47, 89, 109, 150, 186; actions in the Union center, 59, 90–95, 179–84; actions at First Bull Run, 90; actions at Shepherdstown, 121; advance to Sharpsburg, 91; formation of, 90, 143; Humphreys joins the corps at Antietam, 107, 111, 185, 187; positions on 09/18, 107
 Fourth Corps (First Division—Couch), 82, 107, 121, 185
 Ninth Corps (Burnside/Reno/Cox): actions at the lower bridge, 59, 84, 98, 100, 103, 104, 160, 172–75, 179; actions on 09/15 and 09/16, 22, 25, 98, 136, 171; advance from the Antietam, 93, 181, 182; battlefield tour, 170; casualties, 103, 111, 175, 187; counterattacked by A. P. Hill, 89, 95, 183; Cox takes command, 98, 102, 171, 174; Cox commenting on the Ninth's operation, 101, 102, 174; creation of, 97; Jesse Reno killed, 25; McClellan repositions the corps, 98, 172; Rodman crosses Snavely's Ford, 60
 Second Corps (Sumner): action at the Sunken Road, 69, 70, 73, 74, 77, 86, 161, 163, 164, 167; action in the West Woods, 37, 46, 51, 63, 70, 74, 154, 156, 163; actions on 09/15, 134; as a reserve force, 33, 44, 142, 149, 150, 162; battlefield tour, 149; casualties, 111, 187; creation of, 46, 162; crossing the Antietam, 36, 69, 143; part of Sumner's Wing, 150; Richardson kept in reserve, 21, 143; Sumner's after-action report on, 151
 Sixth Corps (Franklin): actions at Crampton's Gap, 13, 130; actions on 09/18, 110, 186; actions on the Union right, 81, 82, 86, 88, 89, 158, 159, 170; as a reserve force, 84, 109, 160, 185, 186; crossing the Antietam, 83; location at the start of the battle, 82; McClellan's plans for, 83, 159; part of Franklin's Wing, 107
 Twelfth Corps (Mansfield/Williams) (a.k.a. Bank's Corps): actions after Antietam, 121; actions on the Union right, 37, 49, 55, 62, 155, 176, 177; advancing to the battle, 36, 42, 44, 143, 147; artillery, 63, 156; casualties, 111, 187; crossing the Antietam, 33, 47, 142; Green's actions, 62, 70, 72, 74, 81, 86, 152, 155, 163; Hooker's options for, 35, 36, 144, 148; Mansfield as commander, 25; Mansfield's wounding, 49, 151; out of action on the 17th, 49, 50, 53, 87; part of Sumner's Wing, 47, 150; position as Hooker's reserve, 33, 34, 142; Sumner orders the corps to Hooker's support, 50, 150; Sumner's after-action report, 47, 150; Williams take command, 151

Index

Army of the Potomac (USA), brigades and divisions
Anderson's Third Brigade, Third Division—First Corps, 145
Buchanan's First Brigade, Second Division—Fifth Corps, 93, 181
Couch's First Division—Fourth Corps: arrival at Antietam, 107, 159; as a reserve force, 109, 136, 185, 186; movement to Williamsport, 121; position on 09/17, 82
Cox's/Scammon's Kanawha Division—Ninth Corps, 100, 172
Crawford's First Brigade, First Division—Twelfth Corps, 49, 62, 70, 152, 156, 163
Dana's Third Brigade, Second Division—Second Corps, 153
Doubleday's First Division—First Corps, 33, 36, 40, 42, 142, 144, 147
Ewing's First Brigade, Kanawha Division—Ninth Corps, 98, 172
Farnsworth's Second Cavalry Brigade, 22, 136
French's Third Division—Second Corps, 68; actions at the Sunken Road, 72–74, 77, 79, 81, 164, 167; Confederate attack on the flank of, 86, 169; crossing the Antietam, 47, 51, 69, 162; organization, 32, 162; Sumner's after-action report, 151; Sumner's options for, 70, 72, 163
Gibbon's Fourth Brigade (a.k.a. the Iron Brigade), First Division—First Corps, 35, 42, 143
Goodrich's Third Brigade, Third Division—Twelfth Corps, 63, 65
Gorman's First Brigade, Second Division—Second Corps, 63, 153
Greene's Second Division—Twelfth Corps, 63; advance into the West Woods, 74, 86; Early's perception of, 62, 65, 68, 155; effect on the Sunken Road, 81; position near the Dunker Church, 49, 62, 70; Sumner's perception of, 49, 70, 73, 152, 163
Hancock's First Brigade, Second Division—Sixth Corps, 84, 93, 160, 182
Hartsuff's Third Brigade, Second Division—First Corps, 35, 143
Howard's Second Brigade, Second Division—Second Corps, 152
Humphreys's Third Division—Fifth Corps: as a reserve force, 107, 109, 185, almost two 186; departure from Washington, 91, 180; experience of the division, 111; location on 09/16 and 09/17, 24, 136
Kanawha Division (Scammon)—Ninth Corps, 98, 100, 101, 120, 121, 172
Kimball's Frist Brigade, Third Division— Second Corps, 79, 163, 164, 169
Lovell's Second Brigade, Second Division— Fifth Corps, 93, 181
Magilton's Second Brigade, Third Division—First Corps, 144, 145
Meade's Third Division—First Corps: action on 09/16, 33, 40, 146; crossing the Antietam, 33, 142; early morning action on 09/17, 36, 42, 143, 147; Meade takes command of the corps, 49, 151; morning advance on 09/17, 35, 143
Morell's First Division—Fifth Corps, 36, 47, 91, 94, 150, 180
Patrick's Third Brigade, First Division—First Corps, 42, 147
Pleasonton's Cavalry Division, 22, 91, 121, 136, 180
Richardson's First Division—Second Corps: actions at the Piper Farm, 86, 160, 164, 167, 168; actions at the Sunken Road, 73, 77–80; advance

288

Index

from South Mountain, 21, 134; as a reserve force, 36, 47, 51, 143, 150

Ricketts's Second Division—First Corps: crossing the Antietam, 33; early morning action on 09/17, 36, 40, 142–44

Rodman's Third Division—Ninth Corps: approach to Snavely's Ford, 84, 160; plan at the lower bridge, 98, 101–4, 172–75

Scammon's Division (Kanawha)—Ninth Corps (*see* Kanawha Division)

Sedgwick's Second Division—Second Corps: actions in the West Woods, 51–53, 55, 59, 63, 69, 86, 152, 153, 177, 179; alternative actions, 39, 53; battlefield tour, 151, 154; crossing the Antietam, 47, 49, 51, 63, 69, 150, 151, 156, 162; French's support of, 70–73, 163; Sumner's options for, 51, 70, 163

Seymour's First Brigade, Third Division—First Corps, 33, 40, 142, 144, 146

Slocum's First Divisio—Sixth Corps, 83, 84, 159

Smith's Second Division—Sixth Corps, 83, 84, 159, 160

Sturgis's Second Division—Ninth Corps, 100, 172

Sykes's Second Division—Fifth Corps, 90, 91, 93, 94, 180, 181

Weber's Third Brigade, Third Division—Second Corps, 73, 163, 164

Army of the Potomac (USA), batteries, infantry, and cavalry regiments

Connecticut: 14th Infantry, 163

New York: 6th Cavalry, 101

Pennsylvania: 4th Reserves, 140; 8th Reserves, 140; 124th Infantry, 62, 66, 156; 125th Infantry, 49, 62, 63, 65, 66, 68, 70, 152, 156, 163; 130th Infantry, 170; 132nd Infantry, 165; Pennsylvania Light, Battery C, 113

Rhode Island: 1st Light, Battery A (Tompkins's Battery), 79, 81, 89, 158

United States: 4th, Battery G (Miller's Battery), 183; 5th, Battery C (Ransom's Battery), 144

West Virginia: 7th Infantry, 165

Army of Virginia (USA), 5, 6

Baltimore, MD, 17, 68

Barksdale, William, Brig. Gen., CSA (Bde Cmdr), 52, 152

Barton, Clara, 140

Battles and Leaders of the Civil War, 101, 174

Beauregard, Pierre Gustave Toutant, Brig. Gen., CSA (Army Cmdr), 2

Belmont, August, 5

Bennett, Risden T., Col., CSA (Reg and Bde Cmdr), 80, 168

Bloody Lane. *See* Sunken Road

Bolivar, MD, 21, 134

Bonaparte, Napoleon, 87

Boonsboro, MD (Boonsborough) battlefield tour, 129, 136; Confederate retreat from South Mountain, 13, 131, 133; Longstreet's march to, 39; Union advance from South Mountain, 22

Boonsboro Turnpike/Pike (a.k.a. Boonsborough Turnpike/Pike) battlefield tour, 129, 175; Burnside's assault, 160; casualties near, 160; Confederate positions, 33, 50, 51, 55, 59; D. H. Hill's position, 76, 166; Lee's observations, 53, 59, 141, 176, 177, 179; Union Fifth Corps actions, 91, 93, 94, 180, 181

Boonsboro Turnpike/Pike (a.k.a. Boonsborough Turnpike/Pike) (*cont.*)
  Union Sixth Corps advance, 84, 88, 161
  See also Maryland Route 34, 31, 139
Boteler's Ford (a.k.a. Blackford's Ford or Packhorse Ford)
  Battle of Shepherdstown, 119, 121, 122
  Confederate retreat from South Mountain, 13, 131, 132
  Lee's position at Sharpsburg, 15, 16
  photos, 122, 193
Bragg, Braxton, Gen, CSA (Army Cmdr—A.T.), 5, 30
Branch Avenue, Antietam National Battlefield, 175
Brockenbrough, John M., Col., CSA (Bde Cmdr), 118, 192
Buchanan, Robert C., Lieut. Col., USA (Bde Cmdr), 93, 181
Buell, Don Carlos, Maj. Gen. USA (Army Cmdr—AO), 5
Burnside, Ambrose, Maj. Gen., USA (Wing Cmdr)
  actions at South Mountain, 22, 136
  actions at the Lower Bridge, 88, 89, 93, 94, 103, 104, 171
  battlefield tour, 170
  before the Maryland Campaign, 96, 97
  biography, 96, 97, 170
  communications from McClellan, 98, 171–73
  final assault, 94, 95, 175, 182, 183
  options at the Lower Bridge, 101–3, 173–75
  photo, 97
  promotion to army command, 123, 124
  relationship with McClellan, 96
  role at Antietam, 97, 98, 140, 171
  tactical situation faced, 98
Burnside's Bridge (a.k.a. Rohrbach Bridge or Lower Bridge)
  advance of the Union Sixth Corps, 84, 88

battlefield tour, 137–39, 165, 170, 175, 176, 189
Burnside's decisions, 96, 102
Burnside's tactical options, 98, 100, 102, 172, 174
Confederate position, 100
Cox's description, 101, 173
Lee's tactical options, 16, 31
McClellan orders to attack, 101, 173
photos, 104, 171
Toombs's report, 100–101, 173
Union assaults, 103, 104, 160, 161, 174, 175, 181
Union tactical situation, 87, 107, 141, 184
Walker redeployed from, 60, 61, 180

California Gold Rush, xvi
Carman, Ezra, xx, 80, 168
Cemetery Hill (Sharpsburg, MD)
  battlefield tour, 175
  Lee commits his reserves, 53, 57, 178
  positions at the Confederate center, 76, 84, 160
  positions at the Union center, 93, 95, 167, 181
  photos, 178
Chancellorsville Campaign, 2
Chantilly, Battle of (a.k.a. Battle of Ox Hill), 6
Chantilly, VA, 6
Charlestown, VA (WV), 58, 179
Chesapeake Bay, 3
Chickahominy River, 116, 192
Chilton, Robert H., Lt. Col., CSA (Chief of Staff), 29
Clara Barton Monument, Antietam National Battlefield, 140
Coast Division (a.k.a. North Carolina Expeditionary Force), 96
Cobb, Howell, Brig. Gen., CSA (Bde Cmdr), 76, 167
Colquitt, Alfred H., Col. CSA (Bde Cmdr), 76, 166, 167

Index

Confederacy, xv, xvii, 1, 3, 5, 8, 46
Cornfield Avenue, Antietam National Battlefield, 139, 149, 154
Cornfield, the (a.k.a. Farmer David R. Miller's Cornfield), 84
  advance of the Union Sixth Corps, 160
  battlefield tour, 139, 140, 149, 176
  Confederate positions at dawn, 33
  Early deploys in the West Woods, 62, 63, 154–56
  Hood counter attacks the, 39, 42–45, 145–48
  Hooker opens the battle, 72, 37–38, 144
  Lee commits his reserves, 54, 176
  McClellan commits Sumner's corps, 150
  photos, 45, 146
Cornfield Trail, Antietam National Battlefield, 140
Couch, Darius N., Maj. Gen., USA (Div Cmdr),
  arriving at Sharpsburg, 107
  as a reserve force, 82, 107, 109, 185
  movement to Sharpsburg, 83
  movement to Williamsport, 121
  position on 09/15 and 09/16, 24, 159
  position on 09/17, 83, 159, 185
Cox, Jacob D., Brig. Gen., USA (Div and Corps Cmdr)
  assault on the Lower Bridge, 98
  assuming command of the Ninth Corps, 98, 102
  command at Antietam, 98, 102, 171, 174
  comments in B&L article, 101, 174
  tactical situation faced, 101, 172, 173
Crampton's Gap
  battles of South Mountain, 9, 13, 18, 133
  Cobb's fight at Sharpsburg, 76, 159
  Confederate retreat from, 12, 76, 130, 167
  Union advance from, 22, 83, 136
Crawford, Samuel W., Brig. Gen., USA (Bde Cmdr), 62, 156

Cumming, Alfred, Col., CSA (Bde Cmdr), 80, 168
Custis, Mary Anna Randolph (Mary Lee), 4

Dana, Napoleon J.T., Brig. Gen., USA (Bde Cmdr), 153
Davis, Jefferson, President, CSA
  Lee's communication to, 8, 18, 119, 123, 132, 193
  placing Lee in command, 4,
  response to Lee's early victories, 6
Democratic Party, 5, 124
Doubleday, Abner, Brig. Gen., USA (Div Cmdr)
  crossing the Antietam, 33, 142
  early morning action, 36, 40, 143
  Longstreet's comments on, 55, 177
  Meade's after-action report, 144
Douglas, Henry Kyd, Lieut. CSA (Assist Adj Gen), 115
Douglass, Marcellus, Col., CSA (Bde and Div Cmdr), 55, 177
Dranesville, VA, 6
Dunker Church Road
  battlefield tour, 137, 139, 140, 142, 145, 149, 154, 158, 170
Dunker Church, the (a.k.a. Saint Mumma Church), Antietam National Battlefield
  battlefield tour, 139, 140, 145, 154, 165, 189
  Confederate advance on French's flank, 79, 169
  Confederate positions before the battle, 31, 142
  Early's actions in the West Woods, 59, 62, 63, 155
  Franklin's advance, 86, 89, 160, 161, 163
  Green's advance, 86
  Hood's after-action report, 148
  Hood's Division in reserve, 40, 42, 45, 146, 155

Dunker Church, the (a.k.a. Saint
    Mumma Church), Antietam
    National Battlefield (*cont.*)
  Hooker opens the battle, 33, 36, 142, 143
  Lee commits his reserves, 84, 87, 179
  photo, 38, 83
  Sumner's tactical observations, 49, 50,
    70, 72, 73, 152

Early, Jubal A., Brig. Gen., CSA (Bde
    and Div Cmdr)
  deploying in the West Woods, 61–68
  Lee's after-action report, 59
  West Point, 29
East Woods, Antietam National
    Battlefield
  actions on 09/16, 33, 142
  battlefield tour, 139, 140, 149, 162
  early morning action, 36–38, 143, 145
  French's advance, 72, 163
  Hood's counterattack, 42–43, 147
  Jubal Early deploys in the West
    Woods, 62, 63, 154–156
  photo, 150
  Sumner attacks the West Woods, 49,
    55, 151, 177
Eastern Theater, the, 2
Elk Ridge, Maryland, 15, 132
Emancipation Proclamation, xvii, 1,
    6, 125
Evans, Nathan G. "Shanks," Brig.
    Gen., CSA (Bde Cmdr), 54, 84,
    93, 160, 176, 181
Ewing, Hugh B., Col., USA (Reg and
    Bde Cmdr), 98, 172

Farnsworth, John F., Col., USA (Bde
    Cmdr Cav), 22, 136
Farragut, David G. Adm, USA, 90
First Bull Run, Battle of (a.k.a. First
    Manassas), 2, 3
Fort Monroe (a.k.a. Fortress Monroe,
    Virginia), 3
Fox's Gap, MD, 15, 22, 98, 136, 171

France, 1, 5
Franklin County, VA, 61
Franklin, William B., Maj. Gen., USA
    (Corps Cmdr)
  actions at Crampton's gap, 21
  actions in Pleasant Valley, 22, 136
  advance at the West Woods, 81, 84,
    86, 159, 170
  comments on the battle, 110, 186
  march to Sharpsburg, 82, 83, 159
  McClellan's communication to
    Halleck, 134
  positions on 09/15 and 09/16, 24, 82,
    83, 159
  Sumner holds back the Sixth Corps,
    50, 87–89, 161
Frederick, MD (Fredericktown), 8, 9,
    17, 18, 39, 133
Fredericksburg, Battle of, 2, 73, 123
Fredericksburg, VA, 123
French, Ephraim, 68
French, William B., Brig. Gen., USA
    (Div Cmdr)
  after-action report, 73
  battle shifts to the Sunken Road,
    68–72, 77, 81, 164, 167
  crossing the Antietam, 36, 47, 143, 150
  part of Sumner's Second, Corps, 47,
    149
  photos, 69
  Sumner's orders for, 51–53, 153, 162, 163
  West Point, 29
Frye, Dennis E., 26

Garland, Samuel, Jr., Brig. Gen. CSA
    (Bde Cmdr), 22, 135
Gettysburg, Battle of, xii, 2, 73, 125
Gibbon, John, Brig. Gen., USA (Bde
    Cmdr), 42, 147
Gillon, Steven M., xvi
Goodrich, William B., Col., USA
    (Bde Cmdr), 62, 66, 156
Gorman, Willis A., Brig. Gen., USA
    (Bde Cmdr), 63, 153

Grant, Ulysses S., Gen. (Army Cmdr/ US Pres.), xi, xvi
Great Briton (England), 1, 5
Greene, George S., Brig. Gen., USA (Div Cmdr)
  advance into the West Woods, 74, 86
  Early's observations, 62, 63, 155
  Sumner's observations, 49, 70, 152, 162
  Sumner's options for, 53, 62,
Grigsby, Andrew J., Col., CSA (Bde and Div Cmdr), 66, 67, 157, 178

Hagerstown, MD, 15, 17, 31, 39, 123, 138, 145
Hagerstown Turnpike (a.k.a. Hagerstown Pike)
  actions at the Sunken Road, 76, 166, 167
  afternoon Union positions, 181
  afternoon Union positions, 93
  battlefield tour, 137, 138, 140, 159
  Confederate position on 09/18, 107, 185
  Confederate positions on Nicodemus Heights, 33, 142, 154
  Early deploys in the West Woods, 62, 63, 66
  Hood counter attacks at the Cornfield, 42–44, 49, 147
  Hooker opens the battle, 35, 37–39, 140, 144
  Lee commits his reserves, 55
  Lee stands at Sharpsburg, 16, 31, 141
  Lee's attempt to move north, 17, 27
  mid-morning Confederate positions, 76, 84, 160
  stand at the Piper Farm, 81, 169
  Sumner attacks the West Woods, 49, 152
  Union mid-morning advance, 156, 177
  Union positions on 09/18, 107, 184
  Union superbattery, 63, 156
  See also Sharpsburg Pike
Halleck, Henry W., Maj. Gen., USA (General in Chief)
  communication from McClellan after the battle, 106, 119, 122, 183, 184, 193
  communication from McClellan before the battle, 21, 22, 90, 134, 135
  communication to McClellan, 123
  evacuation of the Peninsula, 5, 6
  McClellan is relieved of command, 124
Hampden-Sydney College, 75
Hancock, Winfield S., Brig. Gen. USA (Bde and Div Cmdr), 84, 93, 160 182
Harpers Ferry, Battle of (a.k.a. Harpers Ferry Operation), xv, 8, 9, 11, 13, 15, 17, 116, 131, 132
Harpers Ferry, VA (WV)
  A. P. Hill's march from, 61, 93, 103, 175, 181
  Burnside's deployment, 98, 172
  Confederate stragglers, 118, 192
  Franklin's actions on 09/16, 83, 159
  Franklin's communication on 09/15, 22, 136
  Jacksons march from, 24
  Lee commits his reserves, 58
  Lee stands at Sharpsburg, 12, 13, 15, 130, 132
  McClellan launches his attack, 21, 24, 134, 136
  McLaws and Andersons march from, 77, 167, 179
  R. H. Anderson's actions, 75, 167
  Union casualties, 125
  Union reoccupation of, 121
  Union surrender of, 15, 132
Harpers Ferry Road, 95, 107, 139, 183, 185
  battlefield tour, 170, 175, 185
Harpers Ferry Union Garrison, 8, 13, 21, 61, 130, 154
Harrisburg, PA, 17
Harsh, Joseph L., xx, 35, 115, 192
Hartsuff, George L., Brig. Gen., USA (Bde Cmdr), 35, 143

Index

Hartwig, D. Scott, xvii, xx, 125
Hately, John C., Col., CSA (Reg and Bde Cmdr), 80, 168
Hauser's Ridge, 62, 86, 139, 154, 155
Hay, John, 124
Hays, Harry T., Brig. Gen., CSA (Bde Cmdr), 42, 146, 147
Hill, Ambrose Powell (A. P.), Maj. Gen., CSA (Div Cmdr)
  actions at Shepherdstown, 122
  as cadet at West Point, 96
  as a reserve force, 89, 179
  Lee commits his reserves, 58
  Lee stands at Sharpsburg, 18, 58,
  march from Harpers Ferry, 27, 58, 93, 104, 181
Hill, Daniel Harvey (D. H.), Maj. Gen., CSA (Div Cmdr)
  actions at South Mountain, 8
  actions at the Cornfield, 62, 154, 155, 167
  actions at the Sunken Road, 74, 77, 148, 163
  arrival at Sharpsburg on 09/15, 133
  Confederate retreat from South Mountain, 13, 18, 130, 133
  early morning actions, 146
  Harpers Ferry operation, 8
  Lee commits his reserves, 58
  morning message to Lee on 09/17, 57, 178
Hobson, Edwin L., Maj., CSA (Reg Cmdr), 81, 169
Hood, John B., Brig. Gen., CSA (Div Cmdr)
  as a reserve force on 09/17, 33, 40, 42
  bio, 39
  casualties of his division, 54, 148, 176
  comments on 09/18, 113, 114, 190
  Confederate retreat from South Mountain, 13, 131
  counter attack at the Cornfield, 39–45, 62, 145–49, 154, 155
  deployment after the Cornfield fight, 62, 84, 142, 160
  Lee commits his reserves, 57, 178
  photo, 40
  Toombs's after-action reports, 100, 173
Hooker, Joseph (Fighting Joe), Maj. Gen., USA (Corps Cmdr)
  actions at South Mountain, 134
  arriving east of the Antietam on 09/15, 22, 136
  battlefield tour, 129, 140
  bio, 29, 30
  calling for reinforcements, 44, 45, 47, 148, 149, 150
  crossing the Antietam, 18, 26, 33, 137
  Hood's counterattack, 45, 148
  McClellan deploys the Second, Corps, 72, 149, 159, 163
  McClellan's plan for, 84, 98, 171
  opening the battle, 30, 33–38, 83, 140–46, 159
  photo, 30
  Sumner arrives on the field, 55, 177
  Sumner's after-action report, 47, 151
  Twelfth Corps support of, 150
  Union advance to Sharpsburg, 21, 22, 134, 135
  wounding, 49, 50, 55, 151, 177
Hornet's Nest (Shiloh), the, 73
Howard, Oliver O., Brig. Gen., USA (Bde and Div Cmdr), 152
Humphreys, Andrew A., Brig. Gen., USA (Div Cmdr), 91, 107, 111, 185, 187

Indiana, 96

Jackson, Thomas J. "Stonewall," Maj. Gen., CSA (Wing Cmdr), xv
  actions at Shepherdstown, 122
  after-action report, 40, 67, 146
  communications from Lee, 13, 131
  communications to Lee, 15, 17, 18, 132, 133, 178
  conversation with Hood on 09/16, 40, 146

conversation with Hood on 09/18, 114, 190
Early deploys in the West Woods, 62, 63, 66, 156, 157
early morning positions on 09/17, 31, 141
Harpers Ferry operation, 8, 9
Hood counter attacks the Cornfield, 43, 44, 148, 154
Hooker opens the battle, 36, 42, 144, 147, 154, 177
in the Shenandoah, 5
Lee commits his reserves, 51, 57, 148, 178
proposed attack on the Union right, 90
James River, Virginia, 3
Johnston, Joseph E., Gen., CSA (Army Cmdr), 2, 4
Jones, David, R., Brig. Gen., CSA (Div Cmdr)
at the Lower Bridge, 100, 172
casualties, 118, 181, 192
position at the Confederate center, 54, 84, 93, 176, 181
Jones, John R., Brig. Gen., CSA (Div Cmdr)
after-action report, 55, 177
after early morning action, 40, 84, 146, 160
casualties, 54, 176
early morning position, 31, 142,
wounding, 54, 55, 62, 155, 176, 177

Keedysville, MD
battlefield tour, 127, 129
Confederate retreat from South Mountain, 13, 130, 132
McClellan's after-action report, 84
Sixth Corps arrives at Antietam, 83, 159
Twelfth Corps crosses the Antietam, 47, 150
Union advance from South Mountain, 22, 136
Keedysville Road, 31, 138

Kemper, James L., Brig. Gen., CSA (Bde Cmdr), 160
Kentucky, 5, 39
Kershaw, Joseph B., Brig. Gen., CSA (Bde Cmdr), 52, 152
Kimball, Nathan, Brig. Gen., USA (Bde Cmdr), 164

Law, Evander M., Col., CSA (Bde Cmdr), 44, 54, 147, 148, 176
Lawton, Alexander, Brig. Gen., CSA (Div Cmdr)
casualties, 42, 54, 55, 146
early morning deployment on 09/17, 31, 33, 142, 146
early morning actions, 40
Harper's Ferry operation, 61, 154
Hood counter attacks the Cornfield, 42, 147
wounding, 54, 55, 62, 146, 154, 176, 177
Lee, Fitzhugh, Brig. Gen., CSA (Bde Cmdr—Cav)
Confederate retreat from South Mountain, 13, 22, 133, 136
deployment at Sharpsburg, 33, 131, 133, 142
Lee, "Light-Horse" Harry, 4
Lee, Robert E., Gen., CSA (Army Cmdr—ANV), 20, 21, 104, 137, 186, 53, 119
actions after Shepherdstown, 123–25, 193
actions at Chantilly, 6
actions at Second Bull Run, 5
actions at the Battle of Shepherdstown, 121, 122
actions at the Battles of South Mountain, 9, 130
actions at the Confederate center, 89, 94, 95, 96
actions at the Sunken Road, 81, 170
actions before South Mountain, 8, 9
actions in the Battles of the Seven Days, 4

Lee, Robert E., Gen., CSA (Army Cmdr—ANV) *(cont.)*
  actions on 09/18, 106–12, 118, 120, 185, 189
  actions on the Confederate left, 44, 54, 103, 44, 51, 84, 87, 100, 148, 152, 159, 160, 179, 180
  actions on the Confederate right, 93, 98, 104, 172, 181
  actions on the Virginia Peninsula, 4
  advancing to Pennsylvania, 9, 17
  after-action report, 59, 67, 133
  appointed to command, 4
  army organization in September 1862, 8, 13, 22, 43, 46
  attempt to turn the Union right, 18, 89, 90
  battlefield tour, 129
  bio, 4
  committing his reserves, 44, 51, 53–60, 74, 84, 87, 113, 144, 148, 160, 176–80, 189
  communications to A. P. Hill, 93, 181
  communications with Davis, 8, 119, 123, 133
  communications with Jackson, 13, 15, 132
  communications with McLaws, 13, 131–32
  Confederate casualties, 114, 115, 118, 185, 125, 190, 192
  Confederate positions at Sharpsburg, 31
  decision making on 09/18, 115–20, 190–94
  decision to invade the North, 6, 8
  deployment in the center, 93, 95, 181
  deployment of A. P. Hill's Division, 88, 89
  deployment of Hood's Division, 39, 145
  Harpers Ferry operation, 8, 9, 11, 116
  headquarters at Sharpsburg, 189
  Hooker opens the battle, 30, 33–36, 39, 47, 83, 141, 142, 144, 159
  Jacob Cox's description of the battle, 102, 174
  Longstreet comments on, 113, 189
  McClellan launches his attack, 24–27
  McClellan's after-action report, 21, 22
  McClellan's perceptions of, 21, 24–27, 82, 94, 109, 111, 113, 134, 135, 137, 182, 186, 188
  moving Walker's Division from his right to his left, 103, 172, 174
  objectives for the Maryland Campaign, 1, 6–9, 16, 17, 118
  observing the battle, 54, 176
  offering battle at Sharpsburg, 11–16
  organization of corps, xv
  perception of his campaign, 16, 116
  perception of McClellan, 12, 130
  perception of the Army of the Potomac, 8, 15
  photos, 4, 12
  plan of for Antietam, 15–18, 77, 141
  plan to recross the Potomac at Williamsport, 19, 119, 193
  pre-war biography, 4
  quote by John Walker, 119
  replacing Joe Johnston, 4
  reputation in battle, 6, 26
  retreat from Sharpsburg, 19, 60, 61, 115–20, 187, 189–93, 121
  retreat from South Mountain, 11–13, 19, 130–34, 136
  Special Orders (SO) 191, 8, 9, 20
  Sumner's plan at the West Woods, 51
Lee, Stephen D., Col., CSA (Bn Cmdr), 33
  photo, 19
Leesburg, VA, 8
Lightfoot, James N., Lieut. Col. CSA (Reg Cmdr), 81, 168, 169
Lincoln, Abraham, President, USA, xi, 1

action before the campaign, 5
after First Bull Run, 3
after Second Bull Run, 6
communication to McClellan, 25, 137
election of 1862, 124
Emancipation Proclamation, xvii, 5, 6, 125
evacuation of the Peninsula, 6
legacy, 5
letter to August Belmont, 5
meeting McClellan after the battle, 123
photos, 124
placing Burnside in command, 124
placing McClellan in command of the field army, 9
quotes on, xvii
reaction to South Mountain, 24
reaction to the Confederate invasion, 17
removing McClellan from command, 124
Long, Armistead L., Col., CSA (Army Secretary), 46
Longstreet, James, Maj. Gen., CSA (Wing Cmdr)
  assault on French's right, 79, 86, 169
  autobiography, 55, 177
  comments of the battle, 113, 189
  Confederate retreat to Sharpsburg, 18, 130, 133
  Hood's Division, 39
  Second Bull Run, 90
  Special Orders (SO) 191, 8
  stand at the Piper Farm, 86
Lovell, Charles S., Maj., USA (Bde Cmdr), 93, 181
Lower Bridge. *See* Burnside's Bridge

MacRae, William, Lieut. Col., CSA (Reg. and Bde Cmdr), 76, 167
Magilton, Albert L., Col., USA (Bde Cmdr), 144, 145
Main Street (Sharpsburg), 170, 175, 180, 189

Manning, Vannoy, Col., CSA (Bde Cmdr), xv, 86
Mansfield, Joseph, Maj. Gen, USA (Corps Cmdr)
  combat experience, 25
  crossing the Antietam, 47, 151
  early morning actions, 49, 55, 143, 177
  Hood counter attacks the cornfield, 45
  Hooker opens the battle, 34–39
  McClellan's plan for, 98, 171
  mortal wounding of, 49, 55, 144, 151, 177
Mansfield Avenue, Antietam National Battlefield, 139, 140, 145
Marvel, William, 97
Maryland, 2
  casualties, 118, 191
  Confederate invasion of, 8, 17, 116
  Confederate stragglers, 114, 190
  Confederate withdrawal from, 119, 123, 193
  Lee's plan to reenter, 121
  McClellan's action after the battle, 123, 193
  McClellan's campaign objectives, 24, 110, 187
  Pennsylvania Reserve force, 111, 187
  Sears quote, xvii
Maryland Campaign, xii, xiv, xx, 1, 46
  after Antietam, 119
  battlefield tour, 134, 193
  Burnside as wing commander, 97
  casualties, 124, 125
  perspective on McClellan's action in, 19
  quotes on, xvii
Maryland Heights
  Confederate retreat from Crampton's Gap, 12, 130
  Couch's orders to occupy, 83, 136, 159
  McLaws's and Anderson advance to Sharpsburg, 58, 179
  McLaws's and Anderson's position on, 12, 130

Maryland Heights (cont.)
   orders for McLaws to abandon, 13, 131
   Union advance on, 22
   Union occupation after the battle, 121
Maryland Monument, Antietam National Battlefield, 129, 145
Maryland Route 34 (a.k.a. Boonsboro Turnpike or Shepherdstown Pike)
   battlefield tour, 129, 137, 139, 175, 180, 189
   Lee at Cemetery Hill, 53
Maryland Route 65 (a.k.a. Hagerstown Turnpike or Sharpsburg Pike), 137, 138, 142, 170
Mason-Dixon Line, 5
Massachusetts, 29, 46
McClellan, George B., Maj. Gen., USA (Army Cmdr), 59, 97, 101, 103, 113, ,118, 174, 179, 190
   actions after 09/20, 123, 124
   actions at Battles of South Mountain, 9
   actions at Shepherdstown, 12, 121, 122, 193
   actions before South Mountain, 9
   actions on 09/15, 20, 21, 24, 134, 136, 137
   actions on 09/16, 20, 21, 24, 136, 137
   actions on 09/18, 105–13, 119, 183–89, 120
   actions on the Virginia Peninsula, 3, 4
   advance from Washington, 9
   after-action report, 82, 83, 94, 98, 109, 111, 137, 159, 171, 186, 188
   aggressiveness during the Maryland campaign, 11, 15, 16, 20, 130, 132
   appointed to General-in-Chief, 3
   army organization, 46
   asking Halleck to set aside court-marshal proceedings, 90
   battlefield tour, 129, 170
   bio, 3
   casualties, 25, 106, 109–11, 184, 187
   communications to Marry Ellen, 106, 183
   communications with Burnside, 102, 175
   communications with Franklin, 22, 83, 136, 159
   communications with Halleck, 21, 22, 103, 119, 122, 123, 135, 184, 193
   communications with Sumner, 22, 24, 72, 163
   condition of the Army, 25, 111, 187
   Confederate withdrawal from Sharpsburg, 60, 113, 116, 118, 120, 190, 192
   corps does not advance, 93–95, 182, 183
   corps crosses the Antietam, 33, 45, 47, 50, 141, 142, 149, 150, 159
   corps to march to Sharpsburg, 84
   decision to not attack on 09/18, 105–13
   forward headquarters at the Pry house, 24, 50, 129, 136, 170
   Franklin's after-action report, 110, 186
   holding back Richardson's division, 36, 51, 143
   launching his attack at Sharpsburg, 19–27, 134–37
   Lee offers battle at Sharpsburg, 16, 133, 134
   Lee's perception of, 16, 18, 58
   Lincoln's visit to, 123
   making Burnside a wing commander, 97
   not pursuing Lee after Antietam, 19, 61, 183–89
   numbers of Confederates he believed he was facing, 18, 21, 24, 109, 111, 133, 136, 188
   objectives in Maryland, 110, 187
   observing the battle at Antietam, 44, 47, 50
   on Lee's position at Sharpsburg, 25

orders to Hooker on 09/16, 30, 141, 142
perception of Lee, 84, 106, 109, 110, 184, 186
photos, 2, 20, 124
plan of attack for Antietam, 24, 26, 33, 35, 37, 47, 83, 87, 98, 101, 137, 149, 171
plans for the Ninth Corps on 09/17, 98, 171, 172
reaction to Lee's stand at Sharpsburg, 19–27
realigning the Ninth Corps, 98, 171, 172
rebuke of Burnside, 103, 175
relationship with Burnside, 96, 170, 174
relief of Harpers Ferry, 9, 21
relieved of command, 124
reserves and reinforcements at Antietam, 58, 84, 94, 106, 107, 109, 111, 142, 150, 160, 183, 187, 185, 186
response to Hood's attack, 44, 47, 148, 149
Special Orders (SO) 191, 9, 20
Sumner holds back the Sixth Corps, 88, 161
taking command, 1861, 3
taking command, 1862, 9
training of the Army of the Potomac, 3
Union pursuit from South Mountain, 21, 136
Union strength at Antietam, 24, 82
withdrawal from the Virginia Peninsula, 5, 6
McClellan, Mary Ellen, 106, 183, 184
McDowell, Irvin, Brig. Gen. USA (Div Cmdr/Army Cmdr), 2
McKinley, William, xvi
McLaws, Lafayette, Maj. Gen., CSA (Div Cmdr)
  actions at Maryland Heights, 12

actions in the West Woods, 59, 67, 157, 179
advance on the West Woods, 39
as a reserve force, 58, 179
communication from Lee, 13, 131
Confederate retreat from South Mountain, 18
Harpers Ferry operation, 8
Lee offers battle at Sharpsburg, 12, 18, 130, 133
march to Sharpsburg, 58
photo, 57
position after the West Woods fight, 84, 160
McRae, Duncan K., Col., CSA (Reg and Bde Cmdr), 70, 76, 163, 166, 167
Meade, George G., Maj. Gen., USA (Div and Corps Cmdr)
  crossing the Antietam, 33, 142
  early morning actions, 35, 36, 40, 42, 143, 147
  McClellan's after-action report, 112, 188
  taking command of the first corps, 49, 144, 151
Memphis, TN, 5
Middle Bridge, 31
  battlefield tour, 139
  Ninth Corps advance, 93, 181
  photo, 96
  Union advance over, 84, 91, 160, 181
  Union positions, 91, 180
Midterm elections (1862), 1, 5, 124
Miller, Marcus P., Lieut., USA (Btry Cmdr), 183
Miller Farm (David R.), 139, 140, 147
Morell, George W., Maj. Gen., USA (Div Cmdr), 36, 47, 91, 94, 150, 180
Morris, Dwight, Col., USA (Bde Cmdr), 163
Mountain View Cemetery, 176
Muleshoe (Spotsylvania), 73

Mumma Farm (Samuel),
  actions on 09/16, 40, 146, 158
  battlefield tour, 158, 161
  Confederate deployment on 09/17, 31
  photo, 158
  Sumner's actions, 72
  Union positions on 09/18, 107, 184
Mumma Lane, 158
Munford, Thomas T., Col, CSA (Bde Cmdr), 93, 181
Murfin, James V., xvii, 52

National Park Service, xvi, xvii, xx, 97, 129, 158
New York, 5
New York State Monument, 129, 139, 140
Nicodemus Hill (Heights)
  Early's Brigade, 33, 62, 142, 154
  Hooker opens the battle, 35, 37
  Pelham's Battery, 33, 37, 38, 142, 154
North Carolina, 96, 97
North Woods, 140

Observation Tower (Antietam National Battlefield), 139, 161, 165, 176
Old Burnside Bridge Road, 170, 175

Palfrey, Francis, 29, 105
Patrick, Marsena R., Brig. Gen., USA (Bde Cmdr), 42, 63, 147, 156
Pelham, John, Capt., CSA (Cmdr—Horse Arty), 33, 38, 62, 142, 154
Pemberton, John C., Lieut. Gen., CSA (Depart Cmdr—Dept. of the Mississippi), 29
Pender, William D., Brig. Gen., CSA (Bde Cmdr), 118, 192
Pendleton, William N., Brig. Gen., CSA (Arty Res), 13, 121, 122, 130, 170
Peninsula Campaign, 3–6, 25
  3rd Virginia, 75
  Fifth Corps, 90
  Hood's Texas brigade, 39
  Second Corps, 46

Pennsylvania
  1863 invasion, 118, 125, 191
  Lee divides his force, 9, 17, 18
  Lee withdraws to Virginia, 116, 119
  Lee's strategic plan, 1
  McClellan's communication, 119, 123, 193
  reuniting his army at Sharpsburg, 27
  Reynold's militia force, 110, 111, 186, 187
Pennsylvania Monument, 4th Reserves, 140
Pennsylvania Monument, 8th Reserves, 140
Pennsylvania Monument, 130th Infantry, 130
Petersburg, VA, 75
Philadelphia, PA, 3, 17
Philadelphia Brigade Monument, Antietam National Battlefield, 154
Piper Farm (Henry)
  actions at the Sunken Road, 76, 77, 162, 167
  Confederate stand at, 79, 81, 86, 93, 161, 169, 181
Pleasant Valley, 12, 130
  after Crampton's Gap, 12, 130
  Franklin's actions in, 22, 82, 136, 159
  Lee's plan on 09/15, 13
Pleasonton, Alfred, Brig. Gen., USA (Div Cmdr Cav)
  actions at Shepherdstown, 121, 123
  actions at the Middle Bridge, 84, 91, 93–95, 160, 180, 182
  Union advance from South Mountain, 22, 136
Poffenberger Farm (Joseph)
  battlefield tour, 139, 145, 154
  Hooker makes his headquarters, 33, 34, 140, 142, 143
  photo, 141
  positions after the battle, 184
  Twelfth Corps advanced to, 42, 147
Pope, John, Maj. Gen. USA (Army Cmdr—AV), 5, 6, 90

Index

Porter, David, 90
Porter, David Dixon, 90
Porter, Fitz John, Maj. Gen., USA (Corps Cmdr)
  action at Shepherdstown, 122
  action at the Middle Bridge, 93–95, 182, 183
  advance from Washington by his corps, 91
  bio, 90
  charges brought by Pope, 90
  photo, 91
  Second Bull Run, 90
Porter, John, 90
Porter, William D., 90
Posey, Carnot, Col. CSA (Bde Cmdr), 80, 168
Potomac River, 30, 31, 130, 118, 187
  actions at Harpers Ferry, 9
  after the campaign, 123
  Battle of Shepherdstown, 120, 121, 122, 123
  battlefield tour, 138–42, 176
  Confederate crossing at Leesburg, 8
  Confederate crossing at Williamsport, 122, 123, 193
  Confederate withdraw from South Mountain, 12, 13, 130, 132
  Early deploys in the West Woods, 63, 156
  Hooker opens the battle, 35, 38
  illustration, 8
  Lee commits his reserves, 58, 60
  Lee offers battle at Sharpsburg, 15–19, 130, 131, 132
  Lee withdraws to Virginia, 118, 119, 193
  McClellan launches his attack, 20–23, 25, 134, 137
  Pelham's position on Nicodemus Heights, 33
  photos, 122, 193
  Shepherdstown Ford, 15
  Union crossing, 10/26, 123
  Union superbattery, 63, 156
Pry House (Philip Pry Farm) (a.k.a. Pry House Field Hospital Museum)
  actions on 09/15 and 09/16, 24, 47, 136, 149
  battlefield tour, 129, 137, 139, 146, 165, 170
  photos, 27, 130, 131, 135
Pryor, Roger A., Brig. Gen. CSA (Bde and Div Cmdr)
  actions at the Sunken Road, 77, 79–81, 167, 168, 170
  bio, 75
  photo, 76
Pry's Ford, 33, 35, 47, 69, 84
  battlefield tour, 150, 159, 160, 162

Radical Republicans, 5
Rafuse, Ethan S., 20
Ransom, Dunbar R., Capt., USA (Baty Cmdr), 144
Rappahannock River, 123
Reno, Jesse, Maj. Gen., USA (Corps Cmdr)
  action at South Mountain, 21, 134
  death, 25, 98, 102, 100, 171, 174, 184
Republican Party, 124
Revolutionary War, 29, 68
Reynolds, John F., Brig. Gen., USA (Div Cmdr), 111, 187
Richardson, Israel B., Maj. Gen., USA (Div Cmdr)
  action at the Sunken Road, 73, 77, 164, 167
  advance from South Mountain, 21, 22, 134, 136
  as a reserve force, 36, 143
  as part of the Second Corps, 46, 149
  crossing the Antietam, 36, 49, 70
  mortally wounded, 47, 149
  Sumner's deployment of, 74
Richmond, VA, 3, 4, 6, 124
Ricketts, James, Brig. Gen., USA (Div Cmdr), 33, 49, 142, 144, 151

Ripley, Roswell S., Brig. Gen., CSA (Bde Cmdr)
  in support of Hood, 76, 166
  wounding, 55, 177
Rodes, Robert, Brig. Gen., CSA (Bde Cmdr)
  action in the Sunken Road, 77, 80, 81, 167–69
  deployment in the sunken road, 76, 166, 167
  wounding, 75, 166
Rodman, Isaac P., Brig. Gen., USA (Div Cmdr)
  crossing Snavely's Ford, 60
  locating Snavely's Ford, 98, 101–4, 160, 170–75
Rodman Ave., 170
Rohrbach Bridge. *See* Burnside's Bridge
Rohrersville, MD, 82, 159
Roulette Farm (William), 72, 73, 163, 164
  battlefield tour, 158, 161, 165
  photo, 162
Roulette Lane, 165

Scammon, Eliakim P., Col., USA (Bde and Div Cmdr), 100, 172
Scott, Winfield, Maj. Gen. USA (General in Chief), 3
Sears, Stephen W., xvii, xx, 20, 52
Second Bull Run (Second Manassas), Battle of, 5, 6, 75, 94, 182
  Joe Harsh (quoted), 116, 192
  Porter at, 90, 94, 192
Second Manassas, Battle of. *See* Second Bull Run
Sedgwick, John, Maj. Gen., USA (Div Cmdr)
  as part of the Second Corps, 46, 149
  battle shifts to the Sunken Road, 74
  crossing the Antietam, 36, 39, 63, 143, 156

Early deploys in the West Woods, 67, 68, 156, 157
Hooker opens the battle, 39
Sumner attacks the West Woods, 51–53, 66, 152
Sumner holds back the Sixth Corps, 83, 88, 159, 161
West Point, 29
wounding, 47, 154
Semmes, Paul, Brig. Gen., CSA (Bde Cmdr), 52, 67, 152, 157
Seven Days, Battles of, 4, 46, 90
Seymour, Truman, Brig. Gen., USA (Bde and Div Cmdr)
  actions on 09/16, 33, 40, 142, 146
  actions on 09/17, 35, 143, 144
Sharpsburg, Battle of. *See* Battle of Antietam
Sharpsburg, MD, 30, 31
  actions at the Union center, 93, 95, 181, 182
  battle shifts to the Sunken Road, 72, 163
  battlefield tour, 129, 137–40, 145, 165, 170, 175, 189
  Cemetery Hill, 53, 175
  Confederate positions on 09/15, 15
  Confederate positions on 09/18, 107, 185
  Confederate retreat from South Mountain, 39
  Early's march to, 62, 154
  Henry Kyd Douglass quote, 115
  Howard's after-action report, 153
  Jackson's Command arrives at, 136
  Lee offers battle at, 11, 13, 15–19, 132, 133, 145
  Lee withdraws from, 119, 193
  Lincolns visit to McClellan, 123
  McClellan does not attack, 112, 183, 189
  McClellan launches his attack, 26, 27
  McClellan's pan of battle, 98, 171

Message to McLaws, 13, 131, 132
photo, 190
Shepherdstown, 121
Sixth Corps movement on 09/16, 83, 159
Sumner holds back the Sixth Corps, 89
Toombs's after-action report, 100, 173
Union positions on 09/18, 105
Union troops at, 82
Sharpsburg Pike (a.k.a. Hagerstown Turnpike or Maryland Route 65), 137, 138, 142, 170
Sharpsburg Ridge, 93, 182
Shenandoah Valley, VA, 5, 123
Shepherdstown, Battle of, 19, 61, 120, 122, 123, 193
Shepherdstown, VA (WV), 19, 31, 61
actions on 09/15 and 09/16, 21, 132, 135
battlefield tour, 189
Confederate withdrawal from Sharpsburg, 119, 121, 193
Confederates return to, 123
Jackson ordered to move to, 13, 131
McLaws advance to Sharpsburg, 179
Potomac crossing at, 15, 16, 58, 119, 121, 138
road from Sharpsburg, 60, 98, 172, 180
Shepherdstown Pike (a.k.a. Maryland Route 34), 31
battlefield tour, 127, 129, 131, 137, 139, 189
Slocum, Henry W., Maj. Gen., USA (Div Cmdr), 83, 84, 159
Smith, Edmund Kirby, CSA (Maj. Gen.—AET), 5
Smith, William F. "Baldy," Maj. Gen, USA (Div Cmdr), 83, 159
Smoketown Road
battlefield tour, 139, 149
Confederate positions early morning on 09/17, 31
Hood counter attacks the Cornfiled, 40, 42, 44, 45, 145

Hooker opens the battle, 37, 146
Meade's advance on 09/16, 33, 146
photos, 146
Snavely's Ford, 172
battlefield tour, 170
Locating the Ford, 96, 98, 103, 180
Rodman's approach, 84, 160
Walker's division pulled from, 60, 180
South Carolina, 96
South Mountain, xv
battlefield tour, 139
Confederate retreat from, 13, 36, 76, 130, 143
D. H. Hill's position at, 39, 166
Lee divides his army, 8
McClellan crosses over, 136
Union advance from, 20, 134
Union bottlenecked at, 18, 132
South Mountain, Battles of, xv, 111
Confederate reinforcement at, 39, 145
Confederate retreat after, 11, 13
McClellan's decision to not attack on 09/18, 82, 188
Reno's death at, 110, 187
Union advance after, 12, 24, 25, 130, 134
Union advance on 09/14, 9
Spanish-American War, 46
Special Orders (SO) 191 (a.k.a. the Lost Orders), 9, 20, 134
Squires, Charles W., Capt., CSA (Btry Cmdr), 180
Stafford, Leroy A., Col., CSA (Reg and Bde Cmdr), 66, 67, 157
Starke, William E., Brig. Gen., CSA (Bde and Div Cmdr)
death at Sharpsburg, 54, 57, 62, 155, 176, 177
Stone Wall (Fredericksburg), 73
Stotelmyer, Steven R., xx, 20, 82
Stuart, James Earl Brown (JEB), Maj. Gen., CSA (Div/Cav Cmdr)
advance to Williamsport, 121
Harpers Ferry operation, 8

Stuart, James Earl Brown (JEB), Maj. Gen., CSA (Div/Cav Cmdr) (*cont.*)
　holding the confederate flanks, 107, 115, 185, 191
Sturgis, Samuel D., Brig. Gen., USA (Div Cmdr), 100, 172
Sumner, Edwin V., Jr., 46
Sumner, Edwin V., Maj. Gen., USA (Corps Cmdr)
　advance in the Union center, 94–95, 182
　after-action report, 47
　arrival at the Antietam on 09/15, 22, 136
　arrival on the field on 09/17, 39
　as a reserve force, 33, 142
　attack on the West Woods, 49–53, 68, 149–53
　battle shifts to the Sunken Road, 69–74, 162, 164
　bio, 46
　commander of the reserve force, 47
　crossing the Antietam, 44, 45, 47, 149
　division commanders, 46, 149
　holding back the Sixth Corps, 83–90, 158, 159, 161
　McClellan's plan for, 98, 171
　Pleasonton's after-action report, 93, 182
Sumner, Samuel S., Capt. USA (Aide-de-Camp), 46, 73, 164
Sunken Road (a.k.a. Bloody Lane), xiv, 73, 77, 164
　battle shifts to, 68, 70, 72–74, 161, 163, 164
　battlefield tour, 139, 140, 149, 158, 165, 176
　Burnside's attack, 104
　Confederate crisis in, 74, 76, 77, 80, 81, 165–70
　Confederate positions early a.m. on 09/17, 31, 142
　Confederate positions in, 34, 35

D. H. Hill's deployment, 33, 55, 176
Hooker opens the battle, 38, 143–45
Lee commits his reserves, 59, 60, 179, 180
photos, 75, 82, 120, 162, 166
Sumner holds back the Sixth Corps, 83, 84, 86, 87, 159
Sumner's attack at the West Woods, 50, 52, 53, 152, 153, 160
Union advance in the center, 91, 93, 180, 181
Union positions on 09/18, 107, 184
Sykes, George, Brig. Gen., USA (Div Cmdr)
　actions at the Union center, 93, 94, 180, 181, 183
　actions on 09/15 and 09/16, 91
　formation of the Fifth Corps, 90

Tew, Charles C., Col., CSA (Reg and Bde Cmdr), 80, 168
Texas, 39, 44, 148
Tompkins, John A., Capt., USA (Btry Cmdr), 79, 81, 158
　photo, 89
Toombs, Robert A., Brig. Gen., CSA (Bde Cmdr), 100, 104, 172, 173
Turner's Gap
　battles of South Mountain, 9,
　Confederate retrate from, 12, 130
　First Corps action at, 30, 130, 136, 140
　Union advance from, 15, 22, 24. 136

Union, the, xv, 1–9
Union Army, the. *See* Army of the Potomac
United States House of Representatives, 124
United States Senate, 124
University of Virginia, 75
Upper Bridge
　battlefield tour, 160
　Confederate deployment, 31, 141

Index

First Corps crossing the Antietam, 33, 142
Lee's decision to stand at Sharpsburg, 16
Second Corps crossing the Antietam, 84, 15
Twelfth Corps crossing the Antietam, 142

Vermilya, Daniel, xx, xxi
Virginia
  Chantilly battle, 6
  Confederate retreat from South Mountain, 13, 131
  Confederate stragglers, 114, 190
  Confederate wounded, 118, 191
  Jubal Early, 63
  Lee attempts to recross at Williamsport, 121
  Lee bio, 4
  Lee offers battle at Sharpsburg, 15, 16
  Lee withdraws to, 113, 114, 118, 119, 121, 193
  McClellan's communication to Halleck, 123
  Ninth Corps origin, 97
  Roger Pryor, 75
Virginia Peninsula, 3–6, 25, 39, 46

Walker, James A., Col., CSA (Bde Cmdr), xvi
  in relief of Hood on 09/16, 40, 146
  Jackson's after-action report, 40, 146
  wounding, 40, 146
Walker, John G., Brig. Gen., CSA (Div Cmdr), xv, xvi
  actions in the West Woods, 59, 179
  Harpers Ferry operation, 8
  Hooker opens the battle, 39
  position after morning assaults on 09/17, 84, 160
  position at Snavely's Ford, 60, 180
  thoughts on the battle, 119, 192

War Department (USA), 24, 106, 183
Warren, Gouverneur K., Col., USA (Bde Cmdr), 183
Warrenton, VA, 123
Warrenton Turnpike, 90
Washington, Martha, 4
Washington County, MD, 30, 31, 138
Washington, DC
  Confederate advance after Second Bull Run, 4
  Lee withdraws from Maryland, 116
  Lee's advance in to Maryland, 8
  Lincoln's visit to Sharpsburg, 123
  McClellan takes command, 1861, 3
  Union army's advance from, 9, 47, 91, 111, 150, 187
  Union retreat after Second Bull Run, 3, 6
Waugh, John C., 79, 167
Weber, Max, Brig. Gen., USA (Bde Cmdr), 73, 163, 164
West Point, United States Military Academy at, 3, 4, 29, 61, 68, 96
West Woods, xiv
  battle shifts to the Sunken Road, 68–74, 162–64
  battlefield tour, 139, 140, 145, 158, 162
  Confederate positions on 09/18, 107, 185
  Confederate positions early morning on 09/17, 31, 142
  early morning actions on 09/17, 36, 40, 143, 144
  Franklins advance into, 84
  Green's advance into, 86
  Hooker opens the battle, 37, 38, 40, 143, 144, 145
  Jubal Ealy deploys in, 61–68, 154–57
  Lee commits his reserves, 54, 55, 59, 61, 176, 177, 179
  photos, 54, 60, 68, 150, 155
  Sumner holds back the Sixth Corps, 83–86, 88, 89, 159–61

West Woods (*cont.*)
    Sumner's attack, 46, 49, 51–53, 149, 152, 153
Wheatfield (Gettysburg), 73
White House, the, 5
Wilcox, Orlando B., Brig. Gen., USA (Div Cmdr), 172
Williams, Alpheus S., Brig. Gen., USA (Div and Corps Cmdr), 49, 151

Williamsport, MD, 19, 119, 121, 122, 123, 193
Winchester, VA, 123
Wofford, William T., Col., CSA (Bde Cmdr), 44, 148
Wright, Ambrose R., Brig. Gen., CSA (Bde Cmdr), 80, 168

York River, 3